Palgrave Macmillan Studies in Banking and Financial Institutions

Series Editor

Philip Molyneux, Bangor University, Bangor, UK

The Palgrave Macmillan Studies in Banking and Financial Institutions series is international in orientation and includes studies of banking systems in particular countries or regions as well as contemporary themes such as Islamic Banking, Financial Exclusion, Mergers and Acquisitions, Risk Management, and IT in Banking. The books focus on research and practice and include up to date and innovative studies that cover issues which impact banking systems globally.

Jovi Clemente Dacanay ·
Ella Mae Odtuhan Leonida ·
Michaela Nicole E. Meriño

Bank Competition and the Effects on Financial Stability

Insights into the Emerging Banking Markets of the Philippines

palgrave
macmillan

Jovi Clemente Dacanay
School of Economics
University of Asia and the Pacific
Pasig City, Philippines

Ella Mae Odtuhan Leonida
RingCentral
Pasig City, Philippines

Michaela Nicole E. Meriño
First Metro Asset Management, Inc
Makati City, Philippines

ISSN 2523-336X ISSN 2523-3378 (electronic)
Palgrave Macmillan Studies in Banking and Financial Institutions
ISBN 978-3-031-59601-8 ISBN 978-3-031-59599-8 (eBook)
https://doi.org/10.1007/978-3-031-59599-8

Cover credit: shutterstock_City of London

This Palgrave Macmillan imprint is published by the registered company Springer Nature Switzerland AG
The registered company address is: Gewerbestrasse 11, 6330 Cham, Switzerland

Preface

Financial inclusion is the root of sustainable economic development. However, being financially included entails access to a wide range of financial services that respond to one's needs and capabilities.[1] This means targeting seven out of 10 financially excluded Filipinos,[2] which challenges Philippine universal and commercial banks (UKBs) to for-mulate and implement more creative products and services adopted to the needs of low-to-middle income Filipinos who aspire to be financially included.

Taking on this challenge exposes banks to risks and vulnerabilities, as they maintain healthy Basel III and BSP-regulated banking indicators. Yet the local industry managed to achieve this amidst the multiple difficulties posed by the COVID-19 pandemic.

This work took about six years in the making, starting with my dissertation that presented empirical proof to the stability of the Philippine banking system. Ella and Micha, graduate students then, together with their research seminar group mates took up the challenge of investigating important aspects of bank stability, namely bank efficiency and macro stress testing, could no longer be covered in my dissertation, due to time constraints. These research papers served as the seedbed of their individual theses which they successfully accomplished and defended in

[1] BSP. National Strategy for Financial Inclusion (2022–2028), pp. 1–3, (https://www.bsp.gov.ph/Pages/InclusiveFinance/NSFI-2022-2028.pdf).

[2] BSP. Financial Inclusion Survey (2019).

spite of the many COVID-related personal, financial, and health issues that we all had to grapple with. The data gathered, which was open to the public, covering up to the third quarter of 2022, provided sufficient information for us to verify if the banks in this study retained their pre-pandemic stability indicators. They did. This book establishes the theoretical, conceptual, and empirical evidence behind this remarkable phenomenon.

Pasig City, Philippines — Jovi Clemente Dacanay
Pasig City, Philippines — Ella Mae Odtuhan Leonida
Makati City, Philippines — Michaela Nicole E. Meriño

Acknowledgments

This book was made possible through a grant from the Center for Research and Communication via Colin Hubo, Danilo Reyes, and Perry Reyes. The authors would like to thank the invaluable and most effective assistance of Tula Weis, our series editor from Springer Nature, whose untiring encouragement helped the authors to make this book a reality. We also thank Springer Nature's Uma Vinesh, Susan Westendorf, Matthew Savin, and Straive's Jayalakshmi Raju who identified the flaws of the manuscript through their rigorous follow-up and editing.

Our most heartfelt gratitude goes to the expert copy editing of Annie Nisce, whose dedication and patience captured the essence of our message, making our preliminary texts, which were extremely technical, into a coherent, engaging, and readable narrative.

Jovi Clemente Dacanay, Ph.D. I would like to acknowledge the support of the following:

First, my dissertation adviser and mentor, Dr. Fernando T. Aldaba, whose optimism and advice have always provided firm guidance. The content of Chapter 3 would not have been possible without his support and that of Dr. Luis F. Dumlao, who introduced me to the topic of Financial Stability, and Dr. Noel P. De Guzman, my adviser and mentor in my research on Microfinance. To you all I owe the mental discipline to traverse this vast and complex academic field.

Second, I thank my colleagues in the School of Economics of the University of Asia and the Pacific (UA&P), Dr. Peter U and Dr. Victor

Abola, for being available to help me through this project, and to the late Dr. Emil T. Antonio, who first challenged me to go beyond the boundaries of knowledge. His encouraging words and guidance will always be cherished.

Third, I want to cite the contribution of my students in the Industrial Economics Program of the UA&P. Those hours of mentoring and advising them on their research papers and masteral theses prepared me to courageously explore a broad range of literature on banking and microfinance. Their prayers have been a firm support. In particular, I extend my deepest gratitude to my former student, mentee, thesis advisee, and dear friend, Tet Rivera, who generously assisted me in my research needs.

Lastly and most importantly, I thank my parents, Tita and Romulo Dacanay, for simply being there for me. Thank you, Dad, for instilling in me interest in banking and finance. My deepest thanks as well to my siblings, Vivian, Anna, Marita, Windy, and Jerome, and, to my wonderful nieces Francine, Coleen and Adam, Jamie, Morrisey, and Adam for the inspiration. Finally, to my friends for the constant encouragement.

Ella Mae Odtuhan Leonida, I would like to express profound gratitude to the persons who have supported me in this academic journey. I would not have completed Chapter 4 without the help and support of Dr. Victor A. Abola and Dr. Edwin B. Valeroso for their kindness and generosity in sharing their expertise to improve my study. I also thank Ms. Nikka Pesa for her guidance and constant encouragement; and my professors in the School of Economics, Dr. George Manzano, Dr. Cid Terosa, and Dr. Peter U, who instilled in me the intellectual formation during my years at UA&P. I am most thankful for the unfailing support and prayers of my family. Thank you, Mama, Papa, my eldest sister, eldest brother, and Issa. Thank you as well to my pets, Cotton and Mia, for being the best stress-relievers, and to my friends, Cyrus, Emerson, Christian, Trisha, Alyssamae, Nico, and Alma for being the best cheerleaders and for always believing in me. Finally, my thanks go to all the people who helped me complete this study—directly or indirectly.

Michaela Nicole E. Meriño. Chapter 5 is the product of the tireless and selfless support of the following individuals: My brilliant and exceptional mentors, Dr. Victor Abola and Mr. Brillo Reynes, for their valuable input and unfailing guidance and encouragement. My thanks to the SEC Faculty and UA&P Professors for imparting the knowledge, skills, values, and exemplary dedication to their respective fields which helped me launch out into my own career and to become the best version of myself. To all my friends, colleagues, and relatives, thank you for the prayers, encouragement, and inspiration. I dedicate this paper to my parents, Ghing and William, thank you for keeping me grounded and for providing me with more than what I need to finish my studies and aspire for greater ideals. To my younger brothers, Gab and Liam, thank you for the happy moments spent. I promise to strive to be a great role model for you. To my grandpa, Daddy Nick, thank you for stressing that "hard work pays off."

Contents

1 **Growing Literature** 1

2 **Bank Stability and Market Concentration in the Emerging Capital Markets of Southeast Asia** 7
Introduction 7
Emerging Capital Markets and the ASEAN Banking Industry 13
Framework 16
Empirical Methodology 18
Results 20
Bank Stability Trend of the ASEAN 7 33
Annex 35

3 **Bank Competition + Market Concentration = Financial Stability?** 49
Background 49
Review of Related Literature 51
Historical Development 52
Bank Competition and Financial Stability Pertinent to the Asia–Pacific Region 56
Studies Pertinent to the Philippines 56
Policy Issues 58
Theoretical Issues on Bank Competition, Capital Regulation, and Financial Stability 61

Empirical Issues: Industrial Organization Approach to Banking 67
Z-Index 68
Financial Stability Indicator Reflecting a Bank's Resilience From Insolvency: Z-index (ROA) or Z_{ROA} 70
An Alternative Financial Stability Indicator Reflecting a Bank's Resilience From Insolvency: Z-index (ROE) or Z_{ROE} 70
Risk-Based Capital Adequacy Ratio Z-index: Z-index (RCAR) or Z_{RCAR} 71
Herfindahl–Hirschman Index (HHI) 72
Lerner Index 73
Boone Indicator or the Profit Elasticity Indicator 76
Theoretical Framework and Empirical Methodology 77
Hypotheses 78
Theoretical and Conceptual Framework 78
Theoretical Model: Imperfect Competition in the Philippine Banking Industry with a Dominant Bank Model 79
Bank Competition, Concentration, Fragility, and Stability 83
Conceptual Framework 89
Empirical Methodology 98
Empirical Verification of an Imperfectly Competitive Banking Industry 98
Competition, Concentration, and Banking Industry Stability 101
Competition, Concentration, Financial Stability, and Bank Capitalization 107
Results 111
Market Structure and Market Power in the UKB Industry of the Philippines 116
Bank Competition, Market Concentration, and Bank Stability as Indicators of Resilience to Bank Distress or Insolvency 136
Bank Competition, Market Concentration, and Financial Stability as Indicators of Resilience to Regulatory Distress 141
Summary, Conclusion, and Recommendations 156
Appendix 160

4 Does Income Diversification Enhance Bank Efficiency and Stability in Periods of Increased Competition? 167
Background 167

Review of Related Literature 170
Theoretical Studies on Bank Competition, Diversification, and Efficiency 170
Empirical Studies on Bank Competition and Efficiency 171
Bank Competition and Bank Efficiency in the Philippines 173
Bank Competition, Diversification, and Efficiency: Theoretical and Practical Underpinnings of Diversification 173
Empirical Studies on Bank Diversification and Efficiency 176
Diversification and Risk-Taking 176
Theoretical Framework and Empirical Methodology 177
Hypotheses 177
Theoretical Framework 178
Conceptual Framework 184
Empirical Methodology: Computing for Liquidity as a Substitute for Total Output 186
Estimation of Cost and Profit Efficiency Using the Stochastic Frontier Approach 190
Computation of Lerner Index as a Measure of Individual Bank's Market Power 191
Estimating the Effect of Bank Competition on Cost and Profit 195
Efficiency of the Top 20 UKBs in the Philippines 195
Presentation, Interpretation, and Analysis of Results 199
Market Power and Efficiency 200
Market Power and Income Diversification 208
Market power, Income Diversification, and Stability 216
Summary, Conclusion, and Recommendations 224
Appendix 230

5 Macro Stress Testing of the Philippines' Top 10 UKBs: An Analysis of the Effect of Economic Distress on the Bank's Credit Quality 235
Background 235
Review of Related Literature 239
Typology of Macro Stress Testing 239
Formulation of Hypothesis 246
Theoretical Foundations 251
Theoretical and Conceptual Framework 255
Hypotheses 255
Theoretical Framework 256

Theoretical Model 259
The Bank in the Partial Equilibrium Model 259
The Goods-Producing Firm in the Partial Equilibrium Model 261
Partial Equilibrium Model 262
Conceptual Framework 263
Empirical Methodology 265
Model Specification 266
Herfindahl–Hirschman Index (HHI) 267
Vector Autoregressive (VAR) Model 267
Impulse Response Functions (IRF) 268
Generalized Method of Moments (GMM) 269
Data Description 270
Dependent Variable 270
Independent Variables 270
Results 270
Objective 1: Review of the Historical Influence of Macroeconomic Variables and Bank Competition on the Credit Quality of the Top 10 Universal and Commercial Banking Industry of the Philippines 273
Objective 2: Macroeconomic Model 285
Objective 3: Macroeconomic Scenarios 292
Objective 4: Credit Satellite Models 296
Summary, Conclusion, and Recommendations 302
Summary 302
Conclusion 309
Recommendations and Limitations of the Study 311
Appendix 312
Top 10 Banks Based on Total Assets from 2005 to 2020 312

Epilogue 313

Glossary 315

References 325

Index 349

List of Figures

Fig. 2.1	Gross domestic product per capita in current US$ of selected low-to-upper-middle-income countries in ASEAN (*Source* The Global Economy Data https://www.theglobaleconomy.com/)	9
Fig. 2.2	Scatterplot of bank stability, market power, and capitalization (*Source* World Bank)	24
Fig. 2.3	Scatterplot of efficiency, market power, and capitalization (*Source* World Bank)	27
Fig. 2.4	Scatterplot of non-interest income vs market power and capitalization (*Source* World Bank)	30
Fig. 2.5	Return-on-equity of the ASEAN 7 (*Source* World Bank)	31
Fig. 2.6	Bank Z-Score of the ASEAN 7 (2000–2027) (*Source* World Bank and the Global Economy Database. *Note* Actual data from 2000 to 2022, forecasts for RGDP growth rate, and inflation rate from 2023 to 2027 are based on IMF forecasts, as reported in The Global Economy Database)	35
Fig. 3.1	Overlapping dimensions of financial stability: the macroeconomy, financial institutions, and financial markets (*Source* Moenjak 2014, p. 211, and Author's Framework)	53
Fig. 3.2	Short-run implications of a binding risk-based capital requirement among perfectly competitive banks (*Source* VanHoose 2022, p. 165)	64

Fig. 3.3 Long-term effects of a binding risk-based capital ratio with representative competitive banks (*Source* VanHoose 2022, p. 166) 64

Fig. 3.4 Effects of a binding risk-based capital ratio with heterogeneous competitive banks (*Source* VanHoose 2022, p. 175) 66

Fig. 3.5 The structure-conduct-performance hypothesis: a loan market with a dominant bank and a competitive fringe (*Source* VanHoose 2022, p. 43) 81

Fig. 3.6 **a** and **b** The effects of capital regulation and competition on stability (*Source* Schliephake 2016, p. 1789 and the author's theoretical framework) 90

Fig. 3.7 Relevant literature linking capital regulation and competition with market power on stability (*Source* Schliephake 2016, p. 1789 and the author's theoretical framework) 93

Fig. 3.8 The effect of capital regulation and competition with market power on stability (*Source* Schliephake 2016, p. 1789 and the author's theoretical framework) 94

Fig. 3.9 Objectives of the study in the context of capitalization, bank competition and concentration, and bank stability nexus (*Source* Schliephake 2016, p. 1789 and the author's theoretical framework) 102

Fig. 3.10 Return-on-Equity and market concentration (*Source* BSP for basic data and the author's regression results) 110

Fig. 3.11 Herfindahl–Hirschman Index of the 46 BSP-Listed UKBs (*Source* BSP https://www.bsp.gov.ph/SitePages/Statistics/BSFinancialStatements.aspx?TabId=1) 117

Fig. 3.12 Financial Stability and Market Structure using the HHI for Loans and Deposits (*Source* BSP https://www.bsp.gov.ph/SitePages/Statistics/BSFinancialStatements.aspx?TabId=1 for basic data and Author's Regression Results. *Note* HHI < 1000 Unconcentrated and HHI > 1800 Highly Concentrated [Salop 1987]) 118

Fig. 3.13 Bank Capitalization and Market Structure using the HHI for Loans and Deposits (*Source* BSP for basic data) 119

Fig. 3.14 Estimated Equity-to-Assets and Estimated Z_{ROE} with Actual Loans-to-Assets Ratio (2008 Q4 to 2019 Q4) (*Source* BSP for basic data, and Author's estimates) 155

Fig. 3.15 Z_{ROA} and Bank Capitalization Coordinates for the Top 20 Banks (*Source* BSP for basic data, and the author's framework) 156

Fig. 3.16 Equity-to-Assets Ratio and Adjusted Lerner Index of the Top 20 UKBs (2005Q1 to 2019Q4) (*Source* BSP for basic data and the author's regression results) 157
Fig. 4.1 Summary of the theoretical framework (*Source* Author's theoretical framework) 184
Fig. 4.2 Conceptual framework: market power, income diversification, and bank efficiency (*Source* Author's framework) 185
Fig. 4.3 Mean profit efficiency scores (*Source* Author's framework) 185
Fig. 4.4 Mean cost efficiency scores (*Source* Author's framework) 186
Fig. 4.5 Conventional Lerner index (*Source* Author's framework) 201
Fig. 4.6 Adjusted Lerner index (*Source* Author's framework) 201
Fig. 4.7 Scatterplot of cost and profit efficiency vs. conventional Lerner index (*Source* Author's framework) 206
Fig. 4.8 Scatterplot of cost and profit efficiency vs. adjusted Lerner index (*Source* Author's framework) 207
Fig. 4.9 Income diversification index (*Source* Author's framework) 208
Fig. 4.10 Objectives 1 and 2: Relationship of Lerner index, income diversification, and bank efficiency (*Source* Author's framework, **Note* Numbers inside the square brackets are coefficients of the regressions) 213
Fig. 4.11 HHI deposits, loans, and assets of the entire banking industry throughout the sample period (*Source* BSP) 217
Fig. 4.12 Summary of the relationships of the Lerner index, income diversification, and bank stability variables for Objective 3 (*Source* Author's framework, **Notes* Numbers inside the square brackets are coefficients of the regressions) 222
Fig. 5.1 Complete Keynesian model (*Source* Bernard Felderer and Stefan Homburg [1992]) 253
Fig. 5.2 Conceptual map (*Sources* Author's theoretical framework, Vu et al. [2018]) 265
Fig. 5.3 Revised conceptual map (*Sources* Author's theoretical framework, Vu et al. [2018]) 266

Fig. 5.4 Market concentration using the Herfindahl–Hirschman Index (Top 46 UKBs) and Non-performing loans ratio of the entire universal and commercial banks (UKBs) (*Sources* Author's calculations, Bangko Sentral ng Pilipinas (BSP). *Note* Gray portion highlights the movement during the Global Financial Crisis (2008–2009) and the COVID-19 pandemic which started on March 6, 2020, for the Philippines with its first reported COVID-19 case) 277
Fig. 5.5 Non-performing loans ratio of the top 5 universal and commercial banks (*Source* Bangko Sentral ng Pilipinas (BSP). *Notes* (1) Gray portion highlights the movement during the Global Financial Crisis (2008–2009), (2) The NPL ratio of the Philippine National Bank (PNB) is plotted on the right-hand side since it is the only bank from the Top 5 that had NPL higher than 40%) 279
Fig. 5.6 Non-performing loans ratio of the next 5 universal and commercial banks (*Source* Bangko Sentral ng Pilipinas (BSP). *Note* Gray portion highlights the movement during the Global Financial Crisis (2008–2009)) 279
Fig. 5.7 Market shares of the top 46 universal and commercial banks (*Source* Bangko Sentral ng Pilipinas (BSP)) 284
Fig. 5.8 Impulse response function (IRF) results (*Source* Author's Calculations. *Notes* (1) The magnitude of the shock: one standard deviation of x; (2) Red dots represent the standard error (SE) confidence bands. The confidence intervals are computed as +/− 2 SE confidence bands; (3) X axis represents the periods in quarters; Y axis shows the percentage variation) 287
Fig. 5.9 GDP trend in 2019–2021(*Sources* Author's calculations. *Notes* (1) Data for 2021 is computed using VAR; (2) Simulation type: Deterministic, dynamic solution) 289
Fig. 5.10 Inflation Trend in 2019–2021 (*Sources* Author's calculations. *Notes* (1) Data for 2021 is computed using VAR; (2) Simulation type: Deterministic, dynamic solution) 290
Fig. 5.11 Interest rate trend in 2019–2021 (*Sources* Author's calculations. *Notes* (1) Data for 2021 is computed using VAR; (2) Simulation type: Deterministic, dynamic solution) 291

Fig. 5.12 Exchange rate trend in 2019–2021 (*Sources* Author's calculations. *Notes* (1) Data for 2021 is computed using VAR; (2) Simulation type: Deterministic, dynamic solution) 292
Fig. 5.13 Remittances trend in 2019–2021 (*Sources* Author's calculations, Bangko Sentral ng Pilipinas (BSP). *Notes* (1) Data for 2021 is computed using VAR; (2) Simulation type: Deterministic, dynamics: Dynamic solution) 293

List of Tables

Table 2.1	Growth projections for ASEAN and the world	10
Table 2.2	Growth projections for ASEAN 10 and the world	12
Table 2.3	Projected share of global growth for 2023	13
Table 2.4	Banking industry variables per country of the ASEAN 7	21
Table 2.5	Bank stability, efficiency, and capitalization	25
Table 2.6	Cost efficiency and capitalization for ASEAN 7	28
Table 2.7	Profitability and bank stability	32
Table 2.8	Banking industry variables per country	36
Table 2.9	Descriptive statistics relevant indicators	45
Table 2.10	Correlation matrix of relevant indicators	46
Table 2.11	Forecasts: economic growth and inflation	47
Table 3.1	Comparison of Basel III guidelines and proposed BSP regulations	59
Table 3.2	Variable definition	104
Table 3.3	Effect of market power on various dependent variables *i*	108
Table 3.4	Effect of market power on bank capitalization in compliance with Basel III (Competition-Fragility Nexus)	109
Table 3.5	Competition, market concentration, and stability empirical tests: which factors make banks less fragile?	112
Table 3.6	Market power behavior of the Top 20 Top 20 UKBs (2005Q1 to 2019Q4)	121
Table 3.7	Market power behavior of the Top 10 UKBs vs the Next 10 (2005Q1–2019Q4)	122

Table 3.8	Comparison of market power behavior: Top 10 vs Next 10 UKBs (2008Q4–2019Q4)	123
Table 3.9	Market concentration and markups of dominant vs fringe UKBs (2005Q1–2019Q4)	124
Table 3.10	Mark-up elasticity of total loans vs total deposits (2005Q1–2019Q4)	125
Table 3.11	Net income of dominant and fringe banks vs market power (2005Q1–2019Q4)	126
Table 3.12	Results of the empirical verification of an imperfectly UKBs industry using the Monti-Klein and the dominant and fringe models for the Top 20 UKBs	127
Table 3.13	Financial stability using Z_{ROA} of the Top 20 UKBs (2005Q1–2019Q4)	132
Table 3.14	Financial stability using Z_{ROE} of the Top 20 UKBs (2005Q1–2019Q4)	137
Table 3.15	Financial stability using Z_{ROA} of the Top 10 and next 10 UKBs (2005Q1–2019Q4)	138
Table 3.16	Financial stability using Z_{ROE} of the Top 10 and Next 10 UKBs (2005Q1–2019Q4)	139
Table 3.17	Financial Fragility using Equity-to-Assets of the Top 20	142
Table 3.18	Financial fragility using equity-to-assets of the Top 20 UKBs (2005Q1–2019Q4)	143
Table 3.19	Financial fragility using equity-to-assets of the Top 10 and next 10 UKBs (2005Q1–2019Q4)	144
Table 3.20	Financial fragility using the NPL ratio of the Top 20 UKBs (2005Q1–2019Q4)	145
Table 3.21	Financial fragility using non-performing loans ratio of the Top 10 and next 10 UKBs (2005Q1–2019Q4)	147
Table 3.22	Financial stability using Z_{RCAR} of the Top 10 and next 10 UKBs (2007Q3–2019Q4)	148
Table 3.23	Financial stability using Z_{TIER1} of the Top 10 and next 10 UKBs (2007Q3–2019Q4)	149
Table 3.24	Buffer, risk-shifting, and profit-margin effects on the risk-based capital adequacy ratio of the Top 10 and next 10 UKBs (2007Q3–2019Q4)	150
Table 3.25	Inflection Points Estimated from the GMM Regressions (2005Q1–2022Q3)	152
Table 3.26	Bank competition, concentration and financial stability findings	158
Table 3.27	Basis for the dominant and fringe bank grouping	161
Table 3.28	Market share of the Top 46 UKBs (2005–2022)	162

Table 3.29	GMM regression on return-on-equity for the Top 20 UKBs (2005Q1 to 2007Q4)	163
Table 3.30	GMM regression on return-on-equity for the Top 20 UKBs	164
Table 3.31	Descriptive statistics for the Top 20 UKBs (2005 Q1–2019 Q4)	165
Table 3.32	Descriptive statistics for the Top 10 and Next 10 UKBs (2005 Q1–2019 Q4)	166
Table 4.1	Classified accounts with assigned weights	188
Table 4.2	Summary of variables	192
Table 4.3	Regression results for Objective 1: The top 20 banks' profit and cost efficiency as dependent variables	204
Table 4.4	Regression results for Objective 2: The top 10 banks profit and cost efficiency as dependent variables	205
Table 4.5	Regression results for Objective 2: The fringe banks (next 10) profit and cost efficiency as dependent variables	210
Table 4.6	Summary of variables determining bank efficiency using conventional and adjusted lerner index for dominant and fringe banks	215
Table 4.7	Regression results for Objective 3 for dominant banks with Z_{ROA} and Z_{ROE} as dependent variables	219
Table 4.8	Regression results for Objective 3 for fringe banks with Z_{ROA} and Z_{ROE} as dependent variables	221
Table 4.9	Summary of variables determining bank stability using conventional and adjusted Lerner index for dominant and fringe banks	223
Table 4.10	Summary of results	225
Table 4.11	Top 20 banks in terms of assets as of December 2019	230
Table 4.12	Descriptive statistics	231
Table 4.13	Average cost and profit efficiency of the top 20 UKBs in the Philippines from Q1 2005 to Q4 2019	233
Table 5.1	Summary of the developments in macro stress testing (MST)	240
Table 5.2	Summary of the formulation of Hypothesis 1	241
Table 5.3	Summary of the formulation of Hypothesis 2 and 3	243
Table 5.4	List of independent variables	245
Table 5.5	Summary of the empirical methodology	271
Table 5.6	GDP growth rate forecasts of organizations in 2021	294
Table 5.7	Result of GDP shocks using percentile function	294
Table 5.8	Computed GDP growth rate quarterly forecasts for 2021	295
Table 5.9	GMM results of the top 10 UKBs under mild scenario	299

Table 5.10 GMM results of the Top 10 UKBs under moderate scenario 300
Table 5.11 GMM results of the UKB industry under mild and moderate scenarios 301
Table 5.12 Computed results using the forecasted values in 2021 under mild scenario versus actual 2020 data 301
Table 5.13 Computed results using the forecasted values in 2021 under moderate scenario versus actual 2020 data 302
Table 5.14 Results using the forecasted values in 2021 under mild and moderate scenario versus actual 2019 and 2020 data 302
Table 5.15 Summary table of objectives, method and indicators, and results 303

CHAPTER 1

Growing Literature

The five chapters of this book bring together three different studies whose authors worked as an academic team tasked to delve into the industrial organization of the Philippine banking industry, using this structure as a lever to consider the local banking industry as an emerging capital market. All three authors mentored one another, witnessing the reaction and behavior of the universal and commercial banking (UKB) industry to a COVID-19 environment. This study aims to show readers that the Philippine UKB industry demonstrated resilience to this unprecedented economic shock and will continue to withstand the global headwinds affecting the emerging countries of Asia.

The researchers intentionally covered data from 2005 to 2019 due to the irregularity of data pertinent to measure the market power and efficiency indexes from 2020 to 2021. However, the presence of open access data from the Bangko Sentral ng Pilipinas (BSP) website shows that the banking industry is on its way to pre-COVID levels due to their aggressive move to improve capitalization and so withstand anything that would challenge their stability.

First, this book aims to provide empirical verification that market competition and market concentration lead to the financial stability of Philippine UKBs and of the emerging markets in the ASEAN. Second, cost efficiency contributed to the market power of the Top 20 UKBs. In

J. C. Dacanay et al., *Bank Competition and the Effects on Financial Stability*, Palgrave Macmillan Studies in Banking and Financial Institutions, https://doi.org/10.1007/978-3-031-59599-8_1

fact, a Lerner index that is adjusted for cost efficiency strongly explains bank stability. Third, with macro stress testing, one can verify that the Top 10 Philippine UKBs remained stable in spite of the economic distress caused by the pandemic and the regulations regarding the extension of loan payments.

Chapter 2, entitled "Bank Stability and Market Concentration in the Emerging Capital Markets of Southeast Asia," discusses the similarities of macroeconomic policies among the seven selected nations of the Association of Southeast Asian Nations (ASEAN) with regard to achieving financial and economic stability. Sound macroeconomic fundamentals, resilience of financial systems, and bank stability constitute the core of the emerging capital markets of the upper middle-income and low-middle-income countries of the ASEAN. For a region that is vulnerable to external shocks, bank stability arising from the interdependence of the banking sector and the overall health of the capital markets usually characterizes a resilient financial system. This study focuses on the market concentration and stability nexus which signifies that more market concentration leading to higher capitalization in the banking industry of the low-middle countries of the ASEAN leads to more stable banks. One can therefore observe that small developing countries of the ASEAN whose banking industries vary in size and market concentration all manifest stability before and during the pandemic period even if they remained vulnerable to various global headwinds.

Chapter 3, entitled "Does Market Competition and Market Concentration Lead to Financial Stability?" focuses on "competition-stability," a strand of banking literature that affirms that greater market power boosts stability. Martinez-Miera and Repullo (2010) argue that a non-linear, inverted U-shaped relationship between competition and financial stability, and financial stability and fragility can happen at the same time. This study verifies the "competition-stability" view in the context of imperfect competition and a binding bank capitalization regulatory constraint in the banking industry of the Philippines.

With this current environment, does bank competition and concentration lead to financial stability?

Using the techniques of traditional and the new empirical industrial organization literature, the study verified the occurrence of competition-stability in an imperfectly competitive and loans market-concentrated UKB industry under a binding regulatory bank capitalization environment. In a banking industry with dominant and fringe banks, the sampled

Top 20 banks of the Philippines are expected to exercise market power by charging higher loan rates to improve their profit margins and monitoring technology. According to Schliephake (2016), banks resort to this practice to acquire sufficient earnings and so increase their capital buffer.

To test the competition-fragility and competition-stability views, the Z-index (indicator for financial stability vis-à-vis overall bank risk exposure and insolvency), non-performing loans (NPL) to total loans ratio (indicator for portfolio risk), and, the equity to total assets ratio (indicator for bank capitalization) were used as dependent variables and regressed, using the generalized method of moments (GMM). Market power, on the other hand, was measured by the adjusted Lerner index, Herfindahl–Hirschman Index or HHI (for deposits and loans), and other bank-specific control variables, following the methodology used by Berger et al. (2009).

The GMM regression method allows for correction for heteroscedasticity, weak serial correlation, and endogeneity via robust estimators and assumes a non-normal but asymptotic to zero probabilistic distribution for the means of the dependent and independent variables. Varying methods of the financial stability indicator, the Z-index, were used to test resilience from bank insolvency and regulatory distress, i.e., using return-on-assets, return-on-equity, BSP-proposed risk-weighted capitalization ratios.

The results show that in an environment of imperfect competition, dominant banks experience an increase of profit margins through higher markups and a decline in NPL. These combined occurrences lessen the probability of insolvency thereby increasing the stability of the larger banks. However, the strategy of increasing their loans and deposits market shares also exposes them to higher default and market risks, or financial or economic shocks which cause significantly higher equity returns volatility, thereby increasing bank fragility.

The empirical results verify that the profit margin and risk-shifting effects among the Top 10 banks outweigh the buffer effect. On the other hand, the Next 10 banks achieved higher profit margins that were channeled to bigger capitalization ratios. One can therefore hope that as greater market concentration continues, dominant banks will promote a market environment that pursues higher capital ratios to boost stability in the UKB industry.

Chapter 4 "Does Income Diversification Contribute to Achieving Bank Efficiency and Stability in periods of Increased Competition?" tackles how empirical studies churn out ambiguous results regarding the effects of bank competition and income diversification on performance in terms of cost and profit efficiency and stability. This is despite literature that elucidate the importance of cost and profit efficiency to determine a bank's performance. Using the Lerner index as a measure for bank market power and Stochastic Frontier Analysis to estimate bank cost and profit efficiency scores, this study aims to verify whether a high level of income diversification contributes to the efficiency and stability of the Philippines' Top 20[1] UKBs in periods of increased competition.

The GMM panel estimation has shown that competition is negatively related to cost and profit efficiency and stability, which supports the information generation hypothesis and competition-fragility view. The results also show that a high level of income diversification alone is detrimental to bank efficiency and stability. However, when a high level of income diversification comes with a high level of market power, banks improve in efficiency and stability. Due to this, domestic banks, particularly the dominant ones, thrive in an imperfectly competitive market despite their diverse income sources. The erosion of market power adversely affects bank performance, which is more evident in those with highly diversified income. These results imply that a high level of income diversification can intensify the negative impact of market competition on cost and profit efficiency and bank stability.

Chapter 5 "Macro Stress Testing of the Philippines' Top 10 UKBs: An Analysis of the Effect of Economic Distress on the Bank's Credit Quality" intends to address financial instability in emerging markets. A growing share of NPLs in the loan portfolio of banks in developing economies signifies greater risks for banking stability. In the wake of continuing global economic uncertainty, one must understand the importance of macro stress testing to gauge a bank's level of preparedness to manage risks in the financial system. Stress testing, a key technique for quantifying risks, constitutes a series of tests to assess the vulnerability of a financial system to "exceptional but plausible" macroeconomic shocks. Thus, this paper aims to answer the question, "Does increased economic distress, in the context of lower bank competition, lead to lower credit quality?".

[1] From 2005 to 2021, the BSP reports a total of 46 UKBs. The authors consider this as the total number of UKBs in the Philippines. Some failed to submit their records to the BSP from 2020 to 2021, thus list in the BSP database totaled to only 41. As of the first quarter of 2022, 45 UKBs submitted their balance sheets to the BSP. The reduced number was due to the merger of Landbank and United Coconut Planters Bank in 2021.

The research will undertake four different stages that correspond to the following objectives: (1) to review the historical influence of macroeconomic variables and bank competition on the credit quality of the Top 10 Philippine UKBs; (2) to measure the relationship between macroeconomic variables, namely output growth, interest rates, inflation, exchange rate, and remittances; (3) to forecast the macroeconomic indicators under mild and moderate stress scenarios; and (4) to quantify the effect of economic distress on the credit quality of the Top 10 UKBs and the entire industry. The study used the NPL ratio as the empirical measure for credit quality. In terms of scope, it focuses on assessing the relationship between credit quality and the interested macroeconomic variables and does not attempt to predict the probability of a bank failure under stress scenarios.

Given the presence of the top 10 UKBs and bank behavior under the indicated macroeconomic stress scenarios, this chapter shows that lower remittances, GDP growth rate, and inflation, together with an increase in the interest rate and a level of exchange rate, contribute to forecasting an NPL ratio of 1.8%. This is in the scenarios of below 5% forecasts of credit rating agencies and Basel III regulation amidst the pandemic. Considering that the NPL ratio is well within the Basel III regulation of 5%, the UKB industry will continue to be stable.

The chapters look to convince monetary authorities of the emerging markets of the ASEAN to maintain macroeconomic policies that effectively foster financial stability. Such markets are conducive to bank stability resulting from cost-efficient and well-capitalized dominant banks.

CHAPTER 2

Bank Stability and Market Concentration in the Emerging Capital Markets of Southeast Asia

Introduction

Emerging capital markets refer to financial markets in developing countries that are experiencing growth and rapid economic development. Robust capital markets and financial systems, increased foreign investments, improved regulatory frameworks, enhanced financial infrastructure and institutions, and a growing middle class and high-risk and return profiles often characterize these markets. Moreover, they offer investment opportunities in sectors, such as technology, manufacturing, infrastructure, and services.

Governments of emerging market economies often implement economic reforms to attract foreign investments. These reforms may involve deregulation, the privatization of state-owned enterprises, and the opening up of financial markets to foreign investors. The regulatory environment of emerging capital markets may still be evolving, as authorities strive to establish effective regulations and frameworks to support fair and transparent markets. These include regulations on securities offerings, investor protection, corporate governance, and disclosure requirements. Emerging capital markets develop financial institutions, such as stock exchanges, bond markets, and commodity exchanges, to

J. C. Dacanay et al., *Bank Competition and the Effects on Financial Stability*, Palgrave Macmillan Studies in Banking and Financial Institutions, https://doi.org/10.1007/978-3-031-59599-8_2

facilitate capital flows and investment. They may also establish regulatory bodies to oversee and enforce transparency and investor protection measures.

Likewise, the rise of a middle class with increased purchasing power is a key characteristic of emerging markets. Such is the case of Malaysia, Thailand, and, recently, Indonesia whose GDP per capita reached at least US$ 4256 in 2004, 2008, and 2021, respectively, enabling them to achieve upper middle-income status.[1] Figure 2.1 shows per capita GDP of the six selected countries of the Association of Southeast Asian Nations (ASEAN). The selected ASEAN countries in this study have complete databases from 2000 to 2022. In order to see the trend line of the other six ASEAN member countries, high-income Singapore was excluded from the graph as its GDP per capita is double that of Malaysia.

The expanding consumer base creates opportunities for businesses and attracts foreign companies looking to tap into new markets. Emerging capital markets often entail higher risks compared to more developed markets due to factors, such as political instability, currency volatility, and less mature regulatory frameworks. Examples of these are Brazil, Russia, India, China, Mexico, South Africa, and Turkey. However, they also offer possibly higher returns on investment, attracting investors seeking growth opportunities. These markets present opportunities for domestic and international investors looking to diversify their portfolios and participate in the growth of these economies. In particular, Asia is expected to surpass the projected growth of other regions (See Table 2.1).

The emerging capital markets, also referred to as emerging markets in ASEAN, differ from the above-mentioned countries in terms of economic development, regulatory framework, market size, and regional dynamics. Rapid economic growth, an expanding middle class, and increased urbanization typically characterize the markets of Indonesia, Thailand, Malaysia, the Philippines, and Vietnam (see Table 2.2). As of 2022, ASEAN contributed 9.9% to the global economy, much more than Europe (See Table 2.3). ASEAN's emerging markets primarily attract regional and international investors seeking exposure to high-growth economies in Southeast Asia. Emerging capital markets in the ASEAN have been the

[1] In this regard, please refer to the following World Bank classification: less than US$1035 GNI per capita (low-income); $1036–$4085 GNI per capita (lower middle-income); US$4086–$12,615 (upper middle income); over US$12,615 (high income). Upper middle-income countries have a GDP of US$4256–$13,205.

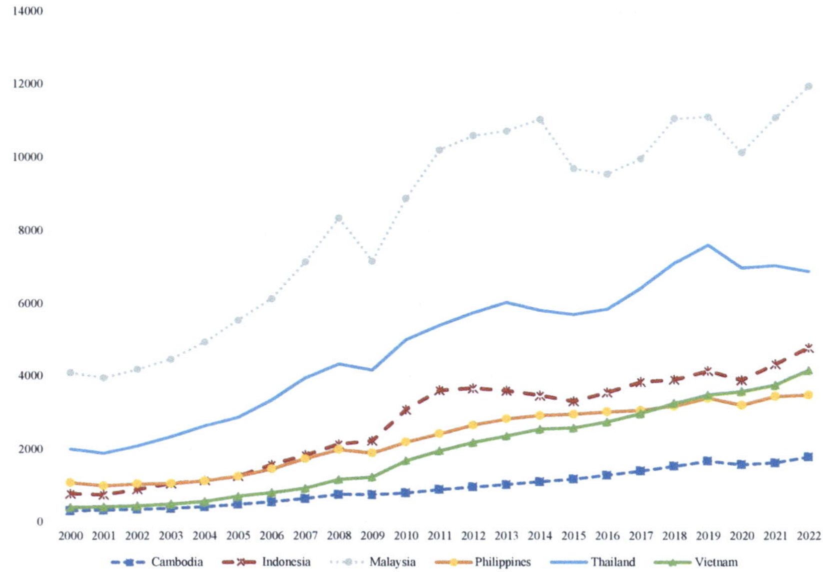

Fig. 2.1 Gross domestic product per capita in current US$ of selected low-to-upper-middle-income countries in ASEAN (*Source* The Global Economy Data https://www.theglobaleconomy.com/)

focal point of investors, policymakers, and financial institutions due to their potential for growth and opportunities. At the same time, their stability remains under scrutiny. Compared to the developed countries, emerging markets often carry higher levels of risk and volatility due to such factors as political instability, currency fluctuations, inadequate regulatory frameworks, and economic uncertainties. Many countries envy the growth of emerging Asian economies even as these fall short of historical standards and are expected to undergo an extended cyclical downturn in 2023–2024. Furthermore, recent shocks have dampened long-term prospects. Several emerging Asian economies are not gaining substantial momentum in terms of investment and exports, indicating that emulating the development trajectories of advanced Asian nations may prove challenging. Achieving the same level of development as advanced Asian countries within the next decade will likely remain beyond the reach of

Table 2.1 Growth projections for ASEAN and the world

	World	*Asia and the Pacific*	*Advanced Economies*	*Emerging Markets and Developing Economies*	*China*	*Japan*	*India*	*Korea*	*Australia*	*Emerging and Developing Asia*	*ASEAN*
2022	3.5	4.1	2.6	4.1	3.0	1.0	7.2	2.6	3.7	4.5	5.7
2023e	3.0	4.4	1.5	4.0	5.0	2.0	6.3	1.4	1.8	5.2	4.2
2024e	2.9	4.1	1.4	4.0	4.2	1.0	6.3	2.2	1.2	4.8	4.6

Source World Economic Outlook, IMF, October 10, 2023

most emerging Asian nations. However, there is hope for some progress through structural and business environment reforms.[2]

Emerging market economies face increasing turbulence in the near future and must reckon with the demand to enhance macroprudential surveillance and address potential sources of financial instability. Ongoing interest rate hikes by the Federal Reserve from 2022 to 2023 have led to local currency depreciation in the ASEAN, driven by expanding interest rate differentials, which complicate the battle against inflation. Central banks of these economies have remained conservative, as they tame core inflation levels. Furthermore, a protracted period of historically low interest rates has resulted in record-high debt levels in the fiscal, corporate, and household sectors. With the gradual phase-out of regulatory relief and forbearance measures and declining monetary policy support, the aftershocks of corporate default and loan loss from the pandemic still occur. The rise of NPL ratios in several regional economies, albeit from a relatively low base, is a case in point. Thus, financial authorities are closely monitoring and taking preemptive action to stave off the accumulation of systemic risks.[3]

The hike of US interest rates elevated borrowing costs even before they occurred. In the era of globalized finance, there is a pressing need for a robust global defense mechanism against financial crises. Strong economic recovery remains the most viable way out. Emerging Asian countries are seizing the opportunities arising from rapid digital transformation to enhance productivity and harness potential gains in economic growth and employment. As a consequence, policy makers in the Region are promoting broader and more equitable access to digital opportunities by enhancing digital infrastructure and expanding human capacities.[4]

[2] https://www.eiu.com/n/a-tougher-growth-outlook-for-emerging-asia/ (27 July 2023).

[3] Cyn-Young Park (2022) "The Implications for Asia of US Monetary Policy," *Asian Development Blog* (https://blogs.adb.org/blog/implications-asia-us-monetary-policy, 7 March 2022).

[4] Ibid.

Table 2.2 Growth projections for ASEAN 10 and the world

	Brunei Darussalam	*Cambodia*	*Indonesia*	*Lao P.D.R*	*Malaysia*	*Myanmar*	*Philippines*	*Singapore*	*Thailand*	*Vietnam*
2022	−1.6	5.2	5.3	2.3	8.7	2.0	7.6	3.6	2.6	8.0
2023e	−0.8	5.6	5.0	4.0	4.0	2.6	5.3	1.0	2.7	4.7
2024e	3.5	6.1	5.0	4.0	4.3	2.6	5.9	2.1	3.2	5.8

Source World Economic Outlook, IMF, October 10, 2023

Table 2.3 Projected share of global growth for 2023

Region		%
Asia and the Pacific		**67.6**
China	34.9	
India	15.4	
Japan	1.8	
Bangladesh	1.8	
Other	3.8	
Selected ASEAN	9.9	
Indonesia	4.4	
Thailand	1.1	
Malaysia	1.1	
Philippines	1.6	
Vietnam	1.7	
Africa		**4**
Europe		**7.1**
Middle East		**7.8**
Western Hemisphere		**13.5**

Source Regional Economic Outlook, April 2023

Emerging Capital Markets and the ASEAN Banking Industry

Emerging capital markets rely on the overall soundness of the banking sector. Banks play a crucial role in financial intermediation by channeling funds from savers to borrowers in emerging capital markets. They provide loans to businesses and individuals, supporting economic growth and development. A stable banking sector ensures the availability of credit and financial services which are vital to the functioning of capital markets and the promotion of investor confidence and liquidity in emerging capital markets. Stable and well-capitalized banks foster liquidity and support trade ventures by acting as market makers and underwriters of securities issuances.

Banks are likewise custodians of customer deposits. This is why banks with strong risk management frameworks help mitigate any negative impact on capital markets and therefore contribute to the stability of the financial system. When banks win the confidence of investors, clients tend to be more engaged in capital market activities, such as investing in stocks and bonds, and so foster more liquidity, attract more foreign investments, and promote overall market stability.

Finally, the stability of the banking sector is crucial to the general resilience of a financial system. Banks that face significant distress in emerging capital markets can set off a domino effect on other financial institutions and the broader economy. Such disruption can lead to market volatility, reduced lending activities, and a decline in investor confidence, affecting the functioning of capital markets. Consequently, macroeconomic stabilization policies, such as those related to the management of flexible exchange and inflation rates, as well as the maintenance of foreign exchange reserves, are crucial to the growth of ASEAN's emerging capital markets.

Regulatory authorities in emerging markets often prioritize the stability and soundness of the banking sector to promote healthy capital markets. They supervise and implement regulations to ensure that banks maintain adequate capital, manage risks effectively, and comply with prudential norms. Additionally, macroeconomic stability, effective governance, and transparency within the banking sector are essential to fostering trust and stability in the banking sector and capital markets in emerging economies.

Efficiency, bank competition and market concentration, liquidity, and macroeconomic stabilization policy interconnect within the broader framework of financial regulation and macroeconomic management. Efficiency in the banking sector refers to the ability of banks to allocate resources effectively, minimize costs, and maximize returns. An efficient banking sector is essential to economic growth and stability because it ensures the productive allocation and use of capital.

Competition drives efficiency and innovation. In an environment of intense competition, banks outdo each other in serving customers by offering better services, lower fees, and more favorable interest rates. However, competition without adequate regulation can give rise to risky behavior and a "race to the bottom" in terms of lending standards. This calls for effective regulatory oversight that strikes a balance between competition and stability.

Liquidity in the banking system refers to the availability of funds to meet short-term financial obligations. It is crucial to the stability of individual banks and the entire financial system. Stabilization policies, such as monetary policy, aim to smoothen economic fluctuation and maintain macroeconomic stability. Central banks and governments use these policies and resort to tools, like open market conditions, to inject or withdraw liquidity and so achieve policy objectives, such as inflation control or stabilization of the financial system during a crisis. Still, efficiency and competition can affect stabilization policies. An efficient banking sector can transmit monetary policy changes more effectively to the broader economy, but the pressures of competition can influence a bank's response to policy measures.

To summarize, efficiency and competition in the banking sector are critical to the proper functioning of financial markets and allocation of resources in the economy, while liquidity is essential to the stability of banks and the financial system. Stabilization policies, including monetary and fiscal measures, aim to maintain overall economic stability but can be influenced by the state of the banking sector. Effective regulation and supervision safeguard financial stability from the negative impact of competition and ensure liquidity that adequately supports the economy in times of need.

Recent studies on the stability of the banking sector focus on the relationship of bank competition, concentration, and efficiency with bank liquidity, solvency, and capitalization. Bank capitalization is the lever through which the Bank for International Settlements via Basel III would regulate the risk-taking tendencies of big banks.

This chapter addresses the question: Is the banking sector of the emerging ASEAN nations stable? First, it aims to verify the bank concentration and stability nexus for the middle- and low-middle countries of the ASEAN. Previous studies have limited the bank concentration and stability nexus only among more concentrated middle-income countries. Second, the study will provide empirical proof that low-middle emerging capital markets of the ASEAN have improved their bank Z-score and cost efficiency, displaying the resilience of their respective financial systems amidst the impact of the pandemic. When banks are stable and well capitalized, they ensure liquidity and support trading activities, thereby contributing to the overall liquidity of the capital markets. Effective risk management practices which contributed to the resilience of the financial systems, as indicated by the bank Z-score, helped mitigate the potential negative effects of market volatility on capital markets.

These favorable characteristics of the selected ASEAN countries shall be empirically verified through a generalized method of moments (GMM) regression of annual data (2000–2021) to measure the bank Z-score, which in turn indicates the solvency of the ASEAN's emerging upper middle capital markets (Malaysia and Thailand) and low-middle-income ones (Cambodia, Indonesia, the Philippines, and Vietnam). As earlier mentioned, the roster excludes high-income Singapore.

Secondary open access, annual data from 2000 to 2022 were obtained from the Global Economy Data website (https://www.theglobaleconomy.com/) for inflation rate, real gross domestic product growth rate, and the Global Financial Development Database of the World Bank for bank-specific data (https://www.worldbank.org/en/publication/gfdr/data/global-financial-development-database). Bank Z-score, cost efficiency, capitalization, and profitability serve as endogenous variables. Market concentration, the previous year's Bank Z-Score, capitalization, other efficiency indicators, liquidity, growth of real gross domestic product (RGDPGR), and inflation rate (INFLRATE) will explain all these. GMM with first differences transformation is the chosen regression procedure because it best responds to the countries' interconnected bank data and cross-section dependence. Moreover, the data used are mostly non-stationary and heteroskedastic.

Despite their vulnerability to post-pandemic external shocks, the bank Z-score of 2024–2027 forecasts stable growth for the selected emerging capital markets. Of note, the banking industries of the developing, low-middle-income countries have proven to be stable before and during the pandemic despite their vulnerability to global headwinds.

Framework

Following the framework of Tran, Nguyen, and Nguyen (2022), this study uses aggregate data (2000–2020) of seven developing and emerging markets within the ASEAN—Cambodia, Indonesia, Malaysia, the Philippines, Singapore, Thailand, and Vietnam. It aims to explore the connection between market concentration, efficiency, and capitalization with bank stability. Criteria for the selection of the seven countries was the availability of macroeconomic, banking, and finance data. Brunei, Myanmar, and Lao PDR lacked the data required for the variables used in the empirical model.[5]

The study confirms that banks operating within a loose oligopoly structure, defined as having Top 3 banks holding a collective market share of at least 40%, tend to exhibit stability. This finding supports the

[5] Tran, S., Nguyen, D. and Nguyen, L., 2022. Concentration, capital, and bank stability in emerging and developing countries. *Borsa Istanbul Review*, *22*(6), pp. 1251–1259 (https://www.sciencedirect.com/science/article/pii/S2214845022000655).

concentration-stability hypothesis, which Chapter 3 will elaborate. Additionally, the research highlights the impact of capital on the financial stability of banks in the said countries, underscoring the pivotal role of capital as their primary source of financing.[6] For developing countries, capital is an important source of funds.

In highly concentrated markets, the larger banks are less susceptible to financial fragility (Schliephake 2016) because larger banks wield more market influence and tend to be more profitable. They are able to maintain a sufficient capital buffer that will shield them from external shocks. Second, larger banks attract and retain a pool of experts who oversee loans and manage investment portfolios. Lastly, larger banks can diversify the risks associated with their loan portfolios across a broader geographical and economic spectrum through cross-border activities. They can very well do so because they enjoy substantial economies of scale and scope inherent to their operations.

In summary, banks that turned out less susceptible to financial fragility demonstrate the following positive relationships: market concentration and sufficient capitalization with bank stability; market concentration and sufficient capitalization with cost efficiency; and bank concentration and operational efficiency with profitability.

Bank concentration that brings about stability and cost efficiency should validate the efficient structure hypothesis. Following Nguyen, et al. (2017), literature on the influence of competition on efficiency closely links to Hicks' "quiet life" hypothesis (1935). This hypothesis suggests that as market power increases, efforts to maximize efficiency decrease, resulting in a negative efficiency impact of market power and a positive efficiency impact of competition. On the other hand, Leibenstein (1966) supports Hicks' argument by explaining the positive effect of competition on cost efficiency. First, competition drives managers to work at avoiding bankruptcy. Second, competition equips owners with superior knowledge to benchmark their firm's performance against that of other firms. This is due to a better flow of information between bank owners and managers.

The evidence suggests that market concentration amplifies the positive influence of capital and efficiency on bank stability (Schaeck and Cihak 2012), underscoring the importance of bank stability in the less

[6] Ibid.

developed financial markets. This holds significant implications to policymakers, bank executives, and financiers. Furthermore, these findings stand when validated against alternative proxies for bank stability and regressions that incorporate market concentration. Subsequent chapters will elucidate this.[7]

Empirical Methodology

The operational and time-series interconnectedness of banks, leading to multicollinearity, as well as the non-stationarity of financial and bank data, leading to autocorrelation, endogeneity problems and heteroskedasticity, require a GMM regression with first differences. The GMM estimator stands out for generating reliable estimates even when dealing with unobservable variations and the dynamic nature of the dependent variable. Meanwhile, the variance–covariance matrices generated within the procedure effectively address endogeneity by incorporating past values of explanatory variables and potentially endogenous predictors. The Arellano-Bond test for autocorrelation and the over-identifying constraints test validate the robustness of the instruments employed and ensure the credibility of the estimation process.

The potential for endogeneity biases arising from reverse causation and unaccounted variables, as noted by Nguyen et al. (2017) poses a significant hurdle for studies that look into the impact of competition on bank efficiency. This research therefore addresses endogeneity by employing a series of methodologies. First, it incorporates a lagged variable to counteract biases associated with reverse causality. Second, it utilizes first differences for the variables to eliminate biases stemming from unaccounted time-invariant factors that might concurrently affect the evolution of efficiency and competition. Finally, it employs a one-step system GMM estimator with robust standard errors, following the framework proposed by Arellano and Bover (1995) to address biases resulting from unaccounted time-varying variables that influence the efficiency and competition variables. This approach effectively manages autoregressive properties within the dependent variable when lagged values are included as variables. It has also proven to be more efficient than the

[7] Ibid.

first-differenced and level GMM methods, as demonstrated by Blundell et al. (2001).

The dynamic model is used, following Tran et al. (2022), while incorporating other explanatory variables to capture the operations of the banks within the ASEAN. Thus, the following formulae:

$$\begin{aligned} \text{BankZScore}_{i,t} = & \text{BankZscore}_{i,t-1} + \text{CR3}_{i,t} + \text{CR3}^2_{i,t} + \text{CR3}_{i,t} * \text{CAR}_{i,t} \\ & + \text{EFFNII}_{i,t} + \text{EFFNIM}_{i,t} + \text{LIQ}_{i,t} \\ & + \text{RGDPGR}_{i,t} + \text{INFLRATE}_{i,t} \end{aligned} \tag{2.1a}$$

$$\begin{aligned} \text{BankZScore}_{i,t} = & \text{BankZscore}_{i,t-1} + \text{CR3}_{i,t} + \text{CR3}^2_{i,t} + \text{CR3}_{i,t} * \text{EA}_{i,t} \\ & + \text{EFFNII}_{i,t} + \text{EFFNIM}_{i,t} + \text{LIQ}_{i,t} \\ & + \text{RGDPGR}_{i,t} + \text{INFLRATE}_{i,t} \end{aligned} \tag{2.1b}$$

With:

Bank Z-Score = non-linear relationship of market concentration using.
CR3, CR3^2 = market share of the Top 3 banks per country (Martinez-Miera, Repullo 2010).
CAR = capital adequacy ratio.
EA = equity-to-assets ratio or capitalization (EA).
EFF = cost efficiency, calculated as operating expenses of a bank as a share of sum of net-interest revenue and other operating income.
EFFNIM = operational efficiency, denoting a bank's capacity to allocate inputs indicated as Net-Interest Margin (%).
EFFNII = non-interest Income (%) of total income.
LIQ = liquid assets to deposits and short-term funding (%).
Macroeconomic variables shall be used as regressors.
RGDPGR = economic growth using the growth rate of real gross domestic.
INFLRATE = inflation rate.

The regression for bank solvency has two versions. The interaction term incorporates the relationship of market concentration of the Top 3 banks with capitalization, using the risk-adjusted capital adequacy ratio and the equity-to-assets ratio. This regression establishes the relationship between market concentration and bank solvency. Table 2.4 lists the definition of the variables while Table 2.8 contains the computations per variable.

Stable banks are a consequence of efficient operations, which is why the next set of equations model efficiency (EFF) are defined as bank cost to income ratio. This indicator focuses on the operating expenses of a bank as a share of the sum of net-interest revenue and other operating income, expressing the cost efficiency of the bank. The explanatory variables are similar to BankZScore.

$$\begin{aligned} \mathrm{EFF}_{i,t} = & \mathrm{BankZscore}_{i,t-1} + \mathrm{CR3}_{i,t} + \mathrm{CR3}^2_{i,t} + \mathrm{CR3}_{i,t} * \mathrm{CAR}_{i,t} \\ & + \mathrm{EFFNII}_{i,t} + \mathrm{EFFNIM}_{i,t} + \mathrm{LIQ}_{i,t} \\ & + \mathrm{RGDPGR}_{i,t} + \mathrm{INFLRATE}_{i,t} \end{aligned} \tag{2.2a}$$

$$\begin{aligned} \mathrm{EFF}_{i,t} = & \mathrm{BankZscore}_{i,t-1} + \mathrm{CR3}_{i,t} + \mathrm{CR3}^2_{i,t} + \mathrm{CR3}_{i,t} * \mathrm{EA}_{i,t} \\ & + \mathrm{EFFNII}_{i,t} + \mathrm{EFFNIM}_{i,t} + \mathrm{LIQ}_{i,t} \\ & + \mathrm{RGDPGR}_{i,t} + \mathrm{INFLRATE}_{i,t} \end{aligned} \tag{2.2b}$$

Another set of equations will establish the relationship between bank profitability as explained by bank stability and efficiency. The abovementioned explanatory variables shall be used except for the interaction term because a bank's profitability allows it to channel funds into capital.

$$\begin{aligned} \mathrm{ROA}_{i,t} = & \mathrm{BankZscore}_{i,t-1} + \mathrm{CR3}_{i,t} + \mathrm{CR3}^2_{i,t} + \mathrm{EFFNII}_{i,t} \\ & + \mathrm{EFFNIM}_{i,t} + \mathrm{LIQ}_{i,t} + \mathrm{RGDPGR}_{i,t} + \mathrm{INFLRATE}_{i,t} \end{aligned} \tag{2.3a}$$

$$\begin{aligned} \mathrm{ROE}_{i,t} = & \mathrm{BankZscore}_{i,t-1} + \mathrm{CR3}_{i,t} + \mathrm{CR3}^2_{i,t} + \mathrm{EFFNII}_{i,t} \\ & + \mathrm{EFFNIM}_{i,t} + \mathrm{LIQ}_{i,t} + \mathrm{RGDPGR}_{i,t} + \mathrm{INFLRATE}_{i,t} \end{aligned} \tag{2.3b}$$

Results

One can say that banks in the low middle-, upper middle- and high-income countries of ASEAN 7 were stable, cost-efficient, and profitable before and during the pandemic period, as noted in the following results that verify the strong link of market power and capitalization with efficiency and stability.

Table 2.4 Banking industry variables per country of the ASEAN 7

Topic	*Name*	*Meaning*	*Short Definition*	*Coverage*	*Source*
Efficiency	EFF	Bank cost to income ratio (%)	Operating expenses as a share of sum of net-interest revenue and other operating incomes	2000–2021	Bankscope (2000–2014) and Orbis (2015–2021), Bureau van Dijk (BvD)
	EFFNIM	Bank net interest margin (%)	Accounting value of net interest revenue as a share of its average interest-bearing (total earning) assets		
	EFFNII	Bank noninterest income to total income (%)	Income generated by non-interest related activities as a percentage of total income (net-interest income plus non-interest income)		
	ROA	Bank return on assets (%, after tax)	After-tax net income to yearly averaged total assets		
	ROE	Bank return on equity (%, after tax)	After-tax net income to yearly averaged equity		
Stability	BANKZ-SCORE	Bank Z-score	Captures the probability of default of a country's commercial banking system. Z-score compares the buffer of a country's commercial banking system (capitalization and returns) with the volatility of those returns		

(continued)

Table 2.4 (continued)

Topic	*Name*	*Meaning*	*Short Definition*	*Coverage*	*Source*
	EA	Bank capital to total assets (%)	Ratio of bank capital and reserves to total assets	1998–2020	International Monetary Fund (IMF)
	CAR	Bank regulatory capital to risk-weighted assets (%)	The capital adequacy of deposit takers, or ratio of total regulatory capital to assets held, weighted according to risk of those assets		
	LIQ	Liquid assets to deposits and short term funding (%)	Ratio of the value of liquid assets (easily converted to cash) to short-term funding plus total deposits	2000–2021	Bankscope, Orbis and BvD
Other	CR3	3-bank asset concentration (%)	Assets of the three largest commercial banks as a share of total commercial banking assets		

Topic	*Name*	*Meaning*	*Short Definition*	*Coverage*	*Source*
	CR5	5-bank asset concentration (%)	Assets of five largest banks as a share of total commercial banking asset		
Economic Data	RGDPGR	Growth of Real Gross Domestic Product	Annual percentage growth rate of GDP at market prices based on constant local currency (2015 prices in US dollars). GDP is the sum of gross value added by all resident producers in the economy plus any product taxes and less subsidies not included in the value of the products. It is calculated without deducting for the depreciation of fabricated assets or for the depletion and degradation of natural resources		Globa Economy Data
	INFLRATE	Inflation Rate	Inflation using the CPI is the annual % change in the cost to the average consumer of acquiring a basket of goods and services that may be fixed or changed at specified intervals (e.g. annual). The Laspeyres formula is generally used		

Source Global Financial Development Database of the World Bank https://www.worldbank.org/en/publication/gfdr/data/global-financial-development-database

Note Results for efficiency and stability indicators are not reported if a country-year has less than three bank-level observations

First, the low-middle-income countries of the ASEAN 7 demonstrate a decidedly positive relationship between market power and capitalization with bank stability (See Fig. 2.2).

The upper middle and high-income countries take on an inverted U-shape relationship with the interaction term for market power and capitalization. As banks strive to increase their market power, their central banks and Basel III set capitalization at the prescribed levels. This verifies the competition-stability hypothesis. Higher levels of market concentration lead to more stable banks. Higher capitalization and greater operational efficiency of banks also make them more stable. However, higher levels of liquidity—short-term funding, in particular—foster fragility, which explains the negative relationship between liquidity and bank stability (Table 2.5).

Second, the interaction between market power and capitalization does not suggest the presence of the "quiet life" but rather a positive relationship with cost efficiency (See Fig. 2.3). Increased capitalization weighted against risk-adjusted assets and coupled with efforts to improve market

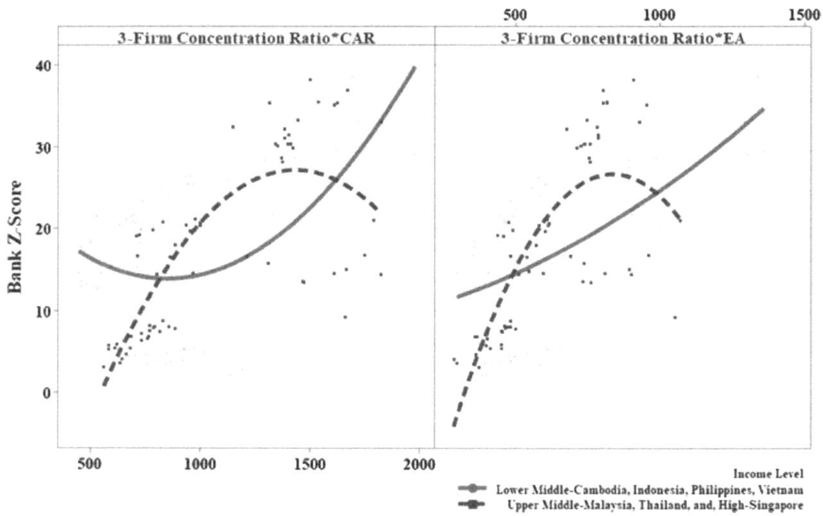

Fig. 2.2 Scatterplot of bank stability, market power, and capitalization (*Source* World Bank)

Table 2.5 Bank stability, efficiency, and capitalization

Method: Panel Generalized Method of Moments with First Differences Transformation
Sample: 2001 2021; Periods Included: 21; Difference specification instrument weighting matrix, Cross-section weights (PCSE) standard errors & covariance (d.f. corrected)
Dependent Variable: Bank Z-Score or Z-index
(Bank Level Indicator of Financial Stability and Solvency)

Regressors/Variable Name	Expected Sign	Capitalization Ratios Used[a,b] Risk-Adjusted Capital Adequacy Ratio	Equity-to-Assets Ratio
Bank Z-Score (−1)	positive	0.15*	0.14*
BANKZSCORE (−1)		(0.10)	(0.09)
Concentration Ratio Top 3	negative	−0.58***	−0.68***
CR3		(0.17)	(0.16)
Concentration Ratio Top 3 squared	positive	0.003**	0.004***
$CR3^2$		(0.001)	(0.001)
CR3 * Capital Adequacy or Equity-to-Assets Ratio	positive	0.01***	0.02***
CR3 * CAR or EA		(0.002)	(0.004)
Bank net interest margin (%)	positive	0.99***	1.01***
EFFNIM		(0.35)	(0.33)
Bank noninterest income to total income (%)	positive	0.09**	0.11***
EFFNII		(0.04)	(0.04)
Liquid assets to deposits & short term funding (%)	negative	−0.21***	−0.23***
LIQ		(0.04)	(0.04)
Real GDP Growth	positive	0.07*	0.05 n.s

(continued)

Table 2.5 (continued)

RGDPGR		(0.06)	(0.06)
Inflation Rate	−/+	0.06 n.s	0.092*
INFLRATE		(0.063)	(0.060)
No. of Cross-Sections / Observations		7/127	7/127
AR(1)	−/+	n.a	−8.42***
AR(2)	negative	−3.44***	−2.24**
Hansen's *J*-Stat	positive	2.70E-26 n.s.	4.73E-26 n.s.

Source Global Financial Development Database and Global Economy Data, World Bank for the inflation rate and the RGDP growth rate

[a]Hansen's *J*-Stat < 1.0 has *p*-value > 0.50

[b]*p*-values: ***[0.00, 0.01]; **[0.01, 0.05]; *[0.05, 0.15]; n.s. not significant or $p > 0.15$

shares positively influence cost efficiency, especially among the low-middle-income countries of the ASEAN 7. One cannot observe the quiet life hypothesis in studies that adjust the market power indicator to costs and operational efficiency. This means that banks that invest in digitalization and the hiring of skilled talent to improve their reach maintain their profitability and stability. In Chapter 4, the Lerner Index serves as a market power indicator, computed using the conventional and efficiency-adjusted forms to reflect the shift from traditional to digitalized banking.

Efficiency, measured by operating expenses as a share of net-interest income and other operating revenues, has a negative relationship with the share of net-interest revenue to the total earning assets, and with increasing liquidity, such as short-term funding. On the other hand, efficiency is positively related to increased market shares and capitalization and non-interest revenues, such as net gains on trading, derivatives, other securities, net fees and commissions, and other operating income (See Table 2.6).

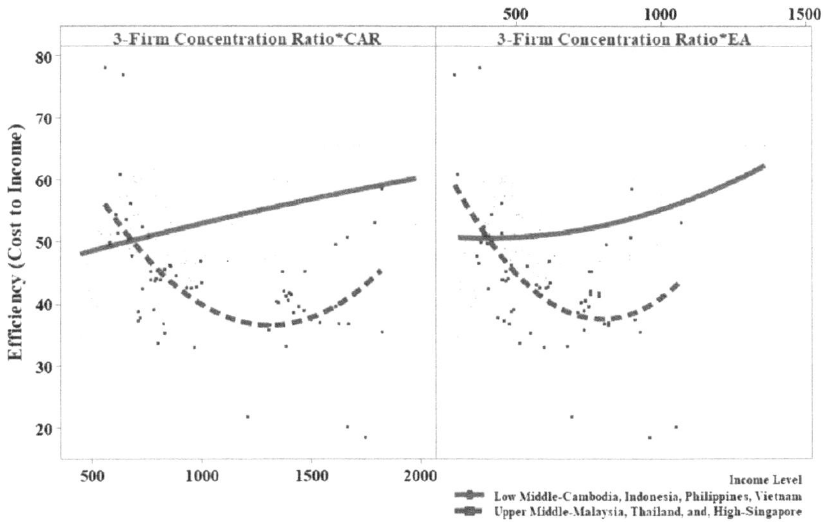

Fig. 2.3 Scatterplot of efficiency, market power, and capitalization (*Source* World Bank)

Table 2.6 Cost efficiency and capitalization for ASEAN 7

Method: Panel Generalized Method of Moments with First Differences Transformation
Sample: 2001 2021; Periods Included: 21; Difference specification instrument weighting matrix,
Cross-section weights (PCSE) standard errors & covariance (d.f. corrected)
Dependent Variable: Efficiency or Bank Cost to Income Ratio
(Operating expenses of a bank as a share of sum of net-interest revenue and other operating income)

Regressors/Variable Name	Expected Sign	Capitalization Ratios Used[a,b] Risk-Adjusted Capital Adequacy Ratio	Equity-to-Assets Ratio
Bank Z-Score (−1)	positive	−0.49**	−0.50***
BANKZSCORE (−1)		(0.19)	(0.19)
Concentration Ratio Top 3	negative	−0.27 n.s.	−0.16 n.s.
CR3		(0.30)	(0.31)
Concentration Ratio Top 3 squared	positive	0.001 n.s.	0.001 n.s.
$CR3^2$		(0.002)	(0.002)
CR3 * Capital Adequacy or Equity-to-Assets Ratio	positive	0.01***	0.01*
CR3 * CAR or EA		(0.005)	(0.008)
Bank net interest margin (%)	−/+	−2.72***	−2.64***
EFFNIM		(0.72)	(0.74)
Bank noninterest income to total income (%)	positive	0.08*	0.11*
EFFNII		(0.08)	(0.08)
Liquid assets to deposits & short term funding (%)	negative	−0.23***	−0.23***
LIQ		(0.08)	(0.08)
Real GDP Growth	positive	0.00 n.s.	0.00 n.s.
RGDPGR		(0.12)	(0.12)

Inflation Rate	negative	−0.15 n.s.	−0.133 n.s.
INFLRATE		(0.136)	(0.135)
No. of Cross-Sections / Observations		7/127	7/127
AR(1)	−/+	−1.13 n.s.	−1.01 n.s.
AR(2)	negative	−2.14**	−2.48**
Hansen's *J*-Stat	positive	9.2E-28 n.s.	4.7E-28 n.s.

Source Global Financial Development Database and Global Economy Data, World Bank for the inflation rate and the RGDP growth rate

[a]Hansen's *J*-Stat < 1.0 has *p*-value > 0.50

[b]*p*-values: ***[0.00, 0.01]; **[0.01, 0.05]; *[0.05, 0.15]; n.s. not significant or $p > 0.15$

Abedifar et al. (2018) identified a potential source of joint production for larger banks, these are non-interest earning services with traditional lending, gains cost, and operational efficiencies. This study asserts that economies of scale come about, not only through traditional lending, but also and alongside non interest-income-earning activities for interest spreads, loan quality, and market economies related to the joint production of such activities.

Smaller banks experience diseconomies from engaging in joint production. Tables 2.5 and 2.6 show that non-interest income significantly contributes to stability and somehow enhances the cost efficiency of the Top 3 banks of the ASEAN.

Figure 2.4 shows the positive relationship of operational efficiency (computed as non-interest income to total income) with market power and capitalization for banks in lower, middle, and high-income countries of the ASEAN 7.

Further, Abedifar et al. (2018) explain that operational efficiencies drive this trend. Said operational efficiencies come from traditional interest-generating activities along with non-interest-income-yielding

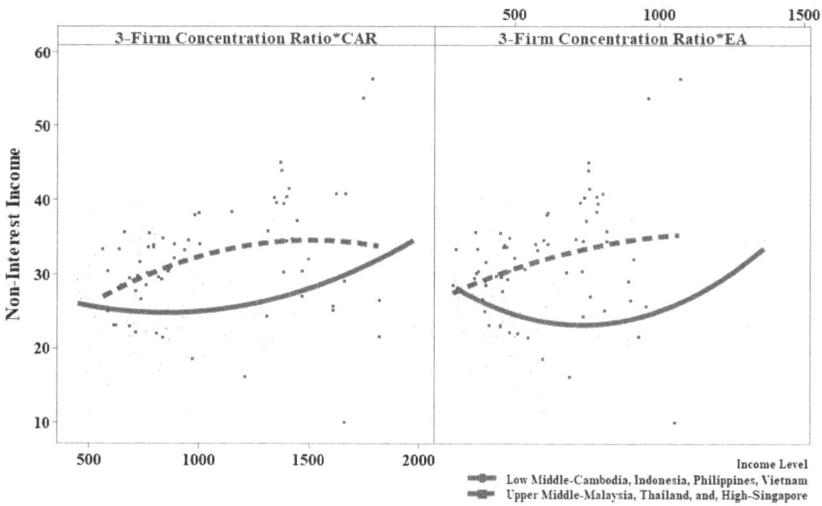

Fig. 2.4 Scatterplot of non-interest income vs market power and capitalization (*Source* World Bank)

services, such as net gains on trading and derivatives, net gains on other securities, and net fees and commissions. This validates the efficient structure hypothesis usually observed in large banks and debunks predictions of the quite life hypothesis for ASEAN 7 banks that have high market power.

Third, efficient and stable banks are profitable. Return-on-assets and return-on-equity are positively related to the share of net-interest margin to total earning assets and to increased real GDP growth (see Fig. 2.5). However, an increase in non-interest income reduces returns-on-equity because non-interest income services charge fees higher than traditional income-generating activities. In 2020–2021, the Top 3 banks of the ASEAN 7 earned sustainable returns-to equity of 5–20% while maintaining the Basel III-prescribed equity-to-asset ratio and the risk-adjusted capital adequacy ratio (see Table 2.7).

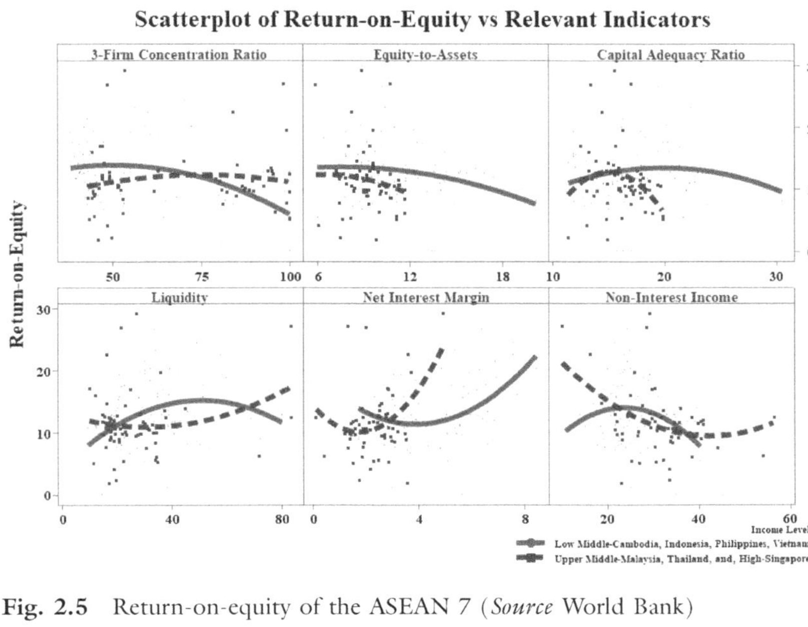

Fig. 2.5 Return-on-equity of the ASEAN 7 (*Source* World Bank)

Table 2.7 Profitability and bank stability

Method: Panel Generalized Method of Moments with First Differences Transformation
Sample: 2001 2021; Periods Included: 21; Difference specification instrument weighting matrix, Cross-section weights (PCSE) standard errors & covariance (d.f. corrected)
Dependent Variable: Return on Assets and Return on Equity
(Commercial banks' after-tax net income to yearly averaged total assets and total equity)

Regressors/Variable Name	**Expected Sign**	**Profitability[a,b]** Return-on-Assets Net of Taxes	Return-on-Equity Net of Taxes
Bank Z-Score (−1)	positive	0.02**	−0.18**
BANKZSCORE (−1)		(0.01)	(0.08)
Concentration Ratio Top 3	negative	−0.05**	0.05 n.s.
CR3		(0.02)	(0.21)
Concentration Ratio Top 3 squared	positive	0.0003*	−0.001 n.s.
$CR3^2$		(0.0002)	(0.001)
Bank net interest margin (%)	−/+	0.42***	2.64***
EFFNIM		(0.051)	(0.471)
Bank noninterest income to total income (%)	−/+	0.0001 n.s.	−0.24***
EFFNII		(0.003)	(0.04)
Liquid assets to deposits & short term funding (%)	positive	0.01 n.s.	0.18***
LIQ		(0.005)	(0.05)
Real GDP Growth	positive	0.02***	0.20**
RGDPGR		(0.01)	(0.09)
Inflation Rate	negative	−0.01 n.s.	0.04 n.s.
INFLRATE		(0.01)	(0.08)
No. of Cross-Sections / Observations		7/127	7/147
AR(1)	−/+	−2.39**	−3.04**
AR(2)	negative	−0.76 n.s.	−0.52 n.s.
Hansen's *J*-Stat	positive	4.0E-01 n.s.	2.5E-28 n.s.

Source Global Financial Development Database and Global Economy Data, World Bank for the inflation rate and the RGDP growth rate
[a]Hansen's *J*-Stat < 1.0 has *p*-value > 0.50
[b]*p*-values: *** [0.00, 0.01]; **[0.01, 0.05]; *[0.05, 0.15]; n.s. not significant or $p > 0.15$

Bank Stability Trend of the ASEAN 7

A survey conducted among executives from the seven selected ASEAN countries reveals the respondents' top perceived risks: living crises, rapid and/or sustained inflation, debt crisis, and severe commodity supply and price crises (World Economic Forum Global Risks Report, 18th Edition, 2023). In addition, the July 2023 report of the International Monetary Fund for East Asia and the Pacific suggests that emerging developing economies will recover smoothly from said risks if they manage the key features of macroeconomic stability—reserves, inflation, and exchange rate. All the countries of the ASEAN 7 have sufficient international reserves because for over a decade, they have engaged in the common practice of accumulating dollar reserves to service their debts and cushion their currencies against the depreciation of the exchange rate (Wiemer 2023, p. 222).

How do the ASEAN 7 manage their exchange and inflation rates? Cambodia, Singapore, and Vietnam anchor their monetary policies onto a basket of foreign currencies. By linking their currencies to the nominal effective exchange rate (NEER), they attain a level of flexibility versus the US dollar and so mitigate fluctuations between their respective currencies and other international currencies when the US dollar experiences significant movements against the latter (Wiemer 2023, p. 216).

In Malaysia, the central bank has a broad mandate that prioritizes price stability while broadly considering economic conditions using an overnight interest rate as its primary tool (Wiemer 2022, p. 218). Singapore's monetary policy aims to "preserve price stability conducive to sustained economic growth." This implies a flexibility in adjusting inflation targets as necessary to support the economy's steady growth trajectory (Wiemer 2023, p. 223). Indonesia, the Philippines, and Thailand have adopted a monetary policy framework known as "inflation targeting." Under this framework, central banks focus on ensuring price stability, resorting to various policy tools to achieve this goal. In all these cases, the exchange rates are floating but not entirely free-floating. This means that even as market forces primarily determine the exchange rates of these economies, the central banks may intervene when circumstances warrant it. While all central banks share a common concern for maintaining low and stable inflation, an inflation-targeting regime explicitly sets a target range for inflation that the central bank commits to achieve with public accountability. This commitment does not rule out other aspects of economic performance when formulating policies, for as long as no measure or action deviates from the overall goal, underscoring resistance to political pressures which may compromise long-term price stability (Wiemer 2023, p. 218).

Werner (2003) describes in detail Vietnam's macroeconomic stabilization framework emphasizing that the country does not manipulate its currency to gain unfair advantage in trade.

> A latecomer to global trade, Vietnam has achieved quick success while yet remaining a small-time player in global capital markets. As a reforming command economy, its recourse to market forces for absorbing shocks is inhibited. Within this context, the country has kept a tight hold on its exchange rate relative to the US dollar even as this has led to changes in reserves that in percentage terms relative to a small base have run to extremes. By 2020, Vietnam had accumulated reserves of just 27.8 percent of GDP, a modest stock by the standards of the region. Before it relaxes its exchange rate control, before it opens its capital markets, before it exposes its economy more fully to international engagement, Vietnam needs to build a reserve position that will allow it to defend its currency should the need arise. Meanwhile, at the time of the manipulator charges, Vietnam was taking on supply chain relocations out of China in response to rising tensions between China and the USA. Such a positive shock to the balance of payments can be absorbed even under a stabilized exchange rate through increased imports or net capital outflows, but these responses take time. As with China then, within a longer-term context of adjustment to shock and the development of market mechanisms, Vietnam's exchange rate policy has been oriented toward macroeconomic stabilization. As such, the behavior does not qualify as 'currency manipulation'. (Wiemer 2023, p. 316)

The macroeconomic policies cited show that the ASEAN 7 are equipped to reach their economic growth targets, thereby ensuring a resilient economy. This has favorable consequences on the banking industry.

Figure 2.6 indicates that with conservative forecasts, or banking dataset at 2021 levels, assuming no drastic changes in market power, cost and operating efficiencies, capitalization, and liquidity, the bank stability indicator would remain at a level that will allow banks to buffer themselves against financial risks. The Bank Z-Score is steady, from Indonesia's lowest

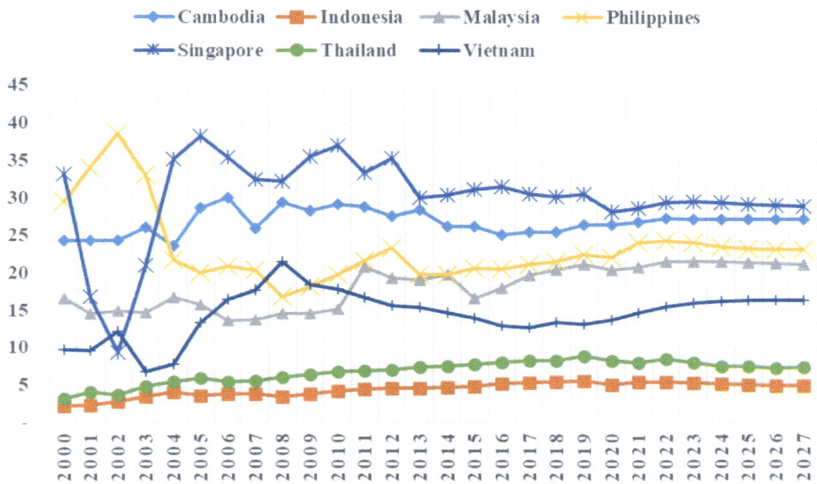

Fig. 2.6 Bank Z-Score of the ASEAN 7 (2000–2027) (*Source* World Bank and the Global Economy Database. *Note* Actual data from 2000 to 2022, forecasts for RGDP growth rate, and inflation rate from 2023 to 2027 are based on IMF forecasts, as reported in The Global Economy Database)

(4.80) to Singapore's highest level (29).[8] A bank Z-Score of 4.80 gives Indonesia much leeway in case massive external shocks cause a significant decline in profitability. Such an event, however, is not likely to occur, given the current management of the Indonesian economy.

Annex

See Table 2.8, 2.9, 2.10, and 2.11.

[8] See Table 2.11 for the economic growth and inflation rate forecasts.

Table 2.8 Banking industry variables per country

Topic	*Name*	*Meaning*	*Short definition*	*Computation*	*Coverage*	*Source*
Efficiency	EFF	Bank cost to income ratio (%)	Operating expenses as a share of sum of net-interest revenue and other operating income	Raw data are from Bankscope and Orbis. The formula applied to Bankscope is data 2090/(data2080 + data2085) and a comparable approach is applied to Orbis. All Numerator and denominator are first aggregated at the country level before division. Note that banks used in the calculation might differ between indicators. Calculated from underlying bank-by-bank unconsolidated data from Bankscope and Orbis	2000–2021	Bankscope (2000–2014) and Orbis (2015–2021), Bureau van Dijk (BvD)

Topic	Name	Meaning	Short definition	Computation	Coverage	Source
	EFFNIM	Bank net interest margin (%)	Accounting value of net interest revenue as a share of its average interest-bearing (total earning) assets	Raw data are from Bankscope and Orbis. The formula applied to Bankscope is data2080[t]/((data2010[t] + data2010[t−1])/2) and a comparable approach is applied to Orbis. All the rest, same as above		
	EFFNII	Bank noninterest income to total income (%)	Income generated by noninterest related activities as percentage of total income (net-interest income plus noninterest income)	Noninterest related income includes net gains on trading and derivatives, net gains on other securities, net fees and commissions and other operating income. Raw data are from Bankscope and Orbis. The formula applied to Bankscope is data2085/(data2080 + data2085) and a comparable approach is applied to Orbis. All the rest are the same as above		

(continued)

Table 2.8 (continued)

Topic	*Name*	*Meaning*	*Short definition*	*Computation*	*Coverage*	*Source*
	ROA	Bank return on assets (%, after tax)	After-tax net income to yearly averaged total assets	Raw data are from Bankscope and Orbis.		
	ROE	Bank return on equity (%, after tax)	After-tax net income to yearly averaged equity	The formula applied to Bankscope is data 2115[t]/((data2025[t] + data2025[t−1])/2) and a comparable approach is applied to Orbis	2000–2021	

Topic	*Name*	*Meaning*	*Short definition*	*Computation*	*Coverage*	*Source*
Stability	BANKZSCORE	Bank Z-score	The probability of default of a country's commercial banking system Z-score compares the buffer of a country's commercial banking system (capitalization and returns) with the volatility of those returns	Estimated as Numerator and denominator first aggregated at country level before division Banks used in the calculation might differ between indicators Calculated from underlying bank-by-bank unconsolidated data from Bankscope and Orbis (ROA+(equity/assets))/sd(ROA); sd (ROA) is the standard deviation of ROA, calculated for country-years with no less than five bank-level observations ROA, equity, and assets are country-level aggregate figures calculated from underlying bank-by-bank unconsolidated data from Bankscope and Orbis		
	EA	Bank capital to total assets (%)	Ratio of bank capital and reserves to total assets	Capital and reserves include funds from owners, retained earnings, general and special reserves, provisions, and valuation adjustments	1998–2020	Financial Soundness Indicators Database (fsi.imf.org), International Monetary Fund (IMF)

(continued)

Table 2.8 (continued)

	Capital includes Tier 1 capital (paid-up shares and common stock), which is a common feature in all countries' banking systems, and total regulatory capital, which includes several specified types of subordinated debt instruments that need not be repaid if the funds are required to maintain minimum capital levels (these comprise tier 2 and tier 3 capital)	
	Total assets include all nonfinancial and financial assets reported by IMF staff. Due to differences in national accounting, taxation, and supervisory regimes, this data is not strictly comparable across countries	

CAR	Bank regulatory capital to risk-weighted assets (%)	The capital adequacy of deposit takers is a ratio of total regulatory capital to its assets held, weighted according to risk of those assets	Also called by the BSP as risk-adjusted capital adequacy ratio as reported by IMF staff The rest are the same as above		
LIQ	Liquid assets to deposits and short term funding (%)	Ratio of the value of liquid assets (easily converted to cash) to short-term funding plus total deposits	Liquid assets include cash and due from banks, trading securities at fair value through income, loans and advances to banks, reverse repos and cash collaterals Deposits and short term funding include total current, savings, and term deposits, and short term borrowing (money market instruments, CDs, and other deposits) Raw data from Bankscope and Orbis The formula applied to Bankscope is data 2075/data2030. A comparable approach is applied to Orbis Numerator and denominator are first aggregated at the country level before division. Calculated from underlying bank-by-bank unconsolidated data from Bankscope and Orbis	2000–2021	Bankscope (2000–2014) and Orbis (2015–2021), Bureau van Dijk (BvD)

(continued)

Table 2.8 (continued)

Other	CR3	3-bank asset concentration (%)	Assets of three largest commercial banks as a share of total commercial banking assets	Total assets include total earning assets, cash and due from banks, foreclosed real estate, fixed assets, goodwill, other intangibles, current tax assets, deferred tax assets, discontinued operations and other assets Raw data from Bankscope and Orbis The formula applied to Bankscope is the sum (data2025) of the three largest banks in Bankscope) (sum data 2025 for all banks) A comparable approach is applied to Orbis. The rest are the same as above	2000–2021

	CR5	5-bank asset concentration (%)	Assets of the five largest banks as a share of total commercial banking assets	Same as above Raw data are from Bankscope and Orbis for the five largest banks in Bankscope)/(sum data2025) for all banks)		
Economic Data	RGDPGR	Growth of Real Gross Domestic Product	Annual percentage growth rate of GDP at market prices based on constant local currency Aggregates based on constant 2015 prices, expressed in US dollars GDP is the sum of gross value added by all resident producers in the economy plus product taxes and less any subsidies excluded in the value of the products Calculated without deducting for the depreciation of fabricated assets or the depletion and degradation of natural resources		2000–2022	Global Economy Data

(continued)

Table 2.8 (continued)

	INFLRATE	Inlflation Rate	Inflation as measured by the consumer price index reflects the annual percentage change in cost on the average consumer's acquisition of a basket of goods and services that may be fixed or changed at specified intervals (e.g. annually) The Laspeyres formula is generally used

Source Global Financial Development Database of the World Bank https://www.worldbank.org/en/publication/gfdr/data/global-financial-development-database

Note Results of the efficiency and stability indicators are not reported if a country-year has less than three bank-level observations

Table 2.9 Descriptive statistics relevant indicators

Variables	*Mean*	*Median*	*Maximum*	*Minimum*	*Std. Dev*	*Observations*
BANKZSCORE	17.4	16.8	38.6	2.1	10.0	161
CR3	60.5	51.5	100.0	37.9	20.7	161
CR5	72.9	67.6	100.0	48.0	16.6	154
EA	10.3	9.7	20.1	5.9	2.5	134
CAR	16.9	16.6	30.5	11.3	3.4	134
EFF	47.2	47.0	78.1	18.6	9.3	154
EFFNII	28.4	27.4	56.3	10.0	7.7	154
EFFNIM	3.7	3.3	8.4	0.2	1.7	154
LIQ	30.7	28.1	83.4	9.7	15.8	154
ROA	1.3	1.2	3.9	−0.4	0.7	154
ROE	12.2	11.7	29.1	0.1	5.1	154
RGDPGR	5.1	5.5	14.5	−9.5	3.2	161
INFLRATE	3.7	2.9	24.1	−1.7	3.7	161

Source Global Financial Development Database of the World Bank https://www.worldbank.org/en/publication/gfdr/data/global-financial-development-database

Table 2.10 Correlation matrix of relevant indicators

Variables	*BANKZSCORE*	*CR3*	*CR5*	*EA*	*CAR*	*EFF*	*EFFNII*	*EFFNIM*	*LIQ*	*ROA*	*ROE*	*RGDPGR*	*INFLRATE*
BANKZSCORE	1.00	0.55	0.51	0.21	0.05	−0.20	0.29	−0.20	0.21	−0.01	−0.25	0.13	−0.20
CR3		1.00	0.96	−0.17	−0.04	−0.26	0.37	−0.40	0.17	−0.35	−0.21	0.02	−0.25
CR5			1.00	−0.22	−0.09	−0.28	0.41	−0.48	0.09	−0.38	−0.23	−0.02	−0.32
EA				1.00	0.77	0.10	−0.20	0.62	0.29	0.44	−0.10	−0.01	−0.02
CAR					1.00	0.01	−0.06	0.52	0.40	0.43	0.02	−0.08	−0.02
EFF						1.00	0.03	0.34	−0.25	−0.20	−0.24	0.03	0.17
EFFNII							1.00	−0.52	0.10	−0.35	−0.30	−0.14	−0.27
EFFNIM								1.00	0.04	0.59	0.25	0.14	0.35
LIQ									1.00	0.20	0.23	−0.01	0.07
ROA										1.00	0.70	0.25	0.15
ROE											1.00	0.23	0.22
RGDPGR												1.00	0.18
INFLRATE													1.00

Source Global Financial Development Database of the World Bank https://www.worldbank.org/en/publication/gfdr/data/global-financial-development-database

Table 2.11 Forecasts: economic growth and inflation

Selected ASEAN Countries		*2022a*	*2023f*	*2024f*	*2025f*	*2026f*	*2027f*
Cambodia	Real GDP Growth Rate	5.01	5.82	6.21	6.38	6.51	6.24
	Inflation Rate	2.88	2.99	3.04	3.04	3.04	3.00
Indonesia	Real GDP Growth Rate	5.31	4.95	5.06	4.97	4.96	4.96
	Inflation Rate	5.51	3.18	2.82	2.67	2.63	2.46
Malaysia	Real GDP Growth Rate	8.69	4.48	4.53	4.36	4.40	3.90
	Inflation Rate	3.78	2.89	3.06	2.56	2.40	2.43
Philippines	Real GDP Growth Rate	7.60	6.03	5.81	6.10	6.22	6.33
	Inflation Rate	8.05	4.53	3.00	3.00	3.00	3.00
Singapore	Real GDP Growth Rate	3.65	1.50	2.12	2.49	2.52	2.49
	Inflation Rate	6.46	5.45	3.48	2.50	1.98	1.99
Thailand	Real GDP Growth Rate	2.64	3.41	3.60	3.26	3.07	3.04
	Inflation Rate	5.89	2.32	1.45	2.54	1.46	2.54
Vietnam	Real GDP Growth Rate	8.02	5.76	6.85	6.76	6.65	6.69
	Inflation Rate	4.61	4.74	4.10	4.05	4.00	4.00

Source The Global Economy Database
Note a-actual; f-forecast

CHAPTER 3

Bank Competition + Market Concentration = Financial Stability?

Background

The evolution of relationship banking and the banking sector's linkages with the real estate and construction sectors generated interest in understanding the credit and liquidity risk of exposure to new alternative financial instruments. To adapt to volatile conditions, Philippine banks must have sufficient buffer against such risks in order to adapt to volatile conditions while acting as a catalyst for economic development.

Indeed, banks have played a direct role in promoting the country's financial stability. However, each of the dominant banks in this study seems to have a specific role in relationship banking due to the presence of imperfect (monopolistic) competition (Pasadilla and Milo 2005) in the industry's competitive market structure. For instance, of the 46 UKBs in the Philippines, the Top 5 account for 38% of deposits and 44% loans from 2020 to 2022 and are family-owned business conglomerates engaged in universal banking, commercial and investment banking, commercial-retail, and industrial real estate. Moreover, the rise of bank mergers and consolidation, which brought about increased market concentration seemed to coincide with a slowdown in the adjustment of monetary policy transmission via the credit channel (Bayangos 2010). Will such mergers lead to more stable banks? Does bank competition and concentration

J. C. Dacanay et al., *Bank Competition and the Effects on Financial Stability*, Palgrave Macmillan Studies in Banking and Financial Institutions, https://doi.org/10.1007/978-3-031-59599-8_3

promote financial stability? This study aims to present empirical evidence, according to the following objectives:

1. determine the market structure of the Philippines UKB industry;
2. establish the relationship between bank competition and financial stability through banks' exposure to risk (Berger et al. 2009; MMR 2010);
3. verify the relationship of bank competition and stability with capitalization (Schliephake 2016) in compliance with the proposed BSP regulation.

The intermediary role of banks affects the monetary and real sectors through liquidity creation. BSP research has proven the existence of a broad lending channel (balance sheet channel and credit channel) of monetary transmission in the Philippines (Bayangos 2010). This means banks influence the speed with which the real sector adjusts to changes in the BSP's policy variables, especially through interest rates. According to the BSP, using the interest rate pass-through, banks seem to pick up the pace in adjusting their long- and short-term market lending rates during the country's inflation-targeting period but slackened again in the wake of bank exits and mergers.

This study will then look into the direct effects of market structure, competitive behavior, and market concentration of banks on risk-taking through the broad lending channel of monetary policy transmission. Further, it will incorporate a theoretical framework for industrial organization to understand the competitive behavior of banks, focusing on bank credit intermediation and the consequent exposure to volatility through increased leverage. This banking scenario will be related to bank competition and concentration and determine if the current competitive behavior of banks promotes stability. Partial equilibrium analysis shall be gleaned from the public archives of the BSP and the PSA.

Extant literature on the state of the industrial organization of banks and bank intermediation yields mixed results with regard to the relationship of bank concentration and competition. However, recent studies claim that such a relationship is non-monotonic (Caminal and Matures 2002; Boyd and De Nicoló 2005; Martinez-Miera and Repullo 2010; Berger et al. 2009) on account of an environment of imperfect competition, i.e., the prevalence of tight-to-lax oligopoly, information asymmetry, and endogenous sunk cost (Kim et al. 2005; Dick 2007). Based on studies on the existence of imperfect competition in the banking industry (Boyd and De Nicoló 2005), this present one will explain financial stability and competitive behavior by comparing the results of two groups—the dominant versus the fringe UKBs ranked by deposits and loans market share. In addition, the authors will present empirical evidence on competitive behavior through:

1. Traditional Methods—HHI, Concentration Measures;
2. Non-Traditional Methods from the New Empirical Industrial Organization (NEIO) using the adjusted Lerner Index, Z-index as a financial stability indicator, and the Boone Indicator to directly measure the market conduct of banks; and,
3. GMM using a random effects model with robust estimators shall be used as the regression estimation procedure of quarterly data for bank-level estimation procedures (2005–2019) from the BSP. GMM allows the correction of data with endogeneity problems, heteroscedasticity, and inherent cross-section correlation of residuals due to interbank lending.

The sample includes only the Top 20 UKBs in the Philippines based on loans and deposits market shares (see Appendix, Table 3.27).

Review of Related Literature

This chapter looks at literature grouped according to discussions on historical development, policy issues, and theoretical and empirical issues. It contains key concepts of financial intermediation, bank competition, and financial stability.

Financial fragility refers to the vulnerability of the financial environment and the macro economy to systemic risks that render banks illiquid and insolvent. This happens when banks expose themselves to risky investments in contingent assets and loaning to risky business ventures. According to Diamond and Dybvig (1983), a bank is inherently prone to runs because it accepts liquid deposits but lends to illiquid projects. The banking system can promote resiliency as well as fragility, depending on the linkage structures, diversity, and density of banking activities (Allen and Gale 2004). In theory, if financial markets function efficiently, then market prices should reflect inherent risks and maintain the stability of the payment system. Stiglitz and Weiss' (1981) reference to inherent information asymmetry can lead to moral hazards, adverse selection, externalities, coordination failures, and principal-to-agent problems. This implies that financial market prices might not reflect inherent risks. As such, the inherent information asymmetry of bank operations causes macroeconomic slowdown and disrupts the flow of payments in the financial system.

Definitions of financial stability often include such elements as the smooth and effective functioning of the financial system, the low probability of default, the absence of stress and disruption in the financial system, and the absence of major financial imbalances in the economy (Moenjak 2014). For this study, financial stability pertains to the capacity of the banking industry to withstand bank and regulatory distress. From the microeconomic standpoint, that is, from the banking industry perspective, it refers to the stability of a financial system.

Bank distress happens when a bank becomes insolvent due to massive loan defaults. Regulatory distress occurs when the largest banks experience numerous runs and/or losses, are unable to create liquidity, and so become insolvent. Financial stability encompasses three interrelated elements:

1. a macro economy that is free of major financial imbalances;
2. a sound and stable system of financial institutions; and
3. smooth functioning financial markets.

These three key elements normally interact with each other in a state of flux. The absence of any one element can cause the other two to fail and lead to financial instability. Figure 3.1 shows how a stable payment system seamlessly stitches them together (Moenjak 2014, p. 211).

Historical Development

Vast academic literature on the topic diverges into two main theoretical branches, "competition-fragility" and "competition-stability."

The traditional competition-fragility view posits that more competitive and less concentrated banking systems are more prone to financial troubles. Advocates of the competition-fragility hypothesis argue that

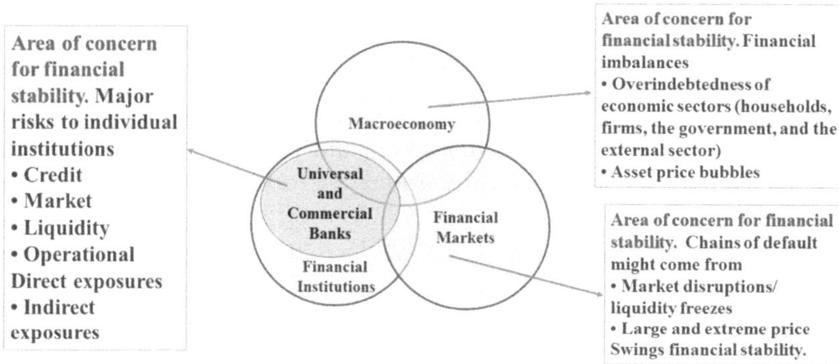

Fig. 3.1 Overlapping dimensions of financial stability: the macroeconomy, financial institutions, and financial markets (*Source* Moenjak 2014, p. 211, and Author's Framework)

increased competition shrinks bank's margins and charter values, which drives more risk-taking behavior (Keeley 1990; Edwards and Mishkin 1995) and reduces the informational rents that banks extract from sustained relationships with clients (Besanko and Thakor 1995; Boot and Greenbaum 1995). Moreover, large banks are usually diversified and more concentrated banking systems, easier to monitor due to the limited number of banks (Allen and Gale 2004).

On the other hand, the alternative "competition-stability" view states that more competition and less concentration improve the soundness of the banks. This argument is based on the risk-shifting paradigm and the "too big to fail" mentality. Boyd and De Nicoló (2005) developed the former, stating that lower lending rates reduce the probability of bankruptcy and risk-taking among borrowers. The latter arises from rescue policies that systematically prevent major banks from failing while implicitly generating incentives to gamble (Mishkin 1999; Boot and Thakor 2019, pp. 63–65).

Several empirical studies support both branches of thought. Those that focus on individual countries present evidence that strongly differ in methodology and sampling (Keeley 1990; Demsetz, Saidenberg, and Strahan 1997; Boyd and De Nicoló 2005), while the majority of cross-country studies highlight a positive relationship between competition and stability as well as between concentration and stability (Beck, Demirgüç-Kunt, and Levine 2003; Schaeck, Cihák, and Wolfe 2009). Such uncertainty triggers inconclusive debate on the effects of different regulatory policies, probably because of the non-monotonic relationship between competition and stability (Martinez-Miera and Repullo 2010; De Nicoló and Lucchetta 2011) or because the studies are too country-specific (Beck et al. 2013).

Vives (2008, 2016), Berger et al. (2009), Berger et al. (2017, p. 187), and Degryse et al. (2019, pp. 797–798) integrate competition-fragility and competition-stability by focusing on the factors that contribute to instability, most of which have something to do with information asymmetry. Banks provide transaction services and risk sharing. They also finance and monitor entrepreneurial projects, which are illiquid and opaque because of asymmetrical information, like adverse selection and moral hazards.

Altogether, banks are central to overcoming asymmetrical information in an economy. They protect entrepreneurs that require financing from the liquidity needs of investors. The standard deposit contracts, redeemable at par, and loan provision to opaque entrepreneurial projects are complementary to the function of a bank. However, their role in liquidity creation leaves banks vulnerable to runs. A deposit redeemable at par exposes banks to failure when returns are low. This possibility has desirable incentive properties but may lead to failure, panic, and systemic crises, with a potentially huge impact on the economy, given the central role of financial intermediation (Vives 2008, 2016).

These operations also allow banks to be highly leveraged. The classical issue of the possible tradeoffs between banking competition and stability would primarily depend on the bank's leverage position, be it exogenous or endogenous. Then, based on its leverage, one can know how banks finance their risks. Thus, a bank's leverage will affect its competitive behavior and the impact of portfolio, insolvency, liquidity, and systemic risks on its financial stability (Freixas and Ma 2014).

With regard to funding and investment policy, once banks hit a certain threshold, heightened competition tends to drive risk-taking incentives and the probability of failure. Intense competition may worsen the excessive risk-taking problem because higher profit serves as a buffer and boosts the bank's charter value (Vives 2008, 2016). In a dynamic setting, market power enhances the bank's charter value, making it more conservative (see Besanko and Thakor 1995, Boot and Greenbaum 1995, and Allen and Gale 2004). With heterogeneous borrowers, tougher competition may lead to a riskier portfolio and a greater probability of failure (Broecker 1990 and Riordan 1995). Yet competition tends to push down the rates that firms pay for loans and may therefore improve the average quality of loan applicants and/or reduce the need to ration credit. This force tends to align competition and stability. Caminal and Matutes (2002), Boyd and De Nicoló (2005), and Martinez-Miera and Repullo (2010) point out that lower rates also reduce banks revenues from non-defaulting loans. When this is incorporated, one obtains a U-shaped relationship between competition and the risk of failure (Vives 2011).

In summary, literature on bank stability usually assumes that banks operate in a perfectly competitive system, disregarding the implications of different banking structures on the safety of the sector. By contrast, competition literature analyzes the operation of the competitive mechanism in the presence of market failures, disregarding the effects on the behavior of agents and depositors. It therefore remains unclear whether greater competition enhances or worsens the stability of the system. Moreover, literature that directly deals with the effects of competition on stability has only recently emerged. The general argument is that competition worsens stability. Higher deposit rates increase the probability of bank runs; lower margins worsen the problem of excessive risk-taking. However, recent views on imperfect competition and key aspects of industrial organization, product differentiation (Dick 2007; Kim et al. 2005), and sunk costs (Vives 2008, 2016; Dick 2007) as endogenous have challenged this stand.

Dick (2007) provided important insights into the competitive behavior of banks and explained the existence of market concentration among the leading banks. Kim et al. (2005) presented similar results and empirical proof of the presence of endogenous sunk costs that give rise to vertical product differentiation and imperfect competition which, in turn, make for less fragile banks.

Bank Competition and Financial Stability Pertinent to the Asia–Pacific Region

Molyneux et al. (2015) studied the competition-stability nexus using cross-country data from 14 Asia–Pacific countries from 2003 to 2010. Market- and accounting-based risk measures determined the fragility of individual banks. Concentration and competition indicators were included in the models to determine their impact on stability. Initial results showed a substantial shift in the average risk exposure of banks over the sample period, accompanied by gradual increases in concentration and competition. The main results not only highlighted the significant negative association between the Lerner Index and individual bank risk but also illustrated the significant positive relationship between concentration ratio and bank fragility. These findings support the neutral view of the competition-stability nexus, indicating that the competition-stability and competition-fragility theories can simultaneously apply to the Asia–Pacific banking markets. The results also confirmed that bank concentration does not adequately measure bank competitiveness. Overall, the findings hold when they control an array of bank-specific, macroeconomic, regulatory, and institutional factors (Molyneux et al. 2015).

In addition, the above-mentioned authors' analyses indicate that a smaller bank has a greater chance of improving its financial soundness. In terms of regulations and institutions, the results show that tougher entry restrictions may enhance bank stability, while stronger deposit insurance schemes negatively influence financial soundness. Unsurprisingly, banks turned out more fragile during the recent financial crisis. These results have immediate effects on the intermediary role of banks (Molyneux et al. 2015). Empirical results suggested a significant and negative bi-causal relationship between liquidity creation and regulatory capital for all the sample banks. However, this relationship varies by bank size. Specifically, the "financial fragility-crowding out" hypothesis works for small banks, while the "risk absorption" and "liquidity substitution" hypotheses favor large banks.

Studies Pertinent to the Philippines

A few recent studies (Guinigundo 2008; Bayangos 2010; Aban 2013) confirmed the presence of a bank lending channel in the Philippines. Banks remain the major source of financing for the private sector, and monetary policy tends to affect loan growth, especially for small banks. Using Aban's (2013) specification, this paper empirically tests the presence of a bank lending channel from the first quarter of 2001 to the third quarter of 2014, with year-on-year growth (YoY) of outstanding loans (net of reverse repurchase) as dependent variable, while the YoY growth of real GDP, YoY inflation, overnight RRP rate, and an error term serve as independent variables. To check the robustness of the regression equation, this exercise used the weighted policy rate that combines the overnight RRP rate and SDA rate as the alternative benchmark rate for pricing loans (Guinigundo 2015).

The estimates revealed bank lending as a significant channel for monetary policy transmission despite the impact of the Global Financial Crisis. In particular, the results, regardless of the use of overnight RRP rate or weighted policy rate, showed significant movement in monetary policy that is inversely related to loan growth (ibid.). Together, these results suggest the impact of monetary policy on bank credit amidst changes in the pattern of financial intermediation (Guinigundo 2015). From these findings, Bayangos (2010) and Aban (2013) recommended further studies on the effects of competitive behavior on loan rates and external finance premiums against the backdrop of heightened concentration among UKBs.

Pasadilla and Milo (2005) investigated this covering the period 1988–2003. While the number of banks and branches increased, the Philippine banking system remains populated by a few large and expanded UKBs and numerous small fringe banks. The asset distribution may be similar to that of the 1980s but the underlying structure is different as the government dominated the sector in the 1980s. Today, the structure is market-driven and largely owned by the private sector. Moreover, the HHI does not point to any undue banking concentration. The ensuing entry of more market players is correlated with a drop in interest spread and profit, which can be telling of many other developments.

For one, there is greater operational efficiency because cost-efficient banks need a relatively lower interest spread than inefficient ones. It also tells of greater confidence in the economic environment or of the possible dissipation of monopoly profits of large commercial banks. Their computation of H-statistics using the Panzar-Rosse (1987) methodology did not reveal monopolistic or oligopolistic behavior. Rather, the behavior was fairly competitive. Further, the trend in the changes of H-stat values showed increased competition with the entry of foreign banks in the

1990s and that stiffer competition existed in loans than in fee-generation. The results of Pasadilla and Milo (2005) require updating while the occurrence of dominant and fringe banks need further verification.

Policy Issues

This section summarizes the regulations for bank supervision in Basel III and their impact (Choudhry and Masek 2011, pp. 304–306). In September 2010, the Basel Committee for Banking Supervision (BCBS) composed of regulators and central bankers from 27 countries, released details of Basel III, or the new banking regulatory capital rules that mandate banks to hold core TIER1 capital higher than that which Basel I and II required:

1. for core TIER1 capital, a minimum of 4.5% for risk-weighted assets versus the 2% required under the Basel II accord;
2. a "capital conservation" buffer of 2.5% to serve as protection during periods of economic and financial stress; and
3. TIER1 "leverage ratio" of 3%.

The above-mentioned additional reserve is not compulsory but non-compliant banks were restricted from paying dividends to shareholders. Thus, for practical purposes, the minimum TIER1 capital ratio is 7%. In addition, a "countercyclical" capital buffer of up to 2.5% was allowed and authorized national regulators to impose it as a necessary response to overheating markets (Parcon-Santos, Bernabe 2012).

Basel III simplified the definition of core TIER1 capital, which covers equity, retained reserves, and undated preference shares. Tier 2 was also simplified to comprise preferred shares, hybrid subordinated debt, and long-term subordinated debt without the incentive to redeem (e.g., step-up coupons).

Basel III sought to increase the quality and required level of bank capital and strengthen the capacity of banks to absorb risks and reduce the probability of future banking crises. Nevertheless, banks have adopted different strategies to comply with the new rules, including hikes in lending rates, which can negatively affect the economy.

The building blocks of Basel III are:

1. higher quality and level of capital;
2. broader risk coverage;
3. prevention of excessive leverage;
4. stronger liquidity:
5. address of systemic risk; and
6. higher standards for risk management and supervision.

All this aims to enhance the capital and liquidity regulations of the banking system and allay the intensity and frequency of financial crises. Given the possible substantial output losses, as observed during the past crises, this new framework can mitigate adverse macroeconomic effects in terms of foregone output (Parcon-Santos, Bernabe 2012).

Table 3.1 shows the Basel III standards for the risk-based capital adequacy framework for UKBs and their subsidiary banks and quasi-banks (QBs) in the Philippines. As approved under Monetary Board Resolution No. 33 on January 5, 2012, the BSP instructed concerned banks to adopt the new minimum ratios starting January 1, 2014, which highly differed from the Basel Committee's recommended staggered implementation. The changes in the BSP guidelines were introduced to UKBs in the first quarter of 2012. Simultaneously with the release of the draft guidelines, banks were requested to participate in the quantitative impact study during the exposure period. The final guidelines were issued by the third quarter of 2012 (Parcon-Santos, Bernabe 2012).

The new Basel III requirement set a CET1 ratio with a conservation buffer of 8.5%. Currently, the BSP has no required CET1 ratio but only a 5.0% TIER1 ratio. With the adoption of Basel III, the BSP proposes a ratio of 10%, even if Basel III guidelines only required 8.5%. Meanwhile,

Table 3.1 Comparison of Basel III guidelines and proposed BSP regulations

Capital requirements	*Under Basel III*	*Proposed BSP guidelines*
a. Common Equity TIER1 (CET1)[a]	7.0	8.5
b. TIER1	8.5	10.0
c. Capital Adequacy Ratio (CAR)	10.5	12.5

Source BSP Memorandum No. M-2012-002

[a]The CET 1 (Common Equity TIER1 or Core capital TIER1) ratio is used in the computation of TIER1 ratio. The TIER1 Capital consists of core TIER1 capital (Common Equity TIER1) and allowable amount of hybrid TIER1 capital as prescribed under BSP circular 688 series of 2010

the new Basel III set the Risk-Based Capital Adequacy Ratio (RCAR) with a conservation buffer of 10.5%. Existing BSP guidelines set it at 10.0% while the proposed BSP requirement set it at 12.5% (Parcon-Santos, Bernabe 2012).

Bank liberalization is another important policy issue that confronts the industry. This section looks into the empirical findings on the entry of foreign banks since 1994 and the subsequent effect of increased industry competition. Manlagñit (2011) observed that the rise of foreign bank presence in the domestic market could produce two offsetting effects from spillovers and increased competition. However, empirical results strongly proved that competition brings about lower profit and overhead costs for domestic commercial banks. This means that the presence of foreign banks seems to exert pressure on domestic banks to lower their profitability and overhead costs as well as to improve on cost efficiency by updating their production technologies and techniques (Manlagñit 2011).

Consistent with findings in the literature, domestic banks no longer earn as much as they used to prior to the upsurge of competition from foreign banks. This suggests that increased foreign presence has compelled domestic banks to step-up and out of the "quiet life" and focus on adopting the superior banking techniques and practices of foreign banks, thereby improving their cost efficiency and reducing overhead costs. Manlagñit (2011) also presented a case study for the broader Asian industry to follow. For example, the Philippine experience would be useful to the Region's banking sectors protected from foreign competition since 2006 (Manlagñit 2011).

From a policy perspective, findings on the effects of competition from foreign banks in the domestic banking system justify the liberalized entry of foreign banks into the Philippines. Manlagñit (2011) demonstrated that a liberalized local banking industry compels homegrown banks to be more competitive and efficient. In addition, easing up restrictions on foreign banks coupled with strengthening domestic prudential regulation and supervision of the commercial banking system can improve the performance of domestic banks (Manlagñit 2011; Phan et al. 2016).

Theoretical Issues on Bank Competition, Capital Regulation, and Financial Stability

Banking institutions have an important function in the economy, which is to provide credit and create liquid deposits. High leverage is not required for them to perform these valuable social functions. In fact, high leverage causes inefficiency and exposes the public to unnecessary risk. Additional distortions arise when distress and insolvency become so unmanageable that the government and the central bank must step in. Current policies end up subsidizing and encouraging banks to choose unrestricted leverage and risk. It would then be highly beneficial to counter these forces with effective equity requirements (Admati and Hellwig 2013).

When substantial increases in equity requirements threaten to damage the economy, growth becomes less of a concern than weak and poorly capitalized banks and a fragile system. The transition to a healthier system is not only possible but also beneficial to the financial sector and the broader economy (Admati and Hellwig 2013).

Schliephake (2016) analyzed the effects of capital requirement regulation on the stability of banks that compete for loans. Regulating the capital structure also changes the competitive environment since more stringent regulations limit entry into the sector and boost a bank's power to set prices. Further, her paper showed how price-setting power reinforced the impact of regulation on the stability of the banking sector. A change in the level of competition influences the ability of banks to consider risk-shifting behavior of borrowers and alters the optimal reaction to increased capital requirements. She also pointed out the disadvantages of imposing capital requirements without considering the adverse effects of a competitive environment and the characteristics of the banking system. These adverse effects occur in highly competitive under-capitalized sectors that invest in risky highly correlated loans with the probability of default that is sensitive to changes in loan interest rates. (Schliephake 2016). Her paper also provided closed-form solutions to critical values of competition and its effect on the efficiency of capital regulation as well as systematically characterized economic states, market environments, and bank characteristics where competition likely affects stability. Further, her analysis brought to light two important conclusions (ibid.).

First, the level of competition does not affect well-capitalized banking sectors with low externalities and low investment risks. In these sectors, higher capital requirements unambiguously boost stability. Since such characteristics most likely apply to healthy banking sectors in periods of economic growth, the policy would likely increase capital requirements during economic booms. Conversely, the second result applies to undercapitalized banks that have invested in risky and highly correlated assets. If these characteristics apply, then an increase in capital requirements for banking sectors that face excess capacities and intense competition can be detrimental to stability. In such a banking sector, higher capital regulation results in riskier lending and higher probability of bank default if the competitive pressure is high. As these characteristics most likely apply to banks during or in the aftermath of economic and financial crises, the results suggest combining a higher capital requirement regulation with a stricter competition policy. In particular, policies that strengthen capital requirements in the aftermath of a crisis should embark on a cleanup of the financial sector to put an end to unprofitable institutions and so reduce excess capacities and unhealthy competition (Schliephake 2016). The results of Schliephake (2016) provided valuable insights to how capital regulation, bank concentration, and competition relate to financial stability. She incorporated the effects of bank market structure and risk-taking behavior to the corresponding changes in bank capitalization in compliance with Basel III, using the assumptions and results of Martinez-Miera and Repullo (2010) and Boyd and de Nicolò (2005). Her study makes for a valuable contribution to the existing body of literature.

Dumlao (2015, 2016) for his part empirically verified that raising the equity-to-assets of the 10 largest banks in the Philippines from a 10% capital ratio to 20–30% would allow banks to have sufficient buffers in the case of a default, thereby making them less fragile. This author (2016) observed that some would argue against increasing capital requirements because this raises the cost of capital. The rationale is that shareholders, more than creditors, require higher rates of return. However, Admati and Hellwig (2013) claim that this is not always true. First, shareholders require higher returns that do not put a business at risk. Hence, banks can take risky ventures and rightfully pay the risk premium. Alternatively, they can opt for safer ventures and rightfully pay less. Second, shareholders require higher returns to the extent of the debt-equity ratio. If a bank wishes to pay shareholders less, then it must earn the privilege by lowering its debt-equity ratio. To quote Miles et al. (2012, p. 12), following the Modigliani–Miller theorem, "as more equity capital is used, the volatility of the return on that equity falls and the safety of the debt rises so that the required rate of return on both sources of funds falls."

Relating the theoretical model of Schliephake (2016) to the empirical results of Dumlao (2015), the banking sector of the Philippines is undercapitalized and risk-prone due to its moderate exposure to investments in real estate. The top two UKBs in the Philippines have a leverage ratio lower than the ASEAN-5. Yet the owners of these banks run the country's top commercial real estate firms. The results of Schliephake (2016) reveal that if the loan defaults of banks are highly correlated and if bank competition is high, then an increase in capital requirements for banking sectors that face intense competition can be detrimental to stability. In such a sector, higher capital regulations drive riskier bank lending and higher probabilities of bank default if the competitive pressure is high. For the Philippines, the correlation of loan defaults among the Top 10 banks may be imperfect. This implies that the level of moral hazard and information asymmetry could be moderate. The relationship between capital regulation, bank competition, bank concentration, and stability theoretically formulated by Schliephake (2016) shall be used in the conceptual framework.

Kopecky and VanHoose (2004a) explain why imperfect competition more likely fosters a stable banking industry with the onset of increased bank capitalization. It also contemplated the impact of binding capital regulation to bank credit supply holding rates of return and allowed adjustments in market interest rates and the addition of bank equity to a bank's balance sheet (VanHoose 2022, p. 165).

Figures 3.2 and 3.3 illustrate the basic conclusions of the Kopecky–VanHoose (2004a) model. The diagrams represent capital-constrained banks. Panel (a) of Fig. 3.2 shows that, in the short run, with bank equity fixed, a binding risk-based capital constraint acts as a quota on bank lending. Thus, loans decline to $\underline{L}$ and the market loan rate rises above the level in an unconstrained equilibrium, at $\underline{r}L$. Panel (b) exhibits the effects of an increase in the level of the risk-free rate that translates into higher interest rates on securities and non-deposit liabilities. In an unconstrained equilibrium, the rise in these interest rates raises the total marginal cost of lending and causes a decline in loan supply. Consequently, the public shifts from securities to bank loans, which causes a rise in loan demand. In an unconstrained equilibrium, lending falls, while the equilibrium loan rate rises. However, in a constrained case, the only impact of the higher level of market rates is an increase in the loan rate, from $\underline{r}L$ to $\underline{r}'L$.

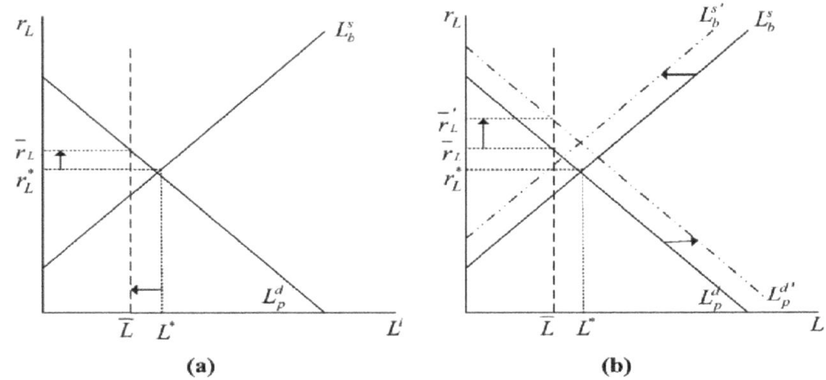

Fig. 3.2 Short-run implications of a binding risk-based capital requirement among perfectly competitive banks (*Source* VanHoose 2022, p. 165)

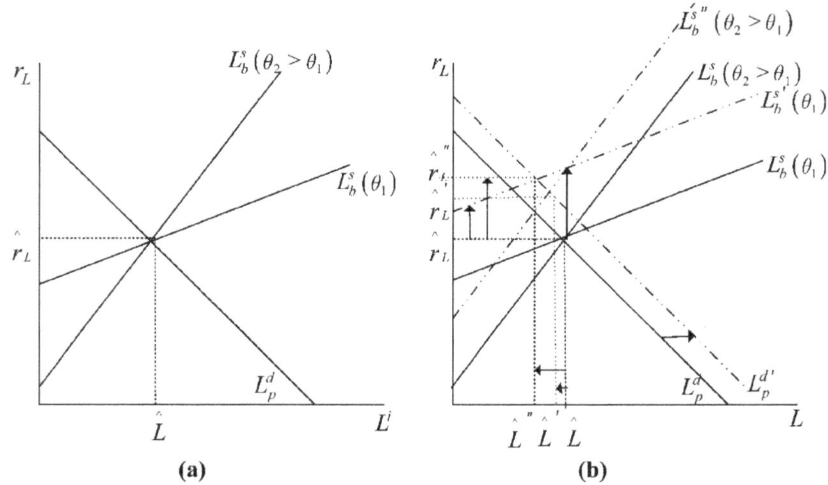

Fig. 3.3 Long-term effects of a binding risk-based capital ratio with representative competitive banks (*Source* VanHoose 2022, p. 166)

Panel (a) of Fig. 3.3 shows that when equity is variable, banks constrained by capital regulation must raise additional higher-marginal-cost equity to support given volumes of lending. Thus, the total marginal costs of lending are steeper with higher required capital ratios. Consequently, an increase in the required capital ratio steepens the market loan supply curve. Panel (b) displays the effects of an increase in the risk-free rate that boosts interest rates on securities on non-deposit liabilities. Again, the rise in other interest rates causes loan supply to dip and the public's loan demand to rise. In the long run, lending declines and the equilibrium loan rate goes up, further accentuated under the higher regulatory capital ratio, $\theta_1 > \theta_2$.

Kopecky and VanHoose (2006) examined the effects of capital regulation with heterogeneous banks where the fraction Ω of competitive banks monitors loans for moral hazard risks while the fraction $1 - \Omega$ does not. In this setting, imposing capital requirements alters the terms of the cost–benefit analysis of constrained banks. Lending responses of capital-constrained banks influence the market loan rate as well as the cost–benefit analysis of unconstrained banks. Kopecky and VanHoose (2006) first considered the case wherein capital regulation binds the entire banking industry and monitoring and non-monitoring banks are constrained by the same balance-sheet decisions. Aggregating this constraint across all banks and combining it with the loan demand function yields the loan market equilibrium (LME) locus. Aggregating this constraint across all banks and combining this with the loan demand function yielded the loan market equilibrium (LME) locus $\hat{r}_L$, which is the horizontal schedule depicted in panel (a) of Fig. 3.4. The loan rate that yields zero economic profits for both monitoring and non-monitoring banks yielded the equal profits (EP) locus depicted in panel (a).

Kopecky and VanHoose (2006) conclude that other things being equal, imposing capital requirements on the entire banking industry reduces the amount of lending, which in turn, reduces risk exposure. At the same time, an all-binding capital regulation reduces levels of loan monitoring and tends to render the industry less safe. On net, the safety-and-soundness effects of capital requirements are ambiguous (VanHoose 2022, p. 176).

Once all-binding capital requirements are in place, raising the required capital ratio causes the equal profit (EP) ratio to shift right. The resulting reduction in constrained bank lending reduces marginal monitoring costs, thereby giving some banks greater incentive to monitor their loans. Thus,

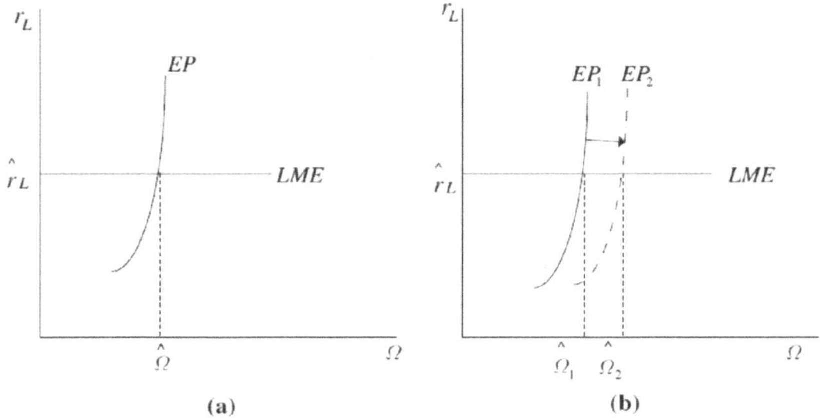

Fig. 3.4 Effects of a binding risk-based capital ratio with heterogeneous competitive banks (*Source* VanHoose 2022, p. 175)

once implemented, a system of capital standards that binds all banks gives the required capital ratio a boost and redounds to a sounder banking industry (VanHoose 2022, p. 176).

This result proves that even if the supply of loans will decrease in the short run, banks that comply with the binding capital requirement choose to improve their monitoring costs by investing in new technology or by hiring personnel. Upon doing so, they slash marginal monitoring costs. Banks can operate in this manner without having to reduce their profits. Thus, the financial stability of the entire banking industry improves if all competing banks comply with binding capital requirements. The industry therefore becomes less fragile because banks lessen their risk exposure by investing in new technology to upgrade their monitoring practices.

For this study, the exercise of market power by the dominant and fringe banks may indicate their capacity to monitor costs and reduce marginal monitoring costs. The results of VanHoose and Kopecky (2004a) explain from the industrial organization point of view why binding capital regulation does not necessarily spell less profit for banks. In fact, the dominant and efficient banks may initiate an increase in capitalization and encourage the efficient fringe banks to follow suit. Schliephake (2016, pp 1806–1807), who looked into the relationship of imperfect competition, market concentration, market power, and binding capital requirements, argued that in a market-concentrated banking industry, with profitable banks bound by strict and consistent regulations, the presence of dominant banks can enhance financial stability. While the analysis of VanHoose (2022, pp. 174–176) applies to a situation of imperfect competition with market concentration where bank regulators consistently implement binding rules for bank capitalization. These factors apply to the Philippine UKB industry.

Empirical Issues: Industrial Organization Approach to Banking

The industrial organization approach to banking, also called "traditional industrial organization" and "new empirical industrial organization," refers to the branch of economics that focuses on the theoretical and methodological ways with which banks address competition. Traditionally, two intellectual paradigms guide the policy-oriented economic analysis of the structure of the banking industry—the structure-conduct-performance (SCP) hypothesis and the efficient structure (ES) theory.

The SCP hypothesis proposes that the level of concentration in the bank market influences bank behavior, which in turn affects loan and deposit quantities, qualities, interest rates, and other market outcomes that determine consumer welfare. The SCP hypothesis implies that greater concentration gives banks greater market power, which leads to fewer loans and deposits, higher loan rates, and lower deposit rates—all of which do not favor the consumer. The ES theory suggests that the cost conditions which banks face play a crucial role in determining the optimal scale of individual banking organizations and the appropriate scope of banking activities. Thus, in contrast to the SCP hypothesis, the ES theory indicates that greater cost efficiencies resulting from the expansion of scale and/or scope can result in expanded loans and deposits with corresponding lower loan rates and higher deposit rates. In practice, therefore, regulators contemplating applications for new banking licenses or, as discussed in the following chapter, bank mergers and acquisitions, have focused on a perceived tradeoff between resulting increases in market power and cost efficiency gains (VanHoose 2022, pp. 70–71).

Criticism leveled against the SCP and the efficiency hypotheses has something to do with the assumed embedded one-way causality from market structure to performance. In other words, most SCP studies do not take into account the conduct of the banks in the market and the impact of bank performance on market structure. Studies have attempted to determine the degree of competition that relies on various indexes of concentration, such as C4 (four-firm concentration ratio) and the HHI, which yielded conflicting results (Degryse et al. 2009, p. 33). The new empirical industrial organization (NEIO) approach circumvents this problem. It does not try to infer the degree of competition from "indirect proxies," such as market structure or market shares, or argue that market structure is the result of the degree of competition. The NEIO aims to infer the banks' behavior regardless of market structure by employing a variety of alternative methodologies with sometimes substantially different data requirements (Degryse et al. 2009, p. 34).

This paper aims to present empirical evidence on the competitive behavior of banks in the Philippines. Competitive behavior will be measured using traditional and new empirical industrial organization (NEIO) methods and tools, such as the *Z*-index, Lerner Index, Boone Indicator, and the HHI, as well as observe four indicators—the Lerner Index, the Boone Indicator or Profit Elasticity Indicator, and, the HHI.

Z-Index

The recent financial crisis has led to a refocus on the importance, impact, and measurement of bank insolvency and liquidity risk. Owing to its relative simplicity and the use of accounting information alone for calculations, the *Z*-score has become popular for measuring insolvency in empirical studies related to banking and financial stability (Lepetit et al. 2015). As such, it is applicable to a wide number of unlisted financial institutions and serves as an indicator for the World Bank in measuring the soundness of financial institutions in its Global Financial Development Database.

The general form of the *Z*-score is attributed to Hannan and Hanweck (1988) while Boyd and Graham (1986) introduced *Z*-scores in the special context of normal return distributions. In 1993, Boyd et al. introduced a general form of the *Z*-Index, allowing for non-normal return distributions. Boyd et al. (1993) initially used it for cross-sectional studies while Bouvatier et al. (2017) gave a refined interpretation of this insolvency risk measure. Starting with Boyd et al. (2005), the *Z*-score is commonly implemented as a time-varying measure in panel studies. Bouvatier et al. (2017) discuss the different approaches to constructing time-varying *Z*-scores in the literature.

One may challenge the popularity of Z-scores on several points. Bouvatier et al. (2017) considered improvements for each one. First, the traditional Z-score is ROA-based and involves implicit scaling by total assets that may introduce spurious variability, which may be avoided and used to skirt an alternative ROE-based measure. Secondly, both ROA- and ROE-based Z-score measures could suffer from measurement bias introduced through banks that potentially engage in income-smoothing behavior. The present study derives an alternative Z-score measure to correct this. Thirdly, returns-based Z-score measures disregard the importance of regulatory capital constraints that banks face.

Bouvatier et al. (2017) consider this aspect by constructing an alternative "regulatory capital" Z-score. The Z-index may be computed in several ways. The volatility of a bank's return-on-assets (ROA), return-on-equity (ROE), risk-based capital adequacy ratio (RCAR), and TIER1 ratio become the weighting measure for the performance indicators. The standard deviation of the bank control variables ROA, ROE, RCAR, and TIER1 will indicate volatility. The bank's performance indicator, net income, shall be combined with its leverage ratio and equity-to-assets. Bank performance and leverage shall then be divided into either Total Assets or Total Equity, depending on the type of Z-index measured. Finally, bank performance and leverage shall be weighted by risk measurement, or volatility, indicated by the standard deviation of ROA, ROE, RCAR, or TIER1.

The calculated Z-index therefore shows the number of standard deviations a bank can have before it experiences default or zero returns. Thus, the higher the Z-index, the more stable a bank is, because it can withstand variations or volatility in its total assets or equity. The Z-index using RCAR (Z_{RCAR}) would be calculated as the difference of the actual RCAR from the BSP-regulated RCAR of 12%, and the Z-index using TIER1 (Z_{TIER1}) as the difference from the BSP-regulated RCAR of 10%. This difference shall be divided by the standard deviation of a bank's actual RCAR or actual TIER1. A higher Z_{RCAR} or Z_{TIER1} would indicate greater capital through the infusion of fresh capital stock and/or increased retained earnings, and/or less volatility or capital that does not vary from the regulated threshold.

Financial Stability Indicator Reflecting a Bank's Resilience From Insolvency: Z-index (ROA) or Z_{ROA}

The bank-level Z-index (ROA) is a measure of a bank's overall exposure to risk or potential insolvency. A higher value indicates greater stability and less overall risk. The Z-index (ROA) is an inverse proxy for the firm's probability of failure. It combines profitability, leverage, and return volatility in a single measure, as provided by the following ratio:

$$Z_{\text{ROA}_i} = \frac{\text{ROA}_i + \frac{EQ}{TA_i}}{\sigma_{\text{ROA}_i}} = \frac{\frac{(\text{Net Income}+\text{Stockholder's Equity})}{\text{Total Assets}}}{\sigma_{\text{ROA}_i}} \tag{3.1}$$

where:

ROA_i	period-average return-on-assets for bank i, performance indicator
$\frac{EQ}{TA_i}$	period-average equity to total assets ratio for bank i, leverage indicator; and
σ_{ROA_i}	standard deviation of ROA over the period under study

The Z-index (ROA) or Z_{ROA} increases with higher profitability and capitalization levels and decreases with unstable earnings as reflected by a higher standard deviation of return-on-assets. It inversely proxies the bank's probability of failure and is an indicator of financial stability. One observation per bank per period (quarter) shall be used.

An Alternative Financial Stability Indicator Reflecting a Bank's Resilience From Insolvency: Z-index (ROE) or Z_{ROE}

Goyeau and Tarazi (1992) first advanced a Z-index measure based on return-on-equity (ROE) in the special context of normal return distributions, defined as:

$$Z_{\text{ROE}_i} = \frac{1 + \text{ROE}_i}{\sigma_{\text{ROE}_i}} = \frac{\frac{(\text{Stockholder's Equity}+\text{Net Income})}{\text{Stockholders' Equity}}}{\sigma_{\text{ROE}_i}} \tag{3.2}$$

Bouvatier et al. (2017) provide a probabilistic interpretation for such a measure that allows for non-normal return distributions. They further argued that an ROE-based *Z*-index or Z_{ROE} measure could be preferable to the more commonly used ROA-based one, as it is constructed to be unaffected by potentially spurious variability in total assets. This could be particularly relevant in the context of time-varying *Z*-index measures.

The loss provisions with an expected decline in earnings may be deliberately understated. However, when earnings are unusually high, banks could opt for discretionary income-reducing accruals. Thus, banks engaged in income-smoothing behavior can reduce the variance of reported earnings, making *Z*-score measures potentially less reliable predictors of bank distress (Bouvatier et al. 2017, pp. 4–5).

Risk-Based Capital Adequacy Ratio *Z*-index: *Z*-index (RCAR) or Z_{RCAR}

Based on the definition of bank distress in the development of returns-based *Z*-score measures, one may argue that a bank is in "regulatory" distress when a particular RCAR drops below a given regulatory threshold (Lepetit et al. 2015). For instance, a bank's total capital ratio drops below 8% or, under Basel III's prescribed TIER1 ratio, below 4.5%.

The "regulatory capital" *Z*-index, is defined as:

$$Z_{\text{RCAR}_i} = \frac{\text{RCAR}_i - 12.5}{\sigma_{\text{RCAR}_i}} \tag{3.3}$$

$$Z_{\text{TIER1}_i} = \frac{\text{TIER1}_i - 10}{\sigma_{\text{TIER1}_i}} \tag{3.4}$$

Since the risk-based capital adequacy ratio *Z*-index or Z_{RCAR} and the *Z*-index Z_{TIER1} are not constructed using returns data, they remain unaffected by the potential measurement problem associated with bank income smoothing. Stable banks have non-zero Z_{RCAR} and Z_{TIER1}, and a small standard deviation (Bouvatier et al. 2017, p. 7).

Table 1.1 lists the existing Basel III regulations and the proposed minimum ratios with conservation buffer for the Philippines. Note that the proposed BSP regulations are higher than what Basel III proposed for the risk-based capital adequacy ratios, common equity TIER1 ratio, and TIER1 ratio. Higher ratios aim to serve as additional buffers in the event of countercyclical events.

This study shall use the risk-based capital adequacy ratio of 12.5% and TIER1 ratio of 10%, as proposed by the BSP. However, the minimum level would be based on the Basel III TIER1 guidelines of 8.5% and 10.5% for RCAR. Finally, the study will use all four methods to calculate the Z-index, Z_{ROA}, Z_{ROE}, Z_{RCAR}, and Z_{TIER1}.

Herfindahl–Hirschman Index (HHI)

Traditionally, the most common measure of bank market concentration has been one-, two-, or three-bank concentration ratios, or the combined assets, loans, or deposits of the top three banks expressed as percentage shares of total market quantities. HHI, which has become more popular in recent years, is the sum of squared percentage shares of assets, loans, or deposits of each of the banks in the market (VanHoose 2022, p. 57).

To assess the degree of concentration in the relevant banking market in the United States, the Federal Reserve follows the prescriptions of the Department of Justice by relying on the HHI, which is the sum of squared percentage market shares of each of the banks in the market. HHI computes pre- and post-merger HHIs and calculates the resulting change in the HHI. In the case of a merger of two rivals, it is equal to twice the product of percentage market shares of the two companies. The pre-merger HHI is equal to $\sum_{i=1}^{n} S_i^2$ where there are n banking institutions in the relevant market and S_i is the market share of bank. The post-merger HHI in the event of a merger by the first two banks, $i = 1, 2$, must be equal to

$$\sum_{i=1}^{n} S_i^2 - S_1^2 - S_2^2 + (S_1 + S_2)^2 = \sum_{i=1}^{n} S_i^2 + 2S_1S_2 \tag{3.5}$$

Subtracting the pre-merger HHI, $\sum_{i=1}^{n} S_i^2$ yields $2S_1S_2$. For regulators, both the post-merger HHI and the change in the HHI are important when assessing a proposed merger (VanHoose 2022, p. 118).

Before 2010, the US Department of Justice's evaluation of planned consolidations of nonfinancial firms considered a market as unconcentrated if the HHI is less than 1000, moderately concentrated if the HHI is between 1000 and 1800, and highly concentrated if the HHI exceeds 1800 (VanHoose 2010, p. 95; Salop 1987). This study shall consider a range of 1000–1500 as moderately concentrated since the massive mergers of Philippine UKBs happened from 2008 to 2013 and from 2021 to 2022. During the said periods, the HHI for loans exceeded 1000.

Moreover, much has changed in the United States, post-2010. The US Department of Justice deemed that a market with an HHI below 1500 was unconcentrated; one with an HHI of 1500–2500, moderately concentrated; and highly concentrated with an HHI higher than 2500 (VanHoose 2022, p. 119). Relying on these classifications of market concentration would imply that many US banking markets, as defined by metropolitan statistical areas, are moderately concentrated. From the late 2000s, on the other hand, a market was considered "highly concentrated" only if it reached a critical HHI value of 1800 (VanHoose 2022, p. 119). These new ranges were used to classify banks that merged, especially after 2010, or after the 2008 US Financial Crisis. Studies in the United States observed the impact of a 0.1 change in the HHI on loan rates. Loan rates in the US increased from 22 to 55 bp in 1996 (Cyrnak and Hannan 1999).

In the absence of accessible data on loan and deposit rates at the bank level, a regression using the adjusted Lerner Index, an indicator of markup, shall be conducted using the HHI on loans and deposits as explanatory variables. The coefficient of the HHI on loans and deposits of the Top 10 Philippine banks when regressed with the adjusted Lerner Index as dependent variables is expected to be significantly higher than that of the Top 20 and Next 10 banks.

Lerner Index

The impact of market structure on risk-taking and financial stability shall be measured using the Lerner Index as a proxy for market power. This is a more direct measure of competition because it focuses on the pricing power in the difference between price and marginal cost, and captures the degree to which a firm can increase its price beyond marginal cost (Berger et al. 2009). The Lerner Index represents the markup of price over marginal costs and indicates the degree of market power (Lerner 1934). It is a "level" indicator of the proportion where price exceeds marginal cost, calculated as:

$$\text{Lerner}_{it} = \frac{\left(P_{TA_{it}} - MC_{TA_{it}}\right)}{P_{TA_{it}}} \tag{3.6}$$

where:

$P_{TA_{it}}$ price of total assets proxied by the ratio of total revenues (interest and non-interest income) to total assets for bank i at time t; and

$MC_{TA_{it}}$ marginal cost of total assets for bank i at time t.

To this day, the Lerner Index remains the most widely used measure for market power and levels of competition (Clerides et al. 2015) because of its simplicity, intuitive interpretation, and relatively mild data requirements. The Lerner Index measures the ability of a bank to charge a price above marginal cost. One can compute the Lerner Index as a simple ratio when data on prices and marginal cost are available. Because marginal cost is rarely available, researchers obtain estimates by measuring a cost function or imposing equilibrium conditions derived from theoretical models. The former was popular in banking literature, while industrial organization economists (Clerides et al. 2015) preferred the latter.

Deriving equilibrium conditions from which the Lerner Index can determine market power requires a regression of the translog cost function. The translog cost function uses the price indicators of personnel compensation, fixed capital, and loan rates. These, along with data on bank-level interest and non-interest income, are not open to the public. Due to the non-availability of open access data at the BSP, the study resorts to an intermediate approach to calculate the production behavior of banks. For example, the cost function shall be derived from balance sheets used in the banking literature, calculating net income from the return-on-equity, and using total assets as the indicator for total revenues. Input and output are specified according to the intermediation model (Sealey and Lindley 1977). Loans, for instance, are considered bank output. A bank's production function uses labor and physical capital, such as ATMs, electronic banking, and bank branches, to attract deposits. Deposits, in turn, fund loans and other earning assets.

Koetter et al. (2012) argued that the conventional approach to computing the Lerner Index assumes profit efficiency (optimal choice of prices) and cost efficiency (optimal choice of inputs by firms). As a result, the estimated price–cost margins do not correctly measure the true extent of market power. The argument reflects a distinction that Lerner himself pointed out: "… for practical purposes we must read monopoly power not as potential monopoly, but as monopoly in force" (Lerner 1934, p. 170. Italics in the original). In other words, the Lerner Index measures actual (exercised) market power, while Koetter et al. (2012) measure potential market power. To this end, the authors propose an adjustment that results in the efficiency-adjusted Lerner Index:

$$\text{adjusted Lerner}_i = \frac{\pi_i + tc_i - mc_i \cdot q_i}{\pi_i + tc_i} \tag{3.7}$$

where

π_i	the profit of bank i,
tc_i	total cost,
mc_i	marginal cost, and
q_i	total output

Unlike the standard Lerner Index, the adjusted one ranges from zero to greater than 1.0, with larger values indicating greater market power. Total cost is calculated from Total Revenues (using Total Assets less Fixed Assets as proxy) less Net Income (using ROE multiplied from Stockholders' Equity).

In the absence of open access loan and deposit rates per bank, this study shall use the adjusted Lerner Index to capture the effect of price-setting power and marginal costs. The adjusted Index shall be computed from individual bank balance sheets using total assets, total loans, total deposits, equity, and return-on-equity as variables to derive net income, total costs, and marginal costs. Marginal cost shall be calculated as the difference per quarter, starting from the second quarter of 2005 to the fourth quarter of 2016. Oduor et al. (2017) undertook a similar procedure in the absence of bank data to complete the translog cost function. Calculation of the adjusted Lerner Index cannot be regressed through a translog function that captures equilibrium levels of input prices where marginal revenue shall equal marginal cost. This indicator will only be considered as a proxy variable for the adjusted Lerner Index to indicate the capacity of banks to charge markups, instead of attributing market power for the indicator.

The adjusted Lerner Index shall be calculated for the study. Breaking down its positive association with the size of monopoly rents, note that the constructed adjusted Lerner Index does not capture risk in the prices of bank products and services. However, it is the only measure of competition in this study computed at the bank level. The adjusted Lerner

Index will serve as a dependent variable to verify the presence of dominant banks, as well as a regressor to explain financial stability and financial fragility through the bank's capacity to mark up its loan rates.

Boone Indicator or the Profit Elasticity Indicator

Boone (2008) proposed a new competition measure called relative profit differences (RPD) to show that most theoretical models for oligopolistic competition between more and less-efficient firms differ in profit as competition among them intensifies. Consider an increase in competition, due perhaps to a decrease in entry costs or to goods becoming closer substitutes. The profit of an efficient firm will increase relative to that of a less-efficient one as stiffened competition severely penalizes the least efficient firm. RPD is a theoretical construct that is difficult to compute. Boone et al. (2005) proposed the profit elasticity (PE) as an empirical analogue of RPD. The PE is the percentage decrease in profits resulting from a one percent increase in the marginal cost:

$$\text{profit elasticity}_i = \frac{\partial \ln \ln \pi_i}{\partial \ln \ln mc_i}. \tag{3.8}$$

The PE, sometimes called the Boone indicator, should be negative because profits and marginal costs are inversely related. An efficient firm will have a lower PE (in absolute value) as its profits will be less affected by a change in marginal cost. For example, if PE is equal to −0.2, a 1% increase in the marginal cost due to reduced efficiency will decrease profits by 0.2%. If PE is equal to −0.5, a 1% increase in marginal cost will decrease profits by 0.5%. A large absolute value of the PE can mean a reduced ability to contain losses due to increased competition. The profit elasticity therefore links bank performance to differences in efficiency in terms of marginal cost (Clerides et al. 2015).

Boone et al. (2005) suggest the following equation to determine the PE:

$$\pi_i = \alpha + \beta_i \ln \ln mc_i \tag{3.9}$$

The coefficient β_i is the desired profit elasticity index of market power. Intuitively, Eq. (3.8) examines the relationship between profits and marginal cost, or the indirect relationship between profit and efficiency.

The profit elasticity can take any value and is therefore a continuous indicator of market power. Equation (3.8) shall be calculated using a GMM regression on Ln (net income) and Ln (adjusted Lerner Index). The adjusted Lerner Index shall serve as a proxy for marginal cost as the balance sheet data used to compute the Lerner Index are total assets, return-on-equity. More data is used to regress vis-à-vis net income. Thus, the result of this estimation procedure will denote a cost advantage, i.e., the ability to profit due to the capacity to achieve a higher markup, rather than the capacity of a dominant bank to operate in an environment where marginal revenues equal marginal cost and a price above marginal cost.

Theoretical Framework and Empirical Methodology

This portion defines the research hypothesis, presents the industrial organization-based theoretical and conceptual framework, and the appropriate empirical model.

Using the techniques of traditional and the new empirical industrial organization literature, the study verified the occurrence of competition-fragility in an imperfectly competitive and loans market-concentrated UKB industry bound by a regulatory bank capitalization environment. In an industry of dominant and fringe banks, the sampled Top 20 UKBs of the Philippines will exercise market power by charging higher loan rates to improve their profit margins and monitoring technology, thereby acquiring enough earnings to increase the capital buffer (Schliephake 2016).

To test the competition-fragility and competition-stability views, the *Z*-index (indicator for financial stability vis-à-vis overall bank risk exposure and insolvency), NPL to total loans ratio (indicator for portfolio risk), and the equity to total assets ratio (indicator for bank capitalization) were the dependent variables. These dependent variables were regressed using the GMM and measures of market power-adjusted Lerner Index, HHI (for deposits and loans), and other bank-specific control variables, following the methodology of Berger et al. (2009).

The GMM regression method allows correction for heteroscedasticity, weak serial correlation, and endogeneity by using robust estimators and assumes a non-normal but asymptotic to zero probabilistic distribution for the means of the dependent and independent variables. Varying methods of the financial stability indicator, like the *Z*-index, tested for a bank's resilience to insolvency and regulatory distress, using return-on-assets, return-on-equity, and BSP-proposed risk-weighted capitalization ratios.

Hypotheses

The study aims to answer the following problem: Does bank competition and concentration lead to financial stability? The solution is based on the following hypotheses:

1. An imperfectly competitive market structure characterizes the Philippine U/KB industry.
2. Market concentration and imperfect competition in the banking industry enable banks to be profitable but expose them to greater risks, making them more fragile.
3. Market concentration and imperfect competition in the banking industry enable banks to increase capitalization, making them more stable.

Theoretical and Conceptual Framework

The industrial organization perspective of banking holds that increased competition drives banks to take more risk (Matute and Vives 2000; Repullo 2004). By reducing a bank's franchise value, competition reduces the penalty for failure and urges the practice of prudence. This literature assumes that banks invest in assets with exogenous distributions of returns. Boyd and De Nicolò (2005), henceforth referred to as BDN, replaced this with the assumption that banks invest in loans. Following the seminal paper on credit rationing by Stiglitz and Weiss (1981), BDN assumed that loans risk an increase in interest rate. Hence, lower loan rates due to greater competition reduce the loans' probability of default. They also assumed that the probability of loan default correlates with the probability of failure. Thus, competition diminishes the risk of failure (Martinez-Miera and Repullo 2010), henceforth referred to as MMR. However, this finding does not necessarily hold in the case of an imperfect correlation of loan defaults, since greater bank competition reduces the interest payments from performing loans, which serve as a buffer against loan loss. Thus, in addition to the risk-shifting effect, there is the contrary margin effect, which renders the risk of bank failure as ambiguous (Martinez-Miera and Repullo 2010).

The basic setup of MMR follows that of BDN, except for the introduction of the imperfect correlation in loan defaults (less than 1.0 but greater than 0.0). Specifically, MMR used a static model of Cournot for competition in a market for entrepreneurial loans where an entrepreneur chooses to risk the probability of loan default. Banks are funded by fully insured deposits and have no capital.

MMR showed that BDN's results do not hold up against even a small deviation from perfect correlation in loan defaults. Specifically, when the number of banks is large enough, the margin effect always dominates the risk-shifting effect and any additional entry would intensify the risk of bank failure.

In less competitive loan markets, the effect is ambiguous, which led MMR to resort to numerical solutions for a large range of parameterizations of the model. MMR pointed out a general U-shaped relationship between competition (measured by the number of banks) and the risk of bank failure. In other words, the risk-shifting effect prevails in very concentrated markets, which reduces the probability of bank failure. On the other hand, the margin effect dominates in very competitive markets, so further entry increases the probability of failure.

To check the robustness of these results, MMR relaxed the assumption that deposits are fully insured. Without deposit insurance, the deposit rate is no longer an exogenous parameter but an endogenous variable derived from the depositors' participation constraint. MMR showed that eliminating deposit insurance increases the risk of bank failure because the higher cost of deposits translates into higher loan rates, which makes loans riskier. However, MMR observed a sustained U-shaped relationship between competition and risk of bank failure.

Theoretical Model: Imperfect Competition in the Philippine Banking Industry with a Dominant Bank Model

The theoretical model in this study combines the effect of market structure on bank competition, concentration, stability, and capitalization. MMR assumed imperfect competition in the banking industry. Thus, an empirical verification of the presence of imperfect competition in the Philippine banking industry shall be done using the Monti-Klein model (Freixas and Rochet 2008) followed by the estimation of the MMR (2010) and Schliephake (2016) model.

The Monti-Klein model shall be used to analyze the market structure of the banking industry. Through this framework, one can verify the existence and exercise of market power in the Philippine UKB industry. The model assumes a monopolistic banking industry and later expands to an oligopolistic banking structure (Freixas and Rochet 2008, pp. 78–79). Under this paradigm, the presence of dominant but efficient banks and less-efficient fringe banks would verify the existence of imperfect competition.

The Monti-Klein model considers a monopolistic bank confronted with a downward-sloping demand for loans $L(r_L)$ and an upward-sloping supply of deposits $D(r_D)$. In fact, it is more convenient to work with their inverse functions, $r_L(L)$ and $r_D(D)$. The bank's decision variables are L (amount of loans) and D (amount of deposits), since its level of equity, α, is assumed to be given. The Monti-Klein model can easily be reinterpreted as a model of imperfect (Cournot) competition between a finite number (N) of banks, which is a more accurate description.

$$\frac{\partial r_L^*}{\partial r} = \frac{1}{1 - \frac{1}{N\varepsilon_L}} \text{ and } \frac{\partial r_D^*}{\partial r} = \frac{1 - \alpha}{1 - \frac{1}{N\varepsilon_D}} \tag{3.10}$$

Although the Monti-Klein model presents a simplified approach to banking activity, it presents particularly natural and appealing conclusions backed by empirical evidence. There are also features of deposit contracts that the model cannot explain but which reasonably states that market power drives banks to quote lower deposit rates and higher loan rates. The empirical findings, an early contribution by Edwards (1964), show that the different interest rates charged on loans can reflect different elasticities of demand, the results of which were derived from Eq. 3.10. Another result derived from said equation is that loan rates are usually higher than deposit rates. This finding shall be used in the empirical methodology of the study. Adachi (2019) theoretically proves that the Monti-Klein model applies to imperfect markets when banks can modify loan rates from deposit rates using the elasticities of demand for loans and deposits.

The Monti-Klein model is consistent with the structure-conduct-performance (SCP) paradigm in banking. Within the SCP paradigm, a dominant bank model takes into account the potential for larger, more cost-efficient banks to engage in market rivalry with smaller, less-efficient banks (VanHoose 2022, pp. 43–44).

Figure 3.5 illustrates the dominant bank framework as applied to a bank loan market. In this market, a large institution (i) and a number of smaller "fringe" banks ($j = 1, \ldots m$) raise funds by issuing non-deposit as well as deposit liabilities. These fringe banks are assumed to face the costs of entering the market, so m is relatively small in number. Both sets of institutions face upward-sloping marginal resource costs. Bank i's total marginal cost of lending is expressed in terms of funds raised via issuance of non-deposit liabilities: $MC_L^i = r_N + C_N^i + C_L^i$, which is the upward-sloping curve, graphed in panel (a) of Fig. 3.5.

The bank's average cost of lending is the curve AC_L^i, assumed to correspond to the bank's long-run efficient scale of operations. If bank i were a monopoly, then it would face the loan market demand curve L^d, marginal revenue curve, MR_M^i, profit-maximizing quantity of loans equal to L_M^i, and monopoly loan rate $r_L^{i,M}$. The bank's profits would be equal to the quantity of lending L_M^i multiplied by the difference between this loan rate

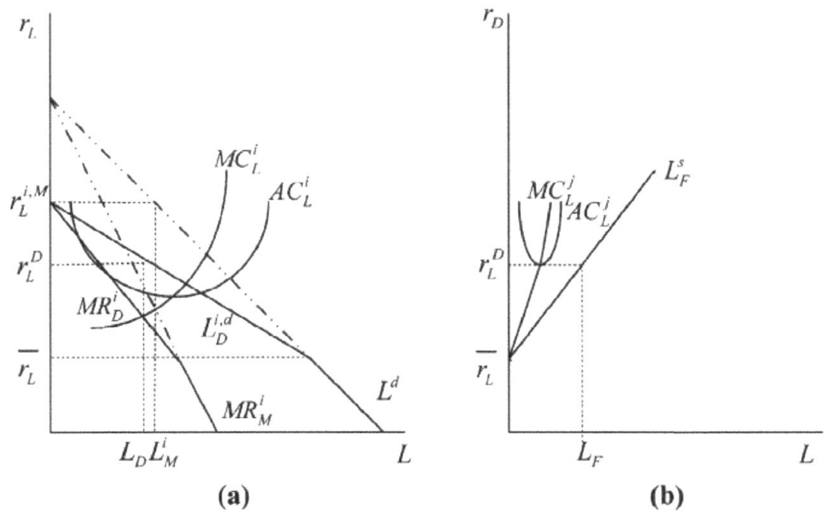

Fig. 3.5 The structure-conduct-performance hypothesis: a loan market with a dominant bank and a competitive fringe (*Source* VanHoose 2022, p. 43)

and the value of AC_L^i evaluated at that amount of lending (VanHoose 2022, pp. 43–44).

Compared with what is available to bank *i*, each of the *m* fringe competitors in the loan market has access to less-efficient technologies for raising and lending funds. For the sake of simplicity, suppose that each of these smaller banks at any given amount of loans faces a higher and identical total marginal cost of lending equal to $MC_L^j = r_N + C_N^j + C_L^j$, as shown in panel (b) of Fig. 3.5. As indicated in the short run, each of the identical fringe banks is willing to lend as long as it earns a loan rate exceeding a reservation loan rate, $\underline{r_L}$ a loan rate that is presumably and sufficiently low such that individual banks cannot cover their variable costs. The amount of lending by each fringe bank is sufficiently small in relation to total market loans that no single fringe bank can affect the market loan rate. Thus, each of these smaller banks takes the loan rate as "given," and the total combined supply of loans by all of these smaller, fringe banks is, as shown in panel (b), given by $L_F^S = \sum_{j=1}^{m} MC_L^j$ (VanHoose 2022, pp. 43–44).

Faced with competition from several smaller institutions, the fringe banks' reservation loan rate $\underline{r_L}$ and the dominant bank *i* do not deal with the entire market demand curve $L_D^{i,d} = L^d - L_F^s$. This means that each possible loan rate above $\underline{r_L}$, or the total quantity of loans demanded by the public from bank *i*, is equal to the market quantity demanded, less the total amount supplied by all fringe banks at that loan rate. This residual demand curve is associated with the marginal revenue curve MR_D^i. Bank *i* therefore maximizes its profits by extending a reduced amount of loans equal to L_D^i. The profit-maximizing loan rate is r_L^D, and bank *i*'s maximum profits from lending drop to the quantity of lending L_D^i multiplied by the difference between r_L^D and the value of AC_L^i evaluated at L_D^i.

The fringe banks take the dominant bank's loan rate r_L^D as the given market loan rate. Hence, the total quantity of loans that they extend is equal to L_F in panel (b), which in turn must be equal to the total market quantity of loans demanded at the loan rate r_L^D less the amount of loans extended by the dominant bank *i*, L_D^i. In the situation depicted in panel (b), each fringe bank *j* earns zero profits, implying the absence of incentives for fringe banks to enter or exit the market under the circumstances depicted in the figure. Thus, Fig. 3.5 illustrates a long-run equilibrium, prior to which there might have been fewer fringe firms in the market and a less elastic aggregate fringe supply curve, a higher profit-maximizing loan rate for the dominant bank, and positive profits for fringe firms that would have encouraged firm entry. Note that in the depicted long-run equilibrium, the dominant banks still rake in positive but not maximized profit due to their cost advantage, while the fringe banks do not.

Like the Monti-Klein model for a monopolist, extended to include N firms, the dominant firm model with fringe banks yielded the following results (VanHoose 2022, p. 44):

1. More market power along with greater market concentration;
2. For dominant firms, an expected higher profit-maximizing loan rate, or the rate at which marginal revenues are equal to marginal cost;
3. Anticipated positive profit for dominant firms due to their cost advantage.

Foreseeable results from the Monti-Klein model (Freixas and Rochet 2008, pp. 78–81) coincided with those of the traditional structure-conduct-performance paradigm, verified by Molyneux et al. (1995). The empirical study of Molyneux et al. (1995) pooled accounting data from banks in 18 European countries from 1986 to 89. The data came from the London-based bank credit rating firm, International Bank Credit Analysis Ltd, and were available for 756 banks in 1986, 1217 banks in 1987, 1538 banks in 1988, and 1265 banks in 1989.

Bank Competition, Concentration, Fragility, and Stability

Focus now will be on the theoretical model of MMR (2010) and Schliephake (2016) on the behavior of banks. At date 0, n identical banks hold fully insured deposits, no capital, and invest in entrepreneurial loans. The supply of deposits is perfectly elastic at an interest rate normalized to zero and without intermediation costs. MMR assumed that banks compete for loans à la Cournot, so the strategic variable of bank $j = 1$, n is its supply of loans l_j. The aggregate supply of loans $L = \sum_{j=1}^{n} l_j$ determines the loan rate $r\ (L)$ which, in turn, determines the probability of failure chosen by the entrepreneurs $p\ (r\ (L))$.

$$\underbrace{q'(L)}_{\substack{\downarrow \\ \text{Slope of the probability} \\ \text{of a bank's survival}}} = \frac{\Phi'(\cdot)}{\sqrt{\rho}}\left[\underbrace{\frac{d\Phi^{-1}(p(r(L)))}{dp}p'(r(L))}_{\substack{\downarrow \\ \text{Risk-shifting} \\ \text{effect (-)}}} - \underbrace{\sqrt{1-\rho}\,\frac{d\Phi^{-1}(\hat{x}(L))}{dx}\hat{x}'(L)}_{\substack{\downarrow \\ \text{Margin effect (+)}}}\right] \quad (3.11)$$

where:

$q'(L)$	slope of the probability of a bank's survival from defaulting loans;
$\Phi'(\cdot)$	survival function;
$d\Phi^{-1}(p(r(L))/dp$	derivative of the survival function for the probability of default of a single loan for a bank;
$p'(r(L))$	derivative of the probability of loan default, $r(L)$;
$d\Phi^{-1}\left(\hat{x}(L)\right)/dx$	derivative of the survival function for the probability of default of a bank;
$\hat{x}'(L)$	derivative of the probability of default for a bank;
ρ	correlation of loan default with a bank's default;

The function $\Phi'(\cdot) > 0$ (normal density) with the sign of $q'\ (L)$ is the same as the sign of the term enclosed in square brackets, which has two components. The first one is negative, since $\frac{d\Phi^{-1}(p(r(L)))}{dp} > 0$, $p'\ (r) > 0$, and $r'\ (L) < 0$, while the second one is positive (whenever $\rho < 1$), since $\frac{d\Phi^{-1}\left(\hat{x}(L)\right)}{dx} > 0$ and $\hat{x}'(L) < 0$.

The negative effect is what Boyd and De Nicolò identified as risk shifting. More competition leads to lower loan rates, which, in turn, lead to lower probability of default, hence safer banks. The positive effect is the so-called margin effect. More competition leads to lower loan rates and, consequently, lower revenues from performing loans, which provide a buffer against loan losses, resulting in riskier banks. Depending on which effect prevails, the impact of competition on the risk of bank failure may be positive or negative.

When $\rho = 1$ (perfectly correlated defaults), the margin effect in Eq. (3.2) disappears, yielding the results stated in BDN—competition always reduces the risk of bank failure. When $p'(r)$ = zero, the risk-shifting effect in Eq. (3.14) disappears and competition always entails the risk of bank failure. When $\rho = 0$ (independent defaults), the default rate is deterministic (a fraction p of the loans default with probability 1) whereby for any number of banks, the probability of failure is zero. For $0 < \rho < 1$ and $p'(r) > 0$, the result is generally ambiguous. In very competitive loan markets, the margin effect always dominates the risk-shifting effect.

In summary, the theoretical model indicates two opposite effects of a non-linear relationship between the risk of bank failure and competition. The risk-shifting effect identified by Boyd and De Nicolò (2005) ensues from increased competition that leads to lower loan rates that, in turn, bring about lower probabilities of loan default, hence safer banks. Results reveal that risk shifting tends to dominate monopolistic markets, while the margin effect prevails in competitive markets; thus, the overall U-shaped relationship between competition and the risk of bank failure. This study aims to establish the relationship between competition and bank insolvency and predicts an inverted U-relationship. At this point, if less competition prevails in the industry, imperfect competition among dominant and fringe banks would have some banks raising their loan rates and increasing their chances of loan default. They could avoid this if the dominant banks can effectively screen and monitor borrowers, hence, lower the probability of loan defaults.

Schliephake (2016) and Schliephake and Kirstein (2013) model the effect of a binding capital requirement in a scenario of imperfect competition. Their theoretical model predicts that banks subjected to a binding regulation and market concentration tend to increase loan rates and improve their monitoring capacity by investing in new technology and hiring skilled loan officers. Once they become more efficient, these dominant banks can hike up loan rates, improve profit, and acquire sufficient capital buffer. On the downside, this move would reduce the supply of loans.

Further, Schliephake and Kirstein (2013) refer to competition of loan rates among capital-regulated banks as a Cournot Duopoly if recapitalization becomes costly. Banks bound by regulatory capitalization cannot compete using prices as a strategic variable. That is, they cannot exercise absolute market power because they risk attracting unreliable borrowers. A Bertrand equilibrium may rake in substantial profit but not serve as a strategic long-term choice. Banks are not likely to increase capitalization indefinitely. Thus, Schliephake and Kirstein (2013) show that under strict regulations, banks compete via a chosen optimal amount of loans at the first stage of the Cournot Duopoly with the corresponding equilibrium loan rates. Subsequently, the second stage sees them competing by increasing loan rates and incorporating the necessary increase in expected profit. This stage has banks targeting the needed equilibrium amount of loans at the corresponding regulated bank capitalization. Banks would expect an increase in marginal costs with an increased capital buffer.

Admati et al. (2013) refute that bank capital is costly to society. They examine the macroeconomic perspective of capital costs, while Schliephake and Kirsten (2013), from a business economics perspective, assume that capital financing is costlier than deposit funding. From the perspective of a single bank, factors, like tax disadvantages, agency conflicts, and the incentive effects of the banking safety net may debunk the Modigliani–Miller theorem. This means that capital financing is more expensive than debt financing per unit, regardless of the time horizon (Schliephake and Kirsten 2013, p. 684).

Finally, contrary to the argument that regulatory capital requirements reduce profits because they increase the cost of offering loans, Schliephake and Kirstein (2013) demonstrate that regulation can enhance profits. A bank's charter value can be in excess of the increased cost of capital. Their theoretical results help explain the occurrence of substantial profits in Bertrand banking markets. Furthermore, they justify the use of the Cournot model in theoretical banking models of imperfect competition even if banks compete in the area of loan interest rates.

The potential welfare effects remain ambiguous. On one hand, increased profits may stabilize the banking sector by reducing risk-taking incentives due to an elevated charter value. On the other hand, reduced competition diminishes borrower rents and may lead to inefficiencies in the loan market. Assuming that the regulator aims at an optimal tradeoff between incentives to foster the competitiveness of bank services and stability in the sector, one should also take into account the collusive effect in designing prudential regulation, especially when considering an increase in capital requirements (Schliephake and Kirstein 2013, p. 698).

Schliephake (2016) generalizes the Cournot competition into n banking firms competing for risky loans to maximize profits. Her model includes a buffer effect combined with the margin and risk-shifting effects of MMR (2008, 2010) and Martinez-Miera (2009), all within the context of imperfect competition. The result is a net effect of capital regulation on a bank's survival from aggregate failure rate in the loan portfolio. She identifies three sources of bank stability—buffer effect, margin effect, and risk-shifting effect, modeled as follows:

Slope of the probability of a bank's survival from an aggregate failure rate in the loan portfolio

$$\overbrace{\frac{dF(\hat{x},p)}{d\beta}} = \left(\frac{1}{\sqrt{\rho}}\right)\phi'\left(\frac{\phi^{-1}(p)-\sqrt{1-\rho}\cdot\phi^{-1}(\hat{x})}{\sqrt{\rho}}\right)$$
$$\times\left[\underbrace{\left(\frac{\sqrt{1-\rho}}{\phi'(\hat{x})}\right)\frac{r_D}{r(L)}}_{\text{buffer effect (+)}}+\left(\underbrace{\frac{\sqrt{1-\rho}}{\phi'(\hat{x})}\,\frac{(1-\beta)(r_D)}{(r(L))^2}}_{\text{margin effect (+)}}-\underbrace{\left(\frac{1}{\phi'(p)}\right)\cdot p'(r)}_{\text{risk-shifting effect (-)}}\right)\underbrace{\frac{dr}{d\beta}}_{\text{competition}}\right] \tag{3.12}$$

Assuming an imperfect correlation of loan defaults, or that not all loans in a loan portfolio default simultaneously, Schliephake (2016) discusses the factors that would explain a bank's survival despite having a certain share of defaults in its loan portfolio. Said share is higher if the equity invested and the marginal profits from non-defaulting loans in the portfolio are higher. The buffer effect, or capital cushion, happens with increased capitalization. It has a direct impact on the bank's probability of failure: the higher the equity funding, the stronger the threshold for failure (Schliephake 2016, pp. 1795–1796).

The indirect effect of capital requirements starts with higher cost and endogenous exits from the market. With this, fewer loans are supplied but at a higher loan interest rate, which leads to risk shifting. When banks charge higher loan interest rates, borrowers react by investing in riskier loans (Schliephake 2016, p. 1797). Assuming that loans do not default at the same time, some banks can charge higher loan rates, which implies higher margins of non-defaulting loans, or the so-called margin effect (Schliephake 2016, p. 1797).

The model indicates that competition directly affects the profit-margin, risk-shifting, and buffer effects. The latter must be substantial enough to outweigh the other two. Competition will affect the capital cushion only if banks acquire enough retained earnings from loans through higher loan rates, interest earnings from invested, risk-weighted assets, or payments of previously NPL. In this sense, Schliephake's (2016) static model indicates that competition has an indirect impact on the buffer effect. The effect of competition on Schliephake's model may increase the bank's capitalization ratio if capital infusion immediately results from increased profits within the same quarter.

The relative size of each component depends on the correlation of defaults, ρ, leverage or 1 minus the bank capitalization ratio, $(1 - \beta)$, idiosyncratic risk of projects, $\left(\frac{1}{\phi'(p)}\right)$, level of competition, $\frac{dr}{d\beta}$, and risk sensitivity of banks to changes in the loan rate, $\left(\frac{1}{\phi'(\hat{x})}\right)$. Three cases with corresponding levels of buffer, risk-shifting, and margin effects are identified and tested to determine which of the three predominates. The results will be the basis for drawing policy prescriptions.

Case 1: Low Risks and Well-Capitalized Banks. The buffer effect is strong in this case if the correlation of loan defaults is low ($\rho \rightarrow 0$) and if the loss-absorbing capacity is high ($\hat{x} \rightarrow 1$). The loss-absorbing capacity increases in the level of equity funding ($\hat{x} \rightarrow 1$ if $\beta \rightarrow 1$). Therefore, the buffer effect is strong in well-capitalized and well-diversified banks with low systemic risk. Case 1 applies to a well-capitalized banking sector with high market discipline, low cost of capital, and investments in assets with low idiosyncratic and systemic risks (Schliephake 2016, pp. 1798–1799). This study will measure the effect using the regression on bank capitalization or equity-to-assets ratio.

Case 2: Low Risks and Undercapitalized Banks. The margin effect prevails in this case, characterized by low levels of idiosyncratic and systemic risk and low-risk shifting. Moreover, in contrast to the buffer effect, which clearly declines as the leverage increases, the margin effect may increase or decrease leverage. Within reasonable parameters, the margin effect increases with higher leverage (lower β). Case 2 describes an undercapitalized banking sector that invests in assets with low correlations and low probabilities of default that are relatively insensitive to changes in loan interest rates. This study will measure the effect using the regression on the Z-index: Z_{RCAR}, Z_{ROA}, and Z_{ROE}.

Case 3: High Risks and Undercapitalized Banks. If correlation is high, $\rho \rightarrow 1$, the risk-shifting effect most likely outweighs the other two marginal effects. When $\rho = 1$, the margin and the buffer effects disappear. Generally, with imperfect correlation $\rho < 1$, the risk-shifting effect is most likely to prevail if the idiosyncratic risk of the assets (probabilities of default) is high, or $p(0) \rightarrow 1$, and if the risk-shifting p' is high. The level of the risk shifting does not depend on the leverage of the banking sector. However, the buffer effect is weaker among the less capitalized banks. Therefore, the indirect effects become more prominent for highly leveraged banks. Case 3 applies to the undercapitalized banking sectors that invest in highly correlated, risky assets, and with default probability that is sensitive to changes in loan rates. This study will measure this effect using the regression on the NPL ratio.

With the presence of imperfect competition and dominant banks, one expects the risk-shifting effect: with less competition, or more concentrated banks, banks are likely to charge higher loan rates and higher loan defaults, causing banks to be less safe. However, the model of Schliephake (2016) adds that enhanced financial stability would arise from the presence of a binding regulatory framework that allows banks to improve their capitalization until 2019 as well as the presence of cost-efficient (cost-advantaged) dominant banks. Compliance with the regulatory framework by cost-efficient (cost-advantaged) banks, therefore, leads to more stable banks.

Conceptual Framework

This study will refer to the conceptual framework of Schliephake (2016) because it counts among the few extant literature that analyze the capital regulation-bank competition-stability nexus from the angle of market structure, capital regulation, and bank performance via the broad lending channel. The succeeding diagrams show the modifications made to the said framework (see Fig. 3.6a) to better accommodate the objectives of this study (see Fig. 3.6b).

Schliephake's (2016) conceptual framework summarizes the literature on the relationship between competition and stability, roughly divided into two streams. Representatives of the competition instability hypothesis argue that more competition erodes stability because it reduces the charter value of the bank and whets the appetite for risk-taking. This charter value effect is the effect (I) in Fig. 3.6a, which Matutes and Vives (2000), Hellmann et al. (2000), Repullo (2004), and Allen and Gale (2000) discuss. Moreover, Allen and Gale (2004) argue that reduced charter value decreases the incentive to improve monitoring and so increases risk. In general, the models for the stability-enhancing charter value effect of competition focus on a bank's liability and take investment risk as an exogenous given (Schliephake 2016).

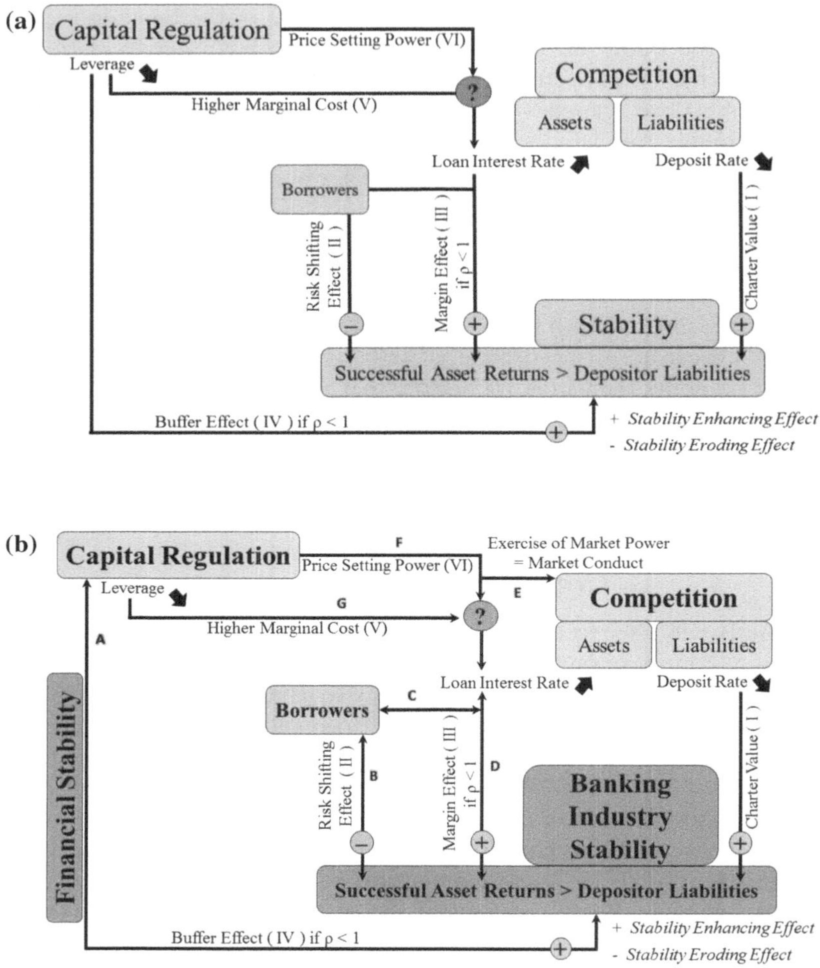

Fig. 3.6 **a** and **b** The effects of capital regulation and competition on stability (*Source* Schliephake 2016, p. 1789 and the author's theoretical framework)

Boyd and De Nicolò (2005) challenged the charter value hypothesis by allowing borrowers, instead of banks, to control the riskiness of loans. They took into account the competition for loan assets and allowed borrowers to react to higher loan interest rates in a Stiglitz and Weiss (1981) environment. Assuming a perfect correlation of loan defaults, they demonstrated how increased competition could reduce the probability of failure, since lower loan rates reduce loan asset risk. This borrower risk-shifting effect is labeled (II) in Fig. 3.6a, b (Schliephake 2016). Martinez-Miera and Repullo (2010) extended the Boyd and De Nicolò (2005) model and allowed for imperfect correlation among the investment projects. As a result, higher loan rates caused an increase in borrower risk shifting and in the bank's margin for non-defaulting loans, labeled (III). If asset default correlation is low, then the higher margins on non-defaulting loans can outweigh borrower risk shifting. Therefore, if not all loans default at the same time, then the impact of competition on banking stability is generally non-monotonous (Schliephake 2016).

The double-edged arrows, labeled **B**, **C**, and **D**, in Fig. 3.6b show what happens in a two-staged Cournot game. From the theoretical model of Schliephake and Kirstein (2013) and extended to *n* players in Schliephake (2016), these arrows denote that banks aim at expected profits at the first stage of the game, where they choose the optimal number of borrowers and loans, given an increase in capitalization. The profit comes in at the second stage of the game. This planning horizon brings about hiked loan rates. Arrows **B** and **C**, both of which originate from borrowers, indicate that borrowers may resort to investing in risky projects for higher profits and so acquiesce to the bank's higher loan rates.

The incorporation of market structure in the analysis of financial stability allows an empirical procedure to verify and compare the buffer, risk shifting, and margin effects for each bank in this study. Thus, the double-edged arrows **B**, **C**, and **D** explain a bank's resilience in the face of distress or insolvency (see Fig. 3.6b). If a bank does not comply with higher capitalization, competition will merely revolve around arrows **B**, **C**, and **D** and likely to increase the risk-shifting effect and end up less stable. The double-edged arrow **A** indicates how bank competition and concentration lead to financial stability. By complying with higher capitalization, the efficient dominant banks may increase loan rates and make decisions that revolve around **A**, **F**, **G**, **D**, and **E**, that is, via a stronger margin effect that enhances stability (see Fig. 3.6b). Overall, the conceptual framework visualizes the possible existence of competition-fragility and competition-stability in the banking sector (Vives 2008, 2016; Berger et al., 2009; Berger et al. 2017, p. 187; Degryse et al. 2019, pp. 797–798). The route covered by arrows **F, G, B, C, D, and A** visualizes competition-fragility, while **F, G, B, C, D, E, and A** indicate competition-stability.

Hakenes et al. (2011) argue that an ambiguous effect on loan rates may arise when banks go for higher capitalization. They assume that the correlation of loan defaults within a bank and among other banks is 1 ($\rho = 1$), which may not assure stability. This can happen when banks invest in high-risk projects and when the depositors differ from the borrowers. This study assumes strict compliance to the BSP's Basel III. Still, Pagaduan and Majuca et al. (2014) aver that UKBs in the Philippines seem under-capitalized and exposed to highly risky projects even as the share of the loans extended to risky ventures amounted to less than 30% of their loan portfolios.

This study uses 48 quarters from the balance sheet data of the Top 20 UKBs in the Philippines, which makes it possible to provide empirical evidence on their market behavior. It likewise altered the conceptual framework (arrow E, Fig. 3.7) of Schliephake (2016) to incorporate the models of Freixas and Rochet (2008) and VanHoose (2022). Freixas and Rochet (2008) and VanHoose (2022) incorporated the behavior of banks exercising market power through a model of imperfect competition with dominant and fringe banks. The exercise of market power, also called market conduct or competitive conduct in the new industrial organization literature, serves as a basis for modelling the competitive behavior of banks. Banks with market power also wield price-setting power. On the other hand, efficient banks can justify higher loan rates because they comply with higher bank capitalization. The effect is an increase in marginal costs (see Fig. 3.7).

Incorporating alterations from the Monti-Klein model of imperfect competition in the market for loans and deposits, Freixas and Rochet (2008) argue that efficient and dominant banks exert market power by charging loan rates higher than the industry standard. While marginal costs may attract and expand loan portfolios, dominant banks still expect higher profits. This result is consistent with VanHoose (2022) who predicts that dominant but efficient banks are more likely to comply with higher capitalization requirements. In the process, investing in better monitoring technology and more skilled loan officers would entail higher loan rates (see arrow F, Fig. 3.7). Nevertheless, an equilibrium level of

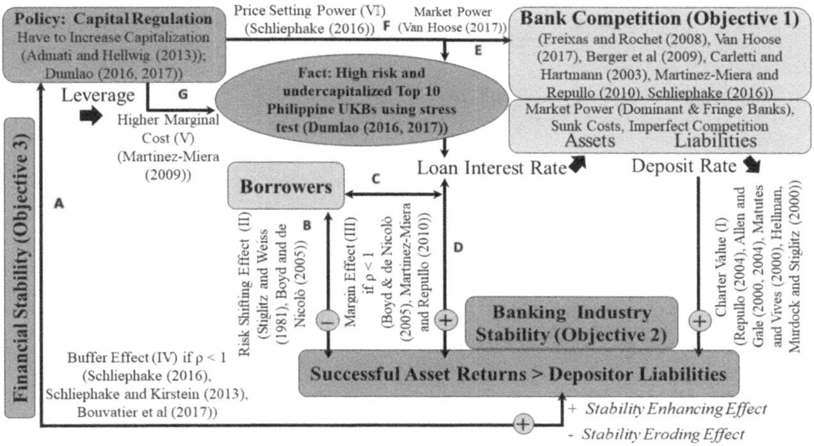

Fig. 3.7 Relevant literature linking capital regulation and competition with market power on stability (*Source* Schliephake 2016, p. 1789 and the author's theoretical framework)

borrowers will eventually pay for an equilibrium level of profit-maximizing loan rates. Efficient fringe banks will follow the level of loan rates charged by dominant banks if they comply with higher capitalization. This means that fringe banks will also invest in better monitoring technology or train and hire skilled credit-investigating loan officers, invest less in risky projects, and hold back on lending to risk-taking entrepreneurs. In the end, the industry benefits from the emergence of efficient players (see Fig. 3.7).

Schliephake (2016) contributed to the literature by describing the competitive banking and economic environments that strictly comply with capital regulation. The strict implementation and incorporation of bank capitalization in a bank's strategic plan (Arrow **A**, Fig. 3.7) likely brings about successful asset returns via the buffer effect. This is why arrow **A** is double-edged. According to Schliephake and Kirstein (2013), banks endogenize the level of bank capitalization that they can absorb through the exercise of market power (arrows **E** and **F**). The strategy eventually results in either a margin or a risk-shifting effect (Arrows **B, C, and D**). The conceptual maps (see Figs. 3.7 and 3.8) integrate literature relevant to the theoretical model and empirical methodology.

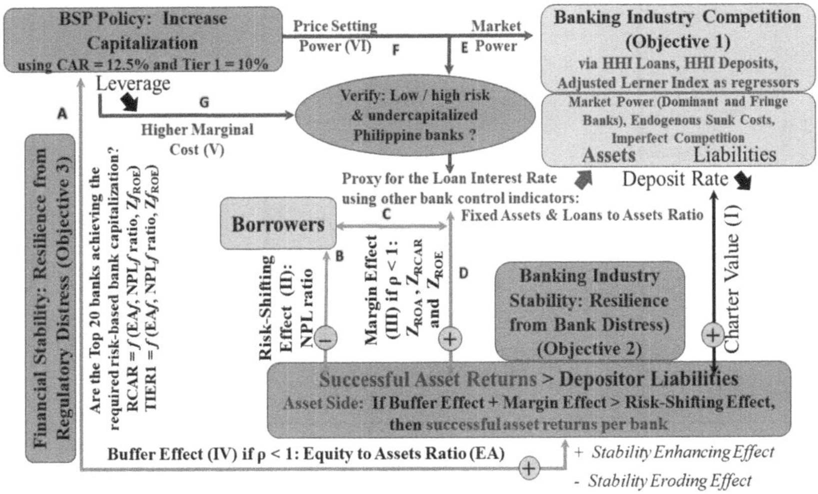

Fig. 3.8 The effect of capital regulation and competition with market power on stability (*Source* Schliephake 2016, p. 1789 and the author's theoretical framework)

Further, she outlined the literature on the net effect of capital regulation on stability, which offered ambiguous results. A higher share of equity funding, *ceteris paribus*, increases the stability of banks because higher equity funding serves as a buffer against losses and reduces the moral hazard of banks similar to the charter value effect of low competition. This is the so-called buffer effect (IV) of equity funding (Arrow **A**, Fig. 3.8). However, changing the refunding structure of banks also changes their investment behavior, given the negative externalities of bank default. If banks were to internalize all costs and benefits of bank equity, then the private optimal capital structure would coincide with the socially optimal capital structure as discussed by Gale (2003). However, banks do not fully internalize the benefits of equity because the banking safety net partly shields them against the risk of their investments. Imposing minimum capital requirements shifts the risks borne by the depositors back to the shareholders and diminishes moral hazard and the incentive for excessive risk-taking, as shown by Hellmann, Murdock, and Stiglitz (2000), Repullo (2004), and Allen, Carletti, and Marquez (2011). Furthermore, Allen and Carletti (2011) note that higher capital requirements minimize the risk of contagion among banks (Schliephake 2016).

For this study, facts that support the assumption of having an imperfect correlation of defaults and possible exercise of market power among high risk and undercapitalized banks in the UKB industry (Dumlao 2015, 2016. See Fig. 3.7) substitute the expected ambiguous effect mentioned by Hakenes et al. (2011).

The requirement to refund investments with more equity increases the bank's marginal cost of financing and reduces perceived profitability, giving rise to higher risk-taking that destabilizes the bank. Higher funding costs decrease the optimal amount of lending, resulting in higher loan interest rates. Higher loan interest rates lead to higher earnings on non-defaulting loans, which can offset losses from defaulting loans (II). On the other hand, higher loan rates reduce the earnings of borrowers, which induce borrower risk shifting (III). The net effect of capital requirement regulation on banking stability depends on which of the described effects prevails. Objective 2 aims to determine this (see Fig. 3.7).

Empirical evidence on the relationship of capital requirements, competition, and financial stability is equally ambiguous. Carletti and Hartmann (2003) provide a good overview of the mixed empirical findings on the relationship between competition and stability (Schliephake 2016). Incorporating market power into the analysis allows one to predict the strategic moves of dominant banks once they comply with the required increase in capitalization. This is why Arrow **A** points at Arrow **F**, which in turn points to market power, signifying banks' reaction to increased loan rates. From the literature (Martinez-Miera and Repullo 2010), more concentrated banking industries tend to resort to risk shifting (Arrow **E**), which Dumlao verifies (2016, 2017).

To verify the overall effect of market power and the strategic decisions of banks to improve expected profits from complying with higher capitalization, the study turns to a financial stability indicator that uses the imposed risk-based capital adequacy ratio and TIER1 ratio. This procedure responds to Objective 3 (see Fig. 3.7).

Only two theoretical papers attempt to analyze the effect of competition and capital regulation on bank stability. Hakenes and Schnabel

(2011) show that the ambiguous effect of competition on banks' risk-taking translates into ambiguous effects of capital requirements on the stability of the banking sector (see Fig. 3.3). Although their model aimed to capture the influence of correlation among loan defaults, this simplified model neglected the buffer and margin effect because all loans default at the same time (Schliephake 2016). Figure 2.4 shows that the study of Dumlao (2016, 2017) specifies the probable high correlation of loan defaults within a bank and among banks, given their exposure to real estate investments. This study would reflect an imperfect correlation of loan defaults in the Philippines.

Schliephake (2016) did not take the competitive environment as a given, but explicitly considered how regulation would change the competitive environment. She also demonstrated that capital regulation affects, not only stability but also the level of competition in the banking sector (Arrow **A** works towards arrows **F** and **E,** Fig. 3.7). A strict imposition of capital requirements to buffer against systemic risks thereby increases a bank's private funding costs and decreases the number of competitors. With higher price-setting power (VI), increased loans, and deposit market penetration, banks tend to avoid risk shifting and endogenize the higher cost of regulation. This is her expected result from a Cournot competition. In the Philippines, banks most likely compete by differentiating their products and services from other banks in their vicinity. Thus, the need to increase their market share for loans and multiply their branches and ATMs to boost deposits. Figure 3.7 reflects this aspect of competition in the Philippines.

Martinez-Miera (2009) analyzed the impact of capital requirement regulation on bank stability under different exogenous market structures when loan defaults are imperfectly correlated. He argued that if the asset risk of a bank's loan portfolio were not perfectly correlated, then the impact of capital requirements on stability and marginal costs (V) would be unclear. He also pointed out the role of competition in determining banking stability (Schliephake 2016). VanHoose (2017) resolved this ambiguity through his model for dominant banks reacting to strictly implemented bank capitalization. Under the condition of dominant but efficient banks, fringe banks tend to mirror the loan rates of dominant banks and aim for efficiency. Assuming the existence of efficient but dominant banks and fringe banks competing in an imperfectly competitive banking industry may nullify the ambiguous results of V and VI.

The model of Monti-Klein, as formulated by Freixas and Rochet (2008), predicts the competitive behavior of dominant banks. These ambiguities signify the need for an empirical model to verify the existence of imperfect competition using a structure, conduct, performance paradigm, and the new industrial economics[1] methodology. As a result, Objective 1 of the study aims to provide empirical proof of existence of imperfect competition in the Philippine U/KB industry.

This research shall refer to the BSP policy to increase the capital-to-equity ratio from 10% to 20%, thereby incorporating bank under-capitalization into the conceptual framework. Due to the ownership and conglomerate structure of the country's biggest UKBs, the exposure of these banks to real estate investment risks signifies that the banking industry has moderate-to-high exposure to credit and default risk. However, banks in the Philippines also have the mandate to develop the financial sector, thus investments in ATMs, electronic banking, and expansion to the provinces probably indicate greater fixed assets. The biggest banks incur endogenous sunk costs because of the need to increase the number of depositors and attract borrowers.

Figure 3.8 summarizes the conceptual framework. The capitalization level that the BSP set shall consider exogenous. The risk and capitalization levels of the Top 10 banks indicate the expected results from Schliephake (2016). From Schliephake's theoretical model (2016), the risk levels of banks are analyzed along with the level of industry competition. This research shall determine whether a competitive or imperfectly competitive banking market structure exists. According to Schliephake (2016), imperfect competition can possibly bring about a higher level of stability in banking industry as banks aim at higher profit margins and shirk engaging in high-risk and high-yield investments.

An environment of imperfect competition is conducive to achieving a strategic combination of a number of loans and borrowers with interest rates set at the profit-maximizing loan rates. The incorporation of endogenous sunk costs may explain the strategy of banks to improve profit margins. This strategy could improve bank charter values in the end. However, this research does not aim to verify the charter value effect but rather the financial stability of UKBs through an increase in asset returns. Successful asset returns refer to the profit margins banks aim for to recover

[1] Industrial organization and industrial economics are used synonymously in this book.

the added financial costs when they increase capitalization. Asset returns are most likely higher than returns on deposit liabilities if the buffer and margin effects are stronger or higher than the risk-shifting effect. This result is likely to achieve bank resilience to insolvency, as verified in Objective 2. Finally, Objective 3 aims to verify whether bank competition and concentration lead to financial stability or resilience to regulatory distress.

Empirical Methodology

This section explains the testing procedure for the above-mentioned relationships. The methodology is broken down into three steps that correspond to the study's objectives.

Empirical Verification of an Imperfectly Competitive Banking Industry

The structure-conduct-performance paradigm and models from the new industrial economics empirical tradition shall be used to verify market power. The empirical test for the first hypothesis verifies the first objective. Monti-Klein's model and Freixas and Rochet (2008, pp. 78–81) will measure imperfect competition among dominant and fringe banks (VanHoose 2022, pp. 43–44) and verify the following:

1. *More market power is observed along with greater market concentration.*

   The following indicate greater market power:
   (a) a positive relationship of market power and market concentration;
   (b) higher markup on loans than deposits; and
   (c) higher profits.
   The following steps will verify this.
   (i) A GMM logarithmic regression of the conventional Lerner Index as a dependent variable will explain the positive relationship of market power and market concentration. The regressor includes the logarithms of HHI Loans, HHI Deposits, and gross national income per capita;
   (ii) Proving the higher markup on loans over deposits:
   (iii) Compare the constants of regressions on loans vis-à-vis the constant regression of deposits for all regressions on the Top 20, Top 10, and Next 10 banks using the regressions from (i);

(iv) From (i), compare the coefficients of HHI Loans with HHI Deposits for the Top 20, Top 10, and Next 10;
(v) Verify if banks have greater market power and profit in an environment of greater market concentration by comparing the regression results of profits (return-on-equity) as the dependent variable, as explained by a market structure indicator and bank controls (Molyneux and Forbes 1995). Greater market concentration happens with greater profits for dominant banks. The period of greater market concentration shall be compared with that of lower market concentration. The results of this comparison shall be the basis for the empirical models or regressions, which will link bank competition, concentration, and financial stability.

In the absence of open access data on loan rates, deposit rates, compensation, and interest earnings per bank, marginal cost (MC) shall then be calculated as the change in total cost per bank per quarter over the change in total output per bank, *i*, per quarter, *t* (Oduor et al. 2017). Total Output would be derived from Total Assets less non-earning assets (fixed assets), and Total Cost (TC) shall be the difference of Total Output (TQ) with Net Income.

Marginal cost is computed as

$$MC_{it} = \frac{\Delta TC_{it}}{\Delta TQ_{it}} \tag{3.13}$$

The adjusted Lerner Index is computed as

$$\text{adjusted Lerner Index } it = \frac{\pi_{it} + tc_{it} - mc_{it} \cdot tq_{it}}{\pi_{it} + tc_{it}} \tag{3.14}$$

where

π_{it} Net Income (ROE multiplied with Stockholders' Equity)
tc_{it} Total Cost (Total Output less Net Income)
mc_{it} Marginal Cost
tq_{it} Total Output (Total Assets less Fixed Assets)

Unlike the standard or conventional Lerner Index, the adjusted Lerner Index ranges from zero to greater than 1, with larger values indicating greater market power. With the use of balance sheet data, the adjusted Lerner Index may exceed 1 because one cannot calculate the cost of inputs, labor, and capital without open access data on loan rates, wages, and interest rates charged per bank.

2. *Dominant firms are expected to achieve a higher profit-maximizing loan rate, that is, the rate at which marginal revenues equal marginal cost.*
   The adjusted Lerner Index shall be a dependent variable and the HHI Loans and HHI Deposits, regressors for the Top 20 banks. The same dependent variable and regressors shall be used for the regression of the Top 10 and Next 10 banks. The coefficient of HHI Loans and HHI Deposits for the Top 10 banks may be significantly higher than the coefficient for the Top 20 and Next 10 banks. This implies that the Top 10 banks have significantly higher markups.
3. *Dominant firms are expected to earn positive profit due to their cost advantage.*
   This procedure shall use the profit elasticity model or the Boone indicator. The logarithm of net income shall be regressed with the logarithm of marginal cost (with the option of adjusted Lerner Index as proxy) for the Top 20, Top 10, and Next 10 banks. The coefficient of the logarithm of marginal cost is the Boone Indicator or the profit elasticity indicator. Greater efficiency would indicate a smaller Boone indicator because net income should not vary much for every increase in marginal cost. The coefficient of the adjusted Lerner Index for the regression on the Top 10 banks is expected to be significantly smaller than that of the adjusted Lerner Index for the regression on the Top 20 and Next 10 banks.

$$\pi_i = \alpha + \beta_i \ln \ln mc_i \tag{3.15}$$

where

Ln π_i	Natural logarithm of Net Income
Ln mc_i	Natural Logarithm of Marginal Cost
β_i	Profit Elasticity

The expected results of these regression procedures would verify the imperfectly competitive market structure and presence of dominant and fringe banks in the Philippine banking industry. Dominant banks can vary their loan rates depending on the specific needs of their borrowers and dictate higher profit-maximizing loan and deposit rates because they can charge higher markups or operate with a cost advantage.

Results from the structure-conduct-performance using traditional and non-traditional indicators of market power will most likely point to an imperfectly competitive industry competing in a concentrated market. This is the aim of Objective 1. Results will be verified after testing Hypothesis 1. Risk-shifting effect and loan default are most likely to occur, since dominant banks will tend to charge higher loan and deposit rates. Profit maximizing, or the buffer and the margin effects, will also likely appear among the dominant banks with efficient operations because they can very well put a cap on loan defaults. In other words, the more efficient banks will more likely experience greater buffer and margin instead of risk shifting. The following section will verify this.

Competition, Concentration, and Banking Industry Stability

Relating bank competition with bank stability will provide empirical proof for Hypothesis 2. The following dependent variables will be used to indicate financial stability: (a) Z-index: Z_{ROA}, Z_{ROE} (indicator for bank distress, in terms of insolvency); (b) NPL to total loans ratio (indicator for loan portfolio risk); and (c) equity to total assets ratio (bank capitalization). These indicators shall be regressed using bank-specific competitiveness characteristics obtained from balance sheet data and appropriate macroeconomic indicators. Another Z-index shall be computed using return-to-equity (ROE) due to the sensitivity of return-on-assets to the bank's income-smoothing performance (Bouvatier et al. 2017).

In addition, the indicator for regulatory distress (Z_{RCAR}) will serve as a dependent variable, regressed over the explanatory variables used in Objective 1. The conceptual framework shown in Fig. 3.9 incorporates these two objectives. As mentioned earlier, the double-ended arrows indicate the decision-making process of banks who base their strategies on the number of loans and loan and deposit rates. The two-stage decision-making process signifies that banks set their intended asset returns and bank default probabilities before deciding on the number of borrowers and loans that they can effectively monitor. This, given their current monitoring technology and loan rates would help them achieve their expected profit.

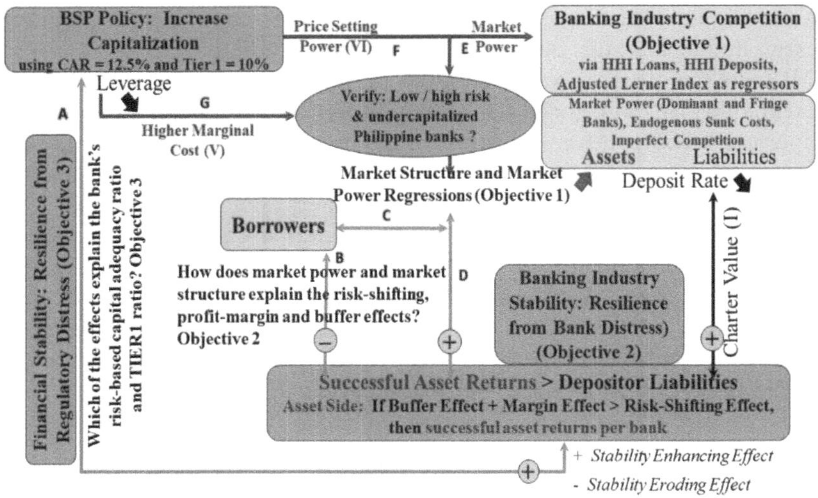

Fig. 3.9 Objectives of the study in the context of capitalization, bank competition and concentration, and bank stability nexus (*Source* Schliephake 2016, p. 1789 and the author's theoretical framework)

Regressing the new industrial economic indicators of market power and stability will verify the relationship between market concentration, financial stability, and fragility. The Z-indexes serve as the dependent variables to indicate financial stability, regressed with the traditional or SCP indicator of market power, HHI, and the adjusted Lerner Index, which is the non-traditional indicator of market power.

Objective 2 aims to determine the relationship between bank competition and financial stability through the bank's exposure to risk (Berger et al. 2009), which is why this section attempts to establish the links of market competition and concentration with stability and fragility.

In Fig. 3.9, red arrows—**E, F, and G**—refer to the variables that will verify market structure, the results of which correspond to Objective 1, while the results from bank competition, concentration, and bank stability nexus intend to satisfy Objective 2. These results shall be verified using the regressions for the NPL ratio, equity-to-assets ratio, Z_{ROA}, Z_{ROE}, and Z_{RCAR}, with market power and bank control indicators as regressors.

Note the multi-faceted nature of financial stability indicators as seen in the number of arrows directed towards it.

Statistically, this signifies that the dependent variables are multivariate and random. In this context, GMM would be appropriate for the regression. Regressing the forecasted value of Z_{RCAR} with the NPL ratio, Z_{ROE}, and equity-to-assets ratio will establish the nexus of bank competition, concentration, and financial stability, as well as the expected results for Objective 3. These results will show if the banking industry is achieving the required capitalization needed for resiliency to regulatory distress.

The implication of market structure on the risk potential of banks using firm-level data will also be tested. The empirical model allows for a non-linear relationship between financial stability and market structure in banking, following MMR (2008 and 2010). The basic GMM regression model is based on a cross-section of banks and has the following general form (Molyneux 1995; Berger et al. 2009):

$$\text{Financial Stability}_i = f\left(a_i, a_i^2, b_i, c_i\right) \tag{3.16}$$

where:

a market structure
b bank controls
c business environment

This functional form shows the occurrence of competition-fragility and competition-stability in the banking industry. Banks can be both fragile and stable. The two concepts do not contradict each other because of the asymmetric information from investment, lending, and borrowing operations. Table 3.2 shows the variables and definitions of the dependent, explanatory, and instrumental variables. The subscript i refers to a bank. Different risk exposure indicators serve as dependent variables to proxy financial stability: the volume of non-performing loans to total loans (*NPLs*) to account for loan portfolio risk, the *Z*-index as an inverse measure of overall bank risk, and equity to total assets (*E/TA*) for the bank's capitalization level. Both *NPLs* and *E/TA* are averaged for each bank over the period under study. To measure industry competition and the percent share of government-owned and foreign-owned banks, the regressions per dependent variable include the adjusted Lerner Index, HHI Deposits, or HHI Loans.

Table 3.2 Variable definition

Variable	*Definition*	*Data source*
Dependent variables		BSP Quarterly data from 2005 to 2019)
NPLs	Bank-level ratio of NPLs to total loans; a higher value indicates a riskier loan portfolio	
Z-Index	Bank-level financial stability indicator A larger value indicates greater stability and less overall risk. Using return-to-assets (Z_{ROA}) and return-to-equity (Z_{ROE}), the difference between the risk-based capital adequacy ratio and the TIER1 ratio from their regulatory levels proposed by the BSP ($Z_{\text{RCAR-12.5}}$ and $Z_{\text{TIER1-10}}$)	
E/TA	The bank-level capitalization ratio, which proxies the leverage ratio is the ratio of equity to total assets; a higher ratio indicates lower bank risk	
Explanatory variables		
Adjusted Lerner Index	A bank-level indicator of market power, calculated as the average bank-level measure of the markup of price over marginal costs with higher values indicating less competition in the banking sector	
HHI Deposits	An annual-level indicator of market power, measured by the Herfindahl–Hirschman Deposits Index with higher values indicating greater market concentration HHI < 1000 unconcentrated, HHI > 1800 highly concentrated (Salop 1987)	
HHI Loans	An annual indicator of market power measured by the HHI Loans Index with higher values indicating greater market concentration HHI < 1000 unconcentrated, HHI > 1800 highly concentrated (Salop 1987)	
Asset Composition	Loans-to-assets and fixed assets to total assets ratios are used as bank controls	
Bank Size	The log value of Total Assets	
Ownership	A dummy variable is set to 1 when total foreign shareholding or government ownership exceeds 50% of total bank ownership	
Ln(GNIPC)	The log value of GNI per capita (nominal)	PSA 2019

Source Molyneux (1995), Berger et al. (2009), Clerides et al. (2015)

In all cases, higher values of the adjusted Lerner Index, HHI Deposits, and HHI Loans imply higher degrees of market power, hence a less competitive environment. Bank size, asset composition, foreign bank ownership, and the log value of GNI per capita are included in all regressions to control variations in the business environment and economic development.

To study the impact of market structure on financial stability, a quadratic term in the estimated equations allows for a non-linear relationship between measures of bank risk/loan risk (i.e., *Z*-index and *NPLR*) and market structure. *Thus, determining whether market concentration and imperfect competition make banks profitable while exposing them to greater risks (Hypothesis 2) calls for regressions on the Z-indexes, bank capitalization, and NPL ratio.* Estimates on the dependent variable for this procedure shall obtain the forecasted value of the *Z*-index using the capital adequacy ratio (Eq. 3.3).

In line with the competition-stability view of Boyd and De Nicolò (2005), the expected findings would show that more market power is associated with riskier loan portfolios. However, even if market power results in riskier loan portfolios, the overall risk need not increase. One must also examine the impact of the degree of competitiveness on the overall bank risk using the *Z*-index (ROA and ROE) as an inverse proxy for overall risk. A higher value for the *Z*-indexes may come from higher earnings or more capital, indicating greater financial stability, while greater variability in earnings reduces the *Z*-indexes and increases the bank's overall risk. "Competition-fragility" or the perspective that greater market power leads to greater exposure to portfolio risk, will be verified by regressing the NPL to total loans (indicator for portfolio risk) as the dependent variable. The market power indicators consist of the adjusted Lerner Index, the HHI Deposits, and HHI Loans. The three market structure indicators along with the U-shaped relationship between market structure and portfolio risk are expected to be positive. The same result is expected with the use of equity to total assets or the indicator for bank capitalization.

Using the *Z*-indexes as the dependent variable to indicate bank insolvency and distress will verify the competition-stability view. Each of the three market structure indicators and loans-to-assets is expected to be positive, but negative for the quadratic form of the market structure indicators and loans-to-assets. This would signify an inverted U-shaped relationship between market structure and overall risk. Tables 2.2 to 2.5 show the various regression estimation procedures on the Top 20, Top 10, and Next 10 sample UKBs.

GMM as the regression method for this study has the following advantages:

1. it corrects endogeneity in the data, does not assume any probability distribution function, and assumes non-normality of data;
2. compared to other estimation procedures, such as ordinary least squares regression and two-staged least squares with instrumental variable technique, it better handles higher moments, such as skewness and kurtosis; and
3. it can calculate robust estimators in an iterative process via a weighting procedure of regressors and an estimation of the covariance matrix that allows the correction of cross-section dependence.

This study will use a White cross-section weighting procedure and a covariance matrix that allows panel-corrected standard errors. The mean of residuals should at least be asymptotically normal. Simulations using GMM techniques can model investment data and Tobin's *q*, which are usually skewed and leptokurtic. The data used in the study have log-normal or log-logistic probability distributions, which usually have skewed fat and longer tails and do not converge to zero. "One particular advantage of this technique is its potential usefulness. The GMM test of the model's over-identifying restrictions can reasonably detect many types of misspecifications, such as heteroskedasticity and nonlinearity" (Roberts and Whited 2013, p. 563). Thus, each variable will undergo unit root tests and variance-ratio tests prior to the actual regression. Diagnostic tests for the relevance (First-Stage *F*-test) and validity of the instruments, endogeneity (using the Sargan statistic or *J* test), and serial correlation (using the Arellano-Bond test) were performed. The presence of heteroscedasticity in the data is expected, hence the use of the GMM estimator, which allows the use of weighting matrices, and a covariance method, which will allow a panel correction of the standard errors. This procedure can yield a robust set of estimators by integrating the GMM weighting matrices (White cross-section) and a covariance matrix method (Cross-section weights of standard errors and covariances that use panel correction of standard errors). This assures the relevance and validity of the instruments of analysis (coefficients of the regression and variables). All the regression diagnostic tests used the E-Views 13 academic/

university version of the software.[2] The scatterplots with a local regression fit and various statistical tests used Minitab 21.4.0.0.[3]

Random effects, usually a time-variant effect of each of the cross-sections that alter the significance of the relevant variables, were tested to establish endogeneity. The significant random effects will be incorporated into the model. Berger et al. (2009) used a fixed effects model because they expected a time-invariant variable, the effect of endogenous sunk costs, across each of the cross-sections. With the inclusion of fixed assets over total assets, the only variable that was not modeled for the control variables on bank operations were the endogenous sunk costs, which were not observable in the balance sheet data.

Competition, Concentration, Financial Stability, and Bank Capitalization

The regression in this section aims to respond to Objective 3 and to test Hypothesis 3, which states that market concentration and imperfect competition in the banking industry enable banks to increase capitalization, making them more stable. This regression will verify if more stable banks have a risk-based capital adequacy ratio (RCAR) not lower than the regulated common equity TIER1 level (TR). In other words, the higher the Z-index for RCAR (Z_{RCAR}), the more stable the bank and the less likely to experience regulatory distress.

Regressions for the Top 20, Top 10, and Next 10 banks shown in Tables 3.3 to 3.4 will obtain inflection points where the estimated inverted U-shaped relationship between competition and stability is increasing, constant, and decreasing. These inflection points shall correspond to a Z-index ROA (Z_{ROA}) level, an equity-to-assets level, and an NPL ratio level. The sets of points shall be the standard for the range of competition and stability measures that will indicate the level of stability or fragility of each of the 20 banks in the sample. The score for each bank represents performance from the first quarter of 2005 to the fourth

[2] EViews 13, Enterprise Edition—June 14, 2023, build; Serial number: 13A00563; Registered to: Jovi C. Dacanay, Ph.D. (for single user, perpetual license).

[3] Minitab 21.4.0.0 (single user, one-year license) Academic Version, Order Number 100738389536, Date Purchased: April 16, 2023; Minitab 16 Windows (Perpetual License) Academic Version, Order Number 100011984794; Date Purchased: March 7, 2011.

quarter of 2019. Specifically, the range of values drawn from the inflection points focuses on the indicators for stability, which will allow banks to reach the targeted bank capitalization ratio of 20% by 2019.

To determine the effect of market power and bank stability on financial stability, the researchers make use of the estimated variables on bank capitalization (buffer effect indicator), NPL ratio (risk-shifting effect indicator), and Z_{ROE} (profit-margin effect indicator) as regressors for the risk-based capital adequacy ratio (RCAR) and the TIER1 ratio. The three regressors, which correspond to Schliephake's three effects (2016) and their corresponding signs, are expected to be significant to the regression of the sample banks. Following are the formulae for comparing the Top 10 and Next 10.

$$\mathrm{RCAR} = f(\underset{(+)}{\mathrm{EA}f}, \underset{(-)}{\mathrm{NPL}f\ \mathrm{ratio}}, \underset{(+)}{\mathrm{Z}f_{\mathrm{ROE}}}) \tag{3.17}$$

$$\mathrm{TIER1} = f(\underset{(+)}{\mathrm{EA}f}, \underset{(-)}{\mathrm{NPL}f\ \mathrm{ratio}}, \underset{(+)}{\mathrm{Z}f_{\mathrm{ROE}}}) \tag{3.18}$$

The regression results from Eqs. 3.17 and 3.18 shall provide empirical evidence on the effects that strongly drive an increase in the risk-based

Table 3.3 Effect of market power on various dependent variables i

Dependent variable: NPL (Indicator for Liquidity Risk) and Expected Signs	*Market power indicator*		
	Model 1 Adjusted lerner index	*Model 2 HHI deposits*	*Model 3 HHI loans*
Degree of Market Power (+)	β_1	γ_1	δ_1
Degree of Market Power Squared (−)	β_2	γ_2	δ_2
Loans-to-assets (+)	β_3	γ_3	δ_3
Loans-to-assets Squared (−)	β_4	γ_4	δ_4
Fixed Assets to Total Assets (+)	β_5	γ_5	δ_5
Bank Size (Ln Total Assets) (−)	β_6	γ_6	δ_6
Foreign Ownership (±)	β_7	γ_7	δ_7
Ln (GNIpc) (+)	β_8	γ_8	δ_8
Constant (±)	β_0	γ_0	δ_0

Source Berger et al. (2009)

Note The dependent variable i refers to (1) NPL (competition-fragility indicator); (2) Z-index: Z_{ROA}, Z_{ROE} (Indicators for Bank Distress or Insolvency, competition-stability indicators); (3) bank capitalization-equity-to-assets ratio (competition-fragility nexus)

Table 3.4 Effect of market power on bank capitalization in compliance with Basel III (Competition-Fragility Nexus)

Dependent variable: Z_{RCAR} & Z_{TIER1} (Regulatory Distress Indicator: RCAR–12.5% & TIER1–10%) & Expected Signs	*Market power measure*		
	Model 1 Adjusted Lerner Index	*Model 2 HHI Deposits*	*Model 3 HHI Loans*
Degree of Market Power (+)	β_1	γ_1	δ_1
Degree of Market Power Squared (−)	β_2	γ_2	δ_2
Loans-to-assets (+)	β_3	γ_3	δ_3
Loans-to-assets Squared (−)	β_4	γ_4	δ_4
Fixed Assets to Total Assets (−)	β_5	γ_5	δ_5
Bank Size (Ln Total Assets) (±)	β_6	γ_6	δ_6
Foreign Ownership (±)	β_7	γ_7	δ_7
Ln(GNIpc) (+)	β_8	γ_8	δ_8
Constant (−)	β_0	γ_0	δ_0

Source Berger et al. (2009) and the author's framework

capital adequacy ratio and TIER1 ratio and support the stability criteria obtained from the inflection points.

To determine whether bank competition and concentration lead to financial stability, this study shall test whether the exercise of market power of the Top 20 UKBs in the Philippines fosters resilience to bank distress or exposes them to default risks. Against the backdrop of the Basel III imposition of a 20% bank capitalization ratio for the next two years and the BSP's proposed TIER1 ratio of 10.5% and risk-based capital adequacy ratio of 12.5%, this study will verify if the operation of the Top 20 UKBs in the current competitive environment drives resilience. In this regard, one may draw policy prescriptions based on Schliephake (2016).

The regressions to be performed all lead to answering the study's three main questions (see Fig. 3.10):

1. Is there imperfect competition present in the Philippine UKB industry?
2. How do market power and market structure explain the risk-shifting, profit-margin, and buffer effects of bank operations?
3. Which of the effects within a bank's operation lead to increased capitalization?

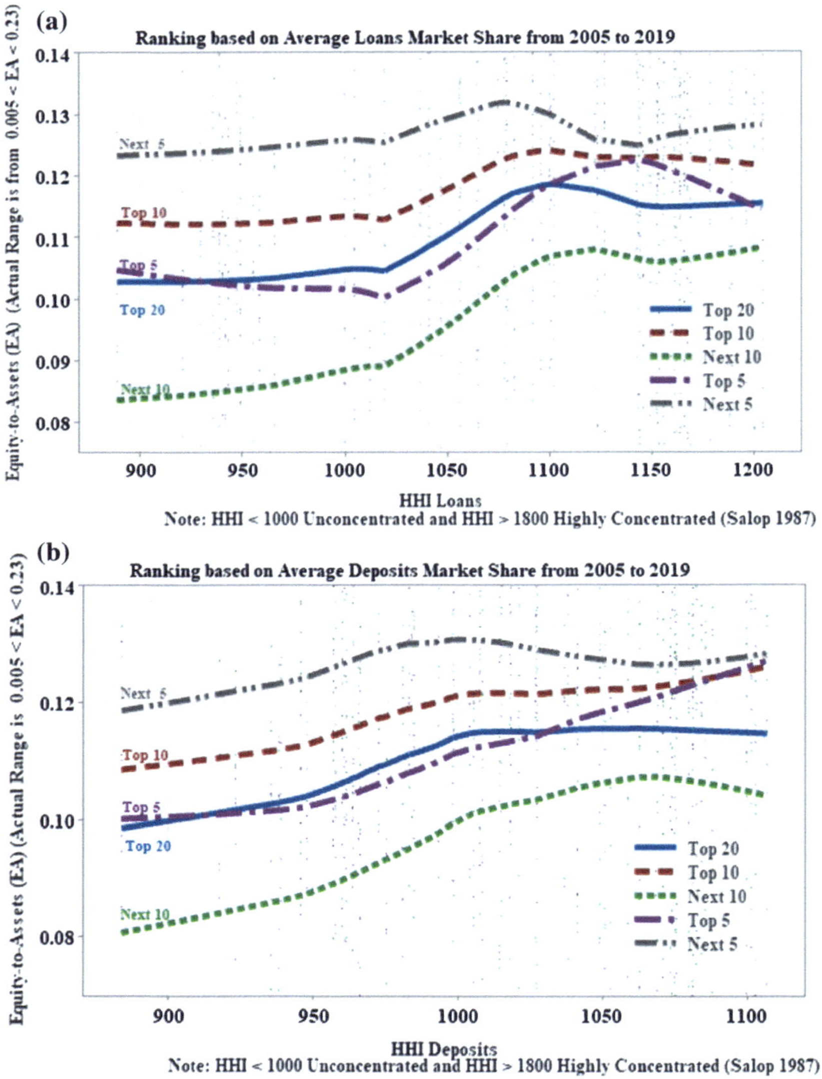

Fig. 3.10 Return-on-Equity and market concentration (*Source* BSP for basic data and the author's regression results)

This procedure uses the risk-based capital adequacy ratio and the TIER1 leverage ratio as indicators of a bank's move to achieve regulatory resilience. Data for the study come from the BSP (https://www.bsp.gov.ph/SitePages/Statistics/BSFinancialStatements.aspx?TabId=1) and the Philippine Statistics Authority (PSA).

Results

Banks are financially stable if the buffer and profit-margin effects outweigh the risk-shifting effect. They would become financially fragile if the profit-margin and risk-shifting effects outweighed the buffer effect. Results seem to point out that in an environment of imperfect competition, dominant banks tend to raise profit margins through higher markups and reduced NPL. These combined occurrences make insolvency less probable and contribute to the stability of the largest banks even if they risk exposure to financial or economic shocks that lead to greater volatility of equity returns. The empirical results verify that the profit-margin and risk-shifting effects among the Top 10 banks outweigh the buffer effect. On the other hand, the Next 10 banks achieved higher profit margins, which they channeled into greater capitalization ratios. With sustained market concentration, the dominant banks are expected to pursue higher capital ratios that promote a market environment and stabilize the UKB industry.

Empirical tests for this study will follow these steps:

1. verify the market structure, concentration, and market power of the banking industry as represented by the Top 20 UKBs and determine their market conduct in terms of higher loan rates and higher profits;
2. determine whether greater market concentration leads to financial stability, or resilience to bank distress and insolvency;
3. find out if operations that are more efficient reduce the ratio of NPL to total assets and increase capitalization.

The Basel III and BSP risk-based capital adequacy ratio and TIER1 ratio render banks less prone to regulatory distress and resilient in the face of systemic risk. The discussion of results shall be based on the proposed objective. Table 3.5 outlines the empirical tests to be performed.

Table 3.5 Competition, market concentration, and stability empirical tests: which factors make banks less fragile?

Assumption: Presence of a competitive banking industry, i.e., HHI < 1000						
Competition-Stability Nexus	**Effects**	**What occurs**	**Competition-Fragility Nexus**	**Effects**	**What should occur**	**Interpretation of Inflection Points**
	Risk Effect (Are NPL and equity-to-assets ratio within range?)	More competition leads to lower loan and deposit rates, less probability of default on borrowers, and more stable banks		Buffer Effect (Z_{RCAR} within the range?)	Maintain a high equity-to-assets ratio, that is, > 11.0%, and a low NPL ratio, i.e., < 5%	Do each of the Top 10 and Next 10 banks have Z_{ROA}, Z_{ROE}, Z_{RCAR}, Equity-to-Assets and NPL ratios that fall within the range of stability? If not, what prevails?

	Margin Effect (Are Z_{ROA} and Z_{ROE} within the range?)	More competition leads to lower loan and deposit rates, less interest earnings on loans, less profits, and more fragile banks		Maintain a risk-based capital adequacy ratio that is $\geq$ 12.5%, TIER1 ratio $\geq$ 10.5%

(continued)

Table 3.5 (continued)

Assumption: Presence of a less competitive banking industry, i.e., more market concentration and 1000 < HHI < 1800						
Competition-Stability Nexus	**Effects**	**What occurs**	**Competition-Fragility Nexus**	**Effects**	**What should occur**	**Interpretation of Inflection Points**
	Risk Effect (NPL and equity-to-assets ratio within the range?)	Less competition leads to higher loan and deposit rates, borrowers taking risks, more probability of default, and more fragile banks		Buffer Effect (Z_{RCAR} within the range?)	Maintain a high equity-to-assets ratio, that is, > 11.0%, and a low NPL ratio, i.e., < 5%	Do each of the Top 10 and Next 10 banks have Z_{ROA}, Z_{ROE}, Z_{RCAR}, Equity-to-Assets and NPL ratios that fall within the range denoting stability? If not, which prevails?

	Margin Effect (Are Z_{ROA} and Z_{ROE} within the range?)	Less competition leads to higher loan and deposit rates, more interest earnings on loans, more profits and more stable banks		Maintain a risk-based capital adequacy ratio that is ≥ 12.5%, TIER1 ratio ≥ 10.5%

Source Berger et al. (2009) and the author's framework

Market Structure and Market Power in the UKB Industry of the Philippines

This section aims to validate Hypothesis 1 by verifying three conjectures from the Monti-Klein model for dominant bank behavior (Freixas and Rochet 2008, pp. 78–81; VanHoose 2022, pp. 43–44):

More Market Power, Greater Market Concentration
The presence of greater market concentration in the UKB industry has dominant banks exercising market power by charging higher markups in the deposits and loans market and varying loan rates to borrowers, vis-à-vis depositors. It can be observed that the profitability of the Top 20, Top 10, Top 5, and Next 10 UKBs increased on the year the HHI Loans reached 1000 (see Fig. 3.10a, b for the scatterplot of return-on-equity (ROE) with HHI Loans and HHI Deposits, respectively).

Berger (2009) indicates that as bigger banks move towards greater concentration, they charge loan rates higher than the smaller banks. Thus, while the Top 10 banks aim to boost their market share for loans, they seem to monitor their creditors better because more market power translates to enhanced profitability, as seen in the less downward-sloping curve for the Top 10 vis-à-vis Next 10 banks. The bigger difference between the ROE of the Top 10 and Next 10 banks as market concentration for loans and deposits increases may be due to the Top 10 banks' charging higher loan rates, operating at lower costs, or enhanced monitoring procedures.

The concurrence of higher market concentration with higher profits can be empirically verified with regression of ROE with market concentration (HHI Loan and HHI Deposits), markup indicator (adjusted Lerner Index), and bank control variables from the first quarter of 2005 to the fourth quarter of 2008 and from the fourth quarter of 2008 to the fourth quarter of 2019. One can observe from the scatterplot in Fig. 3.11 that the ROE of the Top 20 banks started to increase on the year HHI Loans reached 833.

Tables 3.27 and 3.28 present the overall regression for the Top 20 banks. Results show that ROE is significantly higher from the fourth quarter of 2008 to the fourth quarter of 2019. The intercept of the regression loans and deposits in the said period is significantly higher than the ROE regression from the first quarter of 2005 to the fourth quarter of 2008. In that same period, the coefficient during the fourth quarter of 2008 to the fourth quarter of 2019 was higher. In addition, the bank

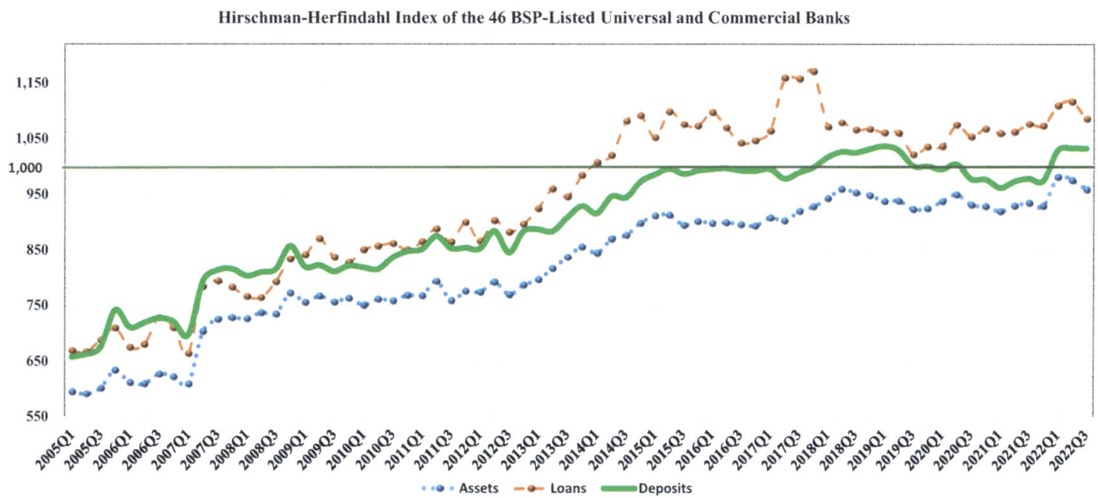

Fig. 3.11 Herfindahl–Hirschman Index of the 46 BSP-Listed UKBs (*Source* BSP https://www.bsp.gov.ph/SitePages/Statistics/BSFinancialStatements.aspx?TabId=1)

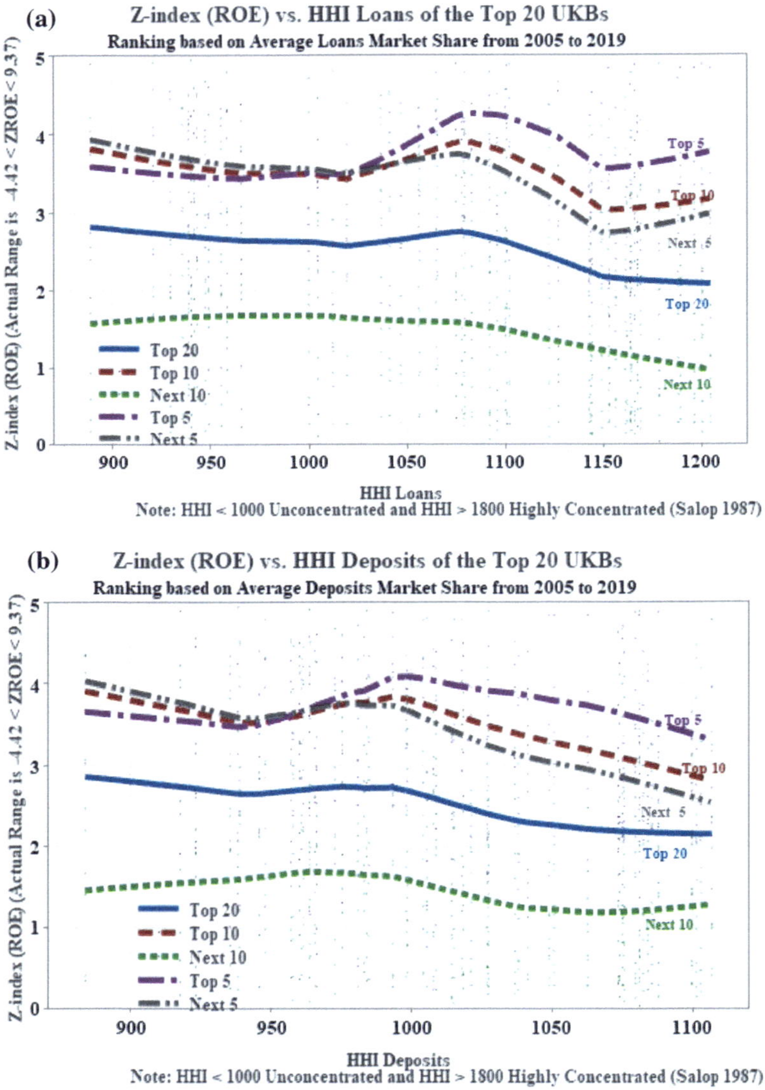

Fig. 3.12 Financial Stability and Market Structure using the HHI for Loans and Deposits (*Source* BSP https://www.bsp.gov.ph/SitePages/Statistics/BSFinancialStatements.aspx?TabId=1 for basic data and Author's Regression Results. *Note* HHI < 1000 Unconcentrated and HHI > 1800 Highly Concentrated [Salop 1987])

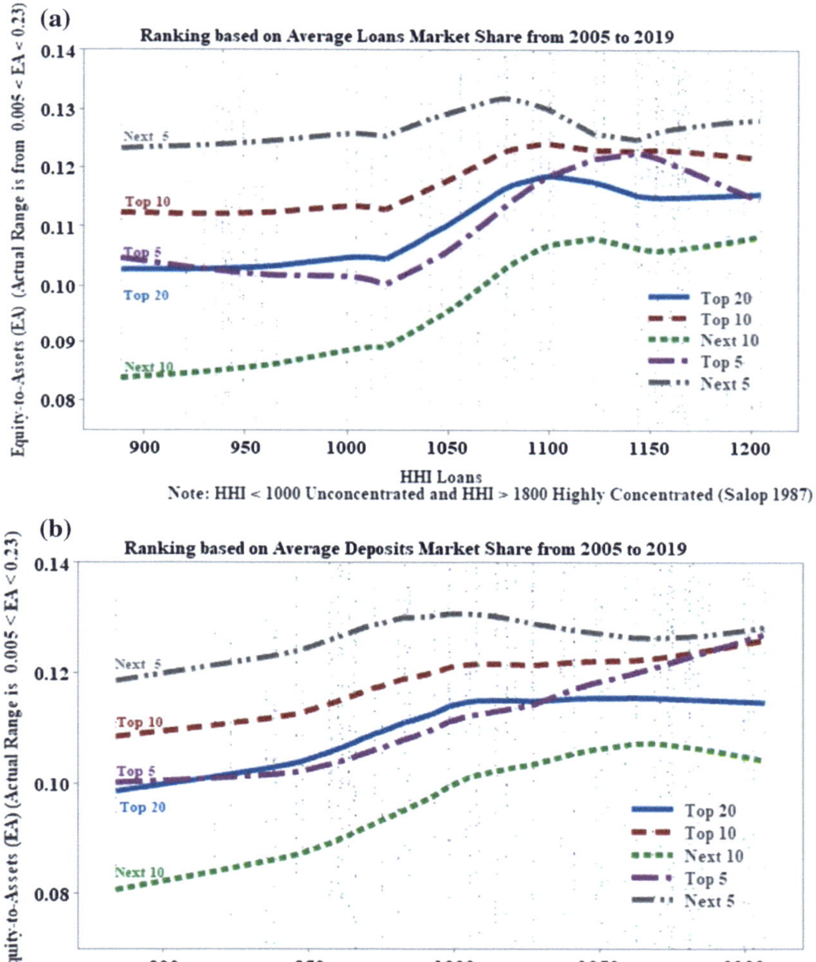

Fig. 3.13 Bank Capitalization and Market Structure using the HHI for Loans and Deposits (*Source* BSP for basic data)

control variables of loans-to-assets and bank size were significant during that said period. All these imply that the Top 20 banks expanded their market share, charged a higher markup and improved profits. However, loans-to-assets of the Top 20 banks moved differently from the first quarter of 2005 to the fourth quarter of 2008. As banks were aiming to increase market size, some banks merged or left the industry, causing a drop in loan supply. This trend changed from the fourth quarter of 2008 to the fourth quarter of 2019, as the remaining banks improved their profit performance and, therefore, their financial stability.

The regression results for ROE verify that market concentration marked the Philippine UKB industry during the said period. The Top 10 banks were able to charge higher markups, as seen in a significantly higher coefficient for the adjusted Lerner Index squared. In addition, the coefficient for HHI Loans and HHI Deposits and the mean ROE of the Top 10 turned out significantly higher than the Next 10 banks (see Table 3.6).

Results in Table 3.7 show that the market power indicators of the Top 10 banks—adjusted Lerner Index and HHI Loans—significantly explain their profit margins. Mergers among the Top 10 banks took place from the fourth quarter of 2008 to the fourth quarter of 2019 (see Table 3.8), raising levels of market power, as presented in the adjusted Lerner Index, and resulting in enhanced profits. In fact, the regression constant for the Top 10 with the adjusted Lerner Index as the market power indicator, had the highest level compared to those of the Next 10. Greater market concentration for loans during this period also contributed to higher ROE for both the Top 10 and the Next 10 banks. Note, however, that as the Top 10 banks increased market share for loans, their loans-to-assets ratio decreased. During this period, their loans-to-assets ratio stayed within 47–50%. While the Next 10 improved their lending capacity and maintained their loans-to-assets ratio within 46–49% in their efforts to boost market share. The next section will explain this result (Table 3.9).

The results in Tables 3.10, 3.11, 3.12, 3.13 show that as the banking industry moves towards greater market concentration, the Top 10 UKBs charge significantly higher loan rates than the other banks. Since banks primarily earn through lending, the results in Table 3.11 show that the Top 20 banks set varying loan rates for borrowers since the markup elasticity for total loans is significantly higher than the markup elasticity for deposits. Thus, the Top 20 banks are able to set loan rates based on the needs and paying capacity of their borrowers.

Table 3.6 Market power behavior of the Top 20 Top 20 UKBs (2005Q1 to 2019Q4)

Method: Panel GMM EGLS (Cross-section random effects) Sample: 2005Q1 2019Q4; Periods Included: 60; white cross-section (cross-section correlation) instrument weighting matrix; Swamy and Arora estimator of component variances; Cross-section weights using panel corrected standard errors (PCSE) & covariance (d.f. corrected) Dependent Variable: Return-on-Equity (ROE) (Bank Level Indicator of Profitability as a Measure of Performance)				
Regressors [(a)]	Expected Sign	Top 20[(a,b)]		
		Adjusted Lerner Index	HHI Deposits	HHI Loans
C	-/+	334.62 ***	367.04 **	168.48 **
		(40.80)	(172.27)	(67.90)
Degree of Market Power	positive	0.52 n.s.	-0.20 n.s.	-0.02 n.s.
		(1.43)	(0.24)	(0.09)
Degree of Market Power^2	negative	0.49 **	8.69E-05 n.s.	-9.06E-06 n.s.
		(0.22)	(0.0001)	(0.00004)
Fixed Assets to Total Assets	negative	-319.11 ***	-321.74 **	-336.42 ***
		(37.07)	(135.06)	(37.57)
Loans to Assets	positive	68.26 ***	72.63 **	71.42 ***
		(20.82)	(33.48)	(20.44)
Loans to Assets^2	negative	-68.88 ***	-73.12 **	-74.97 ***
		(19.91)	(33.35)	(19.54)
Bank Size (Ln Total Assets)	positive	0.73 n.s.	0.85 n.s.	1.35 **
		(0.62)	(1.14)	(0.59)
Ln(GDP per capita)	-/+	-145.78 ***	-110.87 **	-63.47 **
		(18.50)	(45.77)	(24.30)
Government/Foreign Ownership (%)	-/+	-0.06 ***	-0.06 *	-0.06 ***
		(0.02)	(0.04)	(0.02)
No. of Cross-Sections / Observations		20/1200	20/1200	20/1200
AR(1)	negative	-5.41 ***	-5.36 ***	-5.39 ***
AR(2)	negative	-2.14 **	-2.18 **	-2.27 **
Hansen's J-Stat	positive	8.14375E-18 n.s.	4.14E-14 n.s.	2.77E-15 n.s.

Source BSP https://www.bsp.gov.ph/SitePages/Statistics/BSFinancialStatements.aspx?TabId=1 for basic data and Author's Regression Results

[a]Highlighted cells refer to coefficients with signs different from expected and have a significant p-value; Hansen's J-Stat < 1.0 has p-value > 0.50

[b]p-values: ***[0.00, 0.01]; **[0.01, 0.05]; *[0.05, 0.15]; n.s. not significant or $p > 0.15$

Dominant Banks Achieve a Higher Profit-Maximizing Loan Rate

Dominant firms achieve a higher profit-maximizing loan rate, that is, the rate by which marginal revenues approximate marginal cost.

Due to a non-zero adjusted Lerner Index for the Top 20 banks, the results in Table 3.6 verify that the sampled banks are profiting more. This explains the positive coefficient for the square of the degree of market

Table 3.7 Market power behavior of the Top 10 UKBs vs the Next 10 (2005Q1–2019Q4)

Method: Panel GMM EGLS (Cross-section random effects)

Sample: 2005Q1 2019Q4; Periods Included: 60; white cross-section (cross-section correlation) instrument weighting matrix; Swamy and Arora estimator of component variances; Cross-section weights using panel corrected standard errors (PCSE) & covariance (d.f. corrected)

Dependent Variable: Return-on-Equity (ROE) (Bank Level Indicator of Profitability as a Measure of Performance)

Regressors [(a)]	Expected Sign	Top 10[(a,b)] Adjusted Lerner Index	Top 10[(a,b)] HHI Deposits	Top 10[(a,b)] HHI Loans	Next 10[(a,b)] Adjusted Lerner Index	Next 10[(a,b)] HHI Deposits	Next 10[(a,b)] HHI Loans
C	-/+	145.07 ***	20.02 n.s.	59.54 *	347.98 ***	396.65 **	70.50 n.s.
		(28.98)	(104.82)	(38.93)	(54.67)	(190.94)	(112.66)
Degree of Market Power	positive	-14.67 **	0.13 n.s.	0.15 ***	0.30 n.s.	-0.30 n.s.	-0.03 n.s.
		(6.58)	(0.18)	(0.05)	(1.73)	(0.35)	(0.16)
Degree of Market Power^2	negative	9.17 **	-7.17E-05 n.s.	-7.40E-05 ***	0.452 *	1.26E-04 n.s.	-1.67E-05 n.s.
		(3.54)	(0.00009)	(0.00002)	(0.25)	(0.0002)	(0.00008)
Fixed Assets to Total Assets	negative	-89.96 ***	-91.50 ***	-91.77 ***	-429.71 ***	-432.32 ***	-448.75 ***
		(10.90)	(11.21)	(11.25)	(49.51)	(49.34)	(49.30)
Loans to Assets	positive	-18.85 *	-19.73 *	-21.94 **	106.60 ***	114.12 ***	116.73 ***
		(11.13)	(11.39)	(11.04)	(29.79)	(29.43)	(28.65)
Loans to Assets^2	negative	9.48 n.s.	10.57 n.s.	12.47 n.s.	-103.73 ***	-111.02 ***	-118.14 ***
		(10.02)	(10.03)	(9.91)	(30.16)	(29.94)	(29.13)
Bank Size (Ln Total Assets)	positive	-0.41 n.s.	-0.51 n.s.	-0.34 n.s.	0.84 n.s.	1.31 n.s.	2.51 *
		(0.78)	(0.92)	(0.76)	(1.43)	(1.39)	(1.38)
Ln(GDP per capita)	-/+	-47.69 ***	-18.90 n.s.	-47.87 ***	-154.40 ***	-105.33 **	-21.69 n.s.
		(15.62)	(20.85)	(16.18)	(27.31)	(40.34)	(40.52)
Government/Foreign Ownership (%)	-/+	-0.056 ***	-0.04 ***	-0.05 ***	-0.10 **	-0.10 ***	-0.10 ***
		(0.02)	(0.01)	(0.01)	(0.04)	(0.03)	(0.03)
No. of Cross-Sections / Observations		10/600	10/600	10/600	10/600	10/600	10/600
AR(1)	negative	-5.91 ***	-6.14 ***	-5.81 ***	-3.49 ***	-3.45 ***	-3.50 ***
AR(2)	negative	-1.53 *	-1.07 n.s.	-1.63 *	-1.68 *	-1.79 *	-1.76 *
Hansen's *J*-Stat	positive	1.13E-17 n.s.	3.36E-14 n.s.	3.40E-15 n.s.	1.33E-17 n.s.	1.28E-14 n.s.	8.81E-17 n.s.

Source BSP (https://www.bsp.gov.ph/SitePages/Statistics/BSFinancialStatements.aspx?TabId=1 for basic data, and Author's Regression Results

[a]Highlighted cells refer to coefficients with signs different from expected and have a significant *p*-value

[b]*p*-values: ***[0.00, 0.01]; **[0.01, 0.05]; *[0.05, 0.15]; n.s. not significant or $p > 0.15$; Hansen's *J*-Stat < 1.0 has *p*-value > 0.50

Table 3.8 Comparison of market power behavior: Top 10 vs Next 10 UKBs (2008Q4–2019Q4)

Method: Panel GMM EGLS (Cross-section random effects)

Sample: 2008Q4 2019Q4; Periods Included: 45; white cross-section (cross-section correlation) instrument weighting matrix; Swamy and Arora estimator of component variances; Cross-section weights using panel corrected standard errors (PCSE) & covariance (d.f. corrected)

Dependent Variable: Return-on-Equity (ROE) (Bank Level Indicator of Profitability as a Measure of Performance)

Regressors [(a)]	Expected Sign	Top 10[(a,b)] Adjusted Lerner Index	Top 10 HHI Deposits	Top 10 HHI Loans	Next 10[(a,b)] Adjusted Lerner Index	Next 10 HHI Deposits	Next 10 HHI Loans
C	-/+	107.80 ***	-42.21 n.s.	-230.77 ***	78.76 *	-2.31 n.s.	-447.55 **
		(36.62)	(108.30)	(85.25)	(53.34)	(254.06)	(193.47)
Degree of Market Power	positive	-11.94 *	0.20 n.s.	0.64 ***	1.45 n.s.	-0.18 n.s.	0.78 **
		(7.09)	(0.20)	(0.15)	(1.27)	(0.47)	(0.37)
Degree of Market Power^2	negative	6.34 *	-1.06E-04 n.s.	-2.90E-04 ***	2.838 **	6.10E-05 n.s.	-3.72E-04 **
		(3.80)	(0.00010)	(0.00007)	(1.27)	(0.0002)	(0.00016)
Fixed Assets to Total Assets	negative	-117.74 ***	-120.37 ***	-113.14 ***	-169.73 **	-206.43 **	-227.12 ***
		(24.91)	(24.03)	(24.28)	(77.23)	(79.90)	(78.91)
Loans to Assets	positive	-35.70 ***	-34.04 ***	-31.50 **	99.44 ***	97.86 ***	100.13 ***
		(13.71)	(13.24)	(13.08)	(27.54)	(26.34)	(26.13)
Loans to Assets^2	negative	19.07 *	18.79 *	16.74 *	-97.25 ***	-96.52 ***	-100.93 ***
		(11.00)	(10.60)	(10.54)	(28.25)	(27.12)	(26.88)
Bank Size (Ln Total Assets)	positive	-2.61 ***	-2.32 **	-2.45 **	3.21 **	2.41 *	3.03 **
		(1.05)	(1.03)	(1.05)	(1.56)	(1.52)	(1.53)
Ln(GDP per capita)	-/+	-16.49 n.s.	4.15 n.s.	-26.35 n.s.	-55.14 n.s.	38.28 n.s.	-1.58 n.s.
		(20.20)	(21.50)	(20.16)	(26.22)	(36.91)	(32.37)
Government/Foreign Ownership (%)	-/+	-0.059 ***	-0.06 ***	-0.06 ***	-0.03 ***	-0.04 *	-0.04 *
		(0.02)	(0.02)	(0.02)	(0.03)	(0.03)	(0.03)
No. of Cross-Sections / Observations		10/450	10/450	10/450	10/450	10/450	10/450
AR(1)	negative	-5.16 ***	-5.59 ***	-5.39 ***	-2.27 **	-2.25 **	-2.33 **
AR(2)	negative	-1.48 n.s.	-1.01 n.s.	-0.94 n.s.	1.47 n.s.	1.60 n.s.	1.55 n.s.
Hansen's *J*-Stat	positive	1.52E-18 n.s.	5.42E-14 n.s.	4.89E-15 n.s.	1.64E-16 n.s.	3.72E-12 n.s.	2.14E-11 n.s.

Source BSP (https://www.bsp.gov.ph/SitePages/Statistics/BSFinancialStatements.aspx?TabId=1 for basic data, and Author's Regression Results

[a]Highlighted cells refer to coefficients with signs different from expected and have a significant *p*-value

[b]*p*-values: ***[0.00, 0.01]; **[0.01, 0.05]; *[0.05, 0.15]; n.s. not significant or $p > 0.15$; Hansen's *J*-Stat < 1.0 has *p*-value > 0.50

Table 3.9 Market concentration and markups of dominant vs fringe UKBs (2005Q1–2019Q4)

Method: Panel GMM EGLS (Cross-section random effects)
Sample: 2005Q1 2019Q4 or 60 Periods
White cross-section instrument weighting matrix; Cross-section weights (PCSE) standard errors & covariance (d.f.corrected)
Swamy and Arora estimator of component variances

Regressors [(a,b)] with Market Concentration for Loans	**Dependent Variable: Adjusted Lerner Index**						**Dependent Variable: Conventional Lerner Index**					
	Top 20	p-value & *t-stat*	Top 10	p-value & *t-stat*	Next 10	p-value & *t-stat*	Top 20	p-value & *t-stat*	Top 10	p-value & *t-stat*	Next 10	p-value & *t-stat*
C	1.27	**	1.46	***	1.08	n.s.	0.46	***	0.69	***	0.23	*
	(0.53)	*2.38*	(0.23)	*6.32*	(1.04)	*1.04*	(0.08)	*5.80*	(0.09)	*7.71*	(0.13)	*1.79*
Herfindahl-Hirschman Index	0.0003	n.s.	9.94E-05	n.s.	0.001	n.s.	0.0005	***	0.0005	***	0.0006	***
for Loans	(0.0003)	*1.36*	(0.0001)	*0.90*	(0.0005)	*1.19*	(0.00004)	*13.58*	(0.00004)	*11.15*	(0.0001)	*8.95*
Nominal GDP per capita	-0.09	n.s.	-0.07	**	-0.10	n.s.	-0.05	***	-0.07	***	-0.03	**
	(0.07)	*-1.17*	(0.03)	*-2.16*	(0.14)	*-0.72*	(0.01)	*-4.67*	(0.01)	*-5.49*	(0.02)	*-1.92*
Number of Cross-Sections/ Observations	20/1200		10/600		10/600		20/1200		10/600		10/600	
Arellano Bond Correlation Test:												
AR(1)	6.13	***	-1.95	*	4.51	***	-4.77	***	-6.33	***	-0.14	n.s.
AR(2)	-9.18	***	1.70	*	-6.71	***	-0.10	n.s.	-0.43	n.s.	0.24	n.s.
Hansen's *J*-Stat	1.34E-23	n.s.	3.15E-22	n.s.	5.80E-24	n.s.	4.81E-23	n.s.	4.26E-22	n.s.	3.67E-23	n.s.
Regressors [(a,b)] with Market Concentration for Deposits	**Dependent Variable: Adjusted Lerner Index**						**Dependent Variable: Conventional Lerner Index**					
	Top 20	p-value & *t-stat*	Top 10	p-value & *t-stat*	Next 10	p-value & *t-stat*	Top 20	p-value & *t-stat*	Top 10	p-value & *t-stat*	Next 10	p-value & *t-stat*
C	1.28	***	1.25	***	1.31	*	-0.29	***	0.01	n.s.	-0.59	***
	(0.44)	*2.94*	(0.19)	*6.61*	(0.85)	*1.55*	(0.07)	*-4.20*	(0.08)	*0.08*	(0.11)	*-5.26*
Herfindahl-Hirschman Index	0.001	**	-0.0001	n.s.	0.002	**	0.00005	n.s.	0.0001	n.s.	0.00002	n.s.
for Deposits	(0.0004)	*2.28*	(0.0002)	*-0.58*	(0.001)	*2.48*	(0.0001)	*0.71*	(0.0001)	*0.94*	(0.0001)	*0.20*
Nominal GDP per capita	-0.14	**	-0.03	n.s.	-0.26	*	0.07	***	0.04	***	0.10	***
	(0.07)	*-1.97*	(0.03)	*-0.89*	(0.14)	*-1.83*	(0.01)	*6.23*	(0.01)	*3.15*	(0.02)	*5.48*
Number of Cross-Sections/ Observations	20/1200		10/600		10/600		20/1200		10/600		10/600	
Arellano Bond Correlation Test:												
AR(1)	6.18	***	-2.02	**	4.64	***	-4.62	***	-6.19	***	4.64	***
AR(2)	-9.03	***	1.73	*	-6.81	***	-0.52	n.s.	-0.72	n.s.	-6.81	***
Hansen's *J*-Stat	5.46E-24	n.s.	3.37E-23	n.s.	1.63E-22	n.s.	2.44E-24	n.s.	3.07E-24	n.s.	1.29E-23	n.s.

Source BSP (https://www.bsp.gov.ph/SitePages/Statistics/BSFinancialStatements.aspx?TabId=1) for basic data, and Author's Regression Results

[a] ****p*-value [0.00, 0.01]; ***p*-value [0.01, 0.05]; **p*-value [0.05, 0.15]; ns: *p*-value > 0.15; ***Italicized*** numbers are t-statistics. Shaded *t*-statistics refer to their corresponding significant or very significant coefficient parameters when comparing the Top 10 with the Next 10 universal and commercial banks

[b]Hansen's *J*-Stat < 1.0 has *p*-value > 0.50

Table 3.10 Mark-up elasticity of total loans vs total deposits (2005Q1–2019Q4)

Method: Panel GMM EGLS (Cross-section random effects)
White cross-section instrument weighting matrix; Cross-section weights (PCSE) standard errors & covariance (d.f.corrected)
Swamy and Arora estimator of component variances

Dependent Variable: Ln (Total Loans)	Time Period: 2005Q1 to 2019Q4						Time Period: 2008Q4 to 2019Q4					
Regressors [(a,b)]	Top 20	p-value & t-stat	Top 10	p-value & t-stat	Next 10	p-value & t-stat	Top 20	p-value & t-stat	Top 10	p-value & t-stat	Next 10	p-value & t-stat
C	-31.78 ***		-32.98 ***		-29.31 ***		-40.45 ***		-42.48 ***		-38.72 ***	
	(0.92)	-34.6	(1.12)	-29.53	(1.49)	-19.63	(1.28)	-31.63	(1.30)	-32.75	(2.12)	-18.23
Ln (HHI Loans)	0.77 ***		0.21 n.s.		1.04 ***		2.01 ***		1.78 ***		2.34 ***	
	(0.24)	3.13	(0.30)	0.72	(0.39)	2.63	(0.26)	7.66	(0.27)	6.65	(0.44)	5.31
Ln (Conventional Lerner Index)	-0.01 n.s.		0.27 *		-0.02 n.s.		-0.17 *		-0.37 ***		-0.06 n.s.	
	(0.07)	-0.16	(0.15)	1.76	(0.08)	-0.20	(0.10)	-1.73	(0.12)	-3.18045712	(0.12)	-0.50
Ln (Nominal GNI per capita)	16.31 ***		18.93 ***		14.06 ***		16.22 ***		18.11 ***		14.15 ***	
	(0.64)	25.6	(0.74)	25.59	(1.02)	13.78	(0.55)	29.34721469	(0.54)	33.28086755	(0.94)	15.03227725
No. of Periods/Cross-Sections/ Observations	60/20/1200		60/10/600		60/10/600		45/20/900		45/10/450		45/10/450	
Arellano Bond Correlation Test:												
AR(1)	-5.54 ***		-3.62 ***		-3.75 ***		-5.34 ***		-3.78 ***		-3.60 ***	
AR(2)	-2.40 **		-0.13 n.s.		-3.56 ***		-2.84 ***		1.02 n.s.		-3.80 ***	
Hansen's *J*-Stat	9.58E-23 n.s.		9.39E-22 n.s.		1.67E-21 n.s.		1.26E-23 n.s.		1.68E-23 n.s.		1.09E-20 n.s.	
Dependent Variable: Ln (Total Deposits)	**Time Period: 2005Q1 to 2019Q4**						**Time Period: 2008Q4 to 2019Q4**					
Regressors [(a,b)]	Top 20	p-value & t-stat	Top 10	p-value & t-stat	Next 10	p-value & t-stat	Top 20	p-value & t-stat	Top 10	p-value & t-stat	Next 10	p-value & t-stat
C	-26.49 ***		-30.03 ***		-22.59 ***		-29.62 ***		-34.03 ***		-25.29 ***	
	(1.27)	-20.89	(1.38)	-21.71	(22.59)	-10.87	(1.25)	-23.70	(1.33)	-25.57	(2.02)	-12.49
Ln (HHI Deposits)	0.12 n.s.		0.21 n.s.		0.03 n.s.		1.16 ***		1.30 ***		1.05 **	
	(0.31)	0.39	(0.34)	0.63	(0.51)	0.06	(0.30)	3.93	(0.31)	4.14	(0.49)	2.16
Ln (Conventional Lerner Index)	-0.02 n.s.		-0.12 n.s.		0.08 n.s.		0.11 n.s.		-0.09 n.s.		0.21 **	
	(0.06)	-0.32	(0.11)	-1.04	(0.07)	1.27	(0.08)	1.37	(0.10)	-0.87209258	(0.09)	2.27
Ln (Nominal GNI per capita)	16.18 ***		17.74 ***		14.46 ***		14.46 ***		16.23 ***		12.62 ***	
	(0.57)	28.48	(0.61)	28.99	(0.95)	15.27729718	(0.58)	24.79142696	(0.62)	26.26318659	(0.96)	13.13293394
Number of Cross-Sections/Observations	20/1200		10/600		60/10/600		45/20/900		45/10/450		45/10/450	
Arellano Bond Correlation Test:												
AR(1)	-6.17 ***		-3.31 ***		-4.72 ***		-2.37 **		-0.97 ***		-1.63 *	
AR(2)	3.68 ***		3.12 ***		1.92 *		3.46 ***		3.47 ***		1.51 *	
Hansen's *J*-Stat	4.40E-23 n.s.		1.17E-23 n.s.		3.63E-22 n.s.		1.22E-23 n.s.		1.77E-23 n.s.		5.44E-21 n.s.	

Source BSP (https://www.bsp.gov.ph/SitePages/Statistics/BSFinancialStatements.aspx?TabId=1) for basic data, and Author's Regression Results

[a] ****p*-value [0.00, 0.01]; ***p*-value [0.01, 0.05]; **p*-value [0.05, 0.15]; ns: *p*-value > 0.15; Italicized numbers are *t*-statistics. Shaded *t*-statistics refer to their corresponding significant or very significant coefficient parameters when comparing the Top 10 with the Next 10 universal and commercial banks

[b] Hansen's *J*-Stat < 1.0 has *p*-value > 0.50

Table 3.11 Net income of dominant and fringe banks vs market power (2005Q1–2019Q4)

Method: Panel GMM EGLS (Cross-section random effects) White cross-section instrument weighting matrix; Cross-section weights (PCSE) standard errors & covariance (d.f.corrected) Swamy and Arora estimator of component variances												
Dependent Variable: Net Income / Regressor (a,b)	**Time Period: 2005Q1 to 2019Q4**						**Time Period: 2008Q4 to 2019Q4**					
	Top 20	p-value & *t-stat*	Top 10	p-value & *t-stat*	Next 10	p-value & *t-stat*	Top 20	p-value & *t-stat*	Top 10	p-value & *t-stat*	Next 10	p-value & *t-stat*
C	5,128	***	11,698	***	1,067	***	5,882	***	10,902	***	1,225	***
	(1,250)	*4.10*	(2,265)	*5.16*	(274)	*3.9*	(1,512)	*3.89*	(2,573)	*4.24*	(386)	*3.17*
Adjusted Lerner Index	-125	n.s.	-3,130	**	-15	n.s.	190	n.s.	-189	n.s.	134	n.s.
	(98)	*-1.27*	(1,566)	*-2.00*	(56)	*-0.3*	(247)	*0.77*	(1,483)	*-0.1*	(145)	*0.93*
No. of Periods/Cross-Sections/ Observations	60/20/1200		60/10/600		60/10/600		45/20/900		45/10/450		45/10/450	
Arellano Bond Correlation Test:												
AR(1)	-6.30	***	-4.39	***	-5.03	***	-5.38	***	-3.69	***	-5.02	***
AR(2)	-2.09	**	-1.47	n.s.	-1.88	*	-2.07	**	-1.59	*	-0.56	n.s.
Hansen's *J*-Stat	1.26E-31	n.s.	1.86E-29	n.s.	8.43E-31	n.s.	1.56E-30	n.s.	5.38E-29	n.s.	7.55E-31	n.s.
C	-6,246	***	-18,999	***	-2,556	***	-2,705	n.s.	-8,061	*	-1,588	***
	(1,540)	*-4.06*	(3,221)	*-5.90*	(459)	*-5.6*	(2,219)	*-1.22*	(4,950)	*-1.6*	(560)	*-2.8*
Conventional Lerner Index	22,906	***	54,950	***	7,606	***	17,060	***	35,906	***	5,805	***
	(1,936)	*11.83*	(5,257)	*10.45*	(776)	*9.80*	(3,294)	*5.18*	(8,565)	*4.19*	(860)	*6.75*
No. of Periods/Cross-Sections/ Observations	60/20/1200		60/10/600		60/10/600		45/20/900		45/10/450		45/10/450	
Arellano Bond Correlation Test:												
AR(1)	-6.36	***	-4.50	***	-4.93	***	-5.45	***	-3.81	***	-4.98	***
AR(2)	-2.10	**	-1.42	n.s.	-1.82	*	-2.08	**	-1.50	*	-0.53	n.s.
Hansen's *J*-Stat	7.80E-29	n.s.	5.26E-31	n.s.	4.52E-29	n.s.	6.12E-30	n.s.	2.44E-29	n.s.	9.86E-29	n.s.

Source BSP (https://www.bsp.gov.ph/SitePages/Statistics/BSFinancialStatements.aspx?TabId=1) for basic data, and Author's Regression Results

[a] ****p*-value [0.00, 0.01]; ***p*-value [0.01, 0.05]; **p*-value [0.05, 0.15]; ns: *p*-value > 0.15; ***Italicized*** numbers are *t*-statistics. Shaded *t*-statistics refer to their corresponding significant or very significant coefficient parameters when comparing the Top 10 with the Next 10 universal and commercial banks

[b] Hansen's *J*-Stat < 1.0 has *p*-value > 0.50

Table 3.12 Results of the empirical verification of an imperfectly UKBs industry using the Monti-Klein and the dominant and fringe models for the Top 20 UKBs

Indicators		*Empirical model with expected results*	*Actual results*
More market power + greater market concentration (Freixas and Rochet 2008, pp. 78–81)	(a.1) A positive relationship of market power and market concentration	A GMM logarithmic regression of the adjusted and conventional Lerner Indexes as the dependent variable with HHI Loans and HHI Deposits, and gross national income per capita as regressors (see Table 3.11)	The coefficient of the market concentration indicator for loans is significantly higher for the Top 10 UKBs, compared to the Next 10. The conventional Lerner Index for the Top 10 UKBs explains that greater market power comes about through increasing market concentration for Loans

(continued)

Table 3.12 (continued)

Indicators		*Empirical model with expected results*	*Actual results*
	(a.2) Higher markup on loans vs deposits	Expect the coefficient of the price indicator for loan rates to be higher than the coefficient of the price indicator for deposits. The conventional Lerner Index serves as the price indicator (see Table 3.12)	These observations refer to 2008Q4–2019Q4, when the merger of two large UKBs happened • The Top 10 UKBs charge loan rates higher than deposit rates, showing greater market concentration • The Top 10 banks charge loan rates higher than the Next 10 banks due to steeper price elasticity of the demand for loans • The income elasticity of demand for loans and deposits of Top 10 banks is higher than the Next 10 banks

Indicators		Empirical model with expected results	Actual results
	(a.3) Banks with more market power achieve higher profits in an environment of greater market concentration	This is verified by comparing the regression results of profits (return-on-equity) as dependent variable, as explained by a market structure indicator and bank controls (Molyneux and Forbes 1995) (see Table 3.10)	• The regression result on ROE verifies that the **Top 10 banks, upon gaining market power were able to charge higher mark-ups**, as seen by a significantly higher coefficient for the adjusted Lerner Index squared and a higher regression line from the scatter plot for the Top 10 (see Fig. 3.11a) • The coefficient for HHI Loans and the adjusted Lerner Index for the Top 10 is significantly higher than the corresponding coefficient for the Next 10

(continued)

Table 3.12 (continued)

Indicators		*Empirical model with expected results*	*Actual results*
Presence of Dominant and Fringe Banks	An expected higher profit-maximizing loan rate for dominant banks, that is, the rate at which marginal revenues are equal to marginal cost (VanHoose 2022, pp. 43–44)	• The indicator used for profit is net income while the indicator for loan rate is the adjusted and conventional Lerner Indexes (see Table 3.13)	• The Top 10 banks earn significantly higher net income than the Next 10 banks. The higher net income is a result of their ability to charge higher markups or lower their costs, which spells greater efficiency. These results are seen in the higher regression constant of net income for the Top 10 banks, compared with those of Next 10 with the adjusted Lerner Index as an explanatory variable • The regression constant for net income using the adjusted Lerner Index as a regressor and the coefficient for the conventional Lerner Index is significantly higher than the Next 10 • Despite the higher fixed costs, the presence of more nationwide branches and ATMs translates to higher net income for the Top 10 banks

Indicators		*Empirical model with expected results*	*Actual results*
	Positive profit for dominant banks due to their cost advantage	Using a modified Boone indicator where Total Loans serves as an indicator for net income and the HHI as an indicator for markup/market power (see Table 3.12), greater efficiency would indicate a smaller Boone indicator	A 1% change in the markup of the Top 10 banks would result in a 1.78% increase in Total Loans. For the Next 10 banks, a 1% increase in markup would result in a 2.34% increase in Total Loans. The larger wholesale funds position enables the Top 10 banks to charge lower funding costs during periods of low-interest rates

Source Author's Regression Results

Table 3.13 Financial stability using Z_{ROA} of the Top 20 UKBs (2005Q1–2019Q4)

Method: Panel GMM EGLS (Cross-section random effects) Sample: 2005Q1 2019Q4; Periods Included: 60; white cross-section (cross-section correlation) instrument weighting matrix; Swamy and Arora estimator of component variances; Cross-section weights using panel corrected standard errors (PCSE) & covariance (d.f corrected)				
Dependent Variable: Z-index using ROA (ZROA) (Bank Level Indicator of Financial Stability)				
Regressors [(a)]	**Expected Sign**	**Top 20 [(a,b)]**		
		Adjusted Lerner	**HHI Deposits**	**HHI Loans**
C	-/+	17.77 ***	-15.07 n.s.	-15.30 **
		(4.27)	(10.75)	(6.38)
Degree of Market Power	positive	0.29 **	0.03 *	0.04 ***
		(0.15)	(0.02)	(0.009)
Degree of Market Power^2	negative	0.04 *	-1.89E-05 **	-2.01E-05 ***
		(0.02)	(0.00001)	(0.000004)
Fixed Assets to Total Assets	negative	-10.48 ***	-10.11 ***	-10.47 ***
		(1.43)	(1.33)	(1.34)
Loans to Assets	positive	7.84 ***	8.62 ***	8.76 ***
		(1.80)	(1.73)	(1.72)
Loans to Assets^2	negative	-7.80 ***	-8.55 ***	-8.90 ***
		(1.92)	(1.85)	(1.84)
Bank Size (Ln Total Assets)	positive	0.02 n.s	-0.02 n.s.	0.06 n.s.
		(0.11)	(0.10)	(0.10)
Ln(GDP per capita)	-/+	-7.45 ***	0.23 n.s.	-2.12 ***
		(2.18)	(2.48)	(2.41)
Government/Foreign Ownership (%)	-/+	-0.01 **	-0.007 **	-0.008 **
		(0.003)	(0.003)	(0.003)
No. of Cross-Sections / Observations		20/1180	20/1200	20/1200
AR(1)	negative	-8.37 ***	-8.42 ***	-8.38 ***
AR(2)	negative	-2.10 **	-2.24 **	-2.24 **
Hansen's *J*-Stat	positive	1.71 n.s	4.06E-16 n.s.	7.174E-19 n.s.

Source BSP https://www.bsp.gov.ph/SitePages/Statistics/BSFinancialStatements.aspx?TabId=1 for basic data and the author's regression results

[a]Highlighted cells refer to coefficients with signs different from expected and have a significant *p*-value; Hansen's *J*-Stat < 1.0 has *p*-value > 0.50.

[b] *p*-values: ***[0.00, 0.01]; **[0.01, 0.05]; *[0.05, 0.15]; n.s. not significant or *p* > 0.15

power when using the Adjusted Lerner Index, for all the Top 20 UKBs. One can expect higher profits from the higher markups charged by the Top 10 (dominant) banks. The data, however, cannot verify if these banks are operating at a level where marginal revenue is equal to marginal cost. This can only be tested using a translog cost function. If one derives marginal cost from a translog cost function, then, the computed Lerner Index would capture a profit-maximizing level of market power.

The regression result in Table 3.6 shows an optimal level of profits for the Top 20 banks. UKBs begin to decrease their returns-to-equity when the loans-to-assets ratio becomes too high. However, from 2008 to 2019, when evidence of market concentration is noted, the Top 10 banks sustained an increase in their returns-to-equity at a higher loans-to-assets ratio compared to the Next 10. This may imply that the Top 10 banks efficiently monitor their borrowers and thereby provide various options for interest payments on loans. Better monitoring procedures allow the Top 10 and Next 10 banks to charge higher markups through loan interest rates appropriate to the risk levels of their borrowers. From Tables 3.7 and 3.8, increasing market power signified by the adjusted Lerner Index leads to higher returns-to-equity.

The results of the regressions in Table 3.9 and the tests for the difference of constants and coefficients in Table 3.10 provide empirical proof to Monti-Klein's predicted behavior of dominant banks. First, dominant banks charge higher markups as the industry approaches market concentration in the deposits and loans market. Second, dominant banks achieve higher profit-maximizing loan rates where the rate of marginal revenues are equal to marginal cost (Freixas and Rochet 2008, pp. 78–81; VanHoose 2022, pp. 43–44). For the Philippines, the Top 10 banks charge higher loan and deposit rates than the Next 10. From the logarithmic regression on Total Loans and Total Deposits in Table 3.10, note that the constant for the regression on loans and the constant for the regression on deposits are significantly higher than the regression on deposits and loans for the Top 20 and Next 10 banks. This means that the Top 10 enjoy more revenues than the Next 10 through higher markups for deposits and loans or by charging clients various levels of deposit rates. Further, increases in per capita income accrue to higher revenues from loans and deposits for the Top 10, compared to the Next 10. Note that the fringe banks have higher markup elasticity on loans, using the conventional Lerner Index as an indicator for the regression from the fourth quarter of 2008 to the fourth quarter of 2019. This means that fringe banks vary their markups on loan rates more frequently than dominant banks.

Dia and VanHoose (2022) explain that in a low-interest-rate environment, dominant banks have an advantage over fringe banks because they can adjust their wholesale-funds position to respond to shifts in the interest rate on wholesale funds. Wholesale funds refer to funds obtained from external sources, such as other financial institutions and investors. These funds are typically borrowed at an interest rate that is determined by the market. When the interest rate on wholesale funds drops, dominant banks can take advantage of this by adjusting their wholesale funds positions. This means they can borrow more funds at lower rates, which reduces their funding costs. As a result, they can lend out at competitive rates and potentially increase their market share.

Fringe banks, on the other hand, rely more heavily on individual and corporate deposits to finance their lending activities. Fringe banks primarily adjust their deposit positions when changes in the equilibrium deposit rate affect the interest rate on deposits. They may decrease their interest rates on deposits to mitigate their funding costs. However, adjusting deposit positions can be costlier for fringe banks compared to the wholesale-funds alterations made by dominant banks. Fringe banks may face challenges in reducing deposit rates due to competition for deposits from other financial institutions, resulting in higher resource costs that affect their profitability.

Therefore, in a low-interest-rate environment, dominant banks tend to benefit from adjusting their wholesale-funds positions, leading to lower funding costs and potentially higher profitability. They may also gain market share, unlike the fringe banks that may face challenges in adjusting deposit rates and managing their funding costs (Dia and VanHoose 2022).

This explanation sheds light on the greater markup elasticity of fringe banks compared to the Top 10 UKBs when they increased market share for loans and deposits. Both the Top 10 and Next 10 banks can vary their loan and deposit rates but the larger ones obtain greater markups due to higher deposit and loan volumes. The Top 10 also have significantly higher income elasticity of demand for loans and deposits, compared to the Next 10. Income here is represented by per capita gross domestic product. This means that increased income from individuals and institutions, most of whom are clients of the Top 10 banks, redound to a boost in income for all banks. The next section will verify this result.

Dominant Banks Profit Due to Their Cost Advantage
The last predicted behavior of Monti-Klein states that dominant firms earn due to their cost advantage (Freixas and Rochet 2008, pp. 78–81; VanHoose 2022, pp. 43–44). Results in Table 3.13 indicate that the Top 10 banks earn significantly higher net income than the Next 10 banks. The higher net income comes from charging higher markups or lowered costs, which spells more efficiency, as seen in the higher regression constant of net income for the Top 10 banks versus the Next 10 with the adjusted Lerner Index as an explanatory variable. Even if a bank has a smaller markup due to fixed costs and costs of property and equipment, the net income of the Top 10 is higher because said costs allow them to grow their client reach. Fixed costs incurred from expanding nationwide presence through more branches and ATMs eventually generate higher net income.

Using the conventional Lerner Index as an explanatory variable, which excluded fixed and property costs, the constant for the regression turned out negative while the coefficient for the conventional Lerner Index was positive and significantly higher than the coefficient for the conventional Lerner Index of the Top 20 and Next 10 banks. The latter Lerner Index indicates the higher profit margins for the dominant banks.

Competitive behavior of the Top 10 banks in terms of price-setting and profit maximization follows expected outcomes in imperfectly competitive markets where dominant and fringe banks operate. Thus, the results for Objective 1 reveal that the Philippine UKB industry thrives in an imperfectly competitive market structure. Market power is the ability of dominant banks to charge higher markups and obtain higher profits when the industry experienced greater market concentration. However, said results may also be due to better cost management.

Thus, the predicted behavior of dominant and fringe banks through the Monti-Klein model (Freixas and Rochet 2008, pp. 78–81) and VanHoose (2022, pp. 43–44) is empirically verified. Table 3.12 summarizes evidence of an imperfectly competitive UKB industry in the Philippines.

These results have much to do with financial stability as greater market concentration in the Philippine UKB industry leads the dominant banks to exercise market power by charging higher loan rates and markups, as well as varying loan rates vis-à-vis deposit rates and enjoy cost advantage, and so profit more. The market behavior of the dominant banks concurs with greater bank concentration in the loans market from 2008Q4 to

2019Q4. The various regressions that use financial stability indicators as dependent variables will most likely yield a higher coefficient of market power for the dominant banks.

Will the exercise of greater market power in an environment of elevated market concentration bring about more financially stable banks?

Bank Competition, Market Concentration, and Bank Stability as Indicators of Resilience to Bank Distress or Insolvency

This step shall test Hypothesis 2. Market concentration and imperfect competition in the banking industry enable banks to be profitable, but expose them to greater risks, making them more fragile.

Competition, Concentration, and Stability Nexus

The regressions on the two Z-indexes, Z_{ROE} and Z_{ROA}, indicators of solvency and stability, shall be the basis for the verification of the competition and stability nexus. Given that the Top 10 UKBs do exercise market power in the industry, one observes an emerging trend towards less competition and greater market concentration. Given the framework of MMR (2010), less competitive banks tend to focus on the risk-shifting effect, that is, less competition results in greater market concentration. With an HHI greater than 1000, the Top 20 banks have a solvency or stability index (Z_{ROE} and Z_{ROA}) greater than 2.0; and with higher loan rates, borrowers may shift to taking risks in order to settle higher loan rates. This may expose banks to loan defaults and, therefore, fragility; however, the results show otherwise. Figure 3.12a, b show that greater market power allows the Top 20 banks to be more financially stable. Tables 3.15 and 3.16 show that a 1% increase in the adjusted Lerner Index results in a 0.29% increase in the Z_{ROA}, while a 1% increase in the HHI for Loans results in a 0.03%–0.04% increase in the Z_{ROA} and Z_{ROE}. This may be explained by the Top 20 and Top 10 banks' efforts to expand their loans market reach, since bank size increases with the financial stability indicator. In addition, the capacity of the Top 10 banks to charge higher loan rates through higher markups allows them to achieve profit maximization and financial stability during the period of increasing concentration in the loan market (Table 3.14).

Similar to the scatterplot of ROE and HHI, the financial stability indicator, Z_{ROE}, is on an uptrend during the years that HHI Loans and HHI Deposits approached a market concentration level of 1000. From these

Table 3.14 Financial stability using Z_{ROE} of the Top 20 UKBs (2005Q1–2019Q4)

Method: Panel GMM EGLS (Cross-section random effects) Sample: 2005Q1 2019Q4; Periods Included: 60; white cross-section (cross-section correlation) instrument weighting matrix; Swamy and Arora estimator of component variances; Cross-section weights using panel corrected standard errors (PCSE) & covariance (d.f. corrected)				
Dependent Variable: Z-index using ROE (ZROE) **(Bank Level Indicator of Financial Stability)**				
		Top 20[1,2]		
Regressors[1]	**Expected Sign**	**Adjusted Lerner Index**	**HHI Deposits**	**HHI Loans**
C	-/+	28.21 ***	7.85 n.s.	-1.32 n.s.
		(8.18)	(10.32)	(6.11)
Degree of Market Power	positive	-0.09 n.s.	0.01 n.s.	0.03 ***
		(0.18)	(0.02)	(0.01)
Degree of Market Power^2	negative	0.02 n.s.	-9.47E-06 n.s.	-1.76E-05 ***
		(0.02)	(0.00001)	(0.000004)
Fixed Assets to Total Assets	negative	-13.05 ***	-12.79 ***	-13.42 ***
		(2.48)	(1.32)	(1.33)
Loans to Assets	positive	7.79 **	8.37 ***	8.60 ***
		(2.96)	(1.67)	(1.65)
Loans to Assets^2	negative	-8.62 **	-9.07 ***	-9.58 ***
		(3.09)	(1.77)	(1.76)
Bank Size (Ln Total Assets)	positive	0.14 n.s.	0.20 *	0.32 ***
		(0.23)	(0.10)	(0.11)
Ln(GDP per capita)	-/+	-12.13 **	-5.97 ***	-7.47 ***
		(4.48)	(2.45)	(2.37)
Government/Foreign Ownership (%)	-/+	-0.01 *	-0.01 *	-0.014 ***
		(0.007)	(0.004)	(0.004)
No. of Cross-Sections / Observations		20/1180	20/1200	20/1200
AR(1)	negative	-8.51 ***	-8.55 ***	-8.47 ***
AR(2)	negative	-2.49 **	-2.57 ***	-2.70 ***
Hansen's J-Stat	positive	9.4E-18 n.s.	4.0571E-16 n.s.	3.016E-18 n.s.
Notes: 1. Hansen's J- Stat < 1.0 has p-value > 0.50. 2. p-values: *** [0.00, 0.01]; ** (0.01, 0.05]; *: (0.05, 0.15]; n.s. not significant or p > 0.15				

Source BSP https://www.bsp.gov.ph/SitePages/Statistics/BSFinancialStatements.aspx?TabId=1 for basic data, and Author's regression results

scatterplots, the Top 5 UKBs became more financially stable, as verified by the regressions linking competition, concentration, and financial stability.

The intercepts of the Top 10 banks are more negative than the intercepts of the Next 20 banks. Fixed assets and the presence of endogenous sunk costs make up the primary factors to explain the Top 10 banks'

Table 3.15 Financial stability using Z_{ROA} of the Top 10 and next 10 UKBs (2005Q1–2019Q4)

Method: Panel GMM EGLS (Cross-section random effects)

Sample: 2005Q1 2019Q4; Periods Included: 60; white cross-section (cross-section correlation) instrument weighting matrix; Swamy and Arora estimator of component variances; Cross-section weights using panel corrected standard errors (PCSE) & covariance (d.f. corrected)

Dependent Variable: Z-index using ROA (Bank Level Indicator of Financial Stability)

Regressors [(a)]	Expected Sign	Top 10[(a,b)] Adjusted Lerner Index	Top 10[(a,b)] HHI Deposits	Top 10[(a,b)] HHI Loans	Next 10[(a,b)] Adjusted Lerner Index	Next 10[(a,b)] HHI Deposits	Next 10[(a,b)] HHI Loans
C	-/+	37.19 ***	-37.30 *	11.88 n.s.	1.80 n.s.	-12.45 n.s.	-32.69 ***
		(7.27)	(19.42)	(9.37)	(4.61)	(15.12)	(10.64)
Degree of Market Power	positive	-1.91 *	0.07 **	0.05 ***	0.08 n.s.	0.01 n.s.	0.03 *
		(1.21)	(0.03)	(0.01)	(0.14)	(0.03)	(0.016)
Degree of Market Power^2	negative	1.57 **	-3.90E-05 **	-2.33E-05 ***	0.01 n.s.	-6.06E-06 n.s.	-1.47E-05 **
		(0.65)	(0.000017)	(0.000006)	(0.02)	(0.000013)	(0.000007)
Fixed Assets to Total Assets	negative	-23.00 ***	-18.99 ***	-21.91 ***	-7.17 ***	-6.49 ***	-7.15 ***
		(2.71)	(3.55)	(2.77)	(1.53)	(1.54)	(2.44)
Loans to Assets	positive	0.48 n.s.	3.72 n.s.	-0.25 n.s.	8.00 ***	8.12 ***	8.95 ***
		(2.91)	(6.76)	(2.93)	(2.24)	(2.23)	(2.37)
Loans to Assets^2	negative	-1.06 n.s.	-4.32 n.s.	-0.34 n.s.	-7.80 ***	-7.87 ***	-9.06 ***
		(2.85)	(7.35)	(2.88)	(2.48)	(2.47)	(2.74)
Bank Size (Ln Total Assets)	positive	-0.06 n.s.	0.19 n.s.	0.01 n.s.	-0.13 n.s.	-0.16 ***	(0.02) n.s.
		(0.21)	(0.25)	(0.21)	(0.13)	(0.13)	(0.15)
Ln(GDP per capita)	-/+	-13.93 ***	2.88 n.s.	-14.52 ***	-0.22 n.s.	4.55 n.s.	8.93 **
		(4.02)	(5.94)	(4.17)	(2.38)	(3.28)	(4.52)
Government/Foreign Ownership (%)	-/+	-0.004 n.s.	-0.0003 n.s.	-0.005 n.s.	-0.002 n.s.	-0.002 n.s.	-0.002 n.s.
		(0.01)	(0.01)	(0.004)	(0.003)	(0.01)	(0.01)
No. of Cross-Sections / Observations		10/600	10/600	10/600	10/600	10/600	10/600
AR(1)		-5.41 ***	-5.05 ***	-5.56 ***	-6.28 ***	-6.33 ***	-6.33 ***
AR(2)		-1.41 n.s.	-1.30 n.s.	-1.28 n.s.	-1.90 *	-1.86 *	-1.86 *
Hansen's *J*-Stat		3.51E-18 n.s.	5.50E-16 n.s.	2.66E-16 n.s.	6.32E-21 n.s.	2.33E-17 n.s.	1.14E-18 n.s.

Source BSP https://www.bsp.gov.ph/SitePages/Statistics/BSFinancialStatements.aspx?TabId=1 for basic data, and Author's regression results

[a]Highlighted cells refer to coefficients with signs different from expected and have a significant p-value

[b]p-values: ***[0.00, 0.01]; **[0.01, 0.05]; *[0.05, 0.15]; n.s. not significant or $p > 0.15$; Hansen's J-Stat < 1.0 has p-value > 0.50.

Table 3.16 Financial stability using Z_{ROE} of the Top 10 and Next 10 UKBs (2005Q1–2019Q4)

Method: Panel GMM EGLS (Cross-section random effects)							
Sample: 2005Q1 2019Q4; Periods Included: 60; white cross-section (cross-section correlation) instrument weighting matrix; Swamy and Arora estimator of component variances; Cross-section weights using panel corrected standard errors (PCSE) & covariance (d.f. corrected)							
Dependent Variable: Z-index using ROE (Bank Level Indicator of Financial Stability)							
Regressors [(a)]	Expected Sign	Top 10[(a,b)]			Next 10[(a,b)]		
		Adjusted Lerner Index	HHI Deposits	HHI Loans	Adjusted Lerner Index	HHI Deposits	HHI Loans
C	-/+	35.85 ***	3.18 n.s.	13.28 n.s.	26.54 ***	22.15 *	-12.24 *
		(7.58)	(15.02)	(9.50)	(4.42)	(14.41)	(8.25)
Degree of Market Power	positive	-2.01 *	0.03 n.s.	0.04 ***	-0.20 *	-0.01 n.s.	0.02 **
		(1.17)	(0.03)	(0.01)	(0.12)	(0.03)	(0.012)
Degree of Market Power^2	negative	1.33 **	-1.90E-05 *	-2.01E-05 ***	0.001 n.s.	4.59E-06 n.s.	-1.45E-05 **
		(0.62)	(0.000012)	(0.000006)	(0.02)	(0.00001)	(0.000006)
Fixed Assets to Total Assets	negative	-21.51 ***	-20.95 ***	-21.11 ***	-10.44 ***	-10.37 ***	-11.28 ***
		(2.85)	(2.83)	(2.94)	(1.52)	(1.50)	(1.49)
Loans to Assets	positive	-1.83 n.s.	-1.78 n.s.	-2.36 n.s.	9.47 ***	9.80 ***	10.75 ***
		(2.88)	(2.82)	(2.82)	(2.20)	(2.19)	(2.17)
Loans to Assets^2	negative	-0.91 n.s.	-0.85 n.s.	-0.38 n.s.	-9.25 ***	-9.54 ***	-10.97 ***
		(2.79)	(2.72)	(2.71)	(2.47)	(2.46)	(2.43)
Bank Size (Ln Total Assets)	positive	0.05 n.s.	0.07 n.s.	0.15 n.s.	0.17 n.s.	0.24 *	0.43 ***
		(0.22)	(0.22)	(0.23)	(0.13)	(0.13)	(0.13)
Ln(GDP per capita)	-/+	-12.96 ***	-5.57 n.s.	-13.37 ***	-12.30 ***	-7.13 **	-1.33 n.s.
		(4.18)	(4.49)	(4.34)	(2.33)	(3.14)	(3.00)
Government/Foreign Ownership (%)	-/+	-0.014 **	-0.01 **	-0.01 **	-0.004 n.s.	-0.004 n.s.	-0.003 n.s.
		(0.01)	(0.01)	(0.01)	(0.005)	(0.01)	(0.01)
No. of Cross-Sections / Observations		10/600	10/600	10/600	10/600	10/600	10/600
AR(1)		-5.65 ***	-5.87 ***	-5.81 ***	-6.32 ***	-6.27 ***	-6.22 ***
AR(2)		-1.81 *	-1.65 *	-1.63 *	-1.99 **	-2.09 **	-2.15 **
Hansen's *J*-Stat		4.27E-21 n.s.	4.87E-20 n.s.	4.77E-18 n.s.	1.96E-19 n.s.	9.05E-18 n.s.	3.35E-19 n.s.

Source BSP https://www.bsp.gov.ph/SitePages/Statistics/BSFinancialStatements.aspx?TabId=1 for basic data, and Author's Regression Results

[a]Highlighted cells refer to coefficients with signs different from expected and have a significant p-value

[2]p-values: ***[0.00, 0.01]; **[0.01, 0.05]; *[0.05, 0.15]; n.s. not significant or $p > 0.15$; Hansen's J-Stat < 1.0 has p-value > 0.50

source of instability, such as the possibility of greater sunk costs or investments in more ATM machines and bank branches compared to the Next 10 banks (see Table 3.15).

For both regressions for Z_{ROA} and Z_{ROE}, the market structure indicator for the Top 10 has a significantly higher coefficient for HHI Loans and the adjusted Lerner Index than the Next 10. This signifies that, with greater market concentration, the Top 10 banks can become more financially stable by improving their market share through an increase in markups. The aggressiveness of the Top 10, however, also exposes them to greater volatility in equity and asset returns, which makes them less stable. The possibility of decreasing their financial stability, however, does not seem to lessen their loan capacity. From the regression with the adjusted Lerner Index, one observes that while the Top 10 boost their market power and elevate their markups, they have maintained their loans-to-assets ratio at 47–50%. For their part, the Next 10 banks' endeavor to boost market share has improved their lending capacity, putting their loans-to-assets ratio range within 46–49% (see Tables 3.15 and 3.16). Thus, the Top 10 banks are able to extend loans but not to the detriment of stability, or a decrease of not less than 43% and not beyond 67% (see Table 3.24). These indicators signify that the Top 20 banks, whose loans-to-assets ratio did not exceed 50% from the first quarter of 2005 to the fourth quarter of 2019 rigorously screened borrowers in order to reduce credit risks and so be less prone to fragility.

Competition, Concentration, and Fragility Nexus

The regressions on equity-to-assets and non-performing loan ratios shall be the basis for the verification of the competition and stability nexus.

The effect of market power on bank capitalization, as measured by the adjusted Lerner Index and the HHI on loans and deposits, differed from Berger's expected results (2009). For the Top 20 banks, an initial downtrend in bank capitalization occurs with an increase in market power. However, bank capitalization starts to increase with heightened market power, as seen in the regression results for equity-to-assets (see Table 3.19). Figure 3.13a, b show that the bank capitalization levels of the Next 10 banks are lower than the Top 10 banks.

Some results took on unexpected but significant coefficients perhaps due to the Top 20 banks' attempts to expand their market reach, especially in cities outside of Metro Manila. Under such circumstances, increasing their buffer, i.e., equity-to-assets ratio against risks, did not seem to be a priority. Faced with stiff competition, banks focus more on the margin effect or increase in profit, while those that already enjoy a higher market share seem bent on raising their capital cushion, prioritizing the buffer effect, thus improving their equity-to-assets ratio (Tables 3.17 and 3.18).

Greater market concentration helps improve the financial stability of the Top 20 banks but it also exposes them to risk and makes them more fragile, as seen in the negative relationship between bank size and capitalization. The regressions in Tables 3.19 and 3.20 show that increasing loan defaults and NPLs can give rise to fragility. As market share increases, so do the markups on loan rates, as banks want to take advantage of greater market concentration. These results contribute to increasing their NPLs.

Before 2008, HHI Loans were at competitive market structure levels of 600–800. Some of the UKBs had extremely high levels of NPLs. As market concentration began to build up in the UKB industry, one observes a drastic decline in NPLs, or an average of up to 3.57% among the Top 20 banks from 2005Q1 to 2019Q4.

In summary, the Top 20 banks exercised market power through higher markups against the backdrop of intense market concentration from the fourth quarter of 2008 to the fourth quarter of 2019. They also attempted to improve capitalization to obtain an overall average of 11% for the Top 20, 12% for the Top 10, and 10.3% for the Next 10. The NPL ratio also dropped way below the BSP's regulation of 5% or an average of 2.92% for the Top 20; 2.3% for the Top 10; and 3.54% for the Next 10 (Table 3.20).

Bank Competition, Market Concentration, and Financial Stability as Indicators of Resilience to Regulatory Distress

This step shall test Hypothesis 3. Market concentration and imperfect competition in the banking industry enable banks to increase capitalization and therefore promote stability. Tables 3.21 and 3.22 show the combined influence of market power, bank controls, and macroeconomic variables on the *Z*-index, which is a stability and solvency index computed via the risk-based capital adequacy ratio and the TIER1 leverage ratio.[4]

[4] The TIER 1 capital ratio compares a bank's equity capital with its total risk-weighted assets (RWAs). These are a compilation of bank assets weighted by credit risk. TIER 1 capital refers to a bank's core capital reserves used to fund the business of bank clients.

Table 3.17 Financial Fragility using Equity-to-Assets of the Top 20

Method: Panel GMM EGLS (Cross-section random effects)

Sample: 2005Q1 2019Q4; Periods Included: 60; white cross-section (cross-section correlation) instrument weighting matrix; Swamy and Arora estimator of component variances; Cross-section weights using panel corrected standard errors (PCSE) & covariance (d.f. corrected)

Dependent Variable: Z-index using ROE (Bank Level Indicator of Financial Stability)

Regressors [a]	Expected Sign	Top 10 [a,b] Adjusted Lerner Index	Top 10 [a,b] HHI Deposits	Top 10 [a,b] HHI Loans	Next 10 [a,b] Adjusted Lerner Index	Next 10 [a,b] HHI Deposits	Next 10 [a,b] HHI Loans
C	-/+	35.85 ***	3.18 n.s.	13.28 n.s.	26.54 ***	22.15 *	-12.24 *
		(7.58)	(15.02)	(9.50)	(4.42)	(14.41)	(8.25)
Degree of Market Power	positive	-2.01 *	0.03 n.s.	0.04 ***	-0.20 *	-0.01 n.s.	0.02 **
		(1.17)	(0.03)	(0.01)	(0.12)	(0.03)	(0.012)
Degree of Market Power^2	negative	1.33 **	-1.90E-05 *	-2.01E-05 ***	0.001 n.s.	4.59E-06 n.s.	-1.45E-05 **
		(0.62)	(0.000012)	(0.000006)	(0.02)	(0.00001)	(0.000006)
Fixed Assets to Total Assets	negative	-21.51 ***	-20.95 ***	-21.11 ***	-10.44 ***	-10.37 ***	-11.28 ***
		(2.85)	(2.83)	(2.94)	(1.52)	(1.50)	(1.49)
Loans to Assets	positive	-1.83 n.s.	-1.78 n.s.	-2.36 n.s.	9.47 ***	9.80 ***	10.75 ***
		(2.88)	(2.82)	(2.82)	(2.20)	(2.19)	(2.17)
Loans to Assets^2	negative	-0.91 n.s.	-0.85 n.s.	-0.38 n.s.	-9.25 ***	-9.54 ***	-10.97 ***
		(2.79)	(2.72)	(2.71)	(2.47)	(2.46)	(2.43)
Bank Size (Ln Total Assets)	positive	0.05 n.s.	0.07 n.s.	0.15 n.s.	0.17 n.s.	0.24 *	0.43 ***
		(0.22)	(0.22)	(0.23)	(0.13)	(0.13)	(0.13)
Ln(GDP per capita)	-/+	-12.96 ***	-5.57 n.s.	-13.37 ***	-12.30 ***	-7.13 **	-1.33 n.s.
		(4.18)	(4.49)	(4.34)	(2.33)	(3.14)	(3.00)
Government/Foreign Ownership (%)	-/+	-0.014 **	-0.01 **	-0.01 **	-0.004 n.s.	-0.004 n.s.	-0.003 n.s.
		(0.01)	(0.01)	(0.01)	(0.005)	(0.01)	(0.01)
No. of Cross-Sections / Observations		10/600	10/600	10/600	10/600	10/600	10/600
AR(1)	negative	-5.65 ***	-5.87 ***	-5.81 ***	-6.32 ***	-6.27 ***	-6.22 ***
AR(2)	negative	-1.81 *	-1.65 *	-1.63 *	-1.99 **	-2.09 **	-2.15 **
Hansen's *J*-Stat	positive	4.27E-21 n.s.	4.87E-20 n.s.	4.77E-18 n.s.	1.96E-19 n.s.	9.05E-18 n.s.	3.35E-19 n.s.

Source BSP https://www.bsp.gov.ph/SitePages/Statistics/BSFinancialStatements.aspx?TabId=1 for basic data, and Author's Regression Results

[a] Highlighted cells refer to coefficients with signs different from expected and have a significant *p*-value

[b] *p*-values: ***[0.00, 0.01]; **[0.01, 0.05]; *[0.05, 0.15]; n.s. not significant or $p > 0.15$; Hansen's *J*-Stat < 1.0 has *p*-value > 0.50

Table 3.18 Financial fragility using equity-to-assets of the Top 20 UKBs (2005Q1–2019Q4)

Method: Panel GMM EGLS (Cross-section random effects)				
Sample: 2005Q1 2019Q4; Periods Included: 60; white cross-section (cross-section correlation) instrument weighting matrix; Swamy and Arora estimator of component variances; Cross-section weights using panel corrected standard errors (PCSE) & covariance (d.f. corrected)				
Dependent Variable: Equity-to-Assets (Bank Capitalization) (Bank Level Indicator of Financial Fragility)				
Regressors [(a)]	Expected Sign	Top 20[(a,b)]		
		Adjusted Lerner Index	HHI Deposits	HHI Loans
C	-/+	-0.28 ***	-0.29 n.s.	0.003 n.s.
		(0.08)	(0.29)	(0.18)
Degree of Market Power	positive	0.02 ***	2.5E-04 n.s.	-1.16E-04 n.s.
		(0.002)	(0.0005)	(0.0003)
Degree of Market Power^2	negative	0.002 ***	-1.00E-07 n.s.	8.04E-08 n.s.
		(0.0004)	(0.0000002)	(0.0000002)
Fixed Assets to Total Assets	negative	-0.20 ***	-0.19 ***	-0.18 ***
		(0.03)	(0.02)	(0.02)
Loans to Assets	negative	-0.05 n.s.	-0.04 n.s.	-0.04 n.s.
		(0.04)	(0.03)	(0.03)
Loans to Assets^2	positive	0.05 n.s.	0.04 n.s.	0.04 n.s.
		(0.04)	(0.03)	(0.03)
Bank Size (Ln Total Assets)	negative	-0.01 ***	-0.01 ***	-0.01 ***
		(0.002)	(0.003)	(0.003)
Ln(GDP per capita)	-/+	0.22 ***	0.18 ***	0.14 **
		(0.04)	(0.06)	(0.06)
Government/Foreign Ownership (%)	-/+	3.2E-05 n.s.	2.27E-05 n.s.	4.15E-05 n.s.
		(0.0001)	(0.0001)	(0.0001)
No. of Cross-Sections / Observations		20/1200	20/1200	20/1200
AR(1)	negative	-2.14 **	-2.13 **	-2.22 **
AR(2)	negative	-0.52 n.s.	-0.60 n.s.	-0.52 n.s.
Hansen's *J*-Stat	positive	6.4E-21 n.s.	9.3907E-19 n.s.	3.697E-20 n.s.

Source BSP https://www.bsp.gov.ph/SitePages/Statistics/BSFinancialStatements.aspx?TabId=1 for basic data, and Author's Regression Results

[a]Highlighted cells refer to coefficients with signs different from expected and have a significant *p*-value; Hansen's *J*-Stat < 1.0 has *p*-value > 0.50.

[b]*p*-values: ***[0.00, 0.01]; **[0.01, 0.05]; *[0.05, 0.15]; n.s. not significant or $p > 0.15$

As regards the BSP's regulatory capital ratios, all the Top 20 hold a positive *Z*-index from 2009 to 2019 and so comply with the requirements.

It covers common stock, disclosed reserves, and other assets. Along with TIER 2 capital, the size of a bank's TIER 1 capital reserves is used to measure an institution's financial strength. (https://www.bsp.gov.ph/Regulations/Issuances/2013/c781.pdf and https://www.investopedia.com/terms/t/tier1capital.asp).

Table 3.19 Financial fragility using equity-to-assets of the Top 10 and next 10 UKBs (2005Q1–2019Q4)

Method: Panel GMM EGLS (Cross-section random effects)							
Sample: 2005Q1 2019Q4; Periods Included: 60; white cross-section (cross-section correlation) instrument weighting matrix; Swamy and Arora estimator of component variances; Cross-section weights using panel corrected standard errors (PCSE) & covariance (d.f. corrected)							
Dependent Variable: Equity-to-Assets (Bank Capitalization) (Bank Level Indicator of Financial Fragility)							
		Top 10[(a,b)]			**Next 10[(a,b)]**		
Regressors[(a)]	**Expected Sign**	**Adjusted Lerner Index**	**HHI Deposits**	**HHI Loans**	**Adjusted Lerner Index**	**HHI Deposits**	**HHI Loans**
C	-/+	0.04 n.s.	0.12 n.s.	0.15 n.s.	-0.62 ***	-0.58 *	0.02 n.s.
		(0.13)	(0.29)	(0.18)	(0.10)	(0.37)	(0.22)
Degree of Market Power	positive	0.02 n.s.	0.0001 n.s.	0.0001 n.s.	0.02 ***	0.0004 n.s.	-0.0004 n.s.
		(0.03)	(0.0005)	(0.0002)	(0.002)	(0.0007)	(0.0003)
Degree of Market Power^2	negative	0.005 n.s.	-2.50E-08 n.s.	-2.43E-08 n.s.	0.002 ***	-1.55E-07 n.s.	2.44E-07 *
		(0.01)	(0.0000002)	(0.0000001)	(0.000)	(0.0000003)	(0.0000002)
Fixed Assets to Total Assets	negative	-0.21 ***	-0.24 ***	-0.22 ***	-0.17 ***	-0.17 ***	-0.16 ***
		(0.05)	(0.05)	(0.05)	(0.04)	(0.04)	(0.04)
Loans to Assets	negative	0.18 ***	0.16 **	0.17 **	-0.14 **	-0.13 **	-0.14 **
		(0.06)	(0.06)	(0.06)	(0.05)	(0.05)	(0.05)
Loans to Assets^2	positive	-0.12 **	-0.11 *	-0.11 *	0.11 **	0.09 *	0.11 *
		(0.06)	(0.06)	(0.06)	(0.05)	(0.06)	(0.06)
Bank Size (Ln Total Assets)	negative	-0.01 **	-0.01 **	-0.01 **	-0.02 ***	-0.02 ***	-0.02 ***
		(0.00)	(0.003)	(0.004)	(0.003)	(0.003)	(0.003)
Ln(GDP per capita)	-/+	0.04 n.s.	0.01 n.s.	-0.003 n.s.	0.41 ***	0.31 ***	0.25 ***
		(0.07)	(0.08)	(0.08)	(0.05)	(0.08)	(0.08)
Government/Foreign Ownership (%)	-/+	-0.0001 n.s.	0.00001 n.s.	0.00001 n.s.	-0.001 *	-0.001 **	-0.001 **
		(0.0001)	(0.0001)	(0.0001)	(0.0003)	(0.0002)	(0.0002)
No. of Cross-Sections / Observations		10/600	10/600	10/600	10/600	10/600	10/600
AR(1)		-0.23 n.s.	-0.20 n.s.	-0.28 n.s.	-2.02 **	-2.04 **	-2.07 **
AR(2)		-0.17 n.s.	-0.26 n.s.	-0.22 n.s.	-0.53 n.s.	-0.58 n.s.	-0.48 n.s.
Hansen's *J*-Stat		2.24E-20 n.s.	3.16E-17 n.s.	5.77E-17 n.s.	1.69E-22 n.s.	1.55E-19 n.s.	9.51E-20 n.s.

Source BSP https://www.bsp.gov.ph/SitePages/Statistics/BSFinancialStatements.aspx?TabId=1 for basic data, and Author's Regression Results

[a]Highlighted cells refer to coefficients with signs different from expected and have a significant p-value

[b]p-values: ***[0.00, 0.01]; **[0.01, 0.05]; *[0.05, 0.15]; n.s. not significant or $p > 0.15$; Hansen's J-Stat < 1.0 has p-value > 0.50

Table 3.20 Financial fragility using the NPL ratio of the Top 20 UKBs (2005Q1–2019Q4)

Method: Panel GMM EGLS (Cross-section random effects)				
Sample: 2005Q1 2019Q4; Periods Included: 60; white cross-section (cross-section correlation) instrument weighting matrix; Swamy and Arora estimator of component variances; Cross-section weights using panel corrected standard errors (PCSE) & covariance (d.f. corrected)				
Dependent Variable: Non-Performing Loans Ratio (Bank Level Indicator of Financial Fragility)				
Regressors [(a)]	Expected Sign	Top 20[(a,b)]		
		Adjusted Lerner Index	HHI Deposits	HHI Loans
C	positive	39.62 ***	58.95 **	7.70 n.s.
		(9.62)	(27.86)	(16.56)
Degree of Market Power	positive	0.10 n.s.	-0.11 **	-0.03 n.s.
		(0.25)	(0.05)	(0.023)
Degree of Market Power^2	negative	0.02 n.s.	4.96E-05 **	9.91E-06 n.s.
		(0.04)	(0.00002)	(0.00001)
Fixed Assets to Total Assets	positive	8.42 n.s.	7.31 n.s.	3.14 n.s.
		(6.40)	(6.35)	(6.43)
Loans to Assets	negative	-46.19 ***	-44.85 ***	-45.62 ***
		(6.19)	(6.06)	(5.96)
Loans to Assets^2	positive	37.74 ***	36.33 ***	36.19 ***
		(6.00)	(5.87)	(5.78)
Bank Size (Ln Total Assets)	negative	-0.17 n.s.	-0.10 n.s.	0.05 n.s.
		(0.22)	(0.23)	(0.23)
Ln(GDP per capita)	-/+	-9.23 **	9.40 n.s.	13.07 **
		(4.80)	(6.36)	(6.09)
Government/Foreign Ownership	-/+	-0.0101 *	-0.01 n.s.	-0.011 *
		(0.006)	(0.006)	(0.006)
No. of Cross-Sections / Observations		20/1200	20/1200	20/1200
AR(1)	negative	-15.38 ***	-15.41 ***	-15.37 ***
AR(2)	negative	6.39 ***	6.49 ***	6.51 ***
Hansen's *J*-Stat	positive	1.95E-19 n.s.	3.28E-12 n.s.	1.15E-17 n.s.

Source BSP https://www.bsp.gov.ph/SitePages/Statistics/BSFinancialStatements.aspx?TabId=1 for basic data and the author's regression results

[a]Highlighted cells refer to coefficients with signs different from expected and have a significant *p*-value; Hansen's *J*-Stat < 1.0 has *p*-value > 0.50

[b]*p*-values: ***[0.00, 0.01]; **[0.01, 0.05]; *[0.05, 0.15]; n.s. not significant or *p* > 0.15

Only UCPB had difficulty complying with the RCAR and TIER1 leverage ratios from 2007 to 2008.

The results of the ZCAR and ZTIER1 regressions show that the Top 10 banks wield sufficient market power to sustain the required levels for risk-based capital adequacy ratio (RCAR). In fact, from the first quarter of 2005 to the fourth quarter of 2019, all of the Top 20 banks exceeded the required average RCAR of 12.5%, or 16.33% for the Top 20 banks, 15.17% for the Top 10, and 17.5% for the Next 10. All the Top 20 banks held a TIER1 leverage ratio above 10.5%, allowing a 2% countercyclical buffer. The TIER1 leverage ratios for the Top 20, Top 10, and Next 10 are 14.57%, 12.92%, and 16.23%, respectively. This means all the Top 20 banks were sufficiently cushioned against severe financial crises.

The significant effects of bank size to Z_{RCAR} and Z_{TIER1} and of market power squared reflect the Top 20 banks' efforts to reach more markets. This means that all the banks in the sample maximized their market power through higher markups and greater market share. The Next 10 banks appear to be more deeply engaged in expanding their loans and deposits market, as both their loans-to-assets ratio and loans-to-assets ratio squared were significant. Note that financial stability, measured through return-on-assets, return-on-equity, risk-based capital adequacy ratio, or TIER1 leverage ratio, presents an inverted U relationship with market structure and loans-to-assets. Market expansion and growing profit margins expose banks to more risks because these increase the volatility of returns and the difference of the actual RCAR and TIER1 leverage ratios of the bank with the regulated levels.

The final regression aims to plot the behavior of the Top 10 and Next 10 banks with regard to achieving financial stability. The regressions on Z_{RCAR} and Z_{TIER1} using the explanatory variables for market structure and bank controls reflect their competitive behavior and internal operations. The final regressions on RCAR and TIER1 will combine the market conduct and internal operations of the banks from the perspectives of buffer, risk-shifting, and profit-margin effects, and so determine which effect significantly explains compliance with the BSP provision on bank capitalization. The regressions for equity-to-assets, NPL ratios, and ZROE using the variables competition-stability and competition-fragility exogenous variables can explain what a bank is most likely to do to achieve financial stability. Results of the regression in Tables 3.23 and 3.24 reflect a bank's compliance with the regulations.

Table 3.21 Financial fragility using non-performing loans ratio of the Top 10 and next 10 UKBs (2005Q1–2019Q4)

Method: Panel GMM EGLS (Cross-section random effects)

Sample: 2005Q1 2019Q4; Periods Included: 60; white cross-section (cross-section correlation) instrument weighting matrix; Swamy and Arora estimator of component variances; Cross-section weights using panel corrected standard errors (PCSE) & covariance (d.f. corrected)

Dependent Variable: Non-Performing Loans Ratio (Bank Level Indicator of Financial Fragility)

Regressors [a]	Expected Sign	Top 10 [a,b] Adjusted Lerner Index	Top 10 [a,b] HHI Deposits	Top 10 [a,b] HHI Loans	Next 10 [a,b] Adjusted Lerner Index	Next 10 [a,b] HHI Deposits	Next 10 [a,b] HHI Loans
C	-/+	4.82 n.s.	-10.67 n.s.	-20.59 n.s.	62.04 ***	129.00 ***	41.23 *
		(10.26)	(33.04)	(19.78)	(12.30)	(44.15)	(26.10)
Degree of Market Power	positive	0.61 n.s.	-0.03 n.s.	-0.03 n.s.	0.16 n.s.	-0.20 **	-0.04 n.s.
		(2.48)	(0.05)	(0.03)	(0.28)	(0.08)	(0.037)
Degree of Market Power^2	negative	-2.14 *	9.29E-06 n.s.	7.58E-06 n.s.	0.02 n.s.	9.31E-05 **	1.49E-05 n.s.
		(1.32)	(0.00003)	(0.00001)	(0.04)	(0.00004)	(0.00002)
Fixed Assets to Total Assets	negative	14.77 **	9.05 n.s.	-1.24 n.s.	10.20 ***	7.64 n.s.	5.94 n.s.
		(5.97)	(8.32)	(8.53)	(8.26)	(8.34)	(8.44)
Loans to Assets	negative	-44.24 ***	-40.14 ***	-42.60 ***	-52.35 ***	-49.82 ***	-50.35 ***
		(6.63)	(6.58)	(6.56)	(8.36)	(8.14)	(8.03)
Loans to Assets^2	positive	32.33 ***	27.71 ***	28.35 ***	47.83 ***	44.47 ***	44.35 ***
		(6.40)	(6.38)	(6.34)	(8.40)	(8.12)	(8.02)
Bank Size (Ln Total Assets)	negative	-0.39 **	0.01 n.s.	0.36 n.s.	-0.25 n.s.	-0.05 n.s.	0.09 n.s.
		(0.16)	(0.29)	(0.30)	(0.34)	(0.37)	(0.38)
Ln(GDP per capita)	-/+	7.39 *	20.89 **	23.39 ***	-17.89 ***	-1.28 n.s.	0.84 **
		(4.56)	(8.16)	(7.51)	(6.24)	(9.37)	(9.11)
Government/Foreign Ownership (%)	-/+	-0.008 ***	-0.008 *	-0.01 **	-0.03 ***	-0.03 *	-0.03 *
		(0.002)	(0.004)	(0.004)	(0.007)	(0.02)	(0.02)
No. of Cross-Sections / Observations		10/600	10/600	10/600	10/600	10/600	10/600
AR(1)		-12.25 ***	-12.18 ***	-12.41 ***	-9.89 ***	-10.03 ***	-9.69 ***
AR(2)		4.86 ***	4.83 ***	5.42 ***	3.97 ***	4.04 ***	3.77 ***
Hansen's *J*-Stat		6.67E-14 n.s.	1.35E-13 n.s.	4.07E-15 n.s.	1.34E-16 n.s.	4.29E-16 n.s.	2.51E-20 n.s.

Source BSP https://www.bsp.gov.ph/SitePages/Statistics/BSFinancialStatements.aspx?TabId=1) for basic data, and Author's Regression Results

[a] Highlighted cells refer to coefficients with signs different from expected and have a significant *p*-value

[b] *p*-values: ***[0.00, 0.01]; **[0.01, 0.05]; *[0.05, 0.15]; n.s. not significant or $p > 0.15$; Hansen's *J*-Stat < 1.0 has *p*-value > 0.50

Table 3.22 Financial stability using Z_{RCAR} of the Top 10 and next 10 UKBs (2007Q3–2019Q4)

Method: Panel GMM EGLS (Cross-section random effects)

Sample: 2007Q3 2019Q4; Periods Included: 50; white cross-section (cross-section correlation) instrument weighting matrix; Swamy and Arora estimator of component variances; Cross-section weights using panel corrected standard errors (PCSE) & covariance (d.f. corrected)

Dependent Variable: Z-index using Risk-Based Capital Adequacy Ratio (Z-RCAR) (Bank Level Indicator of Financial Stability)

Regressors [1]	Expected Sign	Top 10 [1,2]			Next 10 [1,2]		
		Adjusted Lerner Index	HHI Deposits	HHI Loans	Adjusted Lerner	HHI Deposits	HHI Loans
C	-/+	-8.96 n.s.	-52.41 n.s.	-31.89 **	-9.05 *	-96.78 ***	-8.33 n.s.
		(8.62)	(37.84)	(15.85)	(5.72)	(24.37)	(10.91)
Degree of Market Power	positive	-0.97 n.s.	0.11 *	0.07 **	0.69 ***	0.19 ***	0.02 n.s.
		(0.74)	(0.06)	(0.029)	(0.16)	(0.05)	(0.017)
Degree of Market Power^2	negative	0.80 *	-4.95E-05 *	-2.92E-05 **	0.21 **	-8.98E-05 ***	-7.60E-06 n.s.
		(0.53)	(0.00003)	(0.00001)	(0.09)	(0.00002)	(0.000008)
Fixed Assets to Total Assets	negative	-3.98 n.s.	-4.17 n.s.	-1.38 n.s.	-28.94 ***	-28.68 ***	-28.38 ***
		(4.06)	(3.62)	(3.08)	(3.84)	(4.00)	(4.06)
Loans to Assets	negative	-4.18 n.s.	-3.45 n.s.	-2.95 n.s.	-8.09 ***	-7.33 ***	-7.12 ***
		(3.64)	(3.84)	(3.77)	(2.10)	(2.14)	(2.19)
Loans to Assets^2	positive	2.52 n.s.	2.20 n.s.	2.13 n.s.	6.38 **	5.98 **	5.67 **
		(2.91)	(3.05)	(3.07)	(2.44)	(2.42)	(2.49)
Bank Size (Ln Total Assets)	negative	-0.43 ***	-0.55 ***	-0.55 ***	-0.70 ***	-0.68 ***	-0.68 ***
		(0.14)	(0.13)	(0.12)	(0.18)	(0.15)	(0.16)
Ln(GDP per capita)	-/+	7.45 *	2.64 n.s.	1.74 n.s.	8.85 ***	5.22 n.s.	3.92 n.s.
		(4.16)	(6.73)	(5.34)	(2.92)	(3.70)	(3.35)
Government/Foreign Ownership (%)	-/+	-0.001 n.s.	-0.002 n.s.	-0.001 n.s.	-0.001 n.s.	-0.003 n.s.	-0.003 n.s.
		(0.002)	(0.002)	(0.002)	(0.010)	(0.00)	(0.00)
No. of Cross-Sections / Observations		10/500	10/500	10/500	10/499	10/499	10/499
AR(1)	negative	-6.49 ***	-6.58 ***	-6.37 ***	-3.39 ***	-3.65 ***	-3.26 ***
AR(2)	negative	0.22 n.s.	0.18 n.s.	0.57 n.s.	-3.79 ***	-3.43 ***	-3.55 ***
Hansen's *J*-Stat	positive	2.24E-17 n.s.	1.43E-10 n.s.	3.77E-13 n.s.	1.17E-21 n.s.	1.22E-12 n.s.	1.20E-17 n.s.

Notes:
1. Highlighted cells refer to coefficients with signs different from expected and have a significant p-value
2. p-values: *** [0.00, 0.01]; ** (0.01, 0.05]; *: (0.05, 0.15]; n.s. not significant or $p > 0.15$; Hansen's *J*-Stat < 1.0 has p-value > 0.50.

Source BSP https://www.bsp.gov.ph/SitePages/Statistics/BSFinancialStatements.aspx?TabId=1 for basic data and the author's regression results

Table 3.23 Financial stability using Z_{TIER1} of the Top 10 and next 10 UKBs (2007Q3–2019Q4)

Method: Panel GMM EGLS (Cross-section random effects)

Sample: 2007Q3 2019Q4; Periods Included: 50; white cross-section (cross-section correlation) instrument weighting matrix; Swamy and Arora estimator of component variances; Cross-section weights using panel corrected standard errors (PCSE) & covariance (d.f. corrected)

Dependent Variable: Z-index using TIER 1 (ZTIER1) (Bank Level Indicator of Financial Stability)

Regressors [(a)]	Expected Sign	Top 10 [(a,b)] Adjusted Lerner Index	Top 10 HHI Deposits	Top 10 HHI Loans	Next 10 [(a,b)] Adjusted Lerner Index	Next 10 HHI Deposits	Next 10 HHI Loans
C	-/+	-8.55 n.s.	-105.23 ***	-43.73 ***	-8.93 *	-87.27 ***	-2.56 n.s.
		(9.08)	(26.44)	(12.10)	(5.80)	(24.81)	(11.08)
Degree of Market Power	positive	-1.19 n.s.	0.18 ***	0.0620 ***	0.65 ***	0.1623 ***	0.0031 n.s.
		(1.33)	(0.05)	(0.02)	(0.17)	(0.047)	(0.017)
Degree of Market Power^2	negative	0.797 n.s.	-8.79E-05 ***	-2.98E-05 ***	0.206 **	-7.88E-05 ***	-9.61E-07 n.s.
		(0.74)	(0.00002)	(0.000008)	(0.087)	(0.00002)	(0.000008)
Fixed Assets to Total Assets	negative	-11.62 **	-8.28 *	-11.99 **	-23.75 ***	-23.24 ***	-23.90 ***
		(5.38)	(4.89)	(5.27)	(4.03)	(4.10)	(4.16)
Loans to Assets	negative	-4.52 n.s.	-3.07 n.s.	-4.95 n.s.	-9.57 ***	-8.46 ***	-8.40 ***
		(3.69)	(3.51)	(3.72)	(2.11)	(2.18)	(2.20)
Loans to Assets^2	positive	2.89 n.s.	2.10 n.s.	3.15 n.s.	7.77 ***	6.81 **	6.55 **
		(3.46)	(3.27)	(3.52)	(2.44)	(2.45)	(2.50)
Bank Size (Ln Total Assets)	negative	-0.43 *	-0.29 n.s.	-0.11 n.s.	-0.63 ***	-0.51 ***	-0.52 ***
		(0.29)	(0.25)	(0.26)	(0.18)	(0.16)	(0.16)
Ln(GDP per capita)	-/+	7.56 *	9.24 *	7.06 *	8.60 ***	5.99 *	4.52 n.s.
		(5.11)	(5.17)	(4.90)	(2.96)	(3.77)	(3.41)
Government/Foreign Ownership (%)	-/+	0.013 **	0.007 *	0.005 n.s.	0.004 n.s.	0.002 n.s.	0.002 n.s.
		(0.006)	(0.005)	(0.0048)	(0.009)	(0.004)	(0.004)
No. of Cross-Sections / Observations		10/500	10/500	10/500	10/499	10/499	10/499
AR(1)	negative	-6.37 ***	-6.40 ***	-6.43 ***	-4.49 ***	-4.73 ***	-4.36 ***
AR(2)	negative	0.43 n.s.	0.50 n.s.	0.40 n.s.	-2.75 *	-2.39 **	-2.38 **
Hansen's J-Stat	positive	2.17E-20 n.s.	3.16E-17 n.s.	8.51E-17 n.s.	2.28E-22 n.s.	2.49E-12 n.s.	9.51E-20 n.s.

Source BSP https://www.bsp.gov.ph/SitePages/Statistics/BSFinancialStatements.aspx?TabId=1 for basic data, and Author's Regression Results

[a]Highlighted cells refer to coefficients with signs different from expected and have a significant p-value

[b]p-values: ***[0.00, 0.01]; **[0.01, 0.05]; *[0.05, 0.15]; n.s. not significant or $p > 0.15$; Hansen's J-Stat < 1.0 has p-value > 0.50

Table 3.24 Buffer, risk-shifting, and profit-margin effects on the risk-based capital adequacy ratio of the Top 10 and next 10 UKBs (2007Q3–2019Q4)

Method: Panel GMM EGLS (Cross-section random effects)

Sample: 2007Q3 2019Q4; Periods Included: 50; white cross-section (cross-section correlation) instrument weighting matrix; Swamy and Arora estimator of component variances; Cross-section weights using panel corrected standard errors (PCSE) & covariance (d.f. corrected)

Dependent Variable: TIER 1 (BSP Regulated Ratio)

Regressors [(a)]	Expected Sign	Top 10 [(a,b)] Adjusted Lerner Index	Top 10 HHI Deposits	Top 10 HHI Loans	Next 10 [(a,b)] Adjusted Lerner Index	Next 10 HHI Deposits	Next 10 HHI Loans
C	-/+	-50.19 ***	-51.79 **	-51.50 **	-5.70 n.s.	1.62 n.s.	-37.59 *
		(17.41)	(19.91)	(18.56)	(25.63)	(21.68)	(20.48)
Equity-to-Assets	negative	6.37 ***	5.64 **	5.29 **	-2.56 ***	-7.32 ***	-3.41 ***
forecasted		(2.02)	(2.24)	(1.98)	(0.52)	(0.64)	(0.63)
Equity-to-Assets^2	positive	-0.24 ***	-2.16E-01 **	-2.02E-01 **	0.20 ***	4.20E-01 ***	2.24E-01 ***
forecasted		(0.08)	(0.10)	(0.09)	(0.03)	(0.03)	(0.03)
Non-Performing Loans Ratio	positive	0.12 n.s.	0.42 n.s.	0.39 n.s	-0.17 n.s.	-0.14 n.s.	0.01 n.s.
forecasted		(0.32)	(0.36)	(0.28)	(0.35)	(0.27)	(0.32)
Non-Performing Loans Ratio^2	negative	0.03 n.s.	-0.004 n.s.	0.003 n.s	0.03 *	0.04 **	0.02 n.s.
forecasted		(0.04)	(0.05)	(0.04)	(0.02)	(0.02)	(0.02)
Z-Index ROE (Z_{ROE})	-/+	-0.93 n.s.	-0.74 n.s.	-0.25 n.s	2.14 n.s.	10.20 ***	-0.66 n.s.
forecasted		(0.90)	(0.87)	(0.84)	(1.55)	(0.94)	(1.11)
Z-index ROE (Z_{ROE}^2)	-/+	0.20 *	0.16 *	0.11 n.s	-0.73 *	-3.69 ***	0.29 n.s.
forecasted		(0.12)	(0.11)	(0.10)	(0.48)	(0.29)	(0.34)
Log (Population)	positive	4.78 **	6.07 **	6.24 **	5.03 n.s.	7.41 *	13.13 ***
		(2.30)	(2.37)	(2.23)	(5.32)	(4.85)	(4.51)
No. of Cross-Sections / Observations		10/500	10/500	10/500	10/499	10/499	10/499
AR(1)	negative	-5.79 ***	-5.94 ***	-5.96 ***	-4.71 ***	-4.52 ***	-4.56 ***
AR(2)	negative	0.88 n.s.	0.83 n.s.	0.70 n.s	-0.68 n.s.	-0.65 n.s.	-0.72 n.s.
Hansen's *J*-Stat	positive	4.01E-15 n.s.	1.17E-16 n.s.	1.88E-15 n.s	1.01E-21 n.s.	2.99E-14 n.s.	1.71E-20 n.s.

Source BSP https://www.bsp.gov.ph/SitePages/Statistics/BSFinancialStatements.aspx?TabId=1 for basic data, and the author's regression results

[a]Highlighted cells refer to coefficients with signs different from expected and have a significant *p*-value

[b]*p*-values: ***[0.00, 0.01]; **[0.01, 0.05]; *[0.05, 0.15]; n.s. not significant or $p > 0.15$; Hansen's *J*-Stat < 1.0 has *p*-value > 0.50

The intercepts on the regression for the Top 10 banks are all significant and negative. From the previous regressions using a cross-section random effects model on these variables, the intercepts capture the effect of endogenous sunk costs (Berger et al. 2009). The intercepts consistently show how endogenous sunk costs inversely affect the financial stability of dominant banks (see Tables 3.23 and 3.24). From the results of the adjusted Lerner Index in the above-mentioned tables, one can appreciate how the Top 10 banks took advantage of the intensified market concentration by charging higher loan rates–behavior expected of the dominant banks. The Top 10 improved their financial stability by pegging their NPL ratio at an average of 2.30%. Thus, one can surmise that the Top 10 used capital financing to improve their capital buffer. Results from the regressions for RCAR and TIER1 showed that this strategy reduced the risk exposure of the Top 10 banks.

The buffer effect, as captured by the forecasted value of equity-to-assets, is moderate-to-very significant in all the regressions for the Top 10 and Next 10 banks and for all the market power indicators. Results of said regressions showed that increased profit margins helped improve the capital base. This implies that the Top 10 banks focused on growing capital stock to attain stability in the face of growing market concentration. Infusing fresh capital or sourcing equity through retained earnings became the primary goal of the Top 10 Philippine UKBs. Table 3.24 shows that the capitalization levels of the Top 10 and Next 10 UKBs from 2008Q4 to 2022Q3 were within the stable levels that the forecasting model predicted (Table 3.25). This is also true for the risk-adjusted capital adequacy ratio and the TIER1 capital adequacy ratio. Their asset composition was also maintained at a level that will result to high profit margins. However, the Top 10 and Next 10 banks had to sacrifice their solvency ratios, indicated by the Z-index ROE during the pandemic. The extension of the loan payments period to 60 days exposed them to credit risksthat lowered their solvency ratios.

On the other hand, to gain a better foothold in the struggle for greater market share, the Next 10 banks prioritized the buffer effect. Note that the average risk-based capital ratio and TIER1 Leverage ratio for the Next 10 banks are higher than those of the Top 10 banks. The capacity of the Next 10 to improve their capital base from the fourth quarter of 2008 to the fourth quarter of 2019 outweighed the risk-shifting and profit-margin effects. The results of the regression coefficients for risk-shifting and profit-margin effects show that the Top 10 banks

Table 3.25 Inflection Points Estimated from the GMM Regressions (2005Q1–2022Q3)

Ranges to Compare with the Standard Levels of the Profit-Margin, Buffer and Risk-Shifting Effects and Stability Indicators by Period												
Type of UKBs and Time Periods[5]	Ranges[4] and Indicators											
	Z-Index for Return-on-Equity (ZROE) Profit-Margin Effect		Equity-to-Assets (EA) Buffer Effect		Non-Performing Loans Ratio (NPLR) Risk-Shifting Effect		Loans-to-Assets Ratio (LA) Profit-Margin Indicator		Risk-Based Capital Adequacy Ratio (CAR) Stability Indicator		TIER1 Capital Adequacy Ratio (TIER1) Stability Indicator	
Very Stable (VS)	[3.2, 4.2]		[0.12, 0.13]		< 5%		[0.43, 0.67]		> 12.5		> 10.5	
Stable (S)	[2.2, 3.2)		[0.11, 0.12)									
Moderately Stable (MS)	< 2.2		< 0.11		> 5%		< 0.43 or > 0.67		< 12.5		< 10.5	
Top 20 (S)	ZROET20		EAT20		NPLRT20		LAT20		CART20		TIERIT20	
	Range	Mean[1]	Range	Mean[3]	Range	Mean[2]	Range	Mean[2]	Range	Mean[2]	Range	Mean[2]
Pandemic	[*1.25*, 2.30]	*2.07*	[0.12, 0.13]	0.12	[2.89, 4.60]	4.14	[0.49, 0.54]	0.504	[15.93, 19.0]	17.92	[14.65, 17.86]	16.76
Competition	[2.24, 2.63]	2.51	[0.11, 0.12]	0.11	[2.18, 3.09]	2.92	[0.47, 0.49]	0.475	[15.13, 16.75]	16.38	[13.0, 14.88]	14.49
Top 10 (VS)	ZROET10		EAT10		NPLRT10		LAT10		CART10		TIERIT10	
	Range	Mean[1]	Range	Mean[3]	Range	Mean[2]	Range	Mean[2]	Range	Mean[3]	Range	Mean[2]
Pandemic	[*2.14*, 3.22]	2.90	[0.117, 0.134]	0.123	[2.78, 3.90]	3.49	[0.52, 0.58]	0.54	[14.83, 15.91]	15.76	[13.90, 15.13]	14.68
Competition	[3.16, 3.77]	3.63	[0.118, 0.125]	0.120	[1.75, 2.46]	2.30	[0.47, 0.50]	0.49	[14.74, 15.54]	15.26	[12.38, 13.04]	12.82
Top 5 (VS)	ZROET5		EAT5		NPLRT5		LAT5		CART5		TIERIT5	
	Range	Mean[1]	Range	Mean[2]	Range	Mean[2]	Range	Mean[2]	Range	Mean[2]	Range	Mean[2]
Pandemic	[2.07, 3.77]	3.02	[0.11, 0.13]	0.122	[1.81, 4.11]	3.37	[0.50, 0.61]	0.54	[14.43, 16.27]	15.66	[13.53, 15.37]	14.77
Competition	[3.32, 4.24]	4.00	[0.11, 0.12]	0.113	[1.56, 2.26]	2.08	[0.48, 0.52]	0.51	[13.53, 14.71]	14.39	[11.74, 12.36]	12.12
Next 5 (VS)	ZROEN5		EAN5		NPLRN5		LAN5		CARN5		TIERIN5	
	Range	Mean[3]	Range	Mean[3]	Range	Mean[2]	Range	Mean[2]	Range	Mean[3]	Range	Mean[2]
Pandemic	[*2.01*, 3.23]	2.79	[0.11, 0.14]	0.124	[3.21, 4.15]	3.61	[0.51, 0.58]	0.54	[14.80, 16.52]	15.86	[13.77, 15.27]	14.59
Competition	[2.88, 3.40]	3.25	[0.125, 0.132]	0.128	[1.88, 2.77]	2.52	[0.45, 0.483]	0.47	[15.69, 16.56]	16.12	[12.92, 13.87]	13.52
Next 10 (MS)	ZROEN10		EAN10		NPLRN10		LAN10		CARN10		TIERIN10	
	Range	Mean[3]	Range	Mean[3]	Range	Mean[2]	Range	Mean[3]	Range	Mean[2]	Range	Mean[3]
Pandemic	[*0.73*, *1.54*]	*1.24*	[*0.103*, 0.125]	0.110	[2.80, *5.64*]	4.81	[0.44, 0.53]	0.47	[16.87, 22.23]	20.10	[15.195, 21.02]	18.90
Competition	[*0.98*, *1.52*]	*1.40*	[*0.099*, 0.116]	*0.103*	[2.60, 3.83]	3.54	[0.46, 0.49]	0.46	[15.50, 18.17]	17.49	[13.87, 16.90]	16.17
REMARKS									All means are significantly different from 12.5		All means are significantly different from 10.5	
Notes:	1. Mean[1] refers to the pandemic period mean significantly less than the competition period mean, or $\mu^1 < \mu^2$; Mean[2] refers to $\mu^1 > \mu^2$; Mean[3] refers to $\mu^1 = \mu^2$ 2. Range[4] refers to the combined 95% confidence interval of the mean and the 95% confidence interval for the median 3. Period[5] refers to the pandemic period covering 2020Q1 to 2022Q3, and the competition (mergers started) period covering 2008Q4 to 2019Q4 4. *Italicized numbers* refer to values which are below the levels of bank capitalization and ZROE for financially stable to very stable banks												

Source BSP https://www.bsp.gov.ph/SitePages/Statistics/BSFinancialStatements.aspx?TabId=1for basic data, and the author's regression results primarily relied on lending to improve their equity base. As they charge higher markups, they increase return-on-equity and effectively monitor borrowers, and so reduce the probability of default. The Top 10 banks turned out sufficiently capitalized, as their buffer effect outweighed the margin and risk-shifting effects.

As the Philippine UKBs approached greater market concentration, they sustained their profit margins. The Next 10 banks remained exposed to higher risks. The regression points out that even if their buffer effect outweighed their profit or margin effect, moderate NPL ratios expose them to risk shifting.

In summary, the two previous objectives showed that the market power of dominant banks contributed to the resiliency of the Philippine UKB industry. Yet, banks should still aim at acquiring sufficient capital as a buffer from systemic risk. They can do so through increased capitalization via a higher equity-to-assets ratio and compliance with the BSP-regulated RCAR and TIER1 ratios. As Table 3.24 illustrates, the buffer effect for both the Top 10 and Next 10 banks outweighs the profit or margin effect and the risk-shifting effects.

Dacanay (2017) used data from the first quarter of 2005 to the third quarter of 2016 to show that the Top 20 UKBs were undercapitalized and at high risk. The above results show that from 2017 to 2019, the Top 20 banks aggressively improved their capitalization, strengthening the buffer effect and outweighing the profit and the risk-shifting effects. From 2017 to 2019, interest and inflation rates were kept low to abate the onset of NPLs.

The COVID-19 pandemic challenged the stability of banks. Data in Table 3.24 show that the Top 10 banks managed to strengthen the buffer effect, maintain profit margins, and keep their NPL ratios at 4%. As for the Next 10, profit margins suffered, NPL ratios skyrocketed, and the solvency ratio ZROE declined. To maintain sufficient capitalization, some of these banks resorted to debt financing.

Finally, the inflection points of the non-linear relationship between bank capitalization and financial stability serve to determine which banks were on the road to stability. Table 3.25 contains the inflection points drawn from the regressions with the adjusted Lerner Index ZROE and the bank capitalization ratio. These inflection points refer to an upsurge of values as seen in the scatterplots that use the Kernel Fit (Epanechnikov) Local Regression of the GMM estimated Equity-to-Assets and ZROE with corresponding market power regressors and bank control variables.

For example, on the average, when the estimated bank capitalization ratio is plotted against the ZROE, the Kernel Fit Local Regression curve starts to rise when the ZROE ranges from [2.2422, 3.1674] and the bank capitalization ratio ranges from [11.09%, 13.30%]. The regression derived from the scatterplot of the estimated bank capitalization ratio and estimated ZROE peak when the ZROE reaches 3.1674, with a corresponding bank capitalization ratio of 13.3%. When plotting these values with the loans-to-assets ratio at the abscissa, the loans-to-assets ratio ranges from [43.50%, 67.41%]. Beyond a loans-to-assets ratio of 52%, the bank capitalization ratio starts to fall. Banks can still increase their loans-to-assets ratio up to 67.41% and achieve a ZROE up to 2.24. Beyond a loans-to-assets ratio of 67.41%, bank capitalization, that is, financial stability, rapidly declines. Banks can achieve a wide combination of ratios, from 2.2 to 4.2, or from stable to very stable ZROE, with varying levels of equity-to-assets and net income levels, and still achieve a capitalization ratio of 11.09–13.3% (see Fig. 3.16).

One may deduce financial stability using a Cartesian plane with the estimated equity-to-assets ratio as ordinate and the estimated ZROE as abscissa (see Figs. 3.14 and 3.15). The coordinates coincide at the inflection point of the scatterplot using a Kernel Fit regression of the estimated ZROE and estimated Equity-to-Assets starts that rise until it reaches a maximum of ZROE equal to 3.2 and equity-to-assets ratio of 0.13. This coordinate represents the minimum values for a bank to be considered very financially stable. When ZROE is equal to 2.2 with equity-to-assets ratio of 0.11, banks are considered sufficiently stable. Coordinates below this level signify less stability. These sets of coordinates shall be used to determine if a bank is very stable, stable, or less stable.

The results in Fig. 3.14 show that only BPI, China Bank, RCBC, Asia United Bank, BDO, Bank of Commerce, Phil Trust, and Metrobank prioritized profit margins and equity buffers to achieve financial stability (2008Q4–2019Q4). These banks are labeled "very stable," based on the criteria garnered from the regression results, while PNB, Union Bank, Security Bank, and East West Bank have reached a good level of bank capitalization, or better than 0.11 (2008–2019), and are improving their profit margins. The offshore banks have improved their bank capitalization levels significantly, from 2016 to 2019.

The individual scatterplots for bank capitalization and the Adjusted Lerner Index of the Top 20 banks denote that most of the Top 10 banks have increased capitalization since 2014, as reflected by the smooth,

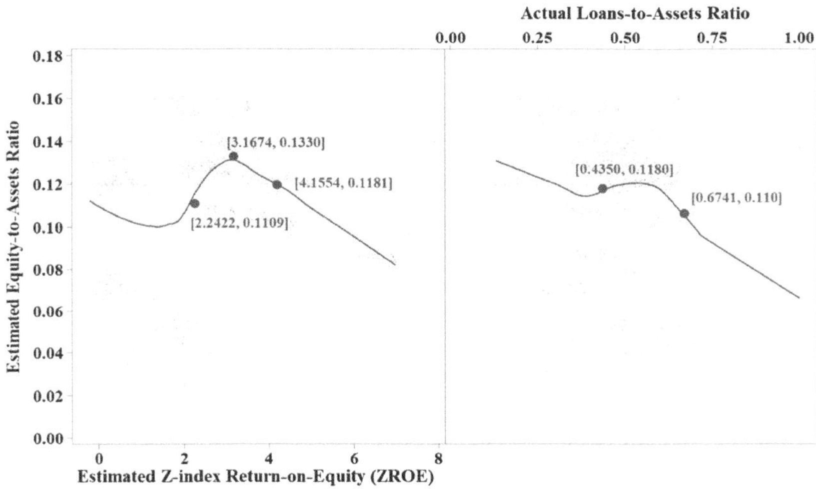

Fig. 3.14 Estimated Equity-to-Assets and Estimated Z_{ROE} with Actual Loans-to-Assets Ratio (2008 Q4 to 2019 Q4) (*Source* BSP for basic data, and Author's estimates)

slightly rising trend across the Top 20 UKBs (see Fig. 3.15). The individual bank cross-sections highlight the positive relationship of the market power indicator, the adjusted Lerner Index, with bank capitalization with almost all the Top 10 banks, except Citibank. This means that charging a higher markup for loan rates increases the likelihood of improved capitalization. In addition, one can determine if the exercise of market power among the Top 10 banks drives efficiency, that is, lowers the share of NPLs to total loans.

The upward trend for capitalization as market power increases can be observed among some of the Next 10 banks. For example, the capitalization of East West and Philippine Trust Bank are at par with the Top 10 banks; however, their financial stability ratio is below the average of the Top 10. Thus, these two banks prioritize improving their capital buffer. Asia United Bank, East West, and Security Bank have been targeting a high equity-to-assets ratio of 10–20% from the first quarter of 2005 to the fourth quarter of 2019. These three banks make for a case study for increasing bank capitalization without sacrificing profits, as they have maintained a Z_{ROE} that averaged 2.5.

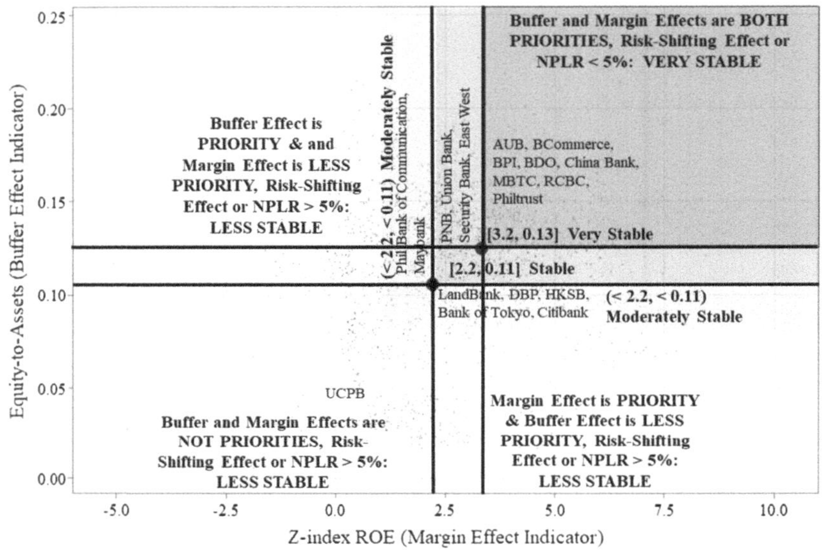

Fig. 3.15 Z_{ROE} and Bank Capitalization Coordinates for the Top 20 Banks (*Source* BSP for basic data, and the author's framework)

In summary, the market power exercised by six of the Top 10 banks and two of the Next 10 banks allowed them to charge higher markups, attain higher profits, and acquire sufficient capitalization. They are constantly improving their profit margins while prioritizing their buffers or capital cushion, which makes them very financially stable. Three of the Top 10 banks and one of the Next 10 banks are likewise stable; two of the Top 10 and five of the Next 10 banks, moderately stable; and one, UCPB, turned out fragile and most vulnerable to bank distress and insolvency. Table 3.25 summarizes the aforementioned findings (Table 3.26).

Summary, Conclusion, and Recommendations

This study uses the conceptual and theoretical model of Schliephake (2016) who formulated a market structure approach to support a binding regulatory capital environment that fosters financial stability. Schliephake built upon the seminal model of Martinez-Miera (2009), Martinez-Miera and Repulo (2010) which established a non-linear U-shape relationship

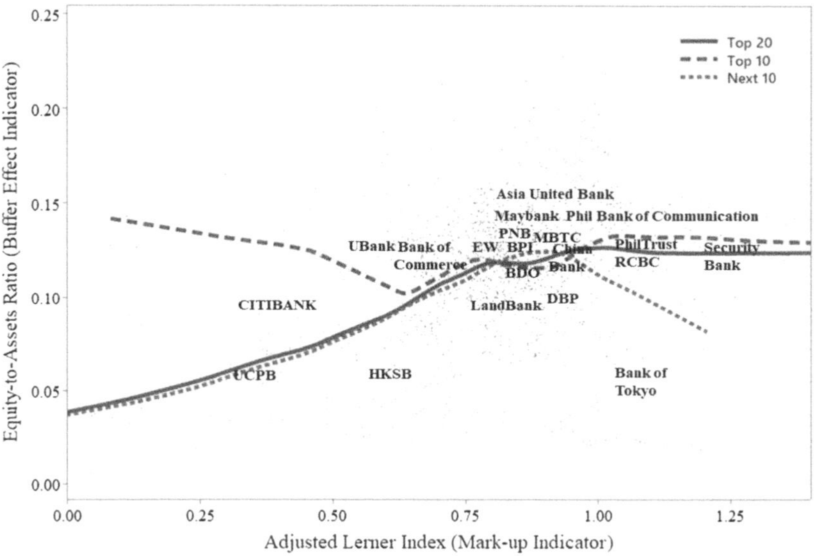

Fig. 3.16 Equity-to-Assets Ratio and Adjusted Lerner Index of the Top 20 UKBs (2005Q1 to 2019Q4) (*Source* BSP for basic data and the author's regression results)

between competition and default risk and, consequently, produced an inverted U-shaped relationship between competition and resilience to insolvency. The empirical model from Berger et al. (2009) verified the dual existence of competition-stability and competition-fragility in an imperfectly competitive banking industry.

Further, this study provided empirical proof of the existence of an imperfectly competitive banking industry that is experiencing a buildup in market concentration. Dominant and fringe banks exercised their market power at a time when market concentration peaked, that is, from the fourth quarter of 2008 to the fourth quarter of 2019. They did so in concurrence, charging higher markups on loans, obtaining higher profits, and operating with improved credit monitoring. The presence of imperfect competition and market concentration bolstered the financial stability or resilience to insolvency and default of the Top 20 banks. In addition, exercise of market power enabled the Top 20 banks to increase their loan

Table 3.26 Bank competition, concentration and financial stability findings

Objectives	*Hypotheses*	*Results*
1. To determine the market structure of the UKB industry in the Philippines	The UKB industry of the Philippines is characterized by an imperfectly competitive market structure	• More intense market concentration in the Philippine UKB industry drives dominant banks to exercise market power by charging higher loan rates • The dominant banks obtain higher profits and can vary loan rates vis-à-vis deposit rates. They have a cost advantage • This market behavior of the dominant banks arose when the loan market experienced greater bank concentration in 2008Q4–2019Q4
2. To determine the relationship between bank competition and financial stability through the bank's exposure to risk (Berger et al. 2009; MMR 2010)	Market concentration and imperfect competition in the banking industry enables banks to be profitable but exposes them to greater risks, making them more fragile	• The Top 20 banks exercised their market power by charging higher markups from 2008Q4 to 2019Q4, thereby increasing market concentration. They have a high financial stability indicator, which allows up to three standard deviations from average ROE, understood as resilience from bank insolvency. The Top 20 banks improved their capitalization and lowered their NPL ratio up to an average of 2.92% • The improvement in bank capitalization, however, only averaged to a significantly higher level of 12% for the Top 10 and a significantly lower 10.3% for the Next 10 banks

Objectives	*Hypotheses*	*Results*
3. To determine the relationship between bank competition and stability with capitalization in compliance with the proposed BSP regulation (Schliephake 2016)	Market concentration and imperfect competition in the banking industry enable banks to increase their capitalization, making them more stable	• The Philippine UKBs achieve financial stability, understood as resilience from insolvency or bank distress, through the exercise of market power of dominant but cost-efficient banks • The dominant Top 10 banks aim to accrue sufficient capital as a buffer from systemic risk. They improved their capitalization through a higher equity-to-assets ratio, maintaining the CAR (15.17%) and TIER1 (12.92%) BSP- and Basel III-prescribed ratios. These ratios significantly differ from the prescribed 10.5% for TIER 1 capital and 12.5% for RCAR. The efforts of the Next 10 banks are not enough despite improvement in capitalization. The average Z_{ROE} of the Next 10 from 2008Q4 to 2019Q4 is 1.40, which is less than 2.0. With dwindling profit margins of some fringe banks, they might not be able to sustain a sufficient level of capitalization

Source Author's GMM Cross-Section Random Effects Regression Results and deposit market shares, strengthen their market power, and obtain and sustain their targeted profit margins. Specifically, the Top 10 banks went on to increase their size and market shares while enhancing their capitalization, thus making them less prone to credit risks. The Next 10 banks, on the other hand, also improved their capitalization as they pursued higher profits and increased market shares. However, their solvency index, Z_{ROE}, shows that they do not have enough profit margins to shield them from market risks. The Top 10 banks managed to improve and sustain their profit margins (profit-margin effect) and reduce their NPLs (risk-shifting effect) through increased risk-weighted bank capitalization. The Next 10 banks may have to improve profit margins to bolster gains in capitalization and not lose these through costly debt financing.

To conclude, the buffer effect outweighed the risk shifting and profit-margin effect among most of the Top 20 banks to reflect better capitalization. The results of the GMM cross-section random effects estimation of the market behavior and stability of the banks revealed a stability-enhancing effect and the pursuit of better capitalization in the behavior of the dominant banks that thrive in an industry of imperfect competition and market concentration. The current level of market concentration among the Top 10 banks allowed them sufficient buffer, while some of the Next 10 banks still need to improve their profitability.

The effect of financial cycles, such as financial booms and busts, may have an impact on how banks pursue their capitalization. Further, Schliephake's theoretical model (2016) can be empirically verified using a dynamic model, that is, by using a difference effects cross-section mode to determine the influence of improved profit margins on equity for succeeding periods. This study is among the first to verify said model through static GMM regression analysis with a covariance matrix using panel-corrected standard errors and a White cross-section weighting matrix.

Appendix

See Tables 3.27, 3.28, 3.29, 3.30, 3.31, and 3.32.

Table 3.27 Basis for the dominant and fringe bank grouping

Rank	*Top 20*	*Average Market Share (%) in terms of Total Assets (2005Q1 to 2022Q3)*
1	Banco de Oro Universal Bank	16.93
2	Metrobank and Trust Company	13.58
3	Bank of the Philippine Islands	12.12
4	Landbank of the Philippines	11.28
5	Philippine National Bank	6.30
6	Development Bank of the Philippines	5.48
7	China Banking Corporation	4.74
8	Rizal Commercial and Banking Corporation	4.56
9	Union Bank of the Philippines	4.15
10	Security Bank Corporation	4.11
11	Citibank, N.A	3.71
12	United Coconut Planters Bank	2.63
13	Hong Kong and Shanghai Banking Corporation	2.15
14	East West Banking Corporation	1.86
15	Bank of Commerce	1.49
16	Phil Trust Company	1.41
17	Asia United Bank Corporation	1.24
18	Philippine Bank of Communication	0.93
19	Maybank	0.67
20	The Bank of Tokyo-Mitsubishi UFJ Ltd	0.67

Source BSP https://www.bsp.gov.ph/SitePages/Statistics/BSFinancialStatements.aspx?TabId=1 for basic data and the author's estimates

Table 3.28 Market share of the Top 46 UKBs (2005–2022)

Rank	*Assets*				*Deposits*				*Loans*			
	2005–2009	*2010–2015*	*2016–2019*	*2020–2022*	*2005–2009*	*2010–2015*	*2016–2019*	*2020–2022*	*2005–2009*	*2010–2015*	*2016–2019*	*2020–2022*
Top 5	27.47	34.59	37.17	37.37	28.73	37.29	39.91	38.21	28.28	39.62	43.00	44.37
Next 5	22.13	21.76	22.40	23.86	20.25	20.18	23.82	25.48	23.64	19.28	18.28	18.14
Next 10	35.43	35.85	36.34	34.19	35.81	35.86	33.23	32.51	33.65	32.99	34.36	33.32
Others	14.97	7.80	4.09	4.58	15.21	6.67	3.05	3.80	14.43	8.11	4.36	4.16
Total Banks = 46 UKBs as of the Third Quarter of 2022												

Source BSP https://www.bsp.gov.ph/SitePages/Statistics/BSFinancialStatements.aspx?TabId=1 for basic data and the author's estimates

Table 3.29 GMM regression on return-on-equity for the Top 20 UKBs (2005Q1 to 2007Q4)

Method: Panel GMM EGLS (Cross-section random effects)				
Sample: 2005Q1 2008Q4; Periods Included: 16; white cross-section (cross-section correlation) instrument weighting matrix; Swamy and Arora estimator of component variances; Cross-section weights using panel corrected standard errors (PCSE) & covariance (d.f. corrected)				
Dependent Variable: Return-on-Equity (ROE) (Bank Level Indicator of Profitability as a Measure of Performance)				
		Top 20[(a,b)]		
Regressors [(a)]	**Expected Sign**	**Adjusted Lerner Index**	**HHI Deposits**	**HHI Loans**
C	-/+	351.59 **	423.70 n.s.	-1253.16 **
		(169.31)	(638.95)	(561.49)
Degree of Market Power	positive	-1.78 n.s.	-0.27 n.s.	2.68 ***
		(4.03)	(1.09)	(1.08)
Degree of Market Power^2	negative	0.03 n.s.	1.41E-04 n.s.	-1.44E-03 ***
		(0.51)	(0.0006)	(0.00057)
Fixed Assets to Total Assets	negative	-185.78 *	-159.39 n.s.	-159.56 n.s.
		(104.97)	(114.51)	(111.69)
Loans to Assets	positive	-35.32 n.s.	-54.55 n.s.	-50.31 n.s.
		(65.68)	(71.72)	(70.01)
Loans to Assets^2	negative	22.35 n.s.	39.91 n.s.	36.01 n.s.
		(64.76)	(70.03)	(68.95)
Bank Size (Ln Total Assets)	positive	1.37 n.s.	0.63 n.s.	0.67 n.s.
		(1.20)	(1.40)	(1.40)
Ln(GDP per capita)	-/+	-147.79 **	-118.99 n.s.	13.79 n.s.
		(75.39)	(99.13)	(94.70)
Government/Foreign Ownership (%)	-/+	0.02 n.s.	0.04 n.s.	0.04 n.s.
		(0.05)	(0.06)	(0.06)
No. of Cross-Sections / Observations		20/320	20/320	20/320
AR(1)	negative	-2.84 ***	-2.79 ***	-2.84 ***
AR(2)	negative	-2.42 **	-2.43 **	-2.46 **
Hansen's *J*-Stat	positive	6.90E-15 n.s.	1.36E-15 n.s.	2.08E-11 n.s.

Source BSP https://www.bsp.gov.ph/SitePages/Statistics/BSFinancialStatements.aspx?TabId=1 for basic data and author's estimates

[a]Highlighted cells refer to coefficients with signs different from expected and have a significant p-value; Hansen's J-Stat < 1.0 has p-value > 0.50

[b]p-values: ***[0.00, 0.01]; **[0.01, 0.05]; *[0.05, 0.15]; n.s. not significant or $p > 0.15$

Table 3.30 GMM regression on return-on-equity for the Top 20 UKBs

Method: Panel GMM EGLS (Cross-section random effects)				
Sample: 2008Q4 2019Q4; Periods Included: 45; white cross-section (cross-section correlation) instrument weighting matrix; Swamy and Arora estimator of component variances; Cross-section weights using panel corrected standard errors (PCSE) & covariance (d.f. corrected)				
Dependent Variable: Return-on-Equity (ROE) (Bank Level Indicator of Profitability as a Measure of Performance)				
Regressors [(a)]	**Expected Sign**	**Top 20[(a,b)]**		
		Adjusted Lerner Index	**HHI Deposits**	**HHI Loans**
C	-/+	90.40 **	-70.90 n.s.	-340.45 ***
		(34.77)	(142.10)	(109.31)
Degree of Market Power	positive	1.12 n.s.	0.13 n.s.	0.75 ***
		(0.93)	(0.26)	(0.20)
Degree of Market Power^2	negative	2.53 ***	-8.29E-05 n.s.	-3.49E-04 ***
		(0.85)	(0.0001)	(0.00009)
Fixed Assets to Total Assets	negative	-130.83 ***	-154.54 ***	-161.72 ***
		(39.67)	(39.28)	(39.23)
Loans to Assets	positive	78.66 ***	76.16 ***	76.06 ***
		(19.30)	(18.41)	(18.33)
Loans to Assets^2	negative	-77.27 ***	-75.91 ***	-76.88 ***
		(18.25)	(17.48)	(17.38)
Bank Size (Ln Total Assets)	positive	0.005 n.s.	0.24 n.s.	0.42 n.s.
		(0.68)	(0.65)	(0.65)
Ln(GDP per capita)	-/+	-41.67 **	6.59 n.s.	-31.35 n.s.
		(16.36)	(21.47)	(19.37)
Government/Foreign Ownership (%)	-/+	-0.04 **	-0.04 **	-0.04 **
		(0.02)	(0.02)	(0.02)
No. of Cross-Sections / Observations		20/900	20/900	20/900
AR(1)	negative	-4.28 ***	-4.44 ***	-4.31 ***
AR(2)	negative	1.25 n.s.	1.48 n.s.	1.38 n.s.
Hansen's *J*-Stat	positive	2.73E-18 n.s.	5.65E-13 n.s.	5.35E-13 n.s.

Source BSP https://www.bsp.gov.ph/SitePages/Statistics/BSFinancialStatements.aspx?TabId=1 for basic data and the author's estimates

[a]Highlighted cells refer to coefficients with signs different from expected and have a significant *p*-value; Hansen's *J*-Stat < 1.0 has *p*-value > 0.50

[b]*p*-values: ***[0.00, 0.01]; **[0.01, 0.05]; *[0.05, 0.15]; n.s. not significant or *p* > 0.15

Table 3.31 Descriptive statistics for the Top 20 UKBs (2005 Q1–2019 Q4)

Variables	*Top 20*				
	Mean	*Median*	*Maximum*	*Minimum*	*Observations*
Adjusted Lerner Index	0.76	0.82	1.57	−8.87	1200
Conventional Lerner Index	0.49	0.49	0.90	0.19	1200
Equity-to-Assets Ratio	0.11	0.12	0.23	0.01	1300
Capital Adequacy Ratio (CAR)	16.33	15.49	50.81	−2.96	1099
CAR TIER 1	14.57	13.37	50.70	−2.96	1099
HHI Total Assets	948	945	1047	824	1300
HHI Total Deposits	1017	1018	1107	884	1300
HHI Total Loans	1080	1096	1205	889	1300
Return-on-Assets	1.11	1.12	6.23	−6.15	1300
Return-on-Equity	9.95	10.81	68.72	−225.34	1300
Stockholders' Equity (Php Billion)	47.07	22.76	399.73	0.61	1300
Non-Performing Loans Ratio	3.34	2.42	29.80	0.00	1300
Total Assets (Php Billion)	418.35	230.50	3261.63	13.15	1300
Total Deposits (Php Billion)	319.06	155.46	2567.31	6.41	1300
Total Loans (Php Billion)	215.40	105.16	2235.56	6.10	1300
Z-Index CAR	0.98	0.94	4.57	−4.52	1010
Z-Index ROA	2.09	2.00	8.32	−5.03	1205
Z-Index ROE	2.54	2.41	10.09	−5.08	1200
Z-Index TIER 1	1.34	1.23	5.57	−3.44	1010
Per Capita Gross Domestic Product	10.22	10.21	10.84	9.63	1200
Government or Foreign Ownership (%)	30.73	0	100	0	1340

Source BSP https://www.bsp.gov.ph/SitePages/Statistics/BSFinancialStatements.aspx?TabId=1 for basic data

Table 3.32 Descriptive statistics for the Top 10 and Next 10 UKBs (2005 Q1–2019 Q4)

Variables	*Mean*		*Median*		*Maximum*		*Minimum*		*Observations*	
	Top 10	*Next 10*	*Top 10*	*Next 10*	*Top 10*	*Next 10*	*Top 10*	*Next 10*	*Top 10*	*Next 10*
Adjusted Lerner Index	0.86	0.66	0.84	0.77	1.57	1.21	0.08	−8.87	600	
Conventional Lerner Index	0.51	0.48	0.51	0.48	0.90	0.81	0.40	0.19	600	
Equity-to-Assets Ratio	0.12	0.10	0.12	0.11	0.19	0.23	0.06	0.01	650	
Capital Adequacy Ratio (CAR)	15.17	17.50	14.99	16.01	25.03	50.81	0.00	−2.96	550	549
CAR TIER 1	12.92	16.23	12.74	14.47	22.47	50.70	0.00	−2.96	550	549
Return-on-Assets	1.47	0.76	1.34	0.68	5.48	6.23	−0.01	−6.15	650	
Return-on-Equity	12.32	7.59	11.78	8.98	34.98	68.72	−0.15	−225.34	650	
Stockholders' Equity (Php Billion)	81.9	12.2	59.2	10.1	399.7	77.2	9.8	0.6	650	
Non-Performing Loans Ratio	2.63	4.05	2.05	2.79	27.00	29.80	0.01	0.00	650	
Total Assets (Php Billion)	704.0	132.7	514.2	105.6	3261.6	665.9	99.9	13.1	650	
Total Deposits (Php Billion)	539.0	99.1	387.1	80.1	2567.3	559.5	44.1	6.4	650	
Total Loans (Php Billion)	368.5	62.3	242.1	43.6	2235.6	239.3	36.9	6.1	650	
Z-Index CAR	1.02	0.94	1.04	0.86	4.44	4.57	−3.71	−4.52	500	510
Z-Index ROA	2.80	1.38	2.71	1.24	8.32	6.78	0.17	−5.03	600	605
Z-Index ROE	3.60	1.48	3.35	1.24	10.09	6.47	0.24	−5.08	600	
Z-Index TIER 1	1.43	1.24	1.30	1.15	5.56	5.57	−3.44	−3.42	500	510

Source BSP https://www.bsp.gov.ph/SitePages/Statistics/BSFinancialStatements.aspx?TabId=1 for basic data

CHAPTER 4

Does Income Diversification Enhance Bank Efficiency and Stability in Periods of Increased Competition?

Background

The global financial crisis of 2007–2009 greatly affected the world's financial system. The past decade saw significant deregulation and integration in the financial industry in both developed and developing countries, prompting banks to engage in new non-traditional businesses. Diversification turned out to be an effective response to competition from non-banking players and served to sustain the competitiveness of individual firms (Edwards and Mishkin 1995). Thus emerged a new topic for debate: diversification versus concentration. Among scholars, efficiency became a popular measure for bank management and performance, as it is widely upheld that the long-term viability of the financial industry depends on how well banks manage their resources (Ibid).

This chapter will identify the effects of market power on the efficiency of the country's top 20 UKBs, as well as determine whether diversification influences bank efficiency and stability. This paper also makes use of the recently developed comprehensive measure of liquidity to account for the total aggregate output of banks. To the best of the authors' knowledge, this is the first-ever study on the Philippine banking industry that makes use of the said tool.

The BSP highly encourages competition in the domestic banking industry. In July 2014, the late President Benigno Aquino III signed

J. C. Dacanay et al., *Bank Competition and the Effects on Financial Stability*, Palgrave Macmillan Studies in Banking and Financial Institutions, https://doi.org/10.1007/978-3-031-59599-8_4

Republic Act 10641, otherwise known as "An Act Allowing the Full Entry of Foreign Banks in the Philippines amending for the purpose Republic Act No. 7721." The amended law liberalizes the Philippine banking industry by allowing the full entry of foreign banks and 100% foreign ownership of domestic banks, thus giving the Philippines a significant advantage in the ASEAN economic integration. Since then, the BSP Monetary Board allowed the entry of 12 foreign banks and the establishment of liaison offices of 11 foreign banks in the country.

According to Gochoco-Bautista (1999), increased competition in the Philippine banking industry drove banks to tap new niche markets and adopt new business strategies, such as turning to finance off-balance sheet activities, thus increasing their share of non-interest income. Based on the individual income statement of the Philippine UKBs, the components of non-interest income include net gains on trading and derivatives, net gains on other securities, net fees and commissions, and other operating incomes. Another study by Meslier et al. (2014) pegged the average share of non-interest income in the total operating income of banks in the Philippines at around 35.92%, covering the sample period 1999–2005. Sanya and Wolfe (2010) also found that Philippine banks had the highest diversification of assets (0.612) and income (0.548) of all the ASEAN countries that they studied using the HHI index. It would therefore be interesting to monitor the growing share of non-interest income in the total operating income of banks in the country.

The theory behind diversification recommends that banks can be more efficient and improve their risk management by generating income from sources other than banking-related activities. However, empirical studies of different markets around the world yield mixed results. Thus, the need to arrive at a definitive consensus on the benefits of diversification in the banking industry.

Since UKBs dominate the local financial industry, it is important to foster an environment that enhances their efficiency in the interest of economic growth. Further, if competition and income diversification hinder the efficient management of bank resources, then inefficiencies must be identified and possible policy tradeoffs, addressed.

Ultimately, this study seeks to determine if greater market power and a high degree of income diversification actually contribute to the efficiency and stability of the country's top UKBs. The authors formulated the following objectives to answer this research question:

1. To determine the effects of greater market power on bank performance in terms of the cost and profit efficiency of the top 20 UKBs in the Philippines;
2. To determine the effects of greater market power and a higher degree of income diversification on cost and profit efficiency of dominant and fringe banks; and
3. To determine the effects of greater market power and a higher degree of income diversification on the stability of dominant and fringe banks.

This study aims to measure the cost and profit efficiency and stability of the Philippine banking industry in order to provide empirical evidence on the effects of market power and income diversification on bank performance. The authors conducted a limited study of emerging markets in the Philippine banking industry to observe how the said variables affect one another. Results were inconclusive, especially those that had to do with identifying the best strategies to improve efficiency and deal with increased competition.

The results of this study may serve as guideposts for the following stakeholders:

1. policymakers tasked with designing future legislations;
2. bank managers and authorities in charge of initiating reforms and design strategic measures; and
3. depositors and other stakeholders seeking guidance on their investment decisions.

Data for this study comes from the BSP database of financial statements reported in the annual reports of the top 20 Philippine UKBs from 2005 to 2019[1] that is publicly available online and from the SEC. The year 2020 is not included in the sample period due to difficulties in obtaining data on interest rates. Moreover, 2020 posed a unique scenario as it was the year of the COVID-19 outbreak, resulting in significant changes in banking behavior and in BSP policies (BSP 2020).

[1] As of 2019, the Philippine totaled 46 UKBs.

Review of Related Literature

Theoretical Studies on Bank Competition, Diversification, and Efficiency

The following discussion focuses on how bank competition, concentration, and efficiency relate to one another. Operational efficiency determines a bank's long-term viability. This is why enhanced competition pushes banks to go all out in efficiently utilizing their resources. Studying the efficiency of banks is crucial to identifying inefficiencies and to fostering an environment conducive to financial activities, especially in the developing economies (Chen 2009).

According to Usman, Wang, Mahmood, and Shahid (2010), "Efficiency refers to the utilization of resources in such a way as to maximize the production. A bank is said to be efficient when it can no longer enhance its output without increasing inputs or cannot produce the same quantity of output by using less quantity of inputs." One achieves efficiency by minimizing the input to produce a specific output or by maximizing the output, given a specific input.

Banking efficiency stands on two pillars: allocative and technical. Allocative efficiency refers to a bank's distribution and use of resources to realize the highest expected value, given the technology available (Ncube 2009). Xu also states, "Allocative efficiency measures the proportional reduction in costs if the bank chooses the right mix of input given the prices." On the other hand, technical efficiency refers to a bank's ability to produce a specific level of output with the least possible input (Falkena et al. 2004). Further, Xu defined technical efficiency as the measurement of "the proportional reduction in input usage that can be attained if the bank operates on the efficient frontier" (Xu 2011). Allocative and technical efficiency of firms can bring about economic or cost efficiency and so contribute to overall economic growth (Hon et al. 2011).

Numerous strands of literature have verified two contrasting and well-known hypotheses on the relationship between market competition and efficiency. These are the Quiet Life Hypothesis quiet life hypothesis (QLH), and the Information Generation Hypothesis (IGH).

QLH, also referred to as the competition-efficiency hypothesis, suggests that competition has a positive effect on bank efficiency. Hicks (1935) proposed that banks enjoy a "quite life" when market power is high in terms of relaxed cost management, enabled by a portion of monopoly rents, thereby reducing cost efficiency. In a more concentrated market, the absence of intense competition has banks enjoying a "quiet life" and managers not pressured to maintain operational efficiency. On the other hand, tight competition forces banks to cut down on costs, diversify to increase profit, shift output, and screen and monitor clients to reduce the number of NPLs (Phan 2015).

On the other hand, the IGH, which is synonymous to the competition-inefficiency hypothesis, establishes a negative link between competition and bank efficiency (Phan 2015). A bank is a special financial intermediary, which allows it to access and analyze the personal information of clients, screen and monitor the paying capacity of borrowers, and so minimize the risk of default. In a more competitive environment, where clients tend to switch banks, the screening of loan applications tends to slacken and retaining old customers as well as attracting new ones become costlier. In a highly competitive business environment, banks must invest in more aggressive marketing tactics as well as new technologies, such as upgraded information systems and more Automated Teller Machines (ATMs). Nevertheless, such investments do not guarantee the delivery of the expected values because banking relationships no longer last as long as they used to, which redounds to declining efficiency (Ibid).

Empirical Studies on Bank Competition and Efficiency

Previous and current studies have proven to a certain extent that market concentration and competition determine bank efficiency. A study of five developed countries in Europe established a positive link between bank competition and efficiency in the EU banking system. By contrast, the study showed a mix of direct and indirect links in the banking systems of developing countries (Casu and Girardone 2006).

For middle-income countries, Chen (2009) found that competition boosted cost efficiency in underdeveloped countries where foreign banks dominate the financial sector. This is a case in point for countries in the Sub-Saharan region. In the same study, Chen used the Panzar-Rosse approach to estimate the degree of competition and the stochastic frontier approach to measure technical efficiency. His paper supports QLH.

For their part, Hauner and Peiris (2008) saw that tighter competition due to economic and financial reforms brought about higher efficiency in Ugandan banks, again supporting the QLH. Uganda is a low-income country where foreign banks dominate its monopolistic financial structure. The Panzar-Rosse (1987) approach measured the degree of competition, the data envelopment analysis determined technical efficiency, and the Tobit model evaluated the model.

Two studies on the Indian banking system yielded different results. Arrawatia et al. (2015) showed a positive link between competition and stability using Granger causality tests. The results pointed to the mutual causality of competition and efficiency. On the other hand, Zhao et al. (2008) concluded that enhanced competition did not translate to efficiency. The Indian banking market underwent a number of reforms in the periods covered by their study. This discrepancy may be due to the different techniques used to measure the efficiency of the Indian banking system. Zhao et al. (2010) used the SFA while Arrawatia et al. (2015) used the DEA in estimating efficiency scores.

The Czech banking industry likewise yielded contrasting results. Pruteanu-Podpiera (2016), Weill, and Schobert (2016) used a Granger causality test to analyze Czech banks. The results rejected the QLH and pointed to a negative relationship between bank competition and efficiency. The causality only ran from competition to efficiency. On the other hand, Řepková and Stavárek (2013) concluded that the Czech banking system exhibited QLH and suggested that competition contributed to efficiency. Interestingly, both studies used the Lerner Index to measure competition and DEA to measure efficiency. In this case, the difference in results can be due to the different periods covered. Pruteanu-Podpiera et al. covered 1994–2005, when the Czech banking system was transitioning and opening up to foreign investors, while Řepková et al. covered 2001–2010, when the same banking system took on a monopolistic structure but with an increasing atmosphere of competition.

Berger and Hannan (1998) conducted a pioneering empirical study on bank competition and efficiency in the United States. Their conclusions supported the QLH, which asserts the positive relationship between market concentration and efficiency. They also claimed that market concentration and reduced competition led to lower cost efficiency due to slackened management. On the other hand, Fungacova et al. (2012) used GMM estimation and the stochastic frontier approach to rule out any significant relation between competition and efficiency in the Chinese banking industry.

Overall, the different levels of competition in different markets or countries, as well as the variety of approaches to measuring competition and efficiency contributed to the divergence of results.

Bank Competition and Bank Efficiency in the Philippines

Most studies on bank efficiency are from the developed countries in the West. Few have focused on developing countries. Phan (2015) covered the six emerging countries in Asia—Bangladesh, India, Indonesia, Malaysia, Vietnam, and the Philippines—from 2005 to 2012. The industry-level result of the Tobit regression and 2SLS showed that concentration is positively and significantly linked to efficiency, hence, rejecting QLH. Moreover, inflation posted a significantly negative link to bank efficiency.

On the other hand, Lim covered the years 2003–2011 to ascertain the link between competition and efficiency. Using the correlational analysis on selected universal banks, the results showed that financial deregulation led to greater competition, less market concentration, and improved efficiency. Alberto et al. (2018) also looked into the effects of foreign bank entry on the performance of domestic banks. Similar to Lim's findings, they concluded that the presence of foreign banks boosted the efficiency of local banks but only on the condition that foreign banks increased their share of ownership in the domestic banking system.

Bank Competition, Diversification, and Efficiency: Theoretical and Practical Underpinnings of Diversification

Berger et al. (2010) define diversification as the expansion of investments into activities that are not perfectly correlated. The portfolio theory suggests that banks diversify to reduce their risk portfolio. Internal diversification will minimize volatility and, therefore, total risk. The scope of banking activities has shifted from traditional intermediation to new lines of business (Clark and Seems 2002). Recent literature claims that banks today diversify, not only to reduce overall risk, but also to expand through "managerial economies of scale, increasing debt capacity, increasing efficiency of resource allocation in internal markets, and exploiting firm-specific assets in different markets" (Meslier et al. 2014). This means that diversifying does not automatically reduce risks. Bank managers and authorities would only agree to incur more risks if high returns are in the offing. Moreover, diversification entails higher costs and risks with poor capital allocation. It is likewise challenging to design optimal compensation schemes for managers.

From a theoretical standpoint, diversifying can be strategic when dealing with competition. According to the market power theory, firms diversify to cushion themselves from interest income risks, gain internal capital market efficiency, and build market power (Meslier et al. 2014). It presumes that market power propels higher profitability and improves efficiency (Ibid). Banks that wield market power harness their resources and position to back their predatory strategies in new markets and to cash in on opportunities arising from diversification. The same data gathered from their lending activities can be used to screen and monitor clients, thus minimizing costs and facilitating the delivery of non-traditional services.

In line with the market power theory, scholars and bank authorities agree that competition drives banks to diversify. According to Meslier et al. (2014), "greater competition in financial markets leads to banks' increasing need to diversify to expand their activities and to develop new lines of businesses besides their traditional interest activities." True enough, the past years have seen banks engage in activities that generate non-interest income, such as underwriting and trading securities, brokerage, and investment banking. These changes seem to address concerns on profitability and risk despite the lack of industry consensus (Ibid). For example, Shoaib Ali et al. (2022) demonstrated the significant impact of market power on macro prudential policies. They found evidence that banks assume more liquidity risk as their market power increases, resulting in lower profit margins. Market power significantly affects economic growth through liquidity creation. However, in light of the new liquidity rules, banks are required to hold more liquid assets. Shoaib's study does not relate liquidity creation and income diversification to efficiency (Ibid) and only applies to member countries of the Arab Gulf Cooperation Council (GCC)—Bahrain, Kuwait, Oman, Qatar, Saudi Arabia, and the UAE.

Furthermore, there is a clear connection between diversification and efficiency as both point to the proper allocation and management of resources as key to lowering costs and raking in profit. Berger et al.

(2010) support this idea, stating that banks are technically efficient if managers organize production (diversification) such that a firm yields maximum output on a given amount of input. Moreover, Iskandar-Datta and McLaughlin (2007) state that "diversified banks can benefit from applying managerial abilities and skills across different products and markets."

There are two opposing hypotheses on the relationship between diversification and efficiency.

First, the conglomeration hypothesis argues that diversification ensures optimal management of the various aspects of banking operations (Iskandar-Datta and McLaughlin 2007; Gambacorta et al. 2014) to bring about economies of scope from cost sharing of multiple products and to ensure steady earnings (Saunders and Walter 1994; Lown et al. 2000; Gambacorta et al. 2014). A bank achieves economies of scope when it establishes a long-term relationship with its clients (Elsas et al. 2010), allowing the use of customer data gathered from its various services. Lastly, for banks with a more diversified intermediary, reusing information from the same set of clients cuts down on data monitoring costs. In turn, this contributes to overall cost reduction even in a risk-neutral economy.

Second, the strategic focus hypothesis states that monitoring businesses and handling soaring firm costs and high earning variations all pose a challenge to diversified firms (Phan 2015). A more common disadvantage of diversification is the increase of agency problems between bank authorities and small stakeholders, as this could adversely affect the market's perception of the firm (Ibid). Designing efficient managerial incentive contracts also pose a challenge because additional benefits encourage managers to expand the range of business activities, regardless of the impact on the firm's performance and market valuation (Jensen and Meckling 1976). Further, adopting new business strategies may dilute bank managers' comparative advantage by making them operate outside of their expertise (Klein and Saidenberg 2010). Finally, diversification could incur devastating costs and consequences on banks that fail to engage new markets in a highly competitive environment. Hence, it is reasonable and less costly to specialize during periods of increased competition (Winton 1999).

Empirical Studies on Bank Diversification and Efficiency

Using the Stochastic Frontier approach in measuring efficiency, Vennet (2002) found that specialized banks have higher cost and profit efficiency compared to diversified banks. Similarly, Alhassan (2015) concluded that initial diversification to non-interest income activities did not improve the efficiency of banks in Ghana over the sample period 2003–2011. In addition, diversification works mostly for larger banks. Hence, in the Ghanaian banking system, diversification strategies among the larger banks achieved better utilization of resources and maximized profit.

Nguyen (2018) used the SFA method to assess the effect of different aspects of banking diversification on cost and profit efficiency. He concluded that income diversification is associated with lower cost efficiency while funding diversification is associated with higher profit efficiency. Asset diversification is only associated with persistently higher profit efficiency. Tarore and Prasetyo (2017) also used SFA to study an emerging market for Indonesian banks. They found that diversification optimized bank output without additional input costs and that the level of capital improved bank efficiency. On the other hand, bank size and the global financial crisis did not affect efficiency at all.

Diversification and Risk-Taking

Some authors argue that spreading bank operations across various products or markets can reduce the risk of bankruptcy. For instance, Boot and Schmeits (2000) aver, "If different business activities are integrated in one firm, the pooled funding cost of the firm only partially represents the risk characteristic of each activity, which means that the business activities coinsure each other." This brings about predictable returns and reduces the possibility of default. In contrast, some scholars believe that even if diversification contributes to greater efficiency, it could be associated with higher income volatility, thus implying higher risk. DeYoung and Roland (2001) support this with empirical findings, stating that a "shift towards non-interest income is related to higher leverage and increased income volatility, which could increase the volatility of bank earnings." This could be because commercial banks are more likely to lose clients in fee-based activities due to higher incidence of "switching costs," or borrowers incurring costs from changing banks. The more common cases of switching costs are monetary in nature. However, psychological, effort-based, and time-based switching costs have emerged in the borrower-bank relationship. Banks also suffer from high earnings volatility when they invest in additional manpower and technology infrastructure in their shift towards fee-based activities (Nguyen 2018).

Empirical studies on developing and developed countries yield mixed results on the impact of bank diversification on risk exposure or profitability. Merciera et al. (2007) and Stiroh and Rumble (2006) found that high exposure to uncertainty and volatility offset the benefits of diversification. Specifically, Lepetit et al. (2008) and Li and Zhang (2013) concluded that a shift to non-interest activities intensifies risk-taking behavior due to the high volatility of these income sources. While Chiorazzo et al. (2008) maintain that income diversification improves the risk/return tradeoff with larger banks benefitting more from the setup. Similarly, Hakimi, and Zaghoudi (2017) found that non-interest income has a significant negative relationship with the level of risk and a positive relationship with profitability. Hence, Tunisian banks are encouraged to diversify. From inconclusive reports on the effects of bank diversification on risks and profitability, Gambacorta et al. (2014) observed an inverted U relationship in the study they conducted on 98 banks in 27 countries from 1994 to 2012. Banks become less profitable when they are more than 30% diversified.

Theoretical Framework and Empirical Methodology

Hypotheses

To answer the study's main problem, the authors propose the following:

> Hypothesis 1: Greater market power increases the efficiency of the top 20 Philippines UKBs because market power allows banks to charge higher loan rates to boost profit and improve efficiency.
> Hypothesis 2: Greater market power and a high degree of income diversification improve the efficiency of dominant and fringe banks. Market power and a high degree of income diversification work enhance the efficiency of dominant and fringe banks through higher charges and economies of scope from the cost sharing of fixed costs over multiple products.

Hypothesis 3: Greater market power and a high degree of income diversification promote the stability of dominant and fringe banks. With greater market power and a higher degree of income diversification, banks reduce their risk of bankruptcy by spreading their operations across different products and markets.

Theoretical Framework

This study will adopt the theoretical framework of Van Hoose (2010, 2017, 2022) which is the SCP paradigm's dominant bank model that is in line with the market power theory.

Dacanay (2017) provided empirical proof that an imperfectly competitive market exists in the domestic banking industry, giving rise to the coexistence of dominant and fringe banks. According to the dominant bank model, an asymmetrical market environment has firms competing side-by-side even if they vastly differ in scale and costs. The dominant bank model assumes that large banks have a huge cost advantage over small banks owing to lower average per unit operating costs and expanded assets or scale. Moreover, lower per unit cost of production could be due to a broader product mix or scope. Under the SCP paradigm, the market power hypothesis posits that dominant banks with a strong competitive advantage in their current market can be just as competitive in new markets since their strength, position, and resources can support their predatory strategies. This theory also suggests that diversification can enhance the financial performance of banks with high market power. Montgomery (1994) identifies three ways by which banks can strengthen their position in new markets through diversification.

First, cross-subsidization has a bank using excess profit from one market to support a new venture. Second, through mutual forbearance, competing firms operating in multiple markets realize their interdependence and ease up on their aggressive strategies against one another. Third is reciprocal buying "where the interrelationships among large, diversified firms foreclose markets to smaller competitions."

Both the dominant bank model and the market power hypothesis assume that banks with greater market power are generally more efficient and profitable. This is because the cost advantage of dominant banks enables them to charge higher loan rates and to generate profit, not just in their current market, but also in new markets, while fringe banks should charge the same loan rate as those of the dominant banks.

Some authors propose other theories to explain the varying efficiency levels of dominant and fringe banks. One is the development of information and financial technologies that will boost the technical efficiency of banks (Berger 2003). In this regard, Hernandez-Murillo et al. (2010) claim that banks also compete in the area of strategic innovation. As Duygon et al. (2013) note, innovation has much to do with a bank's long-term cost and profit efficiency.

Another reason for the difference in efficiency levels is the use of "soft" and "hard" information. Small banks specialize in "soft" or qualitative information when issuing non-standardized loans, while large banks use "hard" or quantifiable information for standardized loans. In line with this, the information generation hypothesis of Marquez (2002) argues that intense competition affects a bank's capacity to generate information, causing a drop in efficiency. Smaller banks have less knowledge of the whole market compared to large banks, which renders them less capable of screening borrowers. In addition, the data gathering process erodes due to the tendency of customers to shift to banks that offer lower costs.

Relating the conduct of dominant and fringe banks to market stability, proponents of the New Industrial Organization (NIO) state that the operation of individual banks is important, if not more important, than concentration when it comes to explaining overall market competition. As mentioned, large and small banks compete in the more concentrated markets with the larger ones having the edge of economies of scale and scope and the potential to better diversify (Diamond 1991). Boyd and De Nicolo (2005) however argue that a more concentrated market can be more fragile because of the capacity of banks to charge higher loan rates and increase the levels of NPLs. On the other hand, Martinez-Miera and Repullo (2010) say that higher loan rates lead to higher interest revenues for banks. Put together, these arguments might result in an inverted U-shaped relationship between bank competition and stability. One may summarize the arguments of Boyd et al. (2005), Martinez-Miera et al. (2010), and Berger et al. (2009) this way: While market power drives banks to take riskier asset portfolios, this does not necessarily imply an increase in overall risks. This is because banks can discover ways to control and offset higher risk exposure, such as increasing equity capital, reducing interest rate risk, and selling credit derivatives.

This study assumes that the information generation hypothesis of Marquez (2002) is happening in the Philippine banking industry. As mentioned, tougher market competition hinders efficiency. As clients tend to hop from one bank to another, retaining old customers and drawing in new ones entail more costs. Moreover, screening and monitoring processes tend to deteriorate as the customer data on which banks base their loan approvals are not updated and founded on long-term relationships alone. The bigger universal banks are more prone to experience such cost switching (Ibid). Since bank relationships tend to be more short-term in a competitive market, investing in new technologies and aggressive marketing strategies do not generate the expected outcome, resulting again in lower efficiency. Moreover, in line with the dominant bank model and market power hypothesis, this study assumes that dominant banks thrive in a concentrated market more than fringe banks do because market power allows them to dictate higher loan rates, achieve economies of scale, and therefore be more profitable (Ibid). It has also been established that the Philippine banking industry is imperfectly competitive, with dominant and fringe banks pitted against one another. For this reason, diversification has become a common practice especially among banks that enjoy more market power. This study assumes that market power and income diversification help banks reduce risks by spreading volatility across different products and markets, as stated by the portfolio theory.

Following the established framework and the hypotheses, this paper will focus on measuring the impact of market power and income diversification on the cost and profit efficiency and stability of the top 20 UKBs in the Philippines. In line with Berger and Mester (1997), the authors distinguish cost from profit efficiency to avoid possible conflict in the results. Cost efficiency measures how a bank's actual costs approximate those provided by best industry practices in producing similar output under comparable conditions. Profit efficiency combines cost and revenue efficiencies to determine a bank's success in maximizing value.

To test how competition, income diversification, bank efficiency, and stability relate to one another, the researchers employed frontier analysis to measure efficiency. This approach estimates an efficient frontier and measures the differences between the sample banks and the "best-practice" bank. Furthermore, following Berger and Mester (1997), the frontier analysis approach involves careful selection of efficiency concepts and measurement techniques to use as well as identification of the functional form and selection of variables. All the sample banks underwent frontier analysis, which requires the specification or construction of cost and/or profit efficiency frontier. The bank seen to best approximate the efficiency frontier served as the benchmark for all other banks.

Berger and Mester (1997) present the three most relevant measures of efficiency: cost, standard profit, and alternative profit. These best serve as the economic foundations for responding to market prices and competition.

In a frontier analysis, cost efficiency measures how a bank's cost closely approximates the bank which best produces the same output under the same conditions. The formula derives from a cost function in which the variable costs consider the prices of variable inputs, the quantities of variable outputs and any fixed input or output, environmental factors, random error, and efficiency:

$$C = C(w, y, z, v, u_c, e_c), \tag{4.1}$$

where:

C = variable costs
w = vector of prices of variable input
y = vector of quantities of variable output
z = quantities of any fixed netput (input or output)
v = a set of environmental or market variables that may affect performance
u_c = an inefficiency factor that may raise costs above the best-practice level
e_c = random error that incorporates measurement error and luck that may temporarily give banks high or low costs

In addition, u_c covers allocative inefficiencies from failing to react optimally to relative prices of inputs (w) and to technical inefficiencies arising from too much input to come up with (y). Simply put, the measurement of inefficiency and the random terms (u_c) and (e_c) are assumed to be multiplicatively separable from the rest of the cost function with both sides of (1) represented in natural logs:

$$\ln C = f(w, y, z, v) + \ln u_c + \ln e_c \tag{4.2}$$

The cost efficiency of bank b is defined as the estimated cost needed to produce bank b's output vector if the bank were as efficient as the best-practice bank in the sample facing the same exogenous variables (w, y, z, v) divided by the actual cost of bank b, adjusted for random error, i.e.,

$$\text{CostEFF}^b = \frac{C^{\min}}{C^b} = \frac{\exp[f(w^b, y^b, z^b, v^b] \times \exp[\ln u_c^{\min}]}{\exp[f(w^b, y^b, z^b, v^b] \times \exp[\ln_c^{\min}]} \tag{4.3}$$

where $u_c^{\min}$ is the minimum u_c^b.

Further, Berger and Mester (1997) state that the cost efficiency ratio can represent a bank's efficient costs and use of resources. For example, a cost efficiency value of 0.7 means that 70% of the bank's costs is efficient while 30% is "wasted" relative to the best-practice bank. On the other hand, the alternative profit efficiency function measures gaps in generating maximum profit, given a bank's output levels and not its output prices (Isik and Hassan 2002). According to Berger and Mester (1997), alternative profit efficiency is preferred to the standard measure because it offers a way to control unaccounted differences in output quality by taking into account the additional revenue that higher quality output can generate. Moreover, the prices of output can vary and influence profit. The alternative profit efficiency holds, given one or more of the following conditions:

1. substantial unmeasured differences in the quality of banking services;
2. output that is not completely variable, such that a bank cannot achieve every output scale and product mix;
3. output markets are not perfectly competitive such that banks may acquire market power over their charged prices; and
4. output prices are not accurately measured and are therefore inaccurate guides to revenue-earning opportunities in the standard profit function.

According to Manlagñit and Lamberte (2004), the abovementioned conditions are present in the Philippine banking industry, which makes the alternative profit efficiency appropriate to this study. The dependent variables for the standard profit function and the exogenous variables in cost function used to measure alternative profit efficiency are as follows:

$$\pi + \theta = C(w, y, z, v, u_c, e_c) \tag{4.4}$$

The translog form represents the alternative profit function:

$$\ln(\pi + \theta) = f(w, y, z, v) + \ln u_{a\pi} + \ln \varepsilon_{a\pi}, \quad (4.5)$$

where

π = variable profit
θ = the constant added to every firm's profit to make the natural log always a positive number
y = vector of prices of variable outputs
$\ln u_{a\pi}$ = inefficiency
And $\ln \varepsilon_{a\pi}$ = random error

The alternative profit efficiency is the ratio of predicted actual profit to the predicted maximum profit of the benchmark bank, expressed as:

$$\text{Alt}\pi\,\text{EFF}^b = \frac{a\pi^b}{a\pi_{\max}} = \frac{\exp[f\left(w^b, y^b, z^b, v^b\right] \times \exp\left[\ln u^b_{a\pi}\right] - \theta}{\exp[f\left(w^b, y^b, z^b, v^b\right] \times \exp\left[\ln^{\max}_{a\pi}\right] - \theta} \quad (4.6)$$

where

$u^b_{\max}$ = maximum value of u^b_π in the sample
$\text{Alt}\pi\,\text{EFF}^b$ = proportion of maximum profit actually earned

An alternative profit efficiency value of 0.7 means that a bank has achieved 70% profit efficiency compared to the best-practice bank.

To summarize, bank efficiency has become a popular gauge of performance because it measures the effective use of resources to maximize output or to minimize costs. Further, banks have increasingly resorted to income diversification as a strategy to boost market power. This is why non-interest income now takes up a bigger share in the total operating income of banks. Note however that the banks that have successfully diversified their products while minimizing risks are those that are efficient and enjoy market power. It therefore seems that the long-term viability of the Philippine banking industry hinges on diversification, which makes the analysis of its effects on bank efficiency and stability an important matter for study. Figure 4.1 summarizes the theories pertinent to the topic.

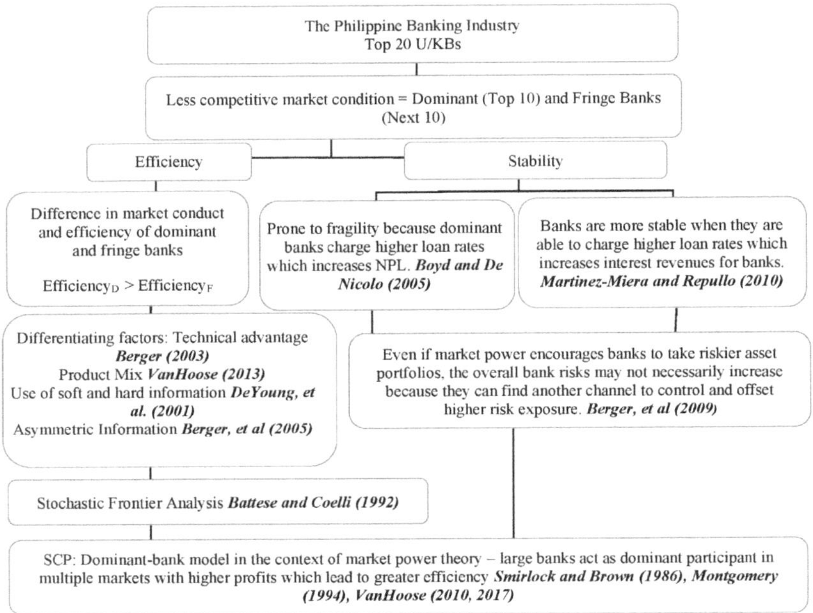

Fig. 4.1 Summary of the theoretical framework (*Source* Author's theoretical framework)

Conceptual Framework

The analysis of this study starts with determining the relationship between bank competition, as measured by the banks' market power and efficiency. Next, the study introduces the income diversification variable to capture its effect on efficiency (See Figs. 4.2 and 4.3). Besides capturing the unique effect of market power and income diversification variables on bank efficiency, the study also tries to discover the combined effect of market power and income diversification through the interaction among the said variables. For instance, competition and income diversification tend to vary with bank size. Hence, bank size will be introduced as a moderator variable and the sample banks classified as dominant (Top 10) UKBs and fringe (Next 10) UKBs.

Strong market power and high levels of income diversification work together to bring about efficiency, especially for the high-earners that

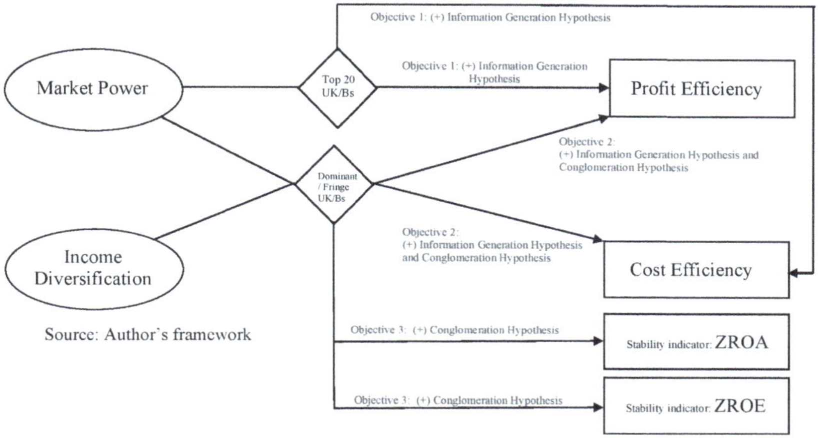

Fig. 4.2 Conceptual framework: market power, income diversification, and bank efficiency (*Source* Author's framework)

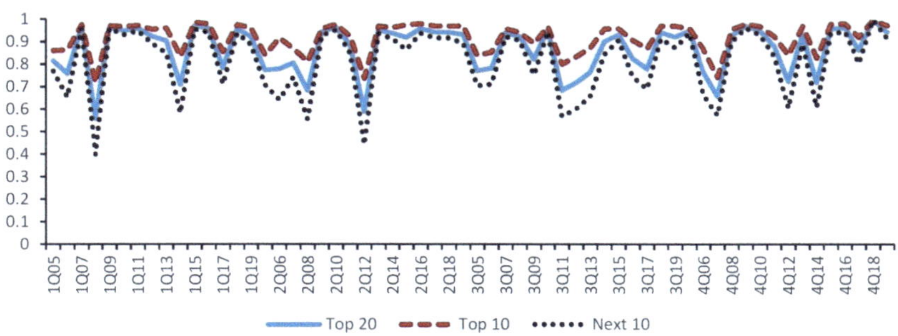

Fig. 4.3 Mean profit efficiency scores (*Source* Author's framework)

charge steeper loan rates and enjoy economies of scope from their diverse income sources. In line with this, the combined effect of market power and income diversification may also lead to financial stability since banks that enjoy market power can properly screen customers and reduce the likelihood of approving loan applications of less capable borrowers. The conglomeration hypothesis supports these assumptions (Fig. 4.4).

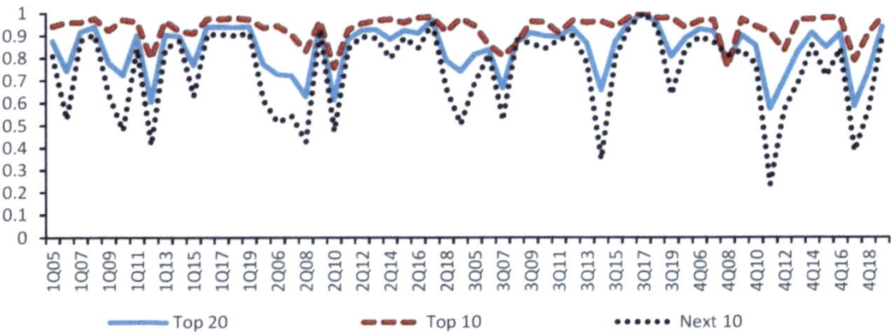

Fig. 4.4 Mean cost efficiency scores (*Source* Author's framework)

Empirical Methodology: Computing for Liquidity as a Substitute for Total Output

The first objective is to determine the effect of greater market power on bank performance in terms of cost and profit efficiency. The total output of the banks in this sample was measured using the new liquidity creation measure of Berger and Bouwman (2009) instead of the traditional total asset (TA) or gross total asset (GTA). Unlike TA and GTA, this comprehensive measure takes into account all on- and off-balance sheet activities, which make up about half of the liquidity creation of banks.

The "cat fat" measurement is favored over the "mat fat" measurement due to the lack of maturity information in the bank balance sheets provided by the BSP. Categorizing the activities in the balance sheet makes it easier to appreciate the ease, cost, and time with which banks obtain funds critical to liquidity creation. Also, the construction of the "cat fat" liquidity creation measure follows Berger and Bouwman's (2009) three steps:

Step 1: Classify all bank activities as liquid, semiliquid, or illiquid.

All the on-balance sheet activities, such as assets, liabilities and stockholder equity, and off-balance sheet activities, such as guarantees and derivatives, are classified into liquid, semiliquid, and illiquid based on the ease, cost, and time for banks to obtain liquid funds.

Classifying Assets. Business loans, leases, premises, and investments in unconsolidated subsidiaries are classified as illiquid because these cannot be quickly sold unless required by the threat of a major loss. On the other hand, receivables, cash, securities, other marketable assets, and other related accounts are relatively easy to secure and classified as liquid. Loans to depositories and government and other related accounts are classified semiliquid because they are comparatively easy to sell or dispose of because the counterparties are large and transparent.

Classifying Liabilities and Stockholder's Equity. Deposit liabilities and payable bills and bonds are liquid liabilities. These can be easily withdrawn without penalizing customers. The semiliquid accounts are based on the subjectivity of the liability accounts per balance sheet where the account may be liquid or illiquid. All accounts under stockholder equity are illiquid because investors cannot demand liquid funds from the bank and the maturity is exceedingly long. Table 4.1 summarizes the specific liability and stockholder equity accounts and their classification.

Classifying Off-Balance Sheet Activities. In classifying guarantees, illiquid bank accounts consist of those that cannot be sold or are used to shelter financial statements from asset ownership and related debt. No liquid and semiliquid off-balance sheet activities are identified because the activities classified in the balance sheets cannot be bought or sold in the market to create liquidity. Finally, the gross fair value of derivatives is classified as a liquid account because these can be easily bought and sold and are functionally similar to liquid securities.

Step 2: Assigning weights to the activities classified in Step 1.

Activities classified according to the liquidity theory assume various weights. Banks create liquidity when they withhold illiquid items and offer liquid items to the public. The higher the volume of loans and deposits, the more liquid the bank. Illiquid assets and liquid liabilities take positive weights because liquidity happens when liquid liabilities finance illiquid assets. On the other hand, liquid assets and illiquid liabilities and equity take a negative weight because illiquid liabilities that finance liquid assets impede liquidity.

Berger and Bouwman (2009) base their weights on a simple "dollar-for-dollar-adding-up" of constraints. Applied to Philippine currency, banks create P1 liquidity when they transform a peso of illiquid assets into a peso of liquid liabilities. The reverse hampers liquidity. A weight of ½ is applied to illiquid assets and liquid liabilities while a weight of −½ is assigned to liquid assets and illiquid liabilities. To achieve maximum liquidity, one peso of liquid liabilities is used to finance one peso of illiquid assets: $0.5*1 + 0.5*1 = 1$. On the other hand, semiliquid activities get a weight of 0 because such activities fall halfway between liquid and illiquid activities. Lastly, for the off-balance sheet activities, the weight of ½ is

Table 4.1 Classified accounts with assigned weights

ASSETS		
Liquid Assets (weight = −1/2) Cash • Due from BSP • Due from other banks • Unquoted debt securities • Net due from head office/branches/ agencies • HTM financial assets • Financial assets at fair value through profit or loss • Available-for-Sale financial assets-net • Investments in non-marketable equity security-net	Semi-liquid Assets (weight = 0) General Loan Loss Provision • Loans to Bangko Sentral ng Pilipinas • Interbank loans receivable • Loans and receivables arising from RA/ CA/PR/SLB • General loan loss provision	Illiquid Assets (weight = 1/2) Other Financial Assets • Bank premises, furniture, fixture, and equipment-net • Real and other properties acquired-net • Non-current assets held for sale • Loans and receivables—others • Equity investment in subsidiaries, associates, and joint ventures-net
LIABILITIES PLUS EQUITY		
Liquid Liabilities plus Equity (Weight = 1/2) • Deposit liabilities • Bills payable • Bonds payable-net	Semi-liquid Liabilities plus Equity (Weight = 0) • Special time deposit • Due to other banks • Redeemable preferred shares • Due to Bangko Sentral ng Pilipinas • Net due to head office/branches/ agencies	Illiquid Liabilities plus Equity (Weight = −1/2) • Unsecured subordinated debt-net • Other financial liabilities • Other liabilities • Retained earnings • Capital stock • Assigned capital and other capital accounts • Financial liabilities at fair value through profit or loss

OFF-BALANCE SHEET ACTIVITIES		
Liquid off-balance sheet activities (weight = −1/2)	Semiliquid off-balance sheet activities (weight = 0)	Illiquid off-balance sheet activities (weight = 1/2) • Letters of credit: performance standby, commercial, financial standby • Commitments • Trade-related guarantees • Trust department accounts • Guarantees issued • Securities held under custodianship by bank proper • Spot foreign exchange contracts
DERIVATIVES		
Liquid derivatives (weight = −1/2)	Semi-liquid derivatives (weight = 0)	Illiquid derivatives (weight = 1/2)

Source Berger and Bowman (2009)

used for illiquid activities and 0 for semiliquid off-balance sheet activities. Similarly, derivatives get −½ because these may be easily bought and sold and are functionally similar to liquid securities. Table 4.1 summarizes Steps 1 and 2.

Step 3: Combining Activities Classified in Step 1 and Weighted in Step 2.

To construct the "cat fat" liquidity creation measure, the researchers combined the accounts that are classified into liquid, semiliquid, and illiquid multiplied by the assigned weights of ½, 0, and −½. The resulting value of the combined on- and off-balance sheet activities will be the liquidity of each bank per quarter or per year.

Estimation of Cost and Profit Efficiency Using the Stochastic Frontier Approach

This study will adopt Battese and Coelli's (1992) empirical model that various scholars use to measure different concepts of bank efficiency for developing countries. For the cost and profit efficiencies, this study will use the Stochastic Frontier Approach (SFA) which benchmarks the performance of an individual bank against another with best practices under similar conditions and which delivers the same output. The SFA measures the functional form of the frontier while the efficiency score is measured separately from the error term. It assumes that a firm deviates from the cost frontier due to inefficiency or to random fluctuation (Maudos et al. 2002). Moreover, this technique measures the minimal cost and efficiency frontiers by specifying a standard cost function with input prices and output factors (Maudos et al. 2002). One disadvantage of SFA is the possible miscalculation of the inefficiency score due to an error in specifying the functional form that the SFA requires. The inefficiency scores will follow a normal symmetrical distribution instead of a half-normal one where the efficiency scores are not constrained. Despite these shortcomings, SFA can overcome the major disadvantages of Data Envelope Analysis, which is a non-parametric approach to measuring efficiency. A number of recent studies on bank efficiency in developing countries use this approach.

This study will employ the translog specification model which Turk-Ariss (2010) used to measure bank efficiency:

$$\ln A = f(\ln Q + \ln W) + \ln e, \tag{4.7}$$

where

A = total operating cost or alternative total profits
Q & W = bank output and input prices

The underlying functional form of the translog cost function is defined in Eq. (4.8). Table 4.2 sums up the variables for measuring bank efficiency.

According to Turk-Ariss, the error term e is decomposed into $v - u$ $(v + u)$ for the profit (cost) model, where v and u are assumed to be multiplicatively separable from the rest of the function. While v is a two-sided disturbance that accounts for uncontrollable (random) factors, u is a one-sided non-negative inefficiency term. Individual cost and profit efficiency of banks in a quarter are measured with the open access software package Frontier 4.1 developed by Battese and Coelli (1992). Cost efficiency benchmarks cost against the best-practice bank in producing the same output bundle under the same conditions. On the same note, standard profit efficiency measures the gaps in producing maximum possible profit on a given level of input and output prices (Ibid). On the other hand, alternative profit efficiency measures a bank's proximity to earning maximum profit given output level and not output prices. Berger and Mester (2003) point out that alternative profit efficiency is preferred to the standard measure because it provides the means to control unaccounted differences in the quality of output quality by considering the additional revenue that higher quality output can generate (Ibid). Alternative profit will be suitable to this study because it will use a comprehensive measure of bank output.

Computation of Lerner Index as a Measure of Individual Bank's Market Power

Lerner (1934) pioneered the Lerner Index. It uses market power as a proxy to reflect the competitive behavior of banks with higher values, implying higher pricing power and less competitive market conditions. The Lerner Index is a well-established measure of the degree of competition at industry and bank levels because it captures the difference between product prices and marginal costs (Ibid). The conventional Lerner Index is measured as the ratio of difference between price and marginal cost to

Table 4.2 Summary of variables

Variables	*Definition*	*Data Source*
Bank Efficiency Estimation		
A	Total operating cost or total operating profit	Financial statements of banks as disclosed in their annual reports
Q	Liquidity creation	Computed using Berger and Bouwman's (2009) 3-step procedure; and BSP Database
W1	Input price of labor defined as the ratio of labor expenses to liquidity creation	Financial statements of banks as disclosed in their annual reports
W2	Input price of physical capital defined as the ratio of operating cost to fixed assets	
W3	Input price of funds or deposits defined as the ratio of interest expense to total deposits	
Objective 1		
Dependent variables		
Cost efficiency Profit efficiency	Measured using Frontier 4.1 software	Financial statements of banks as disclosed in their annual reports
Independent variables		
Portfolio Characteristics		
Market Power (+)	Inverse measure of market competition: Conventional Lerner Index, Adjusted Lerner Index	Financial statements of banks as disclosed in their annual reports
Bank size (+)	Natural logarithmic of total assets	Financial statements of banks as disclosed in their annual reports
Capitalization (+)	Ratio of equity to total assets	
Objective 2		
Dependent variables		
Cost efficiency	Estimated using Frontier 4.1 software	Financial statements of banks as disclosed in their annual reports

(continued)

Table 4.2 (continued)

Variables	*Definition*	*Data Source*
Profit efficiency		
Independent variables		
Portfolio Characteristics		
Market Power (+)	Inverse measure of market competition: Conventional Lerner Index, Adjusted Lerner Index	Financial statements of banks as disclosed in their annual reports
LernerIndex*dIncDiv (+)	Interaction term of market power and income diversification index dummy variable	
IncDiv (+)	Income diversification index	
Bank size (+)	Natural logarithmic of total assets	
Capitalization (+)	Ratio of equity to total assets	
Regulatory environment		
GDP (+)	Ln of per capita GDP	PSA
Objective 3		
Dependent variables		
Z-index	Measure of financial stability used as an inverse proxy for overall risk	Financial statements of banks as disclosed in their annual reports
Independent variables		
Portfolio Characteristics		
Market Power (+)	Inverse measure of market competition: Conventional Lerner Index, Adjusted Lerner Index, HHI Loans	Financial statements of banks as disclosed in their annual reports
LernerIndex*dIncDiv (+)	Interaction term of market power and income diversification index dummy variable	
IncDiv (+)	Income diversification index	
Bank size (+)	Natural logarithmic of total assets	Financial statements of banks as disclosed in their annual reports
Capitalization (+)	Ratio of equity to total assets	
Regulatory Environment		
GDP (+)	Natural logarithmic of per capita GDP	PSA

Source Author's framework

price.

$$\ln TC = \alpha_0 + \alpha_1 \ln y + \frac{1}{2}\alpha_2 (\ln y)^2 + \sum_{j=1}^{3} \beta_j \ln w_j + \sum_{j=1}^{3}\sum_{k=1}^{3} \beta_{jk} \ln w_j \ln w_k + \sum_{j=1}^{3} \gamma_j \ln y \ln w_j + \varepsilon \tag{4.8}$$

where

TC = total cost
y = total assets
w_1 = price of labor (the ratio of staff expenses to the number of employees)
w_2 = price of physical capital (the ratio of the sum of general and administrative expenses, depreciation, and other operating expenses, divided by fixed assets)
w_3 = price of borrowed funds (the ratio of the costs of borrowed funds to borrowed funds)

$$L_{it} = \frac{P_{it} - MC_{it}}{P_{it}} \tag{4.9}$$

where P = price and MC = marginal cost. However, one cannot directly observe and estimate marginal cost, but derive it from the estimated translog cost function.

The total cost is the sum of staff expenses, general and administrative expenses, depreciation, other operating expenses, and costs of borrowed funds. The estimated coefficients of the cost functions are then used to compute the marginal cost, which is presented below. High values of the Lerner Index mean significant market power.

$$MC = \frac{TC}{y}\left(\alpha_1 + \alpha_2 \ln y + \sum_{j=1}^{3} \gamma_j \ln w_j\right) \tag{4.10}$$

Estimating the Effect of Bank Competition on Cost and Profit

Efficiency of the Top 20 UKBs in the Philippines

The GMM panel measurement will determine the magnitude of the relationship among the variables. Aside from this, a GMM measurement system will consider the unobserved bank-specific effects and joint endogeneity of the explanatory variables. This method has the following advantages:

1. It assumes non-normality of data, takes steps to verify probability distribution function, and corrects endogeneity in the data.
2. It calculates robust estimators in an alternative process by measuring the covariance matrix that will allow correction of cross-section dependence. This is why GMM panel estimation is better suited to handling higher moments, such as skewness and kurtosis.

To reduce data errors, GMM uses a cross-section weighting procedure and a covariance matrix that allows panel-corrected errors to account for the heteroskedastic nature of the data. Roberts and Whited stated that the main advantage of the GMM approach is its detection, within reasonable limits, of several types of misspecifications that may affect the regression results, such as heteroskedasticity and nonlinearity (Berger and Bouwman 2009).

To arrive at valid conclusions, several model statistics tested the soundness of the assumptions prior to performing the GMM panel estimation. Unit root tests and variance-ratio tests were performed for every variable in the regressions. A diagnostic test, F-test, or the First-Stage Test checked the relevance and validity of the instruments. To ensure the endogeneity test of the instruments and serial correlation, the J test, Arellano-Bond test, and the Durbin-Wu-Hausman test—also known as the Hausman specification test—validated the autocorrelation of residuals from a statistical regression analysis. All tests used E-Views 12 software, while Minitab 21 software illustrated the scatterplots with a local regression fit of random effects. This may alter the significance of the relevant variables for the entire panel regression.

To determine the impact of bank competition on 118, the study makes use of Turk-Aris' baseline model:

$$Y = f(\text{Market Competition}, \text{Portfolio Characteristics, Regulatory Environment}) \tag{4.11}$$

where the dependent variable Υ measures the cost efficiency and alternative profit efficiency of each bank. Specifically, the regression model for Objective 1 is defined as:

$$Y = f\left(Y_{t-1,}\text{LernerIndex, LernerIndex}^2, \text{BankSize, Capitalization, GDP}\right) \tag{4.12}$$

The study included the lag of the dependent variable to account for the influence of the previous value of the dependent variable on its current value. The Lerner Index was used as a proxy for the degree of market power with higher values, implying greater pricing power and less competitive market conditions. The Lerner Index is preferred for measuring market power because it looks into consistency at the bank level. The computation of the conventional Lerner Index assumes that banks operate at maximum efficiency even as they must deal with unaccounted inefficiencies.

To address this concern, the Lerner index was adjusted as follows:

$$\text{Adjusted Lerner index} = \frac{\pi_i + tc_i - mc_i(q_i)}{\pi_i + tc_i} \tag{4.13}$$

where

π_i = profit of bank
tc_i = total cost
mc_i = marginal cost
q_i = total output.

The adjusted Lerner index checked the strength of the regression results despite the unaccounted inefficiencies. The regression model introduced the squares of market power variables in light of the expected non-linear relationship between market power and bank efficiency. With this, expect the regressions to show a low R^2 value, which indicates a good fit for linear, but not quadratic, relationships. The variables for bank size and capitalization represent bank portfolio characteristics. Bank size indicates economies and diseconomies of scale in the market. Although prior studies were inconclusive, regression results are expected to be positive. On the other hand, bank capitalization, which determines bank cost and profit efficiency, is also expected to have a positive effect. Lastly, the study will employ the per capita GDP, which considers the country's overall economic conditions. Table 4.2 summarizes the variables that determine the effects of bank competition on cost and profit efficiency.

The second objective is to establish the effect of greater market power and a higher degree of income diversification on the cost and profit efficiency of dominant and fringe banks. After estimating the impact of bank competition on bank efficiency, including income diversification measures in the regression model for the first objective, the authors determined if bank competition enhances or deters efficiency, given that they have adopted different levels of income diversification.

Following Toh et al. (2019), the study introduces the LernerIndex*dIncDiv to the baseline model to study the impact of different levels of diversification and competition on cost and profit efficiency. The regression model for Objective 2 is defined as:

$$Y = f(\text{Efficiency}_{t-1,}\ \text{LernerIndex}, \text{LernerIndex}^2, (\text{LernerIndex} * \text{dIncDiv}), \text{IncDiv}, \text{BankSize}, \text{Capitalization}, \text{GDP}) \tag{4.14}$$

where variables in Eqs. 4.12 and 4.13 remain

$$\text{IncDiv} = \text{income diversification index of banks}$$

On the other hand, the coefficient of LernerIndex*dIncDiv will explain if high market power and high-level income diversification enhance or impede bank cost and profit efficiency. The income diversification dummy variable is equal to 1 for highly diversified banks and 0 for less diversified banks. A bank whose income diversification value is above the median index of all the banks is considered highly diversified.

Following Doan et al. (2018), bank diversification measures are computed using the HHI for each bank with total operating income broken down into net interest income (NET), and non-interest income (NON). The main components of non-interest income are fee-based, trading, and other non-interest income. Fee-based income includes bank commissions, service charges/fees, and other commissions, while trading income includes income from trading government securities, private equity/debt; financial futures, forwards, and swaps; profit from the sale of investments; and profit from foreign exchange. The bank's degree of income diversification, IncDiv, is calculated as follows:

$$\text{IncDiv} = 1-(\text{NetShare}^2 + \text{NonShare}^2) \tag{4.15}$$

where NetShare and NonShare are shares of net interest income and of non-interest income from total operating income, respectively, computed as:

$$\text{NetShare} = \frac{\text{NET}}{\text{Total Operating Income}}$$
$$\text{and NonShare} = \frac{\text{NON}}{\text{Total Operating Income}} \tag{4.16}$$

A higher value of IncDiv indicates a more diversified mix. A value of 0 indicates complete concentration, meaning that all income comes from a single source, while 0.5 indicates complete diversification, or an even split between net interest income and non-interest income.

In this objective, bank size is introduced as a moderator variable. The Philippine UKBs will be grouped according to bank size, that is, dominant (Top 10) and fringe (Next 10), to account for the differences in behavior (Dacanay 2017).

The third objective is to determine the effect of greater market power and a higher degree of income diversification on the stability of dominant and fringe banks. The same regression model specification in Objective 2 will be used following the tripod estimation model of Turk-Ariss (2010). However, the measure for financial stability, or the Z-index, replaces the dependent variables of cost and profit efficiency. The former serves as an inverse proxy of the bank's overall risk.

Following is the regression model for Objective 3:

$$\begin{aligned} Z\text{-Index} = f(&Z\text{-Index}_{t-1}, \text{LernerIndex}, \text{LernerIndex}^2, \\ &(\text{LernerIndex} * \text{dIncDiv}), \\ &\text{IncDiv}, \text{BankSize}, \text{Capitalization}, \text{GDP}) \end{aligned} \tag{4.17}$$

The Z-index is used as a proxy for financial stability with larger values indicating more stability and less risk potential. This study will employ two risk-adjusted measures of return for each bank following Merciera et al. (2007):

$$\mathrm{ROR}_{\mathrm{ROA}} = \frac{\overline{\mathrm{ROA}}}{\sigma \mathrm{ROA}} \text{ and } \mathrm{ROR}_{\mathrm{ROE}} = \frac{\overline{\mathrm{ROE}}}{\sigma \mathrm{ROE}}, \tag{4.18}$$

where $\mathrm{ROR}_{\mathrm{ROA}}$ and $\mathrm{ROR}_{\mathrm{ROE}}$ denote risk-adjusted ROA and ROE, respectively (Mercieca et al. 2007).

The estimation of cost and profit efficiencies is considered within the production function the direct measurement of risk-taking behavior (asset and loan portfolios). To study the market structure and the concentration ratio of the Philippine banking industry, the HHI of deposits stood as an alternative measure for competition. The HHI was obtained from the individual market shares of the Top 20 UKBs and the high correlation of HHI of the Top 46 banks with the other explanatory variables of the regression. Table 4.2 summarizes the variables that determine the effect of high-income diversification and market power on cost and profit efficiency and their indicators, as measured by Z-index.

Presentation, Interpretation, and Analysis of Results

The following objectives serve as the springboard for discussing the empirical tests and results of this study.

1. *To determine the effect of bank competition on bank performance in terms of the cost and profit efficiency of the Top 20 UKBs in the Philippines.* Based on the first hypothesis, the significant positive relationship of competition to cost and profit efficiency at bank level as measured by the Lerner Index will establish the cost and profit of banks that wield greater market power.
2. *To determine the effects of greater market power and high levels of income diversification of cost and profit efficiency.* The significant positive relationship of the income diversification index with cost and profit efficiency will verify the benefits of income diversification. Also, the positive effect of the dummy variable that categorizes banks by their level of diversification will verify which ones enjoy

high levels of market power and income diversification in terms of cost and profit efficiency.

3. *To determine the effect of high marker power and bank income diversification on bank stability in terms of* Z_{ROA} *and* Z_{ROE}. The positive interaction of the dummy variable "income diversification" and the Lerner index with bank stability will verify the benefits of increasing the market power of the highly diversified banks.

Ultimately, the results aim to answer the question, "Do greater market power and a high degree of income diversification contribute to bank efficiency and stability?" Data from individual banks in the roster of Top 20 Philippine UKBs covers 95% of the banking industry in terms of total assets. The quarterly panel data covering 2005–2019 came from the public database of the BSP and the SEC as well as from the annual reports of the banks in the sample. The Appendix contains descriptive statistics of the variables used in the study.

Market Power and Efficiency

Objective 1: To determine the effect of greater market power on bank performance in terms of the cost and profit efficiency of the Top 20 UKBs in the Philippines.

Analysis of Profit and Cost Efficiency
The study uses SFA to measure the extent to which a bank achieves efficient frontiers, along with the intermediation approach, which recognizes the role of financial institutions as intermediaries between savers and investors. In the production process, banks channel deposits, loans, and contingent liabilities to deposit holdings, securities, and loans as output (Sealey and Lindley 1977). Banks are multi-input and multi-output institutions. For this reason, Berger and Bouwman's (2009) measure for liquidity creation, which takes into account on- and off-balance sheet activities, serves as the more comprehensive measure for total bank output. Figures 4.5 and 4.6 illustrate the trend in cost and profit efficiency of the Top 20 UKBs in the Philippines.Fig. 4.6Adjusted Lerner index(Source Author's framework)

Note the fluctuation in the mean profit efficiency of the Top 20 UKBs from the first quarter of 2005 to the fourth quarter of 2019. Despite the general uptick, profit efficiency dipped in between increases. The major

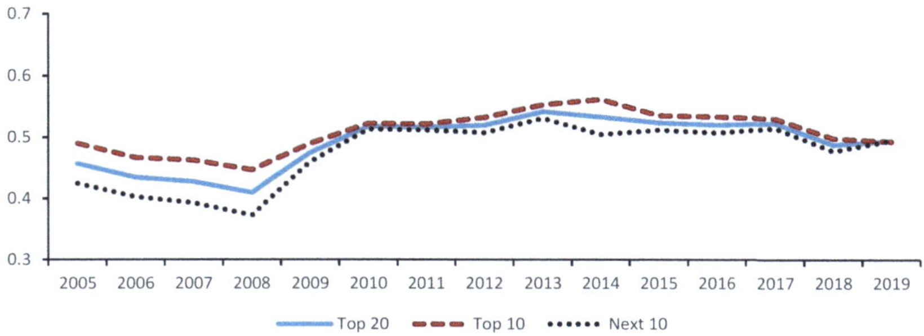

Fig. 4.5 Conventional Lerner index (*Source* Author's framework)

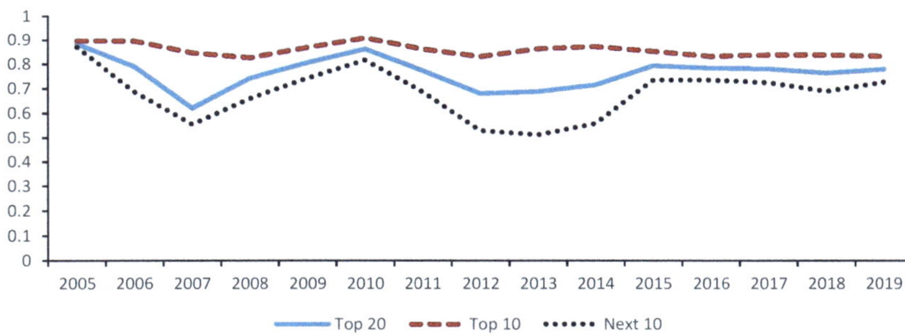

Fig. 4.6 Adjusted Lerner index (*Source* Author's framework)

drop in profit efficiency happened in the first quarter of 2008 and the second quarter of 2012. This trend is most likely due to the sudden surge in total costs of banks in 2008 and 2012, leading to negative profit, especially among the fringe banks. Splitting the sample into dominant and fringe banks may provide insight to the type that delivers the best profit maximization. The graph shows not much difference in the movement of the mean profit efficiencies of the banks studied, with the dominant banks exhibiting an average profit efficiency of 92%, and the fringe banks, 81%.

Similarly, the movement of the mean cost efficiency faltered throughout the sample period. From 2009 to 2011, the banks performed consistently well but the graph for profit efficiency shows a huge drop in cost efficiency in 2008. As earlier mentioned, this may be the direct impact of the sudden surge in the total costs of banks in 2008. Furthermore, from the mean cost efficiencies of dominant and fringe banks, one can deduce minor differences in mean cost efficiencies. The dominant banks scored a higher mean profit efficiency of 83%, while the fringe banks achieved 80%, indicating that the large banks are slightly more profit efficient.

Analysis of the Degree of Market Power of Top 20 UKBs

To study market competition, researchers like Rosse–Panzar (1987) use the aggregate measure of bank competition, while Bresnahan-Lau (1982) uses concentration indices. This study, which required bank-level data or individual measures of competition, used the Lerner Index to measure the degree of market power or as an inverse measure of market competition. Figure 4.5 shows the trend of the annual mean conventional Lerner index over the sample period.

The conventional Lerner Index displayed a rising trend among the sample banks over the sample period even as the mean level of market competition experienced a significant drop in 2008 due to a sudden surge in the total costs of the banks. This influenced the total revenue of banks and was used to compute charges on products and services and marginal costs. Loss of market power was more evident among fringe banks. This could indicate the presence of a competitive market structure in the Philippine banking industry during the raid period. From 2009 to 2014, the domestic banking market was approaching market concentration and less competition, while dominant and fringe banks saw a slight decrease in market power from 2015 to 2018. By 2019, banks started to recover market power (Fig. 4.5).

Unlike the conventional Lerner Index, the efficiency-adjusted Lerner index (Fig. 4.6) responded to the apparent inefficiency of banks. Moreover, the adjusted index took into account the possible endogeneity between efficiency and the Lerner Index, which is a possible mutual causality between these two variables. This is important because two of the study objectives have efficiency scores as the dependent variable and the Lerner index as the independent variable.

Although the movement of the adjusted Lerner index is similar to that of the conventional index, the adjusted index has higher values because it takes into account the total costs and net profit of banks and not total revenues alone. The sudden drop in the adjusted Lerner index in 2007 was due to the relatively low profit of fringe banks—in particular, HSBC,

East West Bank, and UCPB—during the said period. The authors therefore maintain that the market structure of the Philippine banking industry was moving towards more concentration.

The efficiency and market power graphs for the top 20 UKBs support the assumption of Freixas and Rochet's Monte-Klein model (2008) and the dominant bank model of VanHoose (2010, 2017, 2022) which affirm that the Philippine banking industry operates in an imperfect market. In this environment, dominant, competitive, and efficient banks compete alongside smaller, less competitive, and less efficient fringe banks.

Empirical Results for Objective 1

GMM panel estimation with random effects according to the Hausman test used quarterly data. Tables 4.3 and 4.4 present the regression results for Objective 1. Using the two different specifications of the Lerner Index, the lag in profit and cost efficiency turned out significant for the Top 20 banks. This implies that the strategy of banks to maximize profit and minimize costs influences their current profit and cost efficiency.

The degree of market power turned out significant in terms of predicting the profit and cost efficiency using the two specifications of the Lerner index at 1%. The positive coefficients of the Lerner index indicated that the higher the market power, the higher the profit and cost efficiency. This means that banks use their market power to charge higher loan rates and therefore earn much more and are more efficient. The result supports the information generation hypothesis, referred to as the competition-inefficiency hypothesis. However, increased market competition and the erosion of market power may deteriorate bank cost and profit efficiency due to thinner profit margins since the market dictates the prices of bank products. This result is consistent with those obtained by Pruteanu-Podpiera et al. (2016) for the Czech banking industry and Phan (2015), who covered six emerging Asian countries, including the Philippines.

The squares of both the conventional and adjusted Lerner indices were significant in terms of cost and profit efficiency, demonstrating a non-linear relationship between the degree of market power and bank efficiency. This also resulted in low values for R^2 that measured suitability for linear relationships but not for quadratic relationships.

Two opposing signs emerged. The positive sign of the coefficient for the quadratic term for the Top 20 banks using the adjusted Lerner index revealed a parabolic shape to illustrate the relationship between market

Table 4.3 Regression results for Objective 1: The top 20 banks' profit and cost efficiency as dependent variables

Method: Panel GMM EGLS (Cross-section random effects)
Sample (adjusted): 2005Q2 2019Q4; Total panel (balanced) observations: 1180
Cross-section weights instrument weighting matrix; estimator of component variances: Swamy and Arora

Regressors and Expected Signs	Dependent Variable: COST EFFICIENCY [a, b]		Dependent Variable: PROFIT EFFICIENCY [a, b]	
	Model 1: Lerner Index	Model 2: Adjusted Lerner Index	Model 1: Lerner Index	Model 2: Adjusted Lerner Index
C	-0.0212 ns (0.1632)	0.5318 *** (0.1668)	-0.2477 *** (0.0369)	-0.2062 *** (0.0371)
PROFIT/COST EFF (-1) (+)	0.0159 *** (0.0054)	0.0228 *** (0.0049)	0.202 *** (0.0029)	0.2749 *** (0.0032)
LERNER INDEX (+)	2.3587 *** (0.2994)	0.0876 *** (0.0109)	1.3375 *** (0.021)	0.0288 *** (0.0007)
LERNER INDEX^2 (+/-)	-3.0341*** (0.3131)	0.0139 *** (0.0027)	-1.0654 *** (0.02)	0.004 *** (0.0001)
BANK SIZE (+)	0.1086 *** (0.0037)	0.1078 *** (0.0034)	0.039 *** (0.0003)	0.0407 *** (0.0003)
CAPITALIZATION (+)	0.4851 *** (0.1145)	0.6894 *** (0.0923)	0.2038 *** (0.0058)	0.1754 *** (0.0066)
GDP (+)	-0.0922 *** (0.0171)	-0.1161*** (0.017)	0.0045 ns (0.0036)	0.0286 *** (0.0036)
Durbin-Watson Stat	1.901619	1.855801	2.072642	2.131339
J-stat (Sargan statistic)	1.15E-19	1.61E-18	1.37E-18	5.18E-20
AR(1)	-13.04 ***	13.19 ***	13.26 ***	13.23 ***
AR(2)	-1.55 ns	-1.55 ns	0.62 ns	0.73 ns

Notes:
a. The Lerner Index refers to the Conventional Lerner Index. The highlighted cells refer to the rejected sign that was expected to be significant.
b. *** refers to p-value [0.00, 0.01]; ** refers to p-value [0.01, 0.05]; * refers to p-value [0.05, 0.10]

Source of Basic Data BSP, SEC, and bank annual reports

Table 4.4 Regression results for Objective 2: The top 10 banks profit and cost efficiency as dependent variables

Method: Panel GMM EGLS (Cross-section random effects)
Sample (adjusted): 2005Q2 2019Q4; Total panel (balanced) observations: 590
Cross-section weights instrument weighting matrix; Swamy and Arora estimator of component variances

Dominant (Top 10) Banks

Regressors and Expected Signs	Dependent Variable: Cost Efficiency [a, b, c]		Dependent Variable: Profit Efficiency [a, b, c]	
	Model 1: Lerner Index	Model 2: Adjusted Lerner Index	Model 1: Lerner Index	Model 2: Adjusted Lerner Index
C	0.8573 *** (0.0469)	0.6369 *** (0.0352)	0.1114 *** (0.017)	0.1893 *** (0.0163)
COST/PROFIT EFF (-1) (+)	-0.0371 *** (0.0084)	-0.0267 *** (0.009)	0.2028 *** (0.0027)	0.2138 *** (0.0027)
LERNER INDEX (+)	-2.9686 *** (0.2186)	-0.0252 * (0.0149)	1.1191 *** (0.0229)	0.0842 *** (0.004)
LERNER INDEX^2 (+/-)	2.3341 *** (0.2016)	-0.0675 *** (0.0089)	-0.8897 *** (0.0202)	-0.0155 *** (0.0021)
BANK SIZE (+)	0.0499 *** (0.0009)	0.0408 *** (0.0011)	0.0371 *** (0.0003)	0.0397 *** (0.0003)
CAPITALIZATION (+)	0.0329 ns (0.0221)	-0.0432 ns (0.0306)	0.3625 *** (0.0068)	0.3872 *** (0.0069)
GDP (+)	0.0285 *** (0.0033)	-0.0138 *** (0.004)	-0.0199 *** (0.0017)	-0.0053 *** (0.0016)
INCOME DIVERSIFICATION (+)	0.1409 *** (0.0103)	-0.0243 ns (0.0198)	-0.0894 *** (0.0038)	-0.0882 *** (0.0038)
ID*LERNER INDEX (+)	0.0059 * (0.0032)	0.0327 *** (0.0044)	0.0026 *** (0.0009)	0.0029 *** (0.0005)
Durbin-Watson Stat	2.038918	2.00911	2.11291	2.129661
J-stat (Sargan statistic)	1.71E-17	3.15E-17	7.07E-18	2.04E-18
AR(1)	-10.71 ***	-10.68 ***	-9.59 ***	-9.50 ***
AR(2)	2.06 **	1.97 **	0.64 ns	0.57 ns

Notes:
a. The Lerner Index refers to the Conventional Lerner Index. The highlighted cells refer to the rejected signs that were expected to be significant.
b. Numbers inside the parentheses indicate standard error.
c. *** refers to p-value [0.00, 0.01]; ** refers to p-value [0.01, 0.05]; * refers to p-value [0.05, 0.10]

Source of basic data BSP, SEC, and bank annual reports

power and bank efficiency. The negative sign for the quadratic term of market power describes the relationship between market power and profit efficiency. Figures 4.7 and 4.8 verify the results of the regressions.

The graphs illustrate the inverted U relationship between bank efficiency and the conventional Lerner Index. While the scatterplot for bank efficiency against the adjusted Lerner Index demonstrates the U-shaped relationship of the variables, proving the non-linear relationship between market power and efficiency measures. Bank size, proxied by the natural log of total assets, also has a notably positive relationship with profit efficiency in the conventional and the adjusted Lerner indices. This sheds light on the assumption that large banks benefit from economies of scale and scope of operation.

In terms of cost efficiency, bank size is significant for both specifications of the Lerner index. The capitalization ratio of banks in predicting cost and profit efficiency is very significant at 1%. The adjusted Lerner

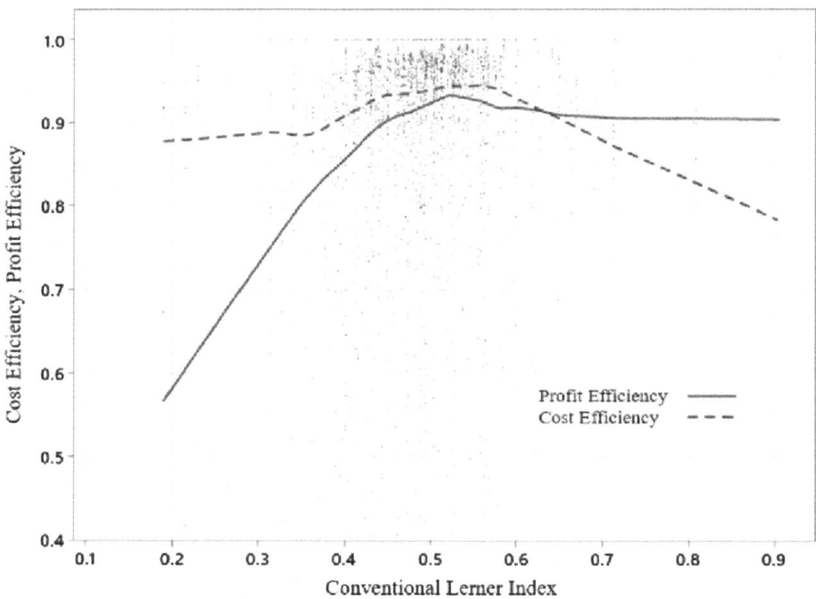

Fig. 4.7 Scatterplot of cost and profit efficiency vs. conventional Lerner index (*Source* Author's framework)

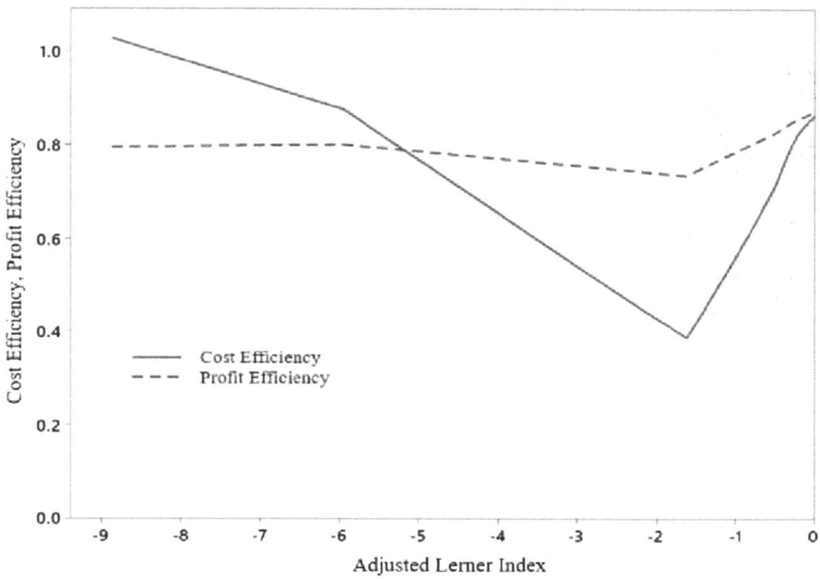

Fig. 4.8 Scatterplot of cost and profit efficiency vs. adjusted Lerner index (*Source* Author's framework)

Index showed that the 1-unit increase in the capitalization ratio had the biggest impact on cost efficiency. This confirms the role of the capitalization ratio as a buffer for future losses and for reducing default costs. One may conclude that banks with high capital are more inclined to minimize costs or to maximize profit.

Lastly, the adjusted Lerner Index showed a positive significant relationship between GDP per capita and profit efficiency. However, increasing GDP showed a negative effect on efficiency as cost management tends to slack in periods of major profit gains.

Market Power and Income Diversification

Objective 2: To determine the effects of greater market power and more extensive diversification on the cost and profit efficiency of dominant and fringe banks.

To verify if market power alone contributes to achieving higher cost and profit efficiency of the Top 20 UKBs, the researchers conducted a preliminary check on the effects of high market power on the cost and profit efficiency of banks, regardless of their level of diversification. The results of the regressions in the first objective showed that an increase in market power improves the banks' capacity to minimize cost and to maximize profit. Objective 2 will shed light on whether bank income diversification enhances the cost and profit efficiency of banks, especially when these enjoy greater market power.

Income Diversification Index of the Top 20 UKBs

The conventional Lerner Index displayed an overall rise over the sample period but with a significant drop in the mean level of market competition in 2008 due to a sudden surge in the total costs of the banks. This influenced total revenue, used to compute charges on products and services, as well as the sample banks' marginal costs. Fringe banks exhibited a greater drop in market power, which may give a clue about the competitive market structure of the Philippine banking industry. From 2009 to 2014, the domestic market was approaching more market concentration and less competition. Market power of dominant and fringe banks slightly dropped from 2015 to 2018 and gradually recovered in 2019 (Fig. 4.9).

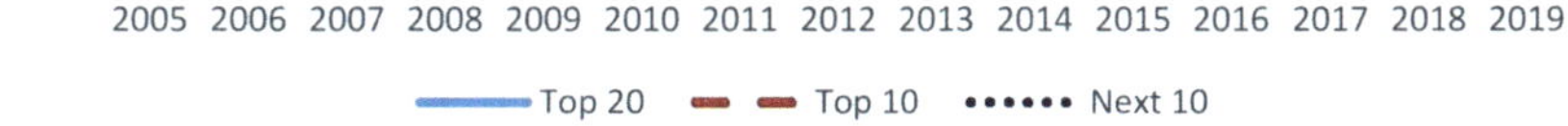

Fig. 4.9 Income diversification index (*Source* Author's framework)

Based on the trend of the mean income diversification index of banks, the Top 10 and Next 10 banks started out as highly income-diversified in 2005, at 42.1 and 45.75%, respectively. As mentioned, the ideal income diversification index should be 0–0.5. In 2006, however, the index of the fringe banks began to drop until it reached an all-time low of –0.10 in 2008 due to losses sustained in the period covered by this study. Most badly hit were Deutsche Bank, which lost millions in net interest income from 2006 to 2009, Bank of Commerce, and Standard Chartered Bank, which suffered losses from non-interest income activities. The fringe banks slowly recovered in 2008 while the dominant banks seemed unaffected even by the global financial crisis and remained highly diversified throughout the sample period.

Empirical Results for Objective 2

The regression model used here is the same as that of the baseline model for Objective 1 save for the introduction of the income diversification index and the interaction term of the dummy variable for the income diversification index and Lerner index. The dummy variable for the income diversification index categorized the banks according to low and high levels of diversification. The interaction term of the dummy variable of the income diversification index and Lerner index captured the effect on cost and profit efficiency of having high market power and a high degree of income diversification. Obtaining a positive sign for the interaction term would verify the benefits of high-income diversification and market power on cost and profit efficiency. Tables 4.4 and 4.5 present the regression results for Objective 2. Again, the baseline result of a lag in profit efficiency is a significant indicator of efficiency within the period covered. The regression results for dominant banks in Table 4.4 verify this.

The two bank groups behaved differently as VanHoose (2013) predicted in his dominant bank model. The degree of market power of dominant banks in the context of the conventional and adjusted Lerner indices exhibited a significant inverse relationship with cost efficiency. Hick's Quiet Life hypothesis (1935), also known as the competition-efficiency hypothesis, comes into play here. Dominant banks with high market power are less pressured to compete. They sustain operations with monopoly rents and tend to be lax in managing costs. Inversely, loss of market power and more intense competition in the banking industry

Table 4.5 Regression results for Objective 2: The fringe banks (next 10) profit and cost efficiency as dependent variables

Method: Panel GMM EGLS (Cross-section random effects)
Sample (adjusted): 2005Q2 2019Q4; Total panel (balanced) observations: 590
Cross-section weights instrument weighting matrix; Swamy and Arora estimator of component variances

Fringe (Next 10) Banks

Regressors and Expected Signs	Dependent Variable: Cost Efficiency [a, b, c]		Dependent Variable: Profit Efficiency [a, b, c]	
	Model 1: Conventional Lerner Index	Model 2: Adjusted Lerner Index	Model 1: Conventional Lerner Index	Model 2: Adjusted Lerner Index
C	-0.9579 ** (0.3975)	0.5282 ns (0.3868)	-0.5211 *** (0.0517)	-0.4902 *** (0.0544)
COST/PROFIT EFFICIENCY (-1) (+)	0.0356 ** (0.017)	0.0771 *** (0.0294)	0.1901 *** (0.0039)	0.301 *** (0.0044)
LERNER INDEX (+)	3.8741 *** (0.6015)	0.1728 *** (0.037)	1.6101 *** (0.0269)	0.0196 *** (0.0008)
LERNER INDEX^2 (+/-)	-5.0381 *** (0.6132)	0.0151 ** (0.0073)	-1.3655 *** (0.0271)	0.0016 *** (0.0001)
BANK SIZE (+)	0.1242 *** (0.0153)	0.1895 *** (0.0178)	0.0362 *** (0.0006)	0.0362 *** (0.0007)
CAPITALIZATION (+)	0.1369 ns (0.2111)	1.096 *** (0.2467)	0.1357 *** (0.0077)	0.1272 *** (0.0078)
GDP (+)	-0.0444 ns (0.0448)	-0.2209 *** (0.0458)	0.0299 *** (0.0051)	0.0597 *** (0.0054)
INCOME DIVERSIFICATION (+)	-0.0464 * (0.0251)	0.0032 ns (0.0163)	-0.0197 *** (0.0016)	0.0308 *** (0.0015)
ID*LERNER INDEX (+)	0.2096 *** (0.0368)	-0.1226 ** (0.0522)	0.0022 *** (0.0014)	-0.0113 *** (0.0008)
Durbin-Watson Stat	1.990511	2.005492	2.060453	2.146071
J-stat (Sargan statistic)	8.70E-19	2.02E-18	1.51E-18	2.66E-20
AR(1)	-9.01 ***	-9.11 ***	-9.34 ***	-9.30 ***
AR(2)	-1.30 ns	-1.21 ns	0.27 ns	0.47 ns

Notes:
a. The Lerner Index refers to the Conventional Lerner Index. The highlighted cells refer to the rejected signs that were expected to be significant.
b. Numbers inside the parentheses indicate standard error.
c. *** refers to p-value [0.00, 0.01]; ** refers to p-value [0.01, 0.05]; * refers to p-value [0.05, 0.10]

Source of basic data BSP, SEC, and bank annual reports

would result in thinning profit margins and most likely push the dominant banks to improve operational efficiency.

On the other hand, the regression for profit efficiency of the dominant banks showed that market power significantly and positively affects profit efficiency. Even if the dominant banks do not take advantage of their market power to increase costs, they harness it to improve profit margins and profit efficiency. Using market power to charge higher loan rates and to earn higher profits compensate for inefficient cost management. Regression results for profit efficiency also imply that an increase in market competition may lead to poorer profit efficiency. This supports the information generation hypothesis, or the competition-inefficiency hypothesis. The market power of banks, as manifested in the capacity to set higher prices, market knowledge, and investment in technology, as well as their monitoring and screening procedures, may deteriorate as market competition intensifies. Banks gather quality client information from long-term relationships with their clients. However, with the onset of more intense competition, relationships tend to be shorter with clients frequently switching banks. Moreover, it becomes costlier for banks to retain old clients and attract new ones. Thus, banks become less efficient as they do not generate the maximum value expected from investing in new technologies and aggressive marketing efforts.

In terms of bank size, the regression for dominant banks in both specifications of the Lerner Index showed a significant positive relationship between total assets and cost and profit efficiency. This is in line with the prior assumption that expansion of assets or scale can be advantageous in terms of lower unit operating costs. Plus, investing in more branches, ATMs, and other technologies that facilitate and speed up transactions make banks more efficient in serving and, ultimately, retaining customers.

On the other hand, capitalization significantly and positively affects the profit efficiency of dominant banks. A well-capitalized bank attracts more customers as people are confident that it can withstand economic downturns. Diversifying income sources however has an opposite effect on cost and profit efficiency, as indicated in the conventional Lerner Index. Income diversification helps dominant banks achieve better cost efficiencies through cost sharing over multiple products or markets, as stated in the conglomeration hypothesis. On the other hand, according to the strategic focus hypothesis, the level of income diversification alone has a significant negative relationship with profit efficiency. These opposing effects mean that dominant banks can benefit from the economies of scale arising from their diversified income sources. In turn, they improve their capability to manage costs. Still, the same effect may not be true for profit because banks may not be reaping the earnings expected from their diversified income sources.

The regression for the interaction term of the level of income diversification and market power showed that the dominant highly diversified banks benefit more if their efficiency improves with increased market power. This means that market power can improve the cost and profit efficiency of banks through greater income diversification. The result also suggests that income diversification alone is not enough to improve efficiency. Dominant banks that venture into other income-generating activities must also have high market power. According to the market power theory, a bank must first have market power and position in its current market to back its successful entry to new markets. In addition, market power allows income-diversified banks to gather more market data to guide their decisions and strategies, such as the proper allocation of resources and smart assessment of activities that generate maximum profit.

Finally, GDP per capita served as a significant indicator of cost and profit efficiency even if the regression yielded opposing signs. The adjusted Lerner Index showed a negative relationship between market power and cost efficiency. One may argue that a thriving business environment negatively affects banks since they tend to relax their cost management procedures. On the other hand, the conventional Lerner index reflects a positive impact since a prosperous economy multiplies opportunities for banks to offer more products and therefore earn more.

For fringe banks, the result of the regressions using the conventional and adjusted Lerner Index for market power is consistent with the result of the baseline regression. As with the dominant banks, market power has a significant positive effect on the cost and profit efficiency of fringe banks. This supports the information generation hypothesis and implies that fringe banks benefit from high market power. Further, increased competition might adversely affect cost minimization and profit maximization. In a more competitive market, declining market power risks loss of longstanding clients, owing to the tendency of customers to switch banks. In addition, decreased capacity to generate market information makes a bank more prone to credit defaults. As seen in Table 4.5, the coefficients of market power are bigger for the regressions with cost efficiency as the dependent variable. This means that fringe banks tend to use their market power to minimize costs as they cannot profit as much as the dominant banks. As the dominant bank model explains, fringe banks only take the price that the market dictates.

With regard to bank size, fringe and dominant banks yielded the same results, reinforcing the assumption that optimizing assets through economies of scale and scope improve cost and profit efficiency. Fringe banks enjoy cost efficiency because they operate at the right scale and do not incur excessive costs. The regression results also revealed the significant positive effect of capitalization on cost and profit efficiency by serving as a buffer for future losses. Banks with high capital are likely to perform better on the efficient cost frontier because of low default costs.

The effects of income diversification on the cost and profit efficiency of fringe banks had mixed results. The conventional Lerner index showed that the income diversification index negatively affected the cost and profit efficiency of fringe banks. As with the dominant banks, this relationship exists among fringe banks because income diversification alone does not contribute to improved efficiency; it can even bloat operating costs because fringe banks are more prone to fail in their efforts at diversification. The combined effect of income diversification and market power improved the cost and profit efficiency of highly diversified fringe banks. This is because highly diversified fringe banks know their market and so deliver the maximum value expected from their new ventures. Figure 4.10 summarizes the interrelationship of the Lerner index, income diversification, and bank efficiency variables.

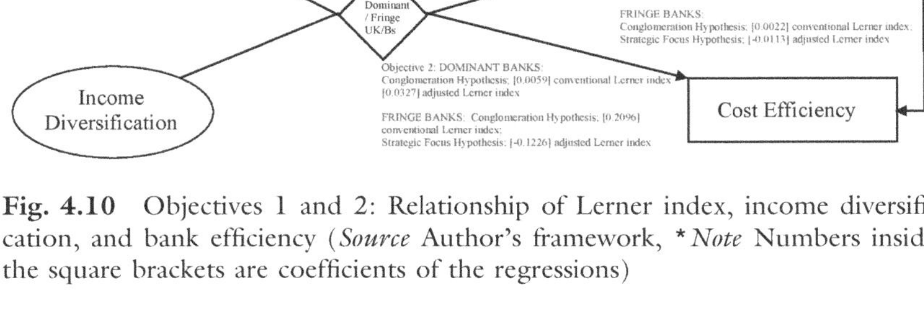

Fig. 4.10 Objectives 1 and 2: Relationship of Lerner index, income diversification, and bank efficiency (*Source* Author's framework, **Note* Numbers inside the square brackets are coefficients of the regressions)

Comparison of Dominant and Fringe Banks in Achieving Cost and Profit Efficiency

Table 4.6 summarizes all significant variables that determine the cost and profit efficiency of dominant and fringe banks. Both dominant and fringe banks benefit from market power in terms of profit and efficiency. This behavior is in line with the dominant bank model which posits that banks, especially the dominant ones, use market power to profit from higher loan rate charges. Consistent with Dacanay's (2017) findings, this result also supports the information generation hypothesis, which proposes a negative link between competition and efficiency. As seen, the information gathering capacity of banks deteriorates in an environment of intense competition. Poor screening and selection of borrowers heighten the inefficiency of banks. Moreover, in an atmosphere of competition, banks can lower their charges to entice customers to switch to one that offers more benefits.

Note that evaluating a dominant bank's cost efficiency also takes into account the coexistence of the QLH and the competition-efficiency view. The dominant bank model may explain this, asserting that banks use market power to charge higher loan rates and therefore profit more. However, market power does not control bank costs. In addition, the QLH asserts that monopoly profits, or the high profits of dominant banks, lead to lax cost management since the high revenue can cover costs. With this, banks definitely reap the benefits of high market power but fail in cost efficiency.

Bank size is also a significant indicator of cost and profit efficiency for dominant and fringe banks. This indicates that both bank groups operate at the right scale without incurring excessive and unnecessary costs and so enhance cost and profit efficiencies. Likewise, dominant and fringe banks benefit from capitalization even if capital is not an indicator of cost efficiency among the dominant banks. Banks are expected to operate efficiently on higher capital and lower default cost. Moreover, high capital holdings allow banks to generate more activity and engage in lending even in a troubled economic environment because they have a sufficient buffer against potential loss.

Income diversification alone does not guarantee efficiency. For dominant banks, income diversification can minimize operational costs but at the expense of profit. For fringe banks, income diversification may harm cost and profit efficiency. These effects can change with combined

Table 4.6 Summary of variables determining bank efficiency using conventional and adjusted lerner index for dominant and fringe banks

Variable/Hypothesis Used	**Dominant Banks** [A, B]		**Fringe Banks** [A, B]	
	Cost Efficiency	**Profit Efficiency**	**Cost Efficiency**	**Profit Efficiency**
Lag of the dependent variable [1, 2]	(+) YES[1, 2]	(+) YES[1, 2]	(+) YES[1, 2]	(+) YES[1, 2]
LERNER INDEX *Competition-Efficiency*	(-) YES [1, 2]	(+) YES [1, 2]	(+) YES [1, 2]	(+) YES [1, 2]
LERNER INDEX^2	(+) YES [1] (-) YES [2]	(-) YES [1,2]	(+) YES [1] (-) YES [2]	(+) YES [1] (-) YES [2]
BANK SIZE	(+) YES [1,2]	(+) YES [2]	(+) YES[1,2]	(+) YES[1,2]
CAPITALIZATION	(-) NO	(+) YES[1,2]	(+) YES[1,]	(+) YES[1,2]
GDP	(+) YES [1] (-) YES [2]	(-) YES[1,2]	(-) YES[2]	(+) YES[1,2]
INCOME DIVERSIFICATION *Conglomeration (C)* *Strategic-Focus (SF)*	(+) YES [1] *(C)*	(-) YES[1,2] *(SF)*	(-) YES[1] *(SF)*	(-) YES [1] *(SF)* (+) YES [2] *(C)*
ID*LERNER INDEX *Conglomeration (C)* *Strategic-Focus (SF)*	(+) YES [1, 2] *(C)*	(+) YES [1, 2] *(C)*	(+) YES [1] *(C)* (-) YES [2] *(SF)*	(+) YES [1] *(C)* (-) YES [2] *(SF)*

Note: (A) Yes/No indicates a variable's significance in determining bank efficiency. (B) The coefficient sign of the variable is enclosed in parentheses. [(1, 2)] Superscripts refer to the model that considers a variable as significant. Model 1 [(1)] used the conventional Lerner Index while Model 2 [(2)] used the adjusted Lerner Index.

Source Author's framework

income diversification and high market power. Table 4.9 shows that dominant and fringe banks can benefit from this combination. According to both specifications of the Lerner index, the said effect is more notable among the dominant banks while, for fringe banks, the result is only true when considered by the conventional Lerner Index. The result is in line with Iskandar-Datta and McLaughlin's conglomeration hypothesis (2007). According to the market power theory, banks with greater market power are more likely to succeed in maximizing opportunities arising from new income-generating activities. A strong foothold in the current market can support their aggressive strategies to penetrate new ones. In addition, customer data gathered from lending activities already serve as a reference for screening and monitoring new clients, thereby minimizing risk and making it easier to offer non-traditional services.

However, the impact of market power and income diversification on cost and profit efficiency can be less. Considering the adjusted Lerner index, they can manifest the effects of the strategic focus hypothesis, which is the opposite of the conglomeration hypothesis. That is, given other inefficiencies, market power and income diversification are not enough to improve the efficiency of fringe banks because more market power does not necessarily equate to influencing set market prices. Fringe banks still have to align with the prices of the dominant banks. Thus, diversifying income sources may even cause more inefficiencies since it costs to enter new markets and monitor a wider range of products.

Since this study uses the Lerner Index to measure market power, it can be deduced that as competition intensifies, the more diversified banks may suffer more than the less diversified ones due to the difficulties and costs incurred from maintaining multiple businesses, ultimately leading to loss of market power.

Market power, Income Diversification, and Stability

Objective 3: To determine the effect of greater market power and a higher degree of income diversification on the stability of dominant and fringe banks.

Building upon the results of the first two objectives, the third one sheds light on the effects of income diversification and market power on stability. The regression model for Objective 2 was used but with Z_{ROA} and Z_{ROE} replacing the dependent variables to measure financial stability.

As proponents of the New Industrial Organization (NIO) claim, concentration measures are important determinants of market structure. Apart from the Lerner index, Objective 3 will verify whether income diversification and market power contribute to bank stability using HHI, which measures market concentration in terms of deposits (see Fig. 4.11).

Figure 4.11 verifies the existence of an imperfectly competitive or moderately concentrated market in the Philippine banking industry with the HHI Deposit value of 1037 in the first quarter of 2019. This value falls under the category of a moderately concentrated market of $1000 \leq HHI \leq 1800$ (Meyer 2018). The regressions for two specifications of the Lerner Index and HHI identify a significant lag in Z_{ROA} and Z_{ROE} among the dominant banks. This indicates that the previous level of stability affects the current state of a bank.

Market power, as indicated by the conventional Lerner Index, has a direct positive effect on bank stability in terms of Z_{ROA} and Z_{ROE}. This result supports the competition-fragility view, which states that as market competition intensifies and market power erodes, banks lose the informational rents from their long-term relationship with clients and experience a decline in profit margins. Consequently, these banks tend to engage

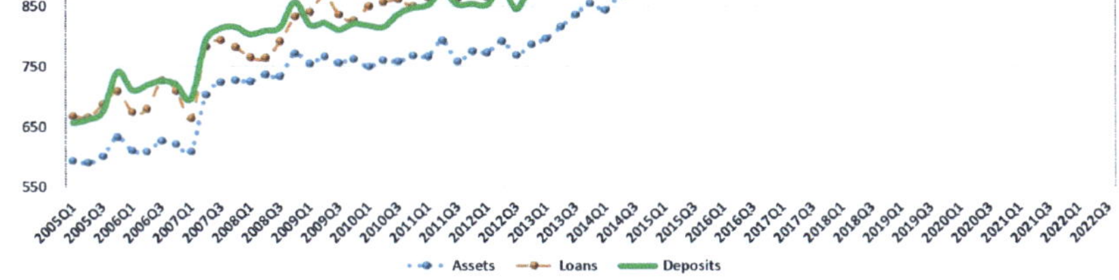

Fig. 4.11 HHI deposits, loans, and assets of the entire banking industry throughout the sample period (*Source* BSP)

in riskier activities. However, a review of the HHI Deposit shows that, as deposits grow, the indicator for financial stability drops. The negative effect of having a higher market share arising from strong market power indicates that as dominant banks increase their profits through higher markups on loan rates, they expose themselves to greater risks, such as credit defaults and NPLs. One can therefore note the coexistence of the competition-stability view and competition-fragility view in the country's dominant banks. The empirical results of the study support the existence of an inverted U relationship between market power and bank stability (Martinez-Miera and Repullo 2010). Banks that charge higher loan rates are more prone to credit defaults and NPLs, even as this practice can lead to higher revenue. Still, the potential of achieving more stability through higher market power is greater than that of acquiring more market shares within a fragile banking system. The overall effect remains positive (see Table 4.7).

Bank capitalization has a very significant positive effect on bank stability as indicated by the regressions using all indicators of market structure. This reinforces the fact that building a capital buffer may be key to lasting stability among dominant banks. Higher capital, especially through liquidity creation, allows banks to expand their capacity to absorb risks and to continue operating. Along with capitalization, the dominant banks can expand their market reach and assets by investing in technologies and physical assets to better serve and retain customers.

Interestingly, GDP per capita has a significantly negative relationship with Z_{ROA} and Z_{ROE} for both specifications of the Lerner index and HHI. GDP was expected to have a positive effect on stability but the results of the regression illustrate a downturn in the business cycle. Thus, banks, especially the big ones, ought to be more cautious and foster stability to withstand potential loss. One can verify this behavior through the notable impact of capitalization on bank stability. Capitalization increases during an economic downturn to cover the increasing risks of credit default.

As for income diversification, the same behavior emerges in the regression that uses cost and profit efficiency as dependent variables. Income diversification alone is not enough to make dominant banks stable. Banks must also possess high market power to improve stability from income diversification. They can do this by properly evaluating the risks that may arise from insufficient knowledge and control of a market.

Table 4.7 Regression results for Objective 3 for dominant banks with Z_{ROA} and Z_{ROE} as dependent variables

Method: Panel GMM EGLS (Cross-section random effects)
Sample (adjusted): 2005Q2 2019Q4; Total panel (balanced) observations: 590
Cross-section weights instrument weighting matrix; Swamy and Arora estimator of component variances

Dominant (Top 10) Banks

Regressors and Expected Signs	Dependent Variable: ZROA [a, b, c]			Dependent Variable: ZROE [a, b, c]		
	Model 1: Lerner Index	Model 2: Adjusted Lerner Index	Model 3: HHI	Model 1: Lerner Index	Model 2: Adjusted Lerner Index	Model 3: HHI
C	4.4054 *** (1.1603)	4.029 *** (1.0159)	4.2228 ns (3.0249)	2.9689 ** (1.4254)	3.4505 *** (1.2054)	-0.2604 ns (0.6889)
ZROA/ZROE (-1) (+)	0.6744 *** (0.0196)	0.708 *** (0.019)	0.6999 *** (0.0228)	0.8236 ** (0.0184)	0.8364 *** (0.0202)	0.8325 *** (0.0184)
LERNER INDEX (+)	8.4506 *** (3.2406)	0.7687 ** (0.3483)	-0.0122 ** (0.0056)	7.4908 * (4.0799)	0.2166 ns (0.8685)	-0.002 ** (0.0011)
LERNER INDEX^2 (+/-)	-7.2142 b (2.9125)	-0.2668 ns (0.1732)	0.000005 * -0.000003	-5.7146 ns (3.6802)	-0.1319 ns (0.4544)	0.00 ns (0.00)
BANK SIZE (+)	0.2041 *** (0.0414)	0.1877 *** (0.0436)	0.2041 *** (0.0404)	0.0986 *** (0.0493)	0.0781 ns (0.0494)	0.0896 ** (0.05)
CAPITALIZATION (+)	6.1847 *** (1.0361)	6.9176 *** (1.0401)	7.321 *** (0.9513)	-1.1468*** (1.2582)	-0.4593 ns (1.1594)	-0.4293 ns (1.2608)
GDP (+)	-0.8891*** (0.1322)	-0.6194*** (0.1238)	-0.4396 *** (0.1351)	-0.5497*** (0.164)	-0.379 *** (0.1314)	-0.1633 ns (0.1883)
INCOME DIVERSIFICATION (+)	-0.6647 * (0.3677)	-0.135 ns (0.3896)	0.259 ns (0.415)	-0.2543 ns (0.6254)	0.1128 ns (0.4873)	-0.626 ns (0.4978)
ID*LERNER INDEX (+)	1.4268 *** (0.517)	-0.2321 ns (0.2739)	-0.0001 ** (0.0001)	-0.1851 ns (0.1651)	-0.1396* (0.0792)	0.0007 ns (0.001)
Durbin-Watson Stat	2.20756	2.215238	2.209583	2.373796	2.376264	2.38077
J-stat (Sargan statistic)	2.26E-16	4.98E-18	4.54E-13	4.70E-17	2.10E-17	2.55E-20
AR(1)	-6.37 ***	-6.43 ***	-6.42 ***	-5.87 ***	-5.80 ***	-6.10 ***
AR(2)	-1.04 ns	-0.92 ns	-1.12 ns	-1.60 ns	-1.85 *	-1.49 ns

Notes:
a. The Lerner Index refers to the Conventional Lerner Index. The highlighted cells refer to the rejected sign that is considered significant.
b. Numbers inside the parentheses are standard error.
c. *** refers to p-value [0.00, 0.01]; ** refers to p-value [0.01, 0.05]; * refers to p-value [0.05, 0.10]

Source of basic data BSP, SEC, bank annual reports

Again, this result supports Iskandar-Datta and McLaughlin's conglomeration theory (2007) and identifies the risks that highly diversified banks open themselves to in an environment of intense competition. Their market power could erode as well as the ability to monitor a wide range of businesses. Under such circumstances, it may be reasonable for dominant banks to focus on their current markets to avoid the consequences of failing to enter a market where they have less advantage and market power.

For fringe banks, market power is also a significant and positive indicator of stability. Despite their relative weakness in the face of the dominant banks, fringe banks can sustain stable operations and higher profit. This result is only true for the regressions using the conventional Lerner Index. The inverted U that defines the relationship of market power to indicators for stability signifies greater risk exposure if said banks charge higher loan rates. While this practice typically invites more credit defaults and NPLs, it also drives the expansion of profit margins and, consequently, stability. Furthermore, just like the dominant banks, capitalization, and size are positive and significant indicators of market power for fringe banks. (See Table 4.8).

On the other hand, the effect of income diversification and market power on the stability of fringe banks had mixed results. Using the conventional Lerner Index, income diversification and market power helped the fringe banks become more stable while the adjusted Lerner index, which takes into account inefficiencies, produced a negative result for the effect of income diversification on bank stability. Both results were negative but the impact observed in the adjusted index turned out less significant than that of the conventional index. Figure 4.12 sums up the relationships noted in this section.

Table 4.9 summarizes the variables that determine the bank stability of dominant and fringe banks for Objective 3. Table 4.9 denotes the competition-fragility hypothesis in both dominant and fringe banks. This means banks thrive in an imperfectly competitive market because market power helps banks achieve financial stability through the expansion of profit margins, which, in turn, adds to the capital buffer of banks. With more competition and less market power, banks may tend to engage in riskier activities to respond to the pressure of competition.

Table 4.8 Regression results for Objective 3 for fringe banks with Z_{ROA} and Z_{ROE} as dependent variables

Method: Panel GMM EGLS (Cross-section random effects)
Sample (adjusted): 2005Q2 2019Q4; Total panel (balanced) observations: 590
Cross-section weights instrument weighting matrix; Swamy and Arora estimator of component variances

Fringe (Next 10) Banks

Regressors and Expected Signs	Dependent Variable: ZROA $^{a, b, c}$			Dependent Variable: ZROE $^{a, b, c}$		
	Model 1: Lerner Index	Model 2: Adjusted Lerner Index	Model 3: HHI	Model 1: Lerner Index	Model 2: Adjusted Lerner Index	Model 3: HHI
C	1.117 ^{ns} (0.7867)	0.2248 ^{ns} (0.7843)	-3.1869 ^{ns} (6.1332)	2.3691 *** (0.8901)	1.1169 ^{ns} (0.8896)	1.9913 * (1.0984)
ZROA/ZROE (-1) (+)	0.7234 *** (0.019)	0.7651 *** (0.0181)	0.7669 *** (0.0251)	0.8006 *** (0.0166)	0.8413 *** (0.016)	0.8401 *** (0.017)
LERNER INDEX (+)	0.802 ** (0.3484)	-0.012 ^{ns} (0.0496)	0.0062 ^{ns} (0.0117)	-1.6848 ^{ns} (1.6646)	0.1248 ** (0.0508)	0.0009 ^{ns} (0.0007)
LERNER INDEX^2 (+/-)	2.5053 * (1.2808)	-0.02 ** (0.0092)	-0.0000 ^{ns} (0.00)	1.847 ^{ns} (1.5667)	-0.0106 ^{ns} (0.0091)	-0.000 ^{ns} (0.00)
BANK SIZE (+)	0.0867 ** (0.0353)	0.0102 ^{ns} (0.037)	0.0316 ^{ns} (0.0506)	0.0579 ^{ns} (0.0378)	0.0168 ^{ns} (0.0343)	0.0031 ^{ns} (0.0507)
CAPITALIZATION (+)	3.3211 *** (0.5418)	2.0658 *** (0.5215)	1.9457 *** (0.6743)	1.2914 ** (0.5442)	0.3133 ^{ns} (0.5171)	0.2615 ^{ns} (0.6087)
GDP (+)	-0.2044 ** (0.0936)	-0.0196 ^{ns} (0.0955)	0.0564 ^{ns} (0.209)	-0.2449 ** (0.1007)	-0.1123 ^{ns} (0.1019)	-0.1767 ^{ns} (0.1286)
INCOME DIVERSIFICATION (+)	-0.0345 ^{ns} (0.1098)	0.0533 ^{ns} (0.1044)	0.0288 ^{ns} (0.1228)	0.088 ^{ns} (0.1112)	0.1096 ^{ns} (0.0947)	0.0662 ^{ns} (0.0772)
ID*LERNER INDEX (+)	1.0376 ** (0.4416)	-0.0963 * (0.051)	-0.000 ^{ns} (0.0001)	1.7921 *** (0.4275)	-0.1221 ** (0.0514)	-0.0003 ^{ns} (0.0007)
Durbin-Watson Stat	2.249414	2.292132	2.287726	2.335716	2.383238	2.360792
J-stat (Sargan statistic)	1.14E-19	1.25E-18	1.63E-16	2.46E-17	1.08E-18	1.56E-16
AR(1)	-6.90 ***	-6.69 ***	-6.61 ***	-6.13 ***	-6.05 ***	-5.96 ***
AR(2)	-0.98 ^{ns}	-1.50 ^{ns}	-1.53 ^{ns}	-1.50 ^{ns}	-1.66 *	-1.49 ^{ns}

Notes:
a. The Lerner Index refers to the Conventional Lerner Index. Highlighted cells (yellow) refer to the rejected expected sign considered significant.
b. Numbers inside the parentheses are standard errors.
c. *** refers to p-value [0.00, 0.01]; ** refers to p-value [0.01, 0.05]; * refers to p-value [0.05, 0.10]

Source of basic data BSP, SEC, and bank annual reports

Furthermore, it is important to note that there exists a negative effect of market power on the stability of the dominant banks. This is also known as the competition-stability view when looking at the negative effects of higher HHI deposits on bank stability. The coexistence of the competition-stability view and the competition-fragility view in the behavior of dominant banks is in line with the findings of Martinez-Miera and Repullo (2010). In an imperfectly competitive market, banks, especially the dominant ones, wield their market power to gain higher profit, increase their capital buffer, and therefore promote stability. On

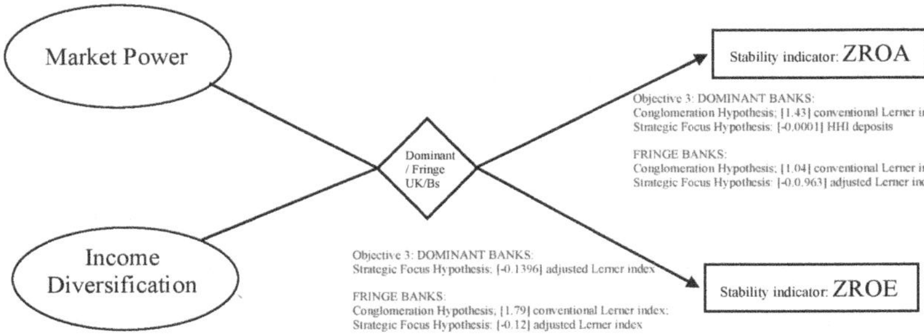

Fig. 4.12 Summary of the relationships of the Lerner index, income diversification, and bank stability variables for Objective 3 (*Source* Author's framework, **Notes* Numbers inside the square brackets are coefficients of the regressions)

the other hand, expanding market share also exposes dominant banks to higher risks, such as credit default. However, efficient monitoring and investing in financial technology may help banks avoid or lessen risk exposure. With this, one can say that stability arising from higher market power is greater than the risks incurred. One can conclude that the benefits of market power through higher profits and capital building on the stability of dominant banks are greater than the negative effect. Dominant banks still thrive in a market with less competition. Bank size is a positive indicator of stability as it has much to do with the goal of dominant banks to expand market reach. By investing in more branches, ATMs, and financial technologies, banks can better monitor and serve clients and so establish a long-term relationship with them. This, in turn, provides banks with informational rents that guide bank officers in their decision-making.

The capitalization ratio also had a positive significant relationship with stability for both dominant and fringe banks. Among all the variables, capitalization had the biggest impact on bank stability across all models. This strongly supports the theoretical assumption that bank capitalization is the main source of stability for all banks as it acts as a buffer for losses and reduces the costs of defaults.

GDP per capita had a significant negative relationship with bank stability. As discussed earlier, when the business cycle is on a downturn, banks tend to be more cautious and focused on stability as their capitalization ratio reflects. In periods of a compressed economy, banks hold more capital that serves as a buffer for losses from expected credit defaults.

Table 4.9 Summary of variables determining bank stability using conventional and adjusted Lerner index for dominant and fringe banks

Variables/Hypotheses	Dominant Banks [A, B]		Fringe Banks [A, B]	
	ZROA	ZROE	ZROA	ZROE
Lag of the dependent variable [1, 2, 3]	(+) YES [1,2,3]	(+) YES [1,2,3]	(+) YES [1,2,3]	(+) YES [1,2,3]
LERNER INDEX *Competition-Stability (CS)* *Competition-Fragility (CF)*	(+) YES [1,2] (-) YES [3] *(CS, CF)*	(+) YES [1] (-) YES [3] *(CS, CF)*	(+) YES [1] *(CF)*	(+) YES [2] *(CF)*
LERNER INDEX^2	(-) YES [1] (+) YES [3]	NO	(+) YES [1] (-) YES [2]	NO
BANK SIZE	(+) YES [1,2,3]	(+) YES [1,3]	(+) YES [1]	NO
CAPITALIZATION	(+) YES [1,2,3]	NO	(+) YES [1,2,3]	(+) YES [1]
GDP	(-) YES [1,2,3]	(-) YES [1,2]	(-) YES [1]	(-) YES [1]
INCOME DIVERSIFICATION	(-) YES [1]	NO	NO	NO
ID*LERNER INDEX *Conglomeration (C)* *Strategic-Focus (SF)*	(+) YES [1] (-) YES [3] *(C, SF)*	(-) YES [2] *(SF)*	(+) YES [1] (-) YES [2] *(C, SF)*	(+) YES [1] (-) YES [2] *(C, SF)*

Note: (A) Yes/No indicates whether the variable is significant in determining bank efficiency (B) The coefficient signs for the variables are inside parentheses. ([1, 2, 3]) Superscripts indicate the variables that are significant to [(1)]Model 1 (conventional Lerner index), [(2)]Model 2 (adjusted Lerner index) or [(3)]Model 3 (HHI of deposits).

Source Author's computations

Again, income diversification did not immediately equate to stability among the dominant banks and insignificant among fringe banks. However, it became significant when the effect of income diversification combined with market power. Similar to the results obtained for bank efficiency, the adjusted Lerner Index proved that enhancing market power through diversification might not sufficiently boost the stability of fringe banks as they risk offering new products without adequate market knowledge or influence.

The empirical results of this study will not explain the behavior of banks during the pandemic period. This study excluded 2020 because the said year experienced unusual policy and regulatory changes. Bayanihan 1 and 2, the government's economic recovery plans, included granting borrowers 30- and 60-day grace periods sans additional interests and charges during the tight lockdowns. Banks were expected to undergo surges in NPLs and deterioration of credit quality. The empirical results of this study will only be consistent once the economic and regulatory environment for banks normalizes, that is, with a regulatory framework similar to that covered in the sample period where Basel regulations governed banks. Table 4.10 summarizes the results for Objectives 1–3.

Summary, Conclusion, and Recommendations

This study, which focuses on the combined effect of market power and income diversification on cost and profit efficiency and stability, confirms the presence of imperfect competition in the Philippine domestic banking industry as seen in the high levels of market power among banks in the sample groups. In addition, the banks classified as the country's Top 20 UKBs are heavily engaged in non-interest income-generating activities apart from their interest income-generating ones. From here arise the following important takeaways:

1. The degree of market power is associated with cost and profit efficiency. Banks can charge higher loan rates and efficiently screen their borrowers. Inversely, increased competition, or less market power causes cost and profit efficiency to drop. One can infer that the information generation hypothesis applies to the domestic banking industry of the Philippines. The result is consistent with the results of Proteanu-Podpiera et al. (2008) and Phan (2015) which

Table 4.10 Summary of results

Objectives	*Hypotheses*	*Results*
1. To determine the effects of greater market power on bank performance in terms of cost and profit efficiency of the Top 20 UKBs in the Philippines	Greater market power increases the efficiency of the Top 20 UKBs	For the Top 20 UKBs, a higher degree of market power is associated with higher cost and profit efficiency. This is in line with the information generation hypothesis This result, which uses the Lerner Index as a proxy for the degree of market power and which serves as an inverse measure of market competition, suggests that bank competition has a negative impact on a bank's cost and profit efficiency
	This is because market power allows banks to charge higher loan rates to profit more and to be more efficient	

(continued)

Table 4.10 (continued)

Objectives	*Hypotheses*	*Results*
2. To determine the effects of greater market power and higher degree of income diversification on cost and profit efficiency of dominant and fringe banks	Greater market power and a higher degree of income diversification increases the efficiency of dominant and fringe banks Market power plus a high degree of income diversification boost the efficiency of dominant and fringe banks by allowing them to charge higher prices and experience the resulting economies of scope from cost sharing of fixed costs over multiple products	Income diversification alone does not guarantee enhanced efficiency. However, dominant and fringe banks with strong market power and highly diverse income sources benefit in terms of cost and profit efficiency because market power allows expansion of their profit margin This result is in line with the conglomeration hypothesis and market power theory which state that a bank must have market power in its current market to successfully penetrate new markets because it has the resources, strength, and positioning to support predatory strategies in the new market Against the backdrop of intensified competition, the effect of income diversification on the cost and profit efficiency of banks will worsen the effects of increased competition. Besides a thinning profit margin, banks will not generate the expected maximum value from investing in new technologies and aggressive market strategies because bank relationships tend to be shorter in a competitive market

Objectives	*Hypotheses*	*Results*
3. To determine the effects of greater market power and higher degree of income diversification on the stability of dominant and fringe banks	Greater market power and a higher degree of income diversification promote stability in both dominant and fringe banks With greater market power and a high degree of income diversification, banks can reduce the risk of bankruptcy by spreading their operations across different products and markets	As with Objective 2, diversifying the income sources for dominant and fringe banks does not automatically improve financial stability. In accordance with the conglomeration hypothesis and market power theory, diversification should come with high market power to achieve stability In the event of intense market competition, the effect of income diversification on stability will worsen the adverse effects of competition. Bank-client relationships tend to be shorter and the capacity to screen clients deteriorates, increasing the chances of granting loans to less capable borrowers. Banks may also encounter difficulties monitoring multiple businesses

Source Author's theoretical framework and results

claim that a bank's screening and monitoring capabilities deteriorate in a competitive market, driving it to grant loans to less capable borrowers, elevating its default costs.

2. Both dominant and fringe banks become more cost- and profit efficient with higher market power. However, dominant banks also experience a negative impact on cost efficiency, which is associated with the QLH. This is because monopoly rents from high market power compensate for high operational costs, causing bank officers to be less vigilant in managing expenses. This can also mean that dominant banks are willing to incur more costs and sacrifice cost efficiency for more profit. On the other hand, a high level of income diversification does not guarantee more profit. To reap the benefits of having highly diverse income sources, this strategy should go with greater market power, as suggested by the conglomeration hypothesis and market power theory. These two posit that market power helps banks penetrate new markets or offer new products because their resources and market position support predatory strategies in new markets. However, the adverse effects are more evident among highly diversified banks should competition intensify. Besides losing clients, such banks are more likely to encounter difficulties in monitoring multiple businesses. Thus, income diversification contributes to the adverse effects of market competition on cost and profit efficiency.
3. Diversification does not automatically equate to financial stability. The combined effect of income diversification and market power yielded mixed results. This can be explained by the coexistence of the competition-stability and competition-fragility views where banks use market power to charge higher loan rates and expand profit margins which, in turn, add up to their capital buffer. However, this behavior also heightens their risk exposure in the form of credit defaults and NPLs. Nevertheless, the likeliness of achieving stability from high levels of income diversification is greater than the adverse effects. One may conclude that loss of market power due to heavy engagement in income diversification may worsen the adverse effect of bank competition on the stability of fringe and dominant banks.
4. The top 20 UKBs in the Philippines remain resilient. Even if a high level of income diversification is associated with a decline in efficiency and stability, these banks, especially the dominant ones, thrive

> because their elevated market power supports their diversification strategies. To succeed in an imperfectly competitive market, great market power must go hand-in-hand with high levels of income diversification. The country's banking industry succeeds in an imperfectly competitive market because it participates in the virtuous cycle of the Lerner index, cost and profit efficiency, capitalization, and bank stability. Since great market power is associated with improved cost and profit efficiency, banks can build up capital to act as a buffer for losses, and so foster stability. With higher capitalization, banks can engage in more banking activities to maximize profit and acquire more market power.

Banks with high market power benefit from being highly diversified. To reap maximum benefits in an imperfectly competitive market, income diversification strategies must come with market power. However, more intense competition in the domestic market may harm the efficiency and stability of dominant and fringe banks due to the loss of market power. Investing in sophisticated banking technologies and operations, like innovations in Information Technology, can improve the risk management and monitoring capabilities of banks as these reduce the risk and adverse effects of increased market competition.

In the area of policy, this study has identified and verified the adverse effects of competition on bank efficiency and stability, which calls for the implementation of balanced pro-competitive measures.

Further studies may employ Z_{CAR} as an alternative measure for bank stability to verify if maintaining or even exceeding the required capitalization will make a bank resilient to financial shocks or regulatory distress. Moreover, the authors recommend introducing other explanatory variables to the regression models, including loan-to-deposit and loan-to-asset ratios, as earlier studies have proven that these variables are significant indicators of stability. Future research may also explore other efficiency measurement techniques for bank cost and efficiency, such as the Data Envelope Analysis, which is similar to SFA. Other studies may also look into cross-country analyses and so contribute to the growing number of studies on bank income diversification and efficiency.

Appendix

See Tables 4.11, 4.12, and 4.13.

Table 4.11 Top 20 banks in terms of assets as of December 2019

Ranking	*Bank*	*Total assets (PHP)*
1	BANCO DE ORO UNIVERSAL BANK	3,069,395
2	METROPOLITAN BANK & TCO	2,116,897
3	LAND BANK OF THE PHILIPPINES	2,033,417
4	BANK OF THE PHIL ISLANDS	1,912,625
5	PHIL NATIONAL BANK	1,067,676
6	CHINA BANKING CORP	866,900
7	SECURITY BANK CORP	788,233
8	RIZAL COMM'L BANKING CORP	762,311
9	DEVELOPMENT BANK OF THE PHIL	761,499
10	UNION BANK OF THE PHILIPPINES	706,867
11	EAST WEST BANKING CORP	382,513
12	UNITED COCONUT PLANTERS BANK	335,181
13	CITIBANK, N.A	327,737
14	ASIA UNITED BANK CORPORATION	260,478
15	HONGKONG & SHANGHAI BANKING CORP	177,209
16	PHIL TRUST COMPANY	160,574
17	BANK OF COMMERCE	144,805
18	MAYBANK PHILIPPINES INCORPORATION	105,056
19	PHILIPPINE BANK OF COMMUNICATIONS	104,739
20	MUFG - THE BANK OF TOKYO	74,079
	Others	760,885
Total Assets		16,919,075

Source BSP https://www.bsp.gov.ph/SitePages/Statistics/BSFinancialStatements.aspx?TabId=1 for basic data

Table 4.12 Descriptive statistics

Variable	*Description*	*Mean*	*Max*	*Min*
Profit Efficiency	Measures a bank's proximity to generating maximum profit, given its output levels	0.8671	1.0000	0.0001
Cost Efficiency	Measures the proximity of a bank's cost to that of the best-practice bank which produces the same output under the same conditions	0.82	1.00	−3.81
Conventional Lerner Index	Used as a proxy for the degree of market power with high values, implying higher pricing power and less competitive market conditions	0.23	0.80	−1.68
Adjusted Lerner Index	Lerner index adjusted to the individual efficiency of banks and to account for the inter-relatedness of market power and bank efficiency in addressing endogeneity concerns	0.77	1.57	−8.87
Bank Size	Measured in terms of total assets (Php Billion)	379	3069	13
Capitalization Ratio	Required amount of shareholder capital expressed in percentage of assets	0.1119	0.2273	0.0053
Income Diversification Index	Indicates the level of diversity of income sources. Zero signifies complete concentration, which means that all income comes from a single source, while 0.5 indicates complete diversification	0.40	0.50	−2.47
Profit	Profit before tax	6323	59,187	−2598
Total Operating Cost	Cost of all resources used	16,614	492,658	96
Liquidity Creation	Represents total output (Php Billions)	102	1367	−175
Price of Labor	Defined as ratio of labor expenses to liquidity creation	−0.13	16.10	−227.43
Price of Physical Capital	Defined as ratio of operating cost to fixed assets	2.38	17.91	0.0023

(continued)

Table 4.12 (continued)

Variable	*Description*	*Mean*	*Max*	*Min*
Price of Funds or Deposits	Defined as ratio of interest expense to total deposits diversification, which means an even split between net interest income and non-interest income	0.02	0.20	0.0003
Z_{ROA}	Measure of financial stability with larger values indicating greater stability and least risk potential; the variable uses ROA	1.95	8.08	−3.22
Z_{ROE}	Measure of financial stability with larger values indicating greater stability and least risk potential; the variable uses ROE	2.60	10.09	−4.77
HHI Deposit	Measure of market concentration in terms of the total banking industry's deposits. It is also used as a measure of market competition in the study	961.49	1165.11	772.28
GDP per capita	Measure of the country's economic output which accounts for population	28,668	51,152	15,272

Source BSP https://www.bsp.gov.ph/SitePages/Statistics/BSFinancialStatements.aspx?TabId=1 for basic data

Table 4.13 Average cost and profit efficiency of the top 20 UKBs in the Philippines from Q1 2005 to Q4 2019

Ranking	*Bank*	*Average of profit efficiency*	*Average of cost efficiency*
1	BANCO DE ORO UNIVERSAL BANK	0.933781587	0.97582019
2	METROPOLITAN BANK & TCO	0.959305335	0.98081016
3	LAND BANK OF THE PHILIPPINES	0.938672665	0.96352577
4	BANK OF THE PHIL ISLANDS	0.968750145	0.97574286
5	PHIL NATIONAL BANK	0.894692838	0.94411484
6	CHINA BANKING CORP	0.905848124	0.9243802
7	SECURITY BANK CORP	0.910139754	0.87785655
8	RIZAL COMM'L BANKING CORP	0.871449871	0.9229978
9	DEVELOPMENT BANK OF THE PHIL	0.908484057	0.86675153
10	UNION BANK OF THE PHILIPPINES	0.912288806	0.92341322
11	EAST WEST BANKING CORP	0.824263396	0.89669601
12	UNITED COCONUT PLANTERS BANK	0.790141275	0.90994405
13	CITIBANK, N.A	0.903377974	0.92425153
14	ASIA UNITED BANK CORPORATION	0.835966579	0.77477327
15	HONGKONG & SHANGHAI BANKING CORP	0.789313369	0.45800876
16	PHIL TRUST COMPANY	0.839278531	0.68802164
17	BANK OF COMMERCE	0.776087492	0.86508393
18	MAYBANK PHILIPPINES INCORPORATION	0.790763488	0.41895341
19	PHILIPPINE BANK OF COMMUNICATIONS	0.809008362	0.76112659
20	MUFG—THE BANK OF TOKYO	0.779414713	0.41336672

Source BSP https://www.bsp.gov.ph/SitePages/Statistics/BSFinancialStatements.aspx?TabId=1 for the basic data and author's estimates

CHAPTER 5

Macro Stress Testing of the Philippines' Top 10 UKBs: An Analysis of the Effect of Economic Distress on the Bank's Credit Quality

Background

The Global Financial Crisis (GFC) of 2008 exposed the vulnerabilities of financial firms that set unrealistic assessments of their risks (SSG 2019). This led to the inability of the firms to secure funding to support their assets under stressed conditions. The event caused huge wealth destruction amounting to $19.2 trillion in household income, eroded confidence in financial institutions and markets worldwide, as well as a plethora of bankruptcies and forced mergers, and caused intensified concerns over liquidity (Silver 2021). This confirms the critical role of banks especially among emerging economies as they are deemed "too big to fail." As a result, this pushed banks at the fore to develop enhanced tools to assess risks and to better understand vulnerabilities in the financial system (Taskinsoy 2020). One of the key techniques for quantifying risks is stress testing.

Macro stress testing refers to a range of techniques used to assess the vulnerability of a financial system to "exceptional but plausible" macroeconomic shocks (Wong et al. 2008). Its main purpose is to evaluate the banks' performance in light of a crisis. It may be performed by an individual bank, a group of banks with some similar characteristics, or the

J. C. Dacanay et al., *Bank Competition and the Effects on Financial Stability*, Palgrave Macmillan Studies in Banking and Financial Institutions, https://doi.org/10.1007/978-3-031-59599-8_5

entire financial system (Vu et al. 2018). In most applications, this requires modeling and analyzing the link between a series of macroeconomic events and the performance of a bank's portfolio of assets (Siddique et al. 2013). It is necessary to conduct macro stress tests to assess the ability of banks to endure the shock, especially given the financial turmoil across the world (Banerjee et al. 2017). In the case of the Philippines, to finance the "Build Build Build" program, one of the main pillars of the current administration's socioeconomic strategy, the government had to increase its borrowings tremendously (FSCC 2019). This tested the capacity of the domestic capital market to provide the government's financing needs as it would heavily rely on domestic sources. On that account, it is crucial to stress test the Philippine banking sector—to understand and assess its risks—since it is the primary supplier of liquidity in the domestic economy (ADB 2012).

One of the key aspects of bank management is asset quality (Lucky et al. 2015). It is also considered to be one of the most critical areas in determining the overall condition of a bank (FDIC 2012). It is a microprudential determinant of the commercial bank's soundness and profitability (Lucky et al. 2015). The stability of the banking system with sound loan asset quality serves as an important tool for capital allocation, stability of the financial system, financial deepening, macroprudential surveillance, and economic development (Arrawatia et al. 2019). A growing share of non-performing loans in the loan portfolio of banks signifies greater risks for banking stability. Consequently, it is important to understand the risks affecting the asset quality of banks as it may influence the financial performance and the soundness of the banking system (Ibid.).

Moreover, the perception and interpretation of various risk exposures are not the same for all investors and banks (Taskinsoy 2020). A particular risk is trivial to one bank but can be significant to another bank and vice versa. In addition, banks need to be aware of the risks of other market players since the collapse of one bank may cause a contagion effect (Singh 2021). Banking institutions are known to be integrated, thus exposure of one bank may pose risks to other banks and the entire financial system (Dungey et al. 2015). This phenomenon was observed during the Global Financial Crisis (GFC) when the fall of Lehman Brothers spurred a full-blown recession (Singh 2021). Therefore, a great deal of prudential effort, such as examining individual banks' risks, must be undertaken to avoid another economic catastrophe.

Essentially, in the light of increasing financial turmoil and the gravity of risk management, it is imperative to determine the influence of adverse macroeconomic conditions on the asset-credit quality of banks—a key institution in fostering economic growth. Hence, the paper aims to create a macroeconomic model to estimate the values of the macroeconomic variables under stress scenarios and then apply a satellite model of credit risk to each bank under the Top 10 Universal and Commercial Banks (UKBs) and the entire industry to evaluate asset-credit quality under adverse conditions.

In the wake of continuing global economic uncertainty, it is necessary to understand the level of preparedness of banks required for managing risks in the financial system by conducting a macro stress test. Such understanding would require identifying the impact of macroeconomic factors on the banks' asset-credit quality historically and under unfavorable stress conditions. The analysis is against the backdrop of the industry's level of competition since the degree of market competition may also influence the risk behavior of banks and consequently, their credit quality. Therefore, the study seeks to answer the question: Does increased economic distress, in the context of lower bank competition, lead to lower credit quality?

To answer this research question, four objectives are proposed.

1. To review the historical influence of macroeconomic variables and bank competition on the credit quality of the Top 10 UKBs individually;
2. To estimate the relationship between macroeconomic variables namely output growth, interest rates, inflation, exchange rate, and remittances;
3. To forecast the macroeconomic indicators under mild and moderate stress scenarios;
4. To quantify the effect of economic distress on the credit quality of the Top 10 UKBs and the entire industry.

This study is significant to the financial industry for several reasons. First, this study will be the first to provide an analysis of the effect of economic distress on the credit quality of the Top 10 Universal and Commercial banks (UKBs) at the individual bank level. At the micro level, it is used by banks for assessing the sustainability of the institution for risk management (Vu et al. 2018).

Second, the study analyzes the effect of macroeconomic stress on the Top 10 UKBs, shedding light on the impact of credit risks individually. Disaggregated data are essential to capture the different responses of banks to stress scenarios (Ibid.). One major shortcoming of econometric models based on aggregate data is that results may conceal significant variation at the portfolio or bank level. More specifically, this procedure fails to detect uncertainty at the bank level.

Third, the study of macro stress testing benefits different stakeholders. For central banks and regulatory authorities, the results of the stress test may provide useful inputs in the formulation and implementation of corrective measures for managing risk (ADB 2012). Understanding financial vulnerabilities will allow policymakers to detect, monitor, and respond to changes in the transmission of the effects from one self-governing area to another (Ibid.). Additionally, this paper is helpful to the Bangko Sentral ng Pilipinas (BSP) as the paper will serve as a guideline that gives the central bank an overview of how macroeconomic variables affect banks. Meanwhile, stress tests are valuable tools for banks as it allows them to better manage and control their risks (Taskinsoy 2020). Understanding and protecting against the vulnerabilities of a financial company's risk-taking activities is one of the major responsibilities of the bank's management (Sorge et al. 2006). Lastly, the analysis of financial risks is important to financial investors. The Global Financial Crisis of 2008 caused the confidence of investors to plummet, thus they need to examine the company's profile for them to minimize their investment losses (Siddique et al. 2013).

This study focuses on the banking industry and its credit risk by looking into the effect of economic distress on the banks' credit quality through its non-performing loans ratio. Credit risk modeling is the area where most of the attention has focused lately (Ibid.). Furthermore, the study is limited to assessing the relationship between credit quality and the interested macroeconomic variables. It will not predict the probability of a bank failure given the stress scenarios. The paper will only look into the Top 10 UKBs as its combined assets already cover 62.51% of the total assets of the entire UKBs as of 2020–2022. It will analyze the credit quality of the Top 10 UKBs in the Philippines individually. The dataset will cover the quarterly balance sheet from the years 2005–2020. The data will be taken from the Bangko Sentral ng Pilipinas (BSP) and the Philippine Statistics Authority (PSA).

Review of Related Literature

The literature review has three sections. The first section discusses the development of macro stress testing from the early stages of its usage to its emergence to be a popular technique in assessing the vulnerability of the financial system. The second section delves into the different theories and literature to formulate the three hypotheses of this study. The last section reviews the different theories to have a deeper understanding of the relationship between macroeconomic indicators and banks' credit quality. These works of literature are indicated in Tables 5.1–5.4.

Typology of Macro Stress Testing

Macro stress testing is an analytical tool for linking macroeconomic variables, risks, and financial system stability (ADB 2012). The results of such stress testing provide a better understanding of the level of preparedness required for managing risks in the financial system, especially in the wake of continuing global economic uncertainty. Thus, early detection of financial vulnerabilities can allow policymakers to take preemptive monetary policy actions, particularly in the formulation and implementation of corrective measures for managing risks, and give market participants in the financial system an opportunity to adjust their business strategies (Ibid.).

There are four distinct periods, explained in Table 5.1, in the evolution of stress testing (Taskinsoy 2020). The early stress tests existed before the early 1990s. Its purpose was to be part of financial risk management to measure the value of a risky asset or portfolio. To do that, analysts would apply assumptions based on an adverse scenario to see how the value of the asset or portfolio would change. Based on the results, management would increase or reduce risk limits.

The second period (1970–1990) in the evolution of stress testing commenced with financial innovation in the 1970s which gave birth to the use of derivatives and securitization of prime mortgages. Securitization of assets became popular because it led to lower funding costs and diversification of risks. This happened because, at the onset of the 1970s,

Table 5.1 Summary of the developments in macro stress testing (MST)

Period	*Events*	*Developments in MST*	*Purpose*
Early 1990s	Normal bank operation	Scenario Analysis	• Financial risk management • To measure the value of a risky asset or portfolio
1970–1990	• Failure of the Bretton Woods fixed exchange rate regime (1970s) • Yom Kippur War (1973) • Oil crisis (1974–1978)	Derivatives and Hedging	• Lower funding costs • Diversification of risks
1990–2007	• Crash of the Nikkei index of Tokyo stock exchange in Japan • Collapse of the European Exchange Rate Mechanism • US-led First Gulf War • Asian Financial Crisis (1997) • Global Financial Crisis (2007)	Value at Risk (VaR)	• Microprudential and supervisory (after AFC) • Macroprudential and crisis-management tool (after GFC)
2009–present	• Global Financial Crisis	"Principles for Sound Stress Testing Practices and Supervision" by the Basel Committee	• Improve stress testing • Serves as a guide for supervisors and banks

Source Author's review of related literature

the world was going through immense turmoil and related disruptions due to the failure of the Bretton Woods fixed exchange rate regime. Under this agreement, gold was the basis for the US dollar, and other currencies were pegged to the US dollar's value (Chen, 2021). This system failed when the US gold supply was no longer adequate to cover the number of dollars in circulation. It resulted in massive volatility in currency markets worldwide causing the dollar to depreciate substantially.

Table 5.2 Summary of the formulation of Hypothesis 1

Hypothesis 1: A more concentrated market is likely to result in higher credit quality of banks

Theory	*Study*	*Key findings*
Competition-Stability	Hicks (1935)	• Quiet life hypothesis ◦ Greater market power is associated with lessened efforts by managers to maximize operating efficiency
	Leibenstein (1966)	• Inefficiencies are reduced by increased competition as managers respond to the challenge
	Hart (1983)	• In oligopolistic or monopolistic environments, banks should be characterized by a lower degree of market discipline which in turn results in operational inefficiency
	Boyd and De Nicoló (2005)	• Risk-shifting effect ◦ Lower lending rates, brought about by increased competition, reduce the probability that borrowers become bankrupt or take on risky projects
	Beck et al. (2006), and Dacanay (2017)	• More competition and less concentration improve the soundness of the banks
Competition-Fragility	Jones (2016)	• Intense competition erodes market power and franchise values, resulting in an increase in incentives to take on risky projects, since forgone future profits in the case of bankruptcy are lower
	Schliephake (2016) and Dacanay (2017), Bayangos (2022)	• Margin effect ◦ increased competition may worsen the excessive risk-taking problem since higher competition reduces bank's margins • Market power enhances the bank's charter value, making it more conservative in its operations • Large banks usually have better-diversified portfolios • It is easier to monitor more concentrated banking systems because of the limited number of banks • This behavior is observed for the UKBs in the Philippines

(continued)

Table 5.2 (continued)

Hypothesis 1: A more concentrated market is likely to result in higher credit quality of banks		
Theory	*Study*	*Key findings*
	VanHoose (2022)	• Greater market power leads banks to boost loan rates and monitoring activities, thus resulting in better asset quality
	Ogura (2006)	• Herding effect ◦ In good economic times as more borrowers qualify for loans, there is a tendency for each bank to extend more loans as its rivals expand their lending ◦ Banks collectively loosening their credit standards during economic booms
	Caminal and Matutes (2002)	• Market power is often associated with a lower probability of a banking failure • Higher lending rates result in lower investment levels and thus a higher expected return of the marginal project, which implies a lower probability of bankruptcy • The higher are the future expected profits of a bank, the larger is the opportunity cost of going bankrupt, which reduces the incentive to overinvest in risky assets • On the deposit side, competition will tend to increase deposit rates pushing the margin further down and failure probabilities up
U-shaped relationship	Martinez-Miera and Repullo (2010) and Dacanay (2017), Bayangos (2022)	• In a highly concentrated market, the risk-shifting effect dominates, thus entry reduces the probability of bank failure (competition-stability) • On the other hand, in a very competitive market, the margin effect dominates, therefore further entry increases the probability of failure (competition-fragility) • This can be observed in the UKBs in the Philippines
	VanHoose (2022)	• The greatest probabilities of failure arise in either highly competitive markets or markets in which banks have greatest market power

Source Author's review of related literature

Table 5.3 Summary of the formulation of Hypothesis 2 and 3

Study	*Objective*	*Key findings*
Hypothesis 2: Development of loan losses is linked to the macroeconomic environment		
Warue (2012)	To investigate the link between NPLs and bank-specific and macroeconomic factors, and establish the extent to which these factors affect the occurrence of non-performing loans in commercial banks in Kenya	• Macroeconomic conditions manifested through economic cycles and had a significant impact on the banking industry's incidence of non-performing loans • Business cycles affect the cash flows of various economic units and consequently credit portfolio performance • Importance of understanding macroeconomic factors in an economy as it aids in effective monitoring and review of credit risk
Greenwald and Stiglitz (1993)	To discuss the different strands of research within old and new Keynesian economics	• Actions of firms are affected by their perceptions of risks • One key factor that influences the risks firms face and their willingness to bear those risks is the overall state of the economy
Foglia (2008)	To review the quantitative methods developed at selected central banks and supervision authorities for stress testing credit risk	• Estimation strategy normally requires the selection of an initial set of macroeconomic and financial variables that affect credit risk
Hypothesis 3: An increase in macroeconomic growth leads to a decrease in NPL		
Warue (2012)	To investigate the link between NPLs and bank-specific and macroeconomic factors, and establish the extent to which these factors affect the occurrence of non-performing loans in commercial banks in Kenya	• During economic distress, failure of borrowers to repay their loans on time or at all constrains the commercial banks' ability to lend to other borrowers • Failure to receive loan repayments on time, results in banks experiencing cash flow problems • Delinquent loans have the potential of creating financial instability which may contribute to the failure of projects thus affecting a country's economy adversely

(continued)

Table 5.3 (continued)

Study	*Objective*	*Key findings*
Arrawatia et al. (2019)	To examine the bank-, industry-, and macroeconomic-specific determinants of asset quality of Indian banks	• A continuous deterioration in the asset quality, brought about by a decline in macroeconomic growth, also deters banks away from lending fresh loans and advances, resulting in a decline in private investment, which affects growth of the economy
Waweru and Kalani (2009)	To investigate the causes of non-performing loans, the actions that bank managers have taken to mitigate that problem, and the level of success of such actions	• Full-blown banking crises are associated more with external developments, and domestic variables are the main leading indicators • National economic downturn was perceived as the most important external factor that contributed to the increase in non-performing loans
Espinoza and Prasad (2010)	To determine the relationship between macroeconomic variables and NPLs in the Gulf Cooperative Council (GCC) banks' books	• NPL ratio worsens as economic growth becomes lower and lending interest rates and risk aversion increase
Flamini et al. (2015)	To understand the determinants of high bank profits in Sub-Saharan Africa and to explore the relationship between profits and equity in the region's commercial banking sector	• Weak economic performance exposes banks to risk while low economic growth promotes the deterioration of credit quality and increases the probability of loan defaults
Kalirai and Scheicher (2002)	To perform macro stress tests for the Austrian banking system, focusing on the impact of credit risk	• A deterioration in economic activity leads to falling incomes, rising payment difficulties, and more business failures and hence default risk rises, causing a decline in the quality of the banking books

Source Author's review of related literature

Table 5.4 List of independent variables

Independent Variables	*Legend*	*Interpretation*	*Expected impact on dependent variable*	*Source*
Bank Competition and Credit Quality (Objective 1)				
Total Assets	TA	The higher the total assets, the bigger the bank size, implying higher market share and less competition	–	BSP
Macro Stress Testing (Objectives 2–4)				
Real GDP growth rate	GDP	An increase in GDP leads to the rise of income, helps decrease unemployment rate, hence supports repayment ability of borrowers	–	PSA
Inflation rate	INF	The higher level of inflation, the lower net value of firms and individuals. Therefore, repayment ability of borrowers will be affected negatively	+	PSA
Exchange rate	EXR	An increase in exchange rate means that national competitiveness is improved. This helps to raise credit quality in the banking system in general	–	BSP
Lending rate[1]	ITR	Increasing interest rates leads to increase in financial burden for borrowed, hence non-performing loan ratio	+	BSP
Remittances	REM	The growth in remittances could increase banks' loanable funds and result in higher credit to the private sector. Thus, it may negatively affect NPLs if they enhance borrowers' capacity to repay	–	BSP

Sources Ebeke et al. (2014), and Vu et al. (2018)

[1] The author estimated the values for interest rate (lending rate) in 2021 due to the unavailability of data. BSP suspended the submission of bank loan and deposit interest rate reports from March to September 2020 as part of the regulatory relief granted to banks during the height of the pandemic following the provisions of the BSP Memorandum No. M-2020-049. Therefore, the values are based on the monthly growth rates of the published lending rates from January 2020 to February 2020.

Under these circumstances, together with the huge surge in oil and food prices, options-based hedging vehicles were developed.

The third period (1990–2007) in the evolution of stress testing was marked by increasing financial turmoil due to the crash of the Nikkei index of the Tokyo stock exchange in Japan, the collapse of the European Exchange Rate Mechanism, and the US-led First Gulf War. Against this background, the Basel Committee was prompted to introduce the 1996 market risk amendment to Basel I under which banks were required to use Value at Risk models (VaR) in their calculation of market risk-weighted and credit risk-weighted capital. At first, it was used for microprudential and supervisory concerns (after the Asian Financial Crisis of 1997), but because of the Global Financial Crisis of 2008, it evolved to become macroprudential and used as a crisis-management tool.

The fourth and final period (2009–present) in the evolution of stress testing began with the implosion of the GFC and its unprecedented costs to societies and economies across the world. Stress tests help bank management form a complete view of a bank's total risk profile. The results of properly designed stress tests containing scenarios built around extreme but plausible events are vital, but particularly more relevant to chief risk officers at banks whose central role is to interpret numerical outcomes of stress tests to set risk limits. During the GFC, the Basel Committee observed that stress testing practices before and during the crisis demonstrated several weaknesses in various aspects of banking intermediation. To improve stress testing and guide both supervisors and banks, the Basel Committee published a guide entitled "Principles for Sound Stress Testing Practices and Supervision."

Formulation of Hypothesis

Bank Competition

It is important to understand the degree of market competition because changes in the level of competition influence the ability of banks to consider the risk-shifting behavior of their borrowers. This changes the optimal reaction of banks when they face increased capital requirements, thereby, affecting banks' asset-credit quality (Schliephake 2016; Dacanay 2017). There are two main strands of literature regarding competition and bank stability namely competition-stability and competition-fragility.

Competition-Stability

There are important theoretical arguments on the negative effects of market power on banks' performance and risk. It states that more competition and less concentration improve the soundness of the banks (Beck et al. 2006; Dacanay 2017).

The starting point in the literature is often Hick's (1935) "quiet life hypothesis." It essentially recognizes that greater market power is associated with lessened efforts by managers to maximize operating efficiency. Therefore, increased concentration should bring about a decrease in efficiency. In addition, Leibenstein (1966) argued that inefficiencies are reduced by increased competition as managers respond to the challenge. Similarly, recent theories have emphasized the importance of the relationship between competition and bank efficiency, as competitive pressures motivate managers to act more efficiently (Hart 1983). In oligopolistic or monopolistic environments, banks should be characterized by a lower degree of market discipline which in turn results in operational inefficiency. When managers fail to monitor and control adequately the operating costs and when loan portfolio management is weak, the result is typically higher numbers of loan loss provisions. Lastly, Boyd and De Nicoló (2005) argued the risk-shifting effect which states that lower lending rates, brought about by increased competition, reduce the probability that borrowers become bankrupt or take on risky projects.

Competition-Fragility

On the other side of the spectrum, competition-fragility states that intense competition erodes market power and franchise values, increasing incentives to take on risky projects, since forgone future profits in the case of bankruptcy are lower (Focarelli et al. 2018).

In addition, increased competition may worsen the excessive risk-taking problem since higher competition reduces banks' margins. This phenomenon is called the "margin effect." Therefore, this lowers the bank's "charter value" (refers to the worth of the bank's capacity to continue operating). In a dynamic setting, market power enhances the bank's charter value, making it more conservative in its operations (Schliephake 2016; Dacanay 2017). Thereby, tougher competition may lead to a riskier bank portfolio and a higher probability of failure. Furthermore, large banks usually have better-diversified portfolios. Also, it is easier to monitor more concentrated banking systems because of the limited number of banks.

Moreover, the structure-conduct-performance paradigm hypothesizes that greater market power leads to higher concentration levels in the banking market, and which influences a bank's market conduct (VanHoose 2022, p. 55). Service differentiation with relationship banking may result leading to higher loan rates and improved monitoring activities, resulting in better asset quality (VanHoose 2022, pp. 52–54). Another paper claimed that an increase in the number of banks leads to more borrowers obtaining loans (Ogura 2006). In good economic times, as more borrowers qualify for loans, there is a tendency for each bank to extend more loans as its rivals expand their lending. The result essentially is a herding effect, with banks collectively loosening their credit standards during economic booms. This is consistent with the facts associated with banking during the 2000s, especially with the Global Financial Crisis of 2008.

Lastly, market power is often associated with a lower probability of a banking failure. Such a negative relationship is usually attributed to various reasons (Caminal et al. 2002). First, higher lending rates result in lower investment levels and thus a higher expected return of the marginal project, which implies a lower probability of bankruptcy. Second, the higher the future expected profits of a bank, the larger the opportunity cost of going bankrupt, which reduces the incentive to overinvest in risky assets. Finally, on the deposit side, competition will tend to increase deposit rates pushing the margin further down and failure probabilities up.

U-Shaped Relationship

Combining these two theories, we now come up with a U-shaped relationship between competition and the risk of bank failure (Martinez-Miera and Repullo 2010; Dacanay 2017; Bayangos 2022). In a highly concentrated market, the risk-shifting effect dominates, thus entry reduces the probability of bank failure (competition-stability). On the other hand, in a very competitive market, the margin effect dominates, therefore further entry increases the probability of failure (competition-fragility). In essence, the greatest probabilities of failure arise in either highly competitive markets or markets in which banks have the greatest market power, resulting in higher loan rates and a decrease in efficiency (VanHoose 2022, p. 75).

This paper applies the competition-fragility theory due to the presence of credit market frictions. In addition, the results of Dacanay (2017) already showed that the Philippine banking industry exhibited imperfect competition, that is, moderate concentration, in the loans and deposits market. This implies that the dominant banks are increasing their profit margins, through higher mark-ups and in turn, decreasing their non-performing loans. Hence, the paper will attempt to verify the hypothesis that "A more concentrated market will more likely result in higher credit quality of banks."

Link Between the Macroeconomic Environment and Bank's Credit Quality

Several studies have proven the existence of a link between macroeconomic indicators and the credit quality of banks. This implies that credit quality is sensitive to changes in macroeconomic factors.

During financial crises, especially the Global Financial Crisis of 2008, it became abundantly clear that macroeconomic conditions manifested through economic cycles and had a significant impact on the banking industry's incidence of non-performing loans (Warue 2012). Business cycles affect the cash flows of various economic units and consequently credit portfolio performance. Effects of the business cycle on the incidence of non-performing loans came to the fore during the global economic recession. During boom periods, interest rates tend to be lower as savings tend to be higher and this tends to bring down the cost of funds. This could lead to excessive borrowing pushing leverage to unsustainable levels. On the other hand, when the bust period sets in and businesses are not making as much sales as they had hoped for and the risk of default starts to go up, lenders raise interest rates to take into account the increased lending risk compounding the borrower's problems. This behavior of banks and investors during boom-and-bust periods leads to exacerbating the business cycle. In addition, Warue (2012) discussed that it is important to understand macroeconomic factors in an economy to aid effective monitoring and review of credit risk.

Greenwald and Stiglitz (1993) argued that the actions of firms are affected by their perceptions of risks. One key factor that influences the risks firms face and their willingness to bear those risks is the overall state of the economy. When the economy goes into a recession, and firms talk about their pessimism or uncertainty, these perceptions have real consequences. Thus, this changes the firm's cash position due to lower profits brought about by the drop in production activities. Consequently, the firm's (borrower) net worth is reduced resulting in a weaker ability to repay existing loans.

Lastly, an estimation strategy normally requires the selection of an initial set of macroeconomic and financial variables that affect credit risk (Foglia 2008). Variables such as economic growth, unemployment, and interest rates contribute to default risk.

Hence, given the support from multiple studies that prove the relationship between macroeconomic indicators and the credit quality of banks, this paper will verify the second hypothesis—"Development of loan losses is linked to the macroeconomic environment."

Inverse Relationship Between the Macroeconomic Environment and Bank's Credit Quality

Researchers often associate the occurrence of banking crises with a massive accumulation of non-performing loans which can account for a sizable share of the total assets of insolvent banks and financial institutions (Warue 2013). The unresolved problem of non-performing loans can compound into a financial crisis the moment these loans exceed bank capital in a relatively large number of banks. Multiple works of literature verify the inverse relationship between macroeconomic factors and the bank's credit quality.

Banks' loan department staff are expected to work out the loan best suited to the applicant's needs to ensure the beneficiary can afford to pay the loan applied for (Warue 2012). During economic distress, the failure of borrowers to repay their loans on time or at all constrains the commercial banks' ability to lend to other borrowers. With increasing default rates, most commercial banks' loan programs fail to achieve their objectives and lead to huge monetary losses. In this regard, failure to receive loan repayments on time results in banks experiencing cash flow problems. Delinquent loans have the potential of creating financial instability which may contribute to the failure of the projects thus affecting a country's economy adversely.

Furthermore, higher loan losses or defaults can jeopardize a bank's existence, which creates distrust in the banking system (Arrawatia et al. 2019). A continuous deterioration in the asset quality, brought about by a decline in macroeconomic growth, also deters banks away from lending fresh loans and advances, resulting in a decline in private investment, which affects the growth of the economy. This proves that asset quality is considered one main concern for any economy in the way of banking stability and the health of the financial system.

Another study by Waweru and Kalani (2009) claimed that full-blown banking crises are associated more with external developments, and domestic variables are the main leading indicators. Results showed that many financial institutions that collapsed in Kenya in 1986 failed due to non-performing loans. In particular, the national economic downturn was perceived as the most important external factor that contributed to the increase in non-performing loans.

The results concur with the findings of Espinoza and Prasad (2010) that the NPL ratio worsens as economic growth becomes lower and lending interest rates and risk aversion increase. Flamini et al. (2015) also argued that weak economic performance exposes banks to risk while low economic growth promotes the deterioration of credit quality and increases the probability of loan defaults. Lastly, Kalirai and Scheicher (2002) stated that a deterioration in economic activity leads to falling incomes, rising payment difficulties, and more business failures, and hence default risk rises, causing a decline in the quality of the banking books. With sufficient evidence that there is an inverse relationship between macroeconomic indicators and the credit quality of banks, this paper will verify the third hypothesis—"An increase in macroeconomic growth leads to a decrease in NPL."

Theoretical Foundations

Neoclassical Synthesis (Complete Keynesian Model)

The complete Keynesian model, also known as the Neoclassical synthesis, is a comprehensive model that encapsulates neoclassical models of the labor market, production function, commodity market, and the Investment-Savings and Liquidity Preference-Monet Supply (IS/LM) model (Felderer et al. 1992). The equations behind the model are depicted simultaneously which allows for graphical consolidation of the models. From the model, we can deduce that macroeconomic factors affect the credit quality of banks.

The standard macroeconomic model does not account for credit frictions because the money supply curve, which indicates monetary liquidity, assumes that all debt instruments can be lumped together in a bond market (Bernanke et al. 1999). Credit frictions have been introduced in the standard Keynesian macroeconomic model, which indicated demand for credit. It relies on the bank lending rate and interest rate. For the bank balance sheet, another asset is added in the form of loans. Since a new asset is added, the real side of the economy will now depend upon the interest rate on deposits and the lending rate. Thus, the loan supply of banks increases with the interest rate on loans and decreases with the interest rate on bonds. On the other hand, banks' demand for loans rises with the interest rate on bonds and falls with the interest rate on loans.

Monetary expansion or an increase in bank reserves would bring about an increase in the quantity of money and in the volume of credit, which stimulates investment demand. The central bank reserves are a shifting parameter of the credit friction curve as reserves influence the effectiveness of the monetary policy. An increase in the reserves available to banks will boost the supply of loans and the demand for bonds. Monetary policy may also affect the external finance premium by shifting the supply of intermediate credit, particularly loans by commercial banks. If the supply of bank loans is disrupted, then bank-dependent borrowers will incur the costs of finding a new lender and establishing a credit relationship. Therefore, a reduction in the supply of bank credit, relative to other forms of credit, is likely to increase the external finance premium and reduce real activity (Fig. 5.1).

In essence, based on the neoclassical synthesis, the model that relates most closely to credit quality would be the IS-LM model. This is due to the model's two key variables, output, and interest rate which will both be considered explanatory macroeconomic variables to the probability of default.

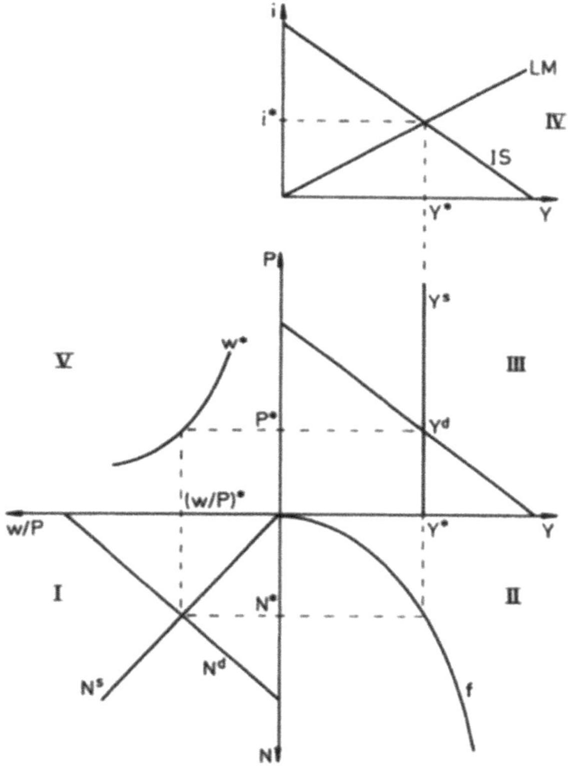

Fig. 5.1 Complete Keynesian model (*Source* Bernard Felderer and Stefan Homburg [1992])

Portfolio Theory

This theory assumes that firms are risk-averse. Under these conditions of uncertainty, firms simultaneously choose all of their actions—prices, wages, employment, production, and so on—taking into account the risk and expected returns with each "portfolio" of decisions (Greenwald et al. 1993). In assessing the consequences of various actions, firms look at the effects that those actions will have on the firm's assets. Thus, changes in economic circumstances—either the firm's willingness to bear risks or its perceptions concerning the riskiness or value of various assets, will lead it to want to change that portfolio. In other words, volatility in the economic environment will in general necessitate changes in some actions of the firm. For instance, if the demand curve for the firm's product shifts to the left (given the drop in macroeconomic activities), it must either change the price it charges, the quantity it sells, or the inventories it holds. If it holds the price constant, the quantity sold must adjust, and conversely. Evaluating what it should do entails an evaluation of the risks associated with each of these changes and the costs of adjustment.

The Portfolio Theory, alongside the assumption of the risk aversion of firms, can explain why each firm's supply curve, and hence the aggregate supply curve—the amount that they are willing to produce at each level of prices (given wages)—should shift markedly as the economy goes into a recession. The riskiness of production has increased, and the firm's willingness and ability to bear that risk has decreased.

This theory can also explain the cyclical behavior of the economy. To maintain the same level of economic activity, with the reduced cash flow from lower profits, firms must borrow more. But increased debt creates a higher probability that future returns will not be sufficient to meet these fixed obligations. As the firm expands its production, it must borrow more, increasing its fixed obligations; there is an increased chance of not being able to meet those increased fixed obligations. Therefore, during economic distress, there is lower demand for goods and services, reducing the firm's profits. This translates to a weaker balance sheet (net worth), thus making it difficult for firms to meet debt obligations.

Lastly, this risk-averse behavior will magnify an initial negative economic shock and make recessions deeper and longer. For banks, when economic conditions worsen, their perceptions of the relative risk of loans increase; and since bad economic conditions are often accompanied by high default rates, banks' net worth decreases, along with their willingness to bear risks. Banks will often be unwilling to raise interest rates, because of a fear that higher rates will have an adverse selection effect of chasing away creditworthy borrowers and adverse incentive effects, inducing them to undertake greater risks. On the other hand, due to the inventory adjustments of firms, the initial shock may have large and persistent effects on the economy. With greater perceived risk and lower wealth, and hence reduced willingness to bear risk, firms cut back on their desired level of inventories. This translates into a further reduction in production.

Modern Intermediation Theory

The environment of banks is where agents are asymmetrically informed (Boyd et al. 1993). This modern intermediation theory predicts that large intermediary firms will be less likely to fail than small ones, becoming more cost-efficient. More importantly, modern intermediation theory forecasts efficiency gains related to size. It predicts economies of scale in intermediation.

The advantage of size means that an intermediary can contract with many borrowers and lenders. Large numbers are assumed to result in diversification, and that is valuable even in environments with all agents risk-neutral. If a large number of investments are made by a single intermediary, the pooled risk is reduced or eliminated, and so is the frequency of costly failure states. What is predicted, then, is an inverse relationship between size and the probability of failure. In that environment, large scale not only reduces contracting costs, it also permits intermediaries to fund the most profitable investments. However, the finding that large intermediaries are more efficient than small ones—even abstracting from risk aversion—is quite general.

Theoretical and Conceptual Framework

This portion begins with the research hypothesis, and, discusses the theoretical framework and theoretical model to be used. It also presents the conceptual framework which serves as a guide that gives coherence to the research process. Several methodologies such as the Herfindahl–Hirschman Index, Vector Autoregressive Regression, Impulse Response Function, and Generalized Method of Moments are to be employed to answer the identified research problems.

Hypotheses

The paper shall attempt to prove the following hypotheses:

1. A more concentrated market will more likely result in higher credit quality of banks.
2. Greater loan losses lead to a less resilient macroeconomic environment.
3. An increase in macroeconomic growth leads to a decrease in NPL.

Theoretical Framework

To understand the link between banks and the real economy in light of the crisis, the financial accelerator is used as the theoretical framework.

Most of the models developed before the crisis presented the role of banks as negligible because banks were not fundamentally independent agents (Dia and VanHoose 2017). They were viewed as merely an intermediation agent with no large implications for the real economy. This can be attributed to the fact that economic theorists during the first few decades after World War II developed general equilibrium models of the economy with complete markets; that is, it assumed a "frictionless" capital market where imperfect information or transaction costs do not exist (De Groot 2018). In this perspective, borrowers do not face an external finance premium (Bernanke 2007). A firm's cash position would be irrelevant to its decision to invest because efficient capital markets would supply the necessary funding for any investment projects expected to yield a positive net return. For instance, the Modigliani–Miller theorem implies that financial structure is both indeterminate and irrelevant to real economic outcomes (Bernanke et al. 1998).

However, historical events proved that credit market frictions may significantly amplify both real and nominal real effects on the economy (Ibid.). The Global Financial Crisis of 2008 is a great example that shows that financial intermediation itself can be the cause of economic downturns (König 2020). Thus, conventional macroeconomics paradigms, as usually presented, do not even give the readers ways of thinking about such effects (Bernanke 2007).

Hence, the financial accelerator is introduced to explain that in the event of an adverse shock, financial conditions worsen significantly, impairing firms' and households' access to credit, and at the same time borrowers' need for external funds may be rising (Bernanke et al. 1998). In other words, it refers to the mechanism by which frictions in financial markets amplify the propagation of shocks through an economy (De Groot 2018).

The key building block of the financial accelerator is the existence of friction in the intermediation of credit (Ibid.). To put it simply, credit friction is the total direct and indirect costs associated with the execution of a financial transaction (Kagan 2020; De Groot 2018). Some examples are information asymmetries and agency costs. With this, banks usually use forms and financial contracts to reduce friction costs (Bernanke et al.

1998). Borrowers, especially consumers and firms with weak balance sheets, who face significant agency costs of borrowing in credit markets are likely to bear the brunt of an economic decline (Bernanke et al. 1996). Following an adverse macroeconomic shock, these borrowers should experience reduced access to credit, relative to other borrowers. Consequently, they should also reduce their economic activity earlier and more sharply than others in the economy. With lower output, the borrower's net worth also tapers, making it difficult to repay existing loans; thereby, affecting the bank's credit quality.

Furthermore, financial friction and lending quality are interconnected in several ways (Chortareas et al. 2011). Information asymmetries may significantly induce managers to undertake more risk by investing in risky projects and increasing the cost of capital. In addition, inefficient banks might perform poor credit screening and monitoring, thus adversely affecting the quality of their loan portfolios. Similarly, various financial frictions such as the lack of market discipline in concentrated markets and moral hazard problems among managers, shareholders, and depositors could also affect the level of credit risk that banks are willing to undertake, therefore resulting in a deterioration of banks' lending quality.

Moving on, with the presence of credit market frictions, the financial accelerator mechanism involves an inverse relationship between external finance premiums and the net worth of potential borrowers (Bernanke et al. 1998). The former is defined as the difference between the cost of funds raised externally and the opportunity cost of funds internal to the firm while the latter refers to the borrower's liquid assets plus the collateral value of illiquid assets less outstanding obligations. The relationship arises because when borrowers have little wealth to contribute to project financing, the potential divergence of interests between the borrower and the suppliers of external funds is greater, implying increased agency costs (in the form of bankruptcy risk) amidst the "flight for quality" (Ibid.). During an economic downturn when exogenous risk increases, credit flows away from borrowers as individuals demand more liquid assets for precautionary reasons (Brunnermeier et al. 2012). With this, lenders must be compensated for higher agency costs by the larger premium (Bernanke et al. 1996). Moreover, the external finance premium that a borrower must pay should depend inversely on the strength of the borrower's financial position, measured in terms of factors such as net worth, liquidity, and current and future expected cash flows (Bernanke 2007).

To paint a picture, in the hypothetical case by Gertler and Bernanke, an adverse productivity shock lowers firms' current cash flows, thereby reducing their ability to finance investment projects from retained earnings (Ibid.). The decline in net worth raises the average external finance premium and the cost of new investments. Declining investment lowers economic activity and cash flows in subsequent periods, amplifying and propagating the effects of the initial shock. In essence, the negative shocks to the economy reduce the net worth of borrowers (or positive shocks increase net worth), and the spending and production effects of the initial shock will be amplified (Bernanke et al. 1996).

As previously discussed, adverse shocks to the economy may be amplified by worsening credit market conditions through the mechanism called financial accelerator (Ibid.). Empirically, the Global Financial Crisis of 2008 proves that fluctuations in the banks' credit may have severe consequences in the real economy. Combining theory and practical experience, it is safe to say that banks provide a crucial supporting role in the economy.

The study uses the financial accelerator mechanism to understand the link between macroeconomic variables and the banks' credit quality amid a crisis. It can be summarized in three points. First, macroeconomic variables directly affect banks' credit quality on account of the borrower's net worth which is procyclical due to the procyclicality of profits and asset prices. This means that when the economy is performing well, as estimated by output growth, the borrowers' net worth increases, moving in the same direction. Thus, during an economic downturn, borrowers will have difficulty accessing and repaying credit. Second, due to the existence of credit market frictions, the mechanism's key building block may lead to the lower credit quality of banks. Asymmetric information can encourage lenders to engage in risky projects, thereby affecting the banks' level of credit risk and in turn, deterioration of their lending quality. Lastly, in the light of a crisis, shocks may be amplified and persist via financial accelerators due to the decline in loan demand and borrowers' net worth. With lower loan demand and borrowers' reduced ability to pay, investment declines, thus augmenting the existing crisis. Consequently, this reduces banks' credit quality.

With these points in mind, it is important to understand and learn more about the banking industry, knowing it has large implications in the real economy. Adverse financial conditions may prevent an economy from reaching its growth potential (Bernanke 2007). A weak banking system grappling with non-performing loans and insufficient capital or firms whose creditworthiness has eroded because of high leverage or declining asset values are examples of financial conditions that could undermine growth. In this paper, the study is limited to comprehending the link between the macroeconomic indicators and banks' loan quality. By understanding such relationships, the probability of having a financial crisis stemming from the low credit quality of banks will be minimized.

Theoretical Model

A simple two-period partial equilibrium model by König (2020) will be used in the analysis to further appreciate the financial accelerator mechanism. The model explains how firms affect banks' net worth through interactions with capital demand. It goes into detail about the link between both factor costs (labor and capital) and the intermediation of credit from banks to goods-producing firms.

Keep in mind that the study is limited to understanding the relationship between macroeconomic indicators to the banks' credit quality. It does not aim to empirically verify the presence of a financial accelerator mechanism.

The Bank in the Partial Equilibrium Model

The model starts with a representative bank with an initial net worth N_1. At the beginning of the first period, the bank provides loans $Q_1 S_1$ to a representative goods-producing firm, where S_1 is the amount of loans and Q_1 is the price of capital. To satisfy the firm's loan demand, the bank receives deposits D_1 from deep-pocket households (savings as the remainder from income minus consumption). Therefore, the bank's balance sheet in the first period is equated by

$$Q_1 S_1 = N_1 + D_1 \tag{5.1}$$

In the second and terminal period, the bank receives a return on loans R_2^k and must pay back its debt to households given the risk-free deposit rate R_2. The financial intermediary maximizes its net present value of future net worth, given the balance sheet constraint (Eq. 5.3) and an incentive constraint (Eq. 5.5).

$$V_1 = \max_{N_2} \beta N_2, \tag{5.2}$$

$$s.t\ Q_1 S_1 = N_1 + D_1, \tag{5.3}$$

$$N_2 = R_2^k Q_1 S_1 - R_2 D_1, \tag{5.4}$$

$$V_1 \geq \lambda Q_1 S_1. \tag{5.5}$$

The incentive constraint $V_1 \geq \lambda Q_1 S_1$ (Eq. 5.5) states that terminal net worth must be larger or equal to a fraction λ of assets. This fraction can be diverted in the initial period by bankers, causing depositing households to suffer a loss and giving rise to a spread between rental rate and risk-free rate (also known as credit spread). This creates an agency problem when the banker transfers the profit back to his household. The bank operates if the expected terminal wealth is larger than, or equal to, the divertible share (Eq. 5.5). Consequently, households will limit the supply of deposits, and, in turn, banks' funds are constrained.

Moving on, the maximization provides us with a term for leverage of

$$\frac{Q_1 S_1}{N_1} = \frac{\beta R_2}{\lambda - \beta(R_2^k - R_2)}, \tag{5.6}$$

which can be rearranged into a term for the contractual rental rate (periodic payments of borrowers to banks in exchange for loans)

$$R_2^k = \frac{\lambda N_1 + (\lambda + \beta R_2) D_1}{\beta(N_1 + D_1)}. \tag{5.7}$$

From the series of equations, banks act as financial intermediaries, providing corporate loans by receiving deposits from saving households. Banks make profits based on the expected difference between the lending rate and the deposit rate. The existing agency problem between savers and banks introduces a countercyclical credit spread. Thus, in the event of an adverse economic shock, an initial deterioration in credit market conditions leads to rising credit spreads, creating an additional weakening of credit market conditions, and resulting in a disproportionately large drop in economic activity (De Groot 2018).

The Goods-Producing Firm in the Partial Equilibrium Model

In the second period, a representative goods-producing firm combines capital and labor to produce the final good under imperfect competition. The firm faces a demand constraint on the world market with $\tilde{P}_2$ denoting the average price level and $\tilde{Y}_2$ the aggregate demand.

$$Y_2(i) = \left(\frac{P_2(i)}{\tilde{P}_2}\right)^{-\varepsilon} \tilde{Y}_2, \tag{5.8}$$

The Cobb–Douglas production function of firm i is defined as:

$$Y_2(i) = (\xi_2 K_2(i))^{\alpha} (L_2(i))^{1-\alpha} \tag{5.9}$$

where ε_2 denotes the quality of capital. The assumption is that the firm must finance its entire capital with loans. The capital stock itself is bought from a capital producer at price Q_1 at the end of period one, and depreciated capital can be sold back at the end of period two at price Q_2. The fully specified maximization problem is then

$$\underset{P_2(i),\, K_2(i),\, L_2(i)}{max} = \frac{\varepsilon - 1}{\varepsilon} P_2(i) Y_2(i) - R_2^k Q_1 K_2(i) - W_2 L_2(i) + Q_2(1-\delta)\xi_2 K_2(i),$$

$$s.t. \;\; Y_2(i) = (\xi_2 K_2(i))^{\alpha} (L_2(i))^{1-\alpha} \tag{5.10}$$

$$Y_2(i) = \left(\frac{P_2(i)}{\tilde{P}_2}\right)^{-\varepsilon} \tilde{Y}_2 \,.$$

The firm takes the real rental rate (cost of employing capital) R_2^k and the real wage w_2 as given. Then, profit maximization for both factor inputs, labor, and capital, can be solved using first-order condition after dropping the index i.

$$L_2 = \frac{\varepsilon - 1}{\varepsilon} P_2(1-\alpha) \frac{\tilde{Y}_2}{W_2} \tag{5.11}$$

$$K_2 = \left(\frac{R_2^k Q_1 - \xi_2(Q_2 - \delta)}{\frac{\varepsilon - 1}{\varepsilon} P_2 \alpha L_2^{1-\alpha} \xi_2^{\alpha}} \right)^{\frac{1}{\alpha - 1}} \tag{5.12}$$

Partial Equilibrium Model

The capital demand of firms must satisfy the loan supply of banks

$$Q_1 S_1 = Q_1 K_2 \tag{5.13}$$

Banks will satisfy the firm's demand by issuing enough loans. To do so, they require a sufficient amount of deposits. Here, the deep-pocketed households will ensure sufficient funding for the banking sector by receiving the risk-free rate, R_2, as its return on provided funds. In other words, it will provide deposits according to the following supply function, which comes from the bank's balance sheets

$$D_1 = Q_1 S_1 - N_1 \tag{5.14}$$

To summarize, intermediate firms combine labor and capital to produce intermediate goods. Capital, in turn, must be bought from competitive capital-producing firms. However, intermediate goods-producing firms must finance their complete capital demand by issuing claims to get loans from financial intermediaries. Banks receive funds from saving households and lend to firms, but intermediation is affected by financial frictions. These credit market frictions, the key building block of the financial accelerator mechanism, are introduced by an agency problem between households and banks. Bankers can divert a certain fraction of assets, transfer the revenue to their households, eroding bank stability, and possibly shut down the bank.

From the model, three points can be deduced that link the theoretical model to the study. First, due to the existence of credit market frictions, bankers can be driven to act on their interests instead of the savers' by transferring funds to their pockets and engaging in risky projects. Thus, this scenario may lead to a decrease in the banks' credit quality.

Second, during an economic downturn, households' savings decrease; therefore, savers will deposit less. Consequently, the provision of loans by banks is reduced since household deposits are one of the factors contributing to its supply. With less credit available, households will engage in fewer economic activities, lowering their net worth. As a result, this reduces the banks' credit quality.

Lastly, firms are also affected by an adverse shock. To expand and modernize their plants and increase their staff, most firms must turn to financial institutions to secure these essential inputs (Bernanke 2007). With less credit available due to a macroeconomic decline, firms are not able to acquire funds to pay for the said inputs. As a result, the output of the firm is significantly reduced. This weakens the firm's balance sheet or in other words, its net worth. In this case, it impairs the firm to repay existing loans, thus resulting in a decline in the banks' credit quality. For these reasons, the study will try to analyze such links by understanding how such macroeconomic indicators affect the Top 10 UKBs' credit quality. Hence, this paper will employ the following model:

$$Probability\ of\ Default_i = f(output\ growth,\ inflation\ rate,\ interest\ rate,\ exchange\ rate,\ remittances)$$

where the Probability of Default (PD, or credit quality indicator) of an individual bank is specified as a function of key macroeconomic variables that represent macroeconomic conditions (Dua et al. 2017). This study uses the NPL ratio as an empirical measure of the probability of default. Furthermore, the model indicates that sounder economic conditions, which are determined by specific metrics on macroeconomic development, implies lower default rate and better credit quality (PD).

Conceptual Framework

The following diagram attempts to illustrate the flow of the entire study. It serves as a guide on how the study will arrive at the answer to the research problem—"Does increased economic distress, in the context of lower bank competition, lead to lower credit quality?".

The first objective of the study aims to review the historical influence of macroeconomic variables and bank competition on the credit quality of the Top 10 UKBs individually as represented by the green box. As discussed, there are two strands of literature regarding competition and bank stability: competition-fragility and competition-stability. The former argues that increased competition erodes market power, decreases profit margins, and results in reduced franchise value. In turn, this encourages banks to take on riskier projects to increase returns and may eventually lead to bank failure (Berger et al. 2017; Dacanay 2017). Meanwhile, the latter posits that more competition, meaning less concentration and market power, improves the soundness of the banks. It is beneficial to the borrowers as competition tends to push down the rates that firms pay for loans and may, therefore, improve the average quality of loan applicants. In addition, banks become more efficient as managers are motivated to act more efficiently due to competitive pressures (Chortareas et al. 2011). With these concepts in mind, the study will try to determine the effect of market competition on the banks' credit quality as portrayed by the green arrow. The Herfindahl–Hirschman Index (HHI) will be used to answer the first objective.

The focus of this study is to use the concept of macro stress testing to analyze the relationship between macroeconomic indicators and the banks' asset-credit quality. To meet this requirement, the first process is to create a macroeconomic model that will capture the link of the variables (Objective 2) using the Vector Autoregressive (VAR) model as represented by the blue diagram. VAR models have appeal because they are a flexible and relatively simple way of producing a set of mutually consistent shocks (Foglia 2008). The variables included are real gross domestic product (GDP), interest rate (lending rate), exchange rate, inflation, and remittances.

After determining the relationship, the next objective is to forecast new values of macroeconomic indicators after subjecting them to mild and mild stress scenarios (Objective 3). To achieve this, the gravity of shocks under these conditions must first be computed using the percentile function as represented by the purple rectangle. The mild scenario is established as the probability of 1 occurring every 10 years while the moderate scenario is the probability of 1 occurring every 25 years (Vu et al. 2018). The stressed events can come from domestic macroeconomic factors making them vulnerable (Banerjee et al. 2017). The following step is to forecast the macroeconomic influences under stress as explained by the purple arrow pointing to the blue diagram.

The last step is to quantify the effect of economic distress on the asset-credit quality of the Top 10 UKBs and the entire industry as represented in the figure through the blue arrow pointing to the yellow rectangular box (Objective 4). To satisfy this objective, a credit satellite model will

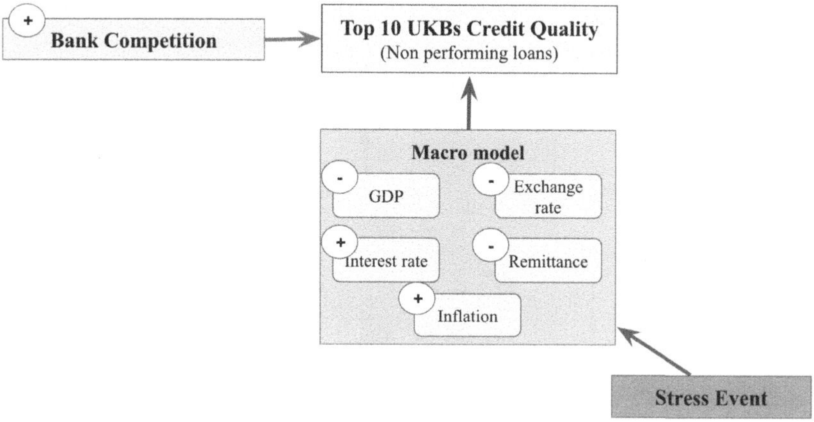

Fig. 5.2 Conceptual map (*Sources* Author's theoretical framework, Vu et al. [2018])

be devised per bank using the Generalized Method of Moments (GMM). The expected relationship between the macroeconomic variables to credit quality is seen in Fig. 5.2. An increase in interest rates and inflation will lead to an increase in NPL, in turn, a decrease in the banks' credit quality. On the other hand, the rise in output growth, exchange rate, and remittances will result in a decline in NPL, consequently, an increase in the bank's credit quality.

By linking the objectives, methodologies, concepts, and hypotheses, the researcher now comes up with a complete conceptual framework for coherence in the research process as depicted in Fig. 5.3. The first hypothesis will be verified in the first objective. Meanwhile, the remaining hypotheses will be confirmed in the fourth objective.

Empirical Methodology

Banking crises have erupted periodically and more frequently in the twenty-first century (Banerjee et al. 2017). This highlights the need for robust econometric models to test the ability of banks to withstand stress from macroeconomic forces. To answer the problems posed by the

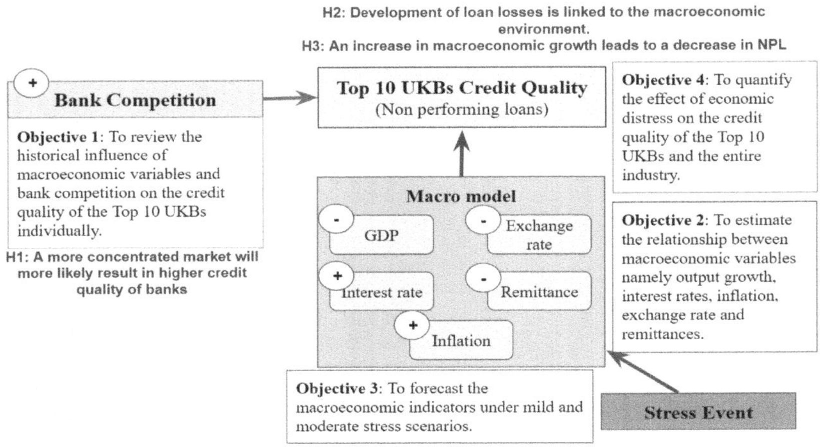

Fig. 5.3 Revised conceptual map (*Sources* Author's theoretical framework, Vu et al. [2018])

study regarding the impact of unfavorable macroeconomic events on the asset-credit quality of UKBs, the following methodologies will be applied.

Model Specification

To empirically verify objective 1, which is to review the historical influence of macroeconomic variables and bank competition on the credit quality of the Top 10 UKBs individually, the following step shall be done.

Herfindahl–Hirschman Index (HHI)

In determining the level of competition in the banking industry, the Herfindahl–Hirschman Index (HHI) will be used. It is a measure of the concentration of the entities on the market where a decrease in concentration reflects an increase in the level of competition and vice versa. The structure of competition in the industry may lead to a change in the conduct of individual banks operating in the market. HHI requires the market shares of the banks. It requires the entire size of the industry as well as its total assets. These will be used to determine the type of market structure, ranging from perfectly competitive to monopolistic.

The study will employ the metric used by Dacanay (2017) and Meyer (2018). A market is unconcentrated if its HHI is less than 1000. Otherwise, it is deemed to be moderately concentrated if its HHI is between 1000 and 1800; and highly concentrated if its HHI is greater than 1800. Thus, by determining if bank competition does indeed increase in NPL formation, meaning HHI is less than 1000, then the first hypothesis is satisfied. It will be done by observing the past trends of NPL in connection with market concentration.

To empirically verify objective 2, which is to estimate the relationship between macroeconomic variables namely output growth, interest rates, inflation, exchange rate, and remittances, and, objective 3, which is to forecast the macroeconomic indicators under mild and moderate stress scenarios, the following steps shall be employed.

Vector Autoregressive (VAR) Model

To obtain a more detailed picture of the relationship between macroeconomic indicators, the vector autoregressive model will be applied (Objective 2). Several studies use this model to study the dynamic relationships that exist among financial and macroeconomic indicators (ADB 2012). The VAR, developed by Sims in 1980, is an extension of the univariate autoregressive models which is a much superior alternative to the conventional dynamic simultaneous equation models used traditionally for multivariate regressions (Banerjee et al. 2017). Since the VAR model employs time-series data, the Unit Root Test and the Lag Length Criteria Test need to be conducted to assure the stationary of macro variables and appropriate lag for the model, respectively (Vu et al. 2018).

The VAR model that will be estimated in this study can be formalized in vector and matrix form in the following manner:

$$\begin{aligned}
x_{t,1} &= \alpha_2 + \beta_{11}x_{t-1,1} + \beta_{12}x_{t-1,2} + \beta_{13}x_{t-1,3} + \beta_{1,4}x_{t1,4} + \beta_{1,5}x_{t-1,5} + \varepsilon_{t,1} \\
x_{t,2} &= \alpha_2 + \beta_{21}x_{t-1,1} + \beta_{22}x_{t-1,2} + \beta_{23}x_{t-1,3} + \beta_{2,4}x_{t1,4} + \beta_{2,5}x_{t-1,5} + \varepsilon_{t,2} \\
x_{t,3} &= \alpha_3 + \beta_{31}x_{t-1,1} + \beta_{32}x_{t-1,2} + \beta_{33}x_{t-1,3} + \beta_{3,4}x_{t1,4} + \beta_{3,5}x_{t-1,5} + \varepsilon_{t,3} \\
x_{t,4} &= \alpha_4 + \beta_{41}x_{t-1,1} + \beta_{42}x_{t-1,2} + \beta_{43}x_{t-1,3} + \beta_{4,4}x_{t1,4} + \beta_{4,5}x_{t-1,5} + \varepsilon_{t,4} \\
x_{t,5} &= \alpha_5 + \beta_{51}x_{t-1,1} + \beta_{52}x_{t-1,2} + \beta_{53}x_{t-1,3} + \beta_{5,4}x_{t1,4} + \beta_{5,5}x_{t-1,5} + \varepsilon_{t,5}
\end{aligned} \tag{5.15}$$

where:
x_1 = Real Gross Domestic Product growth rate (GDP),
x_2 = Inflation Rate (INF),
x_3 = Exchange Rate (EXR),
x_4 = Lending Rate (ITR),
x_5 = Remittances (REM),
α = constant term,
β = coefficient,
$\mathcal{E}$ = error term
After identifying the relationship between variables, the results will be used to forecast the macroeconomic influences under stressed conditions: mild and moderate scenarios (Objective 3) (Vu et al. 2018). The model is not only used to determine the dynamic relationship but is also commonly used to explain and forecast systems of interrelated time series (ADB 2012).

Impulse Response Functions (IRF)

Impulse Response Functions will be employed to complement the VAR results of macroeconomic indicators and to provide a deeper analysis. Through an IRF, a VAR model it is possible to analyze the dynamic impact of shocks on the system of variables (Ibid.). It traces the effect of a one-time shock to one of the innovations on the current and future values of the endogenous variables. For instance, it shows the response of one variable of interest to a shock in another variable of interest while holding other variables constant (ADB 2012).

To empirically verify objective 4, which is to quantify the effect of economic distress on the credit quality of the Top 10 UKBs, the following procedure shall be done.

Generalized Method of Moments (GMM)

The next step after estimating the new values of macroeconomic variables under stress is to link the previous model with a credit satellite model. The model chosen to reach this objective is GMM since the model addresses some data problems such as heteroscedasticity and multicollinearity (Vu et al. 2018). It uses lagged variables as well as a differencing method. Based on the assumption that the first difference of instrument variables is not related to fixed effects, the model allows applying more instrument variables, hence, this helps to increase the effectiveness of the model.

$$\begin{aligned} \Delta \mathrm{NPL}_{i,t} = &\alpha_0 + \alpha_1 \Delta \mathrm{GDP}_t + \alpha_2 \Delta \mathrm{INF}_t + \alpha_3 \Delta \mathrm{EXR}_t \\ &+ \alpha_4 \Delta \mathrm{ITR}_t + \alpha_5 \Delta \mathrm{REM}_t + e \end{aligned} \tag{5.16}$$

where:
NPL = Non-Performing Loans Ratio
GDP = Real Gross Domestic Product
INF = Inflation Rate
EXR = Exchange Rate
ITR = Lending Rate
REM = Remittances
e = Error term.

With the results of GMM, the second hypothesis, which states that the development of loan losses is linked to the macroeconomic environment, is therefore satisfied. This implies that changes in the macroeconomic indicators significantly affect the banks' credit quality. In addition, the results may also evaluate the third hypothesis—an increase in macroeconomic growth leads to a decrease in NPL. This is accomplished by observing if the relationship between GDP and NPL is inversely related.

Data Description

The sample to be used in this study consists of the non-performing loans ratio (NPL) of the Philippines' Top 10 UKBs. The study will utilize the data from 2005 to 2020 (16 years). Data such as market share will be computed by the author. Meanwhile, the remaining variables of interest will be extracted from Bangko Sentral ng Pilipinas (BSP).

Dependent Variable

The core business of any bank is to receive deposits from customers and to lend these funds to borrowing customers (Warue 2013). One of the difficulties in lending is to precisely predict whether a loan will be paid in full. This implies that lending involves credit risk (or the probability of default). Several studies have indicated that the non-performing loan (NPL) ratio is considered one of the most common indicators to measure credit risk (Ibid.). This specific risk is concentrated on the impact of defaults and hence on loan losses arising from the inability of a debtor to repay a loan (Kalirai et al. 2002). Thus, the higher the credit risk, which is estimated by the NPL ratio, the lower the asset-credit quality.

A loan is non-performing when payments of interest and principal are past due for over 90 days or more and are other good reasons to doubt that payments will be made in full (Warue 2013). NPL is calculated by dividing non-performing loans over gross loans.

Independent Variables

The following table lists down the independent variables (See Table 5.4) that would be used in the study, including their expected impact, interpretation, and references (See Table 5.5).

Results

The results of the study shall be based on the objectives proposed. To recapitulate, the first objective is to review the historical influence of macroeconomic variables and bank competition on the credit quality of the Top 10 Universal and Commercial Banks (UKBs) individually. To proceed with the macro stress testing, the second objective aims to estimate the relationship between macroeconomic variables namely output

Table 5.5 Summary of the empirical methodology

Research Question	*What was the behavior of the credit quality of Top 10 UKBs, in connection with market concentration, during unfavorable macroeconomic events?*	*How do macroeconomic variables affect each other?*	*What is the effect of the shock scenarios on the macroeconomic factors?*	*Under stressed conditions, do macroeconomic factors have a significant influence on banks' asset quality?*
Objectives	To review the historical influence of macroeconomic variables and bank competition on the credit quality of the Top 10 UKBs individually	To estimate the relationship between macroeconomic variables namely output growth, interest rates, inflation, exchange rate, and remittances	To forecast the macroeconomic indicators under mild and moderate stress scenarios	To quantify the effect of economic distress on the credit quality of the Top 10 UKBs
Hypothesis	1. A more concentrated market will more likely result in higher credit quality of banks	2. Development of loan losses is linked to the macroeconomic environment 3. An increase in macroeconomic growth leads to a decrease in NPL		

(continued)

Table 5.5 (continued)

Research Question	*What was the behavior of the credit quality of Top 10 UKBs, in connection with market concentration, during unfavorable macroeconomic events?*	*How do macroeconomic variables affect each other?*	*What is the effect of the shock scenarios on the macroeconomic factors?*	*Under stressed conditions, do macroeconomic factors have a significant influence on banks' asset quality?*
Empirical Methodology	Herfindahl–Hirschman Index (HHI)	Unit Root Test, Lag Length Criteria Test, Vector Autoregressive Model (VAR), Impulse Response Function (IRF)	Percentile Function, Vector Autoregressive Model (VAR)	Generalized Method of Moments (GMM)
Expected Results	• NPL significantly increases during a crisis • The relationship between competition and credit quality is inverse ◦ A higher market share, resulting in a higher market concentration, will lead to a reduction in NPL formation	• Unit Root test to check for stationarity of variable • Lag Length Criteria Test to find out the appropriate lag • VAR will be used to estimate the relationship between the macroeconomic variables • IRF to complement the VAR results	• Percentile Function will be used to compute the gravity of the shocks under mild & moderate scenarios • VAR will be employed in order to forecast the macro variables after subjecting it to the shocks	• GDP, exchange rate, and remittances have a negative relationship with NPL • Interest rates and inflation have a positive relationship with NPL

Source Author's framework

growth, interest rates, inflation, exchange rate, and remittances. The third objective seeks to forecast the macroeconomic indicators under mild and moderate stress scenarios. Lastly, the fourth objective intends to quantify the effect of economic distress on the credit quality of the Top 10 UKBs individually and the entire UKB industry under the two scenarios.

Objective 1: Review of the Historical Influence of Macroeconomic Variables and Bank Competition on the Credit Quality of the Top 10 Universal and Commercial Banking Industry of the Philippines

In this review, it is important to highlight the macroeconomic environment and its effect on the banks' credit quality during two major crises: the Global Financial Crisis (GFC) of 2008 and the Coronavirus Pandemic (COVID-19) of 2020. It is critical to make the distinction between the two events. The former originated from financial sector vulnerabilities while the latter was caused by a direct shock to the real economy, to supply chains, and to the welfare of families and individuals (Diokno 2020b). The Philippines, and the rest of the world, had to impose strict lockdowns to save lives, therefore limiting economic activity.

Economic Environment and Credit Quality of UKBs During the Global Financial Crisis

The Philippine economy remained resilient in 2008 as its strong fundamentals enabled it to withstand global macroeconomic headwinds arising from record oil and rice prices that led to a spike in inflation and a liquidity crisis that pummeled financial markets worldwide (BDO 2009). It spawned a business climate fraught with uncertainty and pessimism. Fortunately, a record performance in 2007 gave the country its position of strength going into 2008. The country managed a 4.4% rise in real GDP in 2008, albeit slower than the 6.5% expansion in 2007. Furthermore, GDP inched up by 1.4% in 2009, a sizable difference from the world GDP as economies across the globe contracted by –1.7% (World Bank, https://data.worldbank.org/indicator/NY.GDP.MKTP.KD.ZG?end=2020&start=2004).

Foreign exchange reserves had been built up to record highs, providing a buffer against severe market volatility, thus strengthening the external payments position of the country. Meanwhile, the consumption-driven nature of the economy and the sustained growth in Overseas Filipino Worker (OFW) remittances shielded the country from a floundering external demand. The government actively pursued pump-priming activities to mitigate the impact of the global crisis. Moreover, the country's banking system remained in good shape, as evidenced by the bank's strong capital positions, declining non-performing loans, minimal exposure to toxic financial instruments, and the availability of domestic liquidity sources. These positive factors cushioned the Philippines from the full adverse impact of the global challenges.

Moving on, global commodity price surges sent the country's headline inflation rate accelerating to double digits in early 2008, before slowing down toward the end of the year due to lower demand. At the same time, interest rates mirrored the movements in inflation. Bangko Sentral ng Pilipinas (BSP) raised its policy rates by a total of 100 basis points (bps) from June to August 2008, bringing the overnight borrowing rate to 6% and the overnight lending rate to 8% to temper rising prices. However, subsiding inflation pressures during the latter part of the year prompted the BSP to revert to a more accommodative monetary policy, reducing banks' reserve requirements by 200 bps to 19%, and cutting its key rates by 50 bps in December.

Erratic movement and intermittent volatility characterized the currency markets in 2008, resulting in the peso's weaker performance vis-à-vis its record appreciation in 2007. The peso started the year strong, breaching the Php 40 level in February. However, the appreciation was not sustained due to large capital outflows on heightened investor risk aversion to emerging markets.

Local banks were not immune to the pronounced market volatility and its significant impact on their balance sheets and profitability. Nevertheless, due to financial reforms initiated by BSP and the government, banks were generally better positioned to face the crisis compared to their Asian counterparts—with better capitalization, lower loans-to-deposit ratios, lower NPL ratios, and healthier loan loss coverage ratios. Hence, even as bank profit levels declined across the board, the banking industry ended 2008 with surprisingly robust loan growth (BDO 2009).

Economic Environment and Credit Quality of UKBs Amid the Coronavirus (COVID-19) Pandemic

The Philippines saw a difficult start to 2020, with the eruption of Taal Volcano in January and the beginning of the novel coronavirus outbreak in February (Diokno 2020a). By mid-March, the COVID-19 crisis had turned into a global health crisis, prompting governments and central banks around the world to deploy measures to limit the spread of the virus and mitigate its adverse impact on households and businesses. The government imposed a lockdown to curb the transmission of the disease (Ibid.). The restrictions on the movement of people and the stoppage of business operations dampened domestic and global demand. Its impact on tourism, manufacturing, livelihood, and employment was severe as the enhanced community quarantine (ECQ), the most stringent lockdown, extended up to the second quarter of 2020.

With this, the country's GDP plunged by an unprecedented 9.5% in 2020 due to the COVID-19 pandemic, interrupting 21 years of positive growth since the 0.5% dip in 1998 in the aftermath of the Asian Financial Crisis. This marks the deepest decline in over three decades. Economic performance in Q1 2020 was weak at –0.7% dragged down by the Taal Volcano eruption in January, before plummeting by a record low of 16.9% in Q2 2020 as severe mobility restrictions under the Luzon-wide ECQ imposed in mid-March crippled business and consumption activities. Meanwhile, trade activity stagnated due to the collapse in global (exports) as well as domestic (import) demand. Despite the lack of demand-side pressures, the inflation rate inched up to 2.6% triggered by supply-side constraints. In addition, the Philippine peso made strong gains and remained within the Php 48 level from the Php 50.69 close at the start of the year.

BSP cut key policy rates by a total of 200 basis points and deployed regulatory relief measures to complement fiscal stimulus and help stimulate the domestic economy (BSP 2021). The BSP also purchased P300 billion worth of government securities (GS) and extended over P500 billion in advances to the National Government to help sustain liquidity in the real economy. In addition, BSP enacted the Financial Institutions Strategic Transfer Bill (FIST) which can help ease banking system stress through a joint government and private sector undertaking. It encourages corporations to acquire and manage non-performing assets (NPAs) and to restructure the debt of financial institutions to moderate the spillover effects on the real economy (BSP 2020).

2020 was a very challenging year for the global economy amid the triple shock brought by the COVID-19 pandemic: a health crisis, strict lockdown measures, and a global recession of unprecedented scale (World Bank 2020).

Despite the differences between the two significant crises, there are still some commonalities between the two. First, stemming from the

GFC, recognition of inter-sectoral effects is crucial (BSP 2020). The GFC highlighted the importance of macro-financial linkages such as the interactions between the real economy and the financial sector. The importance of these interactions has resurfaced considering the developments involving the COVID-19 crisis. Slow economic activity reduces the profits of businesses and the incomes of households, magnifying default probabilities that weaken the balance sheets of banks and other financial institutions. When households have a lot of debt, their spending decreases. When firms become highly indebted, hiring and investing slow down. The confluence of these events not only weakens financial and macroeconomic conditions but also hurts the growth potential of the economy (Ibid.). Second, the need for structural reforms to address fissures that became apparent during the GFC and this current pandemic must be pursued. This requires refocusing resources and fine-tuning goals. However, basic principles need not change. Lastly, crisis events change mindsets and institutions. Schumpeter's "creative destruction" highlights how a crisis dismantles longstanding practices and ushers innovation. Behavioral changes and government protocols caused by the COVID-19 crisis were disruptive for some businesses, but others were able to find and create opportunities from them. For instance, due to mobility restrictions, the increased preference for online activities has prompted businesses to shift to online platforms to promote and sell their products.

Market Power and Credit Quality in the Universal and Commercial Banking Industry of the Philippines

To test the first hypothesis—a more concentrated market will more likely result in a higher credit quality of banks—the author employed the Herfindahl–Hirschman Index (HHI) method to determine the level of competition in the Universal and Commercial Banking Industry (UKBs) and to estimate the degree of market share of the Top 10 UKBs since 2005. This is done by plotting the non-performing loans (NPL) and HHI together to identify their movements.

As seen in Fig. 5.4, the NPL ratio of the whole UKBs exhibited a downward trend since 2008 thanks to the strict compliance of banks to submit credit stress tests and to adhere to the Basel III reforms as mandated by BSP.

Only recently, due to the COVID-19 pandemic, did the NPL ratio begin to rise. UKBs posted a significant increase in NPL ratio to 2.4%

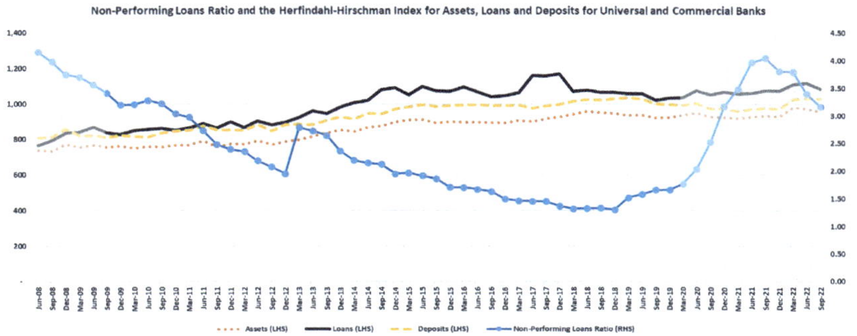

Fig. 5.4 Market concentration using the Herfindahl–Hirschman Index (Top 46 UKBs) and Non-performing loans ratio of the entire universal and commercial banks (UKBs) (*Sources* Author's calculations, Bangko Sentral ng Pilipinas (BSP). *Note* Gray portion highlights the movement during the Global Financial Crisis (2008–2009) and the COVID-19 pandemic which started on March 6, 2020, for the Philippines with its first reported COVID-19 case)

in 2020, more than double compared to the 1.6% average during the past five years (2015–2019). Its growth was the combined effect of the pandemic, African swine flu, and Rice Tariffication Law (Ibid.). Despite heightened levels, the UKB industry has seen recovery and improvement of credit quality as the NPL ratio ranged from 1 to 2% (versus the levels during the GFC of 3% to 4%).

On the other hand, the Herfindahl–Hirschman Index (HHI) for loans grew over the years, reaching a level above 1000 starting in the first quarter of 2014 until the third quarter of 2022. This indicates that the loan market for the universal and commercial banks has moved from a competitive market environment to a moderately concentrated market. Consistent with the results from Dacanay (2017), the Philippine UKB industry exhibits imperfect competition in which the dominant banks are increasing their profit margins through higher markups while also decreasing their delinquent loans. These phenomena were due to the dominant firms' superior performance in competitive markets (Qureshi 2019), even during the pandemic. Numerous works of literature support this claim wherein during periods of distress or economic decline, investors, depositors, and stakeholders tend to transfer their assets to "safer" places, which in this case, the big banks (OECD 2009). This is attributable to the fact that these banks are less likely to fail than small banks, thereby increasing the confidence and trust of depositors in dominant banks.

Moving forward, the Philippine UKB industry may continue to face significant financial and operating challenges such as sharp increases in the level of NPLs, variations of asset and credit quality, significant compression in bank margins, and low loan growth as domestic and global risks are still present (DBP 2020). In addition, Philippine banks are generally exposed to higher credit risks and greater market volatility due to several reasons (UBP 2018). First, there is greater uncertainty associated with the Philippine regulatory, political, legal, and economic environment. Second, the economy is vulnerable to a severe global downturn as it impacts the export sector, employment in export-oriented industries, and more importantly, OFW remittances. Lastly, fluctuations in interest rates and dollar-peso exchange rates may lead to higher credit risk as it can increase the cost of capital.

The Top 20 banks proved to be resilient. As of 2021 to the third quarter of 2022, the non-performing loans ratio of the Top 20 banks had an average of 4.61%. Of the top 20 UKBs, only 5 banks have non-performing loans ratios ranging from 5.5% to 13%, during the pandemic.

To observe trends of UKBs, the author grouped the banks into two: the top 5 and the next 5. The groupings were based on the total assets of banks from 2005 to 2020. By comparing Figs. 5.5 and 5.6, it is evident that the NPL ratios of the Top 5 are not as volatile as the Next 5. In addition, the former's NPL ratios settle in the same range as its peers. Meanwhile, the NPLs of the next 5 display erratic movements, and their fluctuations are more pronounced than the Top 5. This shows that even within the Top 10 banks, some banks (particularly the Top 5 UKBs) demonstrate superior performance in terms of credit quality management. In this regard, bigger banks achieve better credit quality, but they also have greater exposure to risks.

Moving on, the next section observes the movement and interaction of credit quality and market share at the individual bank level. The graph of annual market share and non-performing loans ratio per individual bank is not shown.[2]

[2] Can be requested from the author.

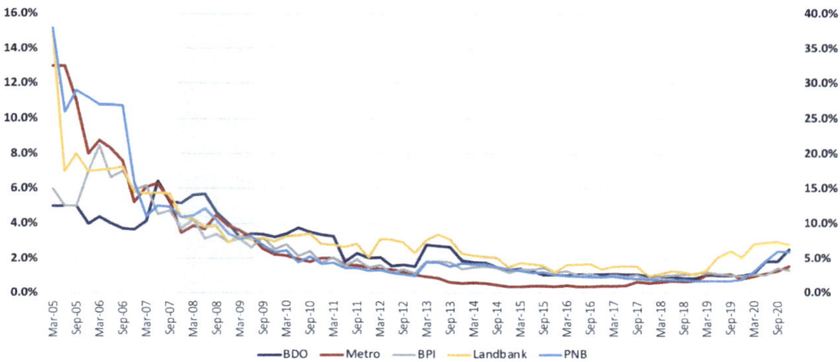

Fig. 5.5 Non-performing loans ratio of the top 5 universal and commercial banks (*Source* Bangko Sentral ng Pilipinas (BSP). *Notes* (1) Gray portion highlights the movement during the Global Financial Crisis (2008–2009), (2) The NPL ratio of the Philippine National Bank (PNB) is plotted on the right-hand side since it is the only bank from the Top 5 that had NPL higher than 40%)

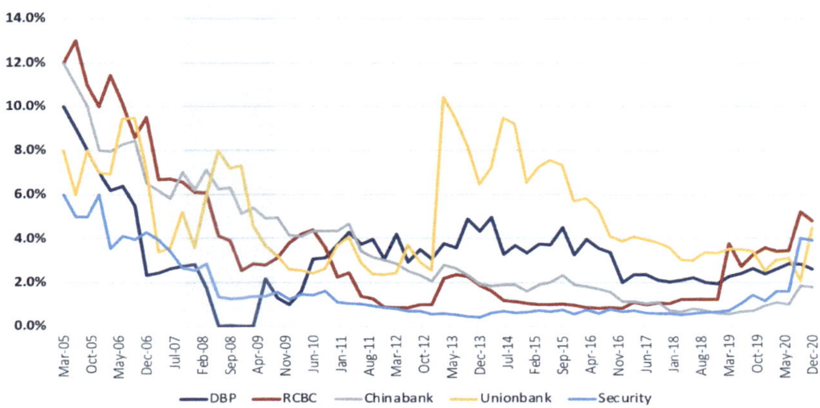

Fig. 5.6 Non-performing loans ratio of the next 5 universal and commercial banks (*Source* Bangko Sentral ng Pilipinas (BSP). *Note* Gray portion highlights the movement during the Global Financial Crisis (2008–2009))

Banco de Oro Universal Bank (BDO)

The first bank is Banco de Oro Universal Bank (BDO), a universal bank, under the SM Group. BDO consistently ranks as the top bank in terms of total assets since 2007 due to its merger with Equitable PCI, one of the biggest UKBs in terms of assets in the 2000s. It was a controversial acquisition since Equitable PCI possessed more assets than BDO.

BDO managed its credit quality well and its NPL ratio never reached double digits (BDO 2019). It even recorded its NPL at 0.8% in Q4 2018 despite facing challenging economic conditions due to the government's implementation of TRAIN Law I and BSP's policy rate increases (Ibid.). In addition, BDO improved its credit quality significantly during GFC from 6% in 2007 to 3% in 2009.

The bank's credit quality and market share moved in the opposite direction 51% of the time. This indicates that NPL is lower during times of higher market share, and vice versa. In terms of market share, it shot up by 112.5% in Q2 2007 from the previous quarter. As a result, it snatched the top spot from Metrobank and afterward, consistently ranked first. It maintained its market-leading position and continued to grow its market share as BDO expanded to new markets (Ibid.).

Metropolitan Bank & TCO (Metrobank)

Established in 1962, Metropolitan Bank & TCO (Metrobank) is the second largest bank and belongs to GT Capital Holdings, Inc. Its credit quality and market share moved in the opposite direction 54% of the time. Its NPL ratio started with double digits and remarkably declined from Q2 2007 onward due to the bank's aggressive campaign to reduce delinquent loans (MBTC 2009). Furthermore, its credit quality remained strong amid the COVID-19 pandemic as the NPL ratio stood at 2.4% in 2020 (vs 1.6% in 2019), better than the industry average of 2.6%. Meanwhile, Metrobank's market share was at its peak during the GFC and stayed in the 10% to 12% range.

Bank of the Philippine Islands (BPI)

Bank of the Philippine Islands, also known as BPI, is the first bank in Southeast Asia and is affiliated with Ayala Corporation. Its credit quality and market share moved in a separate direction 78% of the time. Noticeably its NPL exhibited a "seesaw" trend from 2006 until 2013. Nonetheless, it outperforms its peers as the bank never registered double-digit NPL ratios. Moreover, BPI saw an increase in the level of NPL in

2020 attributable to the temporary/permanent closure of certain businesses, suspended business operations, and limited travel and exchange of goods because of the COVID-19 pandemic (BPI 2021). On the other hand, it maintained its top position with its market share ranging from 10 to 11% while it hit its peak at 13% during the GFC.

Land Bank of the Philippines
Land Bank of the Philippines, or simply Landbank, is a government financial institution that strikes a balance in fulfilling its social mandate of promoting countryside development while remaining financially viable (LandBank, https://www.landbank.com/about-us/about-landbank/performance-highlights). Its NPL ratio and market share moved in the opposite direction 63% of the time. Landbank managed its NPL below double digits but began its ascent in 2019. In particular, its NPL shot up by 57% in Q2 2019. On the other hand, its market share displayed an upward trend and switched hands with Metrobank as it placed second in terms of the number of assets in 2020.

Philippine National Bank (PNB)
Another government-owned financial institution is the Philippine National Bank (PNB). Its NPL and market share moved in a separate direction 49% of the time. NPL shot up by 82% month-on-month (m-o-m) to 4% in Q1 2013 and at the same time, its market share bloated by 64% to 7% due to the merger with Allied Banking Corporation (ABC). Furthermore, PNB managed to control its NPL below double digits after Q4 2008. In 2020, NPL stood at 4.9%, the highest published among the Top 10 UKBs. With this, PNB booked P16.9 billion in provisions for credit losses, more than 5 times the year-ago level, as a proactive approach to addressing potential delinquencies that may arise from the impact of the prolonged pandemic (PNB 2021).

Development Bank of the Philippines (DBP)
The last government-owned bank on the list is the Development Bank of the Philippines (DBP). Its NPL and market share moved in a separate direction 70% of the time. Compared to its peers, its credit quality is characterized by big fluctuations in NPL. However, the bank managed to stabilize its movement from 2017 onward. Moreover, PNB's total NPL ratio in 2020 was at 2.7%, slightly higher than the industry average of 2.6%. It is noted that DBP's array of borrower profiles differs from a

regular bank's borrower profile since the bank is more focused on development financing (DBP 2020). Meanwhile, its market share was at its peak in 2008 at 8% and its movements were relatively flat until Q4 2019.

China Banking Corporation (Chinabank)
China Banking Corporation (Chinabank) was established in 1920 as one of the first privately owned local commercial banks and is an affiliate of the SM Group. Its market share and NPL ratio moved in a separate direction 56% of the time. Chinabank's market share started at 3% and ended at 5% in 2020. Its credit quality is better than the industry average as the bank was able to transform its double-digit NPL ratios to as low as 0.5% in Q1 2019, the lowest recorded NPL. Although in Q3 2020, its NPL ratio shot up by 84% from 1% in the previous quarter to 1.8% due to the effects of the COVID-19 pandemic.

Rizal Commercial Banking Corporation (RCBC)
Rizal Commercial Banking Corporation (RCBC) is among the largest private domestic banks in the country in terms of assets and is majority-owned by the Yuchengco Group of Companies (YGC) (https://www.rcbc.com/our-company). Its market share and credit quality moved in a separate direction 49% of the time. The former stood at 4% to 5% in the given period. In 2019, RCBC merged with its thrift unit, RCBC Savings Bank which resulted in a larger asset base and stronger financial standing (Ibid.). Consequently, its market share and NPL ratio soared by 30% m-o-m to 3.6% from 3.3% and 203% to 4.5% from 3.5%, respectively, in Q4 2019.

UnionBank
UnionBank started its operations in 1981 with Aboitiz Group, Insular Life, and Social Security System as its major shareholders (https://www.unionbankph.com/about-us/who-we-are). Its market share and credit quality moved in a separate direction 70% of the time. Its NPL ratio fluctuates frequently and even zoomed up by 309% in Q1 2013 to 10% from 2.6% in the previous quarter. It was particularly boosted due to its acquisition of a thrift bank named CitySavings in 2013 (UBP 2013). Additionally, the bank's credit quality (NPL) deteriorated to 3.2% in 2020 as it was not spared from the adverse effects of the pandemic.

Security Bank Corporation
Established in 1951, Security Bank Corporation was the first private and Filipino-controlled bank of the post-World War II period (https://www.securitybank.com/about-us/business-profile/). Its market share and credit quality moved in a separate direction 57% of the time. Similar to BPI, its asset quality remained strong as its NPL ratio never reached double digits. Although in Q3 2020, its NPL spiked by 154% to 4% from the previous month given the challenges arising from the pandemic and the resulting economic impact. Meanwhile, its market share significantly rose in 2016 due to its partnership with the Bank of Tokyo-Mitsubishi UFJ (MUFG), Japan's largest bank. With this, Security Bank received P36.9 billion from MUFG making it the largest equity investment in a Philippine financial institution by a foreign investor (Ibid.).

In summary, three main points can be deduced from the first objective. First, there is an inverse relationship between the NPL ratio and market concentration. This implies that increasing market concentration, marked by higher market share, would result in lower NPLs, hence an improvement in credit quality, and vice versa. For instance, BDO registered low NPL ratios despite being the largest bank in terms of asset size. Therefore, the first hypothesis—a more concentrated market will more likely result in higher credit quality of banks—is accepted.

Second, the results of HHI for loans (HHI greater than 1000) showed that the Philippine UKB industry exhibits imperfect competition, i.e., moderate concentration (Fig. 5.4). According to BSP, there are 46 domestic and foreign UKBs operating in the Philippines as of 2022. Out of 46 banks, the Top 20 UKBs accounted for 95–97%, and the Top 10 accounted for 55% to 62% of the computed market share for deposits, loans, and assets from 2005 to 2022Q3, signifying the presence of dominant banks. In addition, these dominant Top 10 banks manifest market power, that is, a moderate level of market concentration. Increased competition may make it difficult to increase the size of the banks' loan portfolio and deposit base which affects their credit quality and have a material adverse effect on their margins (Fig. 5.7).

Lastly, historically, macroeconomic factors affect the banks' credit quality, particularly in periods of economic decline during the GFC and COVID-19 pandemic. Accordingly, economic difficulties in the Philippines that have a significant adverse effect on Philippine consumers resulted in reduced growth and deterioration in the credit quality of the bank's consumer loan portfolios. In other words, economic distress

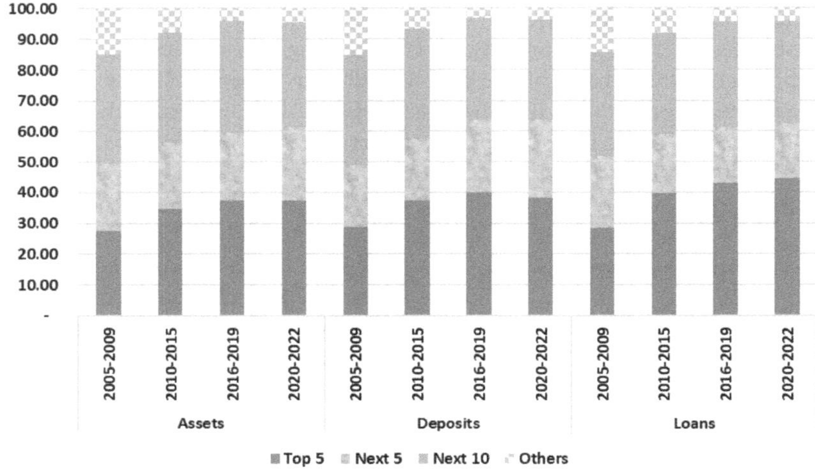

Fig. 5.7 Market shares of the top 46 universal and commercial banks (*Source* Bangko Sentral ng Pilipinas (BSP))

caused uncertainty regarding their ability to fulfill their loan obligations, and in effect, increased the banks' exposure to credit risk. For example, a rise in unemployment or an increase in interest rates harmed the ability of borrowers to make payments, which increased the likelihood of loan defaults, while reducing demand for consumer loans. Furthermore, the impact of economic growth on the ratio of non-performing loans varies per crisis. During the GFC, banks' credit quality improved, while the opposite happened during the COVID-19 Pandemic. This might be due to several reasons. One, the Philippines did not experience the full impact of the financial crisis compared to other countries whose GDP contracted significantly. On the other hand, the Philippines had a difficult time in 2020 as GDP decreased to –9.5%. It took the full brunt of the crisis as the country is significantly dependent on its domestic activity for growth. Another reason is that the Philippine banking system has remained resilient despite the heightened level of global financial distress. There was a limited exposure of domestic banks to the US subprime fallout and other related securitized assets, which accounted for only 0.4% of the banking system's total assets as of June 2008 (Guinigundo 2011). Moreover, banks recorded solid performances in terms of asset quality, capital position, and profitability, partly due to the improvements in risk and liquidity management and the strengthening of supervisory and regulatory systems during this period. Lastly, the NPL ratios were high (even double digits) before the GFC, however, this was not the case in 2020. NPL ratios rose in 2021 due to the lapse of the Bayanihan Act I, the continued muted demand, and the tightening of credit standards (BPI 2021). However, as the COVID-19 restrictions eased by the second quarter of 2022, one can observe a decrease in the NPL ratios by the third quarter of 2022 (See Fig. 5.4).

Objective 2: Macroeconomic Model

To assess the vulnerability of a financial system to "exceptional but plausible" macroeconomic shocks (macro stress testing), the first step is to create a macroeconomic model that will capture the dynamic interactions among the macroeconomic variables namely output growth, interest rates, inflation, exchange rate, and remittances. This relationship is measured by a Vector Auto Regression (VAR) method. The model includes two dummy variables to account for the significant variations in data during the GFC and COVID-19 pandemic.

It is common practice to subject the variables to pre-tests for unit roots to determine the appropriate transformations that render the data stationary (Vu et al. 2018). This is an important specification issue for time-series regression modeling. The stationarity of a series implies that its mean, variance, and covariance are constant over time. In other words, the movement of the variable after it has been subjected to a shock to its equilibrium or steady state may be traced. Furthermore, the assumption behind VAR is that all variables are stationary. Therefore, each variable was tested using the Unit Root Test by Augmented Dickey–Fuller (ADF). Under this test, the null hypothesis states that the variable has a unit root, indicating it has non-stationary properties. The results of these tests are not shown.[3]

In summary, the results of the vector autoregression indicate that GDP is greatly affected by interest rate and itself and influences the same variables. On the other hand, inflation is influenced by the exchange rate and itself and has a minor impact on the exchange rate. Meanwhile, changes

[3] Can be requested from the author.

in GDP and exchange rate significantly affect interest rates and impact GDP and remittances. Additionally, the exchange rate has a strong influence on other variables as it affects inflation, interest rate, remittances, and itself but is unaffected by others. On the contrary, the level of remittances is relatively sensitive to the changes in macroeconomic conditions, but it does not influence other variables. Dummy variables such as GFC affect the inflation rate and GDP while COVID-19 significantly influences GDP, interest rate, and remittances.

Since VAR results are difficult to interpret, the Impulse Response Function[4] (IRF) is also calculated. IRF presents the time path (current and future values) of the variables in the model to a one-unit increase in the current value of a variable, showing the dynamic response to the shock. In other words, it answers the question "what is the effect of one unit shock in x on y?". With this, changes of one standard deviation in one variable will have an impact on the remaining variables. Furthermore, it is useful in being able to explain the sign of the relationship as well as how long these effects require to take place.

The analysis of the IRF results is limited to the response of the macroeconomic variables on the shock of GDP in a span of 8 periods (2 years) which is seen in the second column of Fig. 5.8. It focuses mainly on the GDP shock since the paper will employ a similar scenario in the next objective. Moving on, Fig. 5.9 shows that a shock in GDP on itself exhibits a "W" pattern. In particular, it hits its lowest in the 3rd period (Q3 2021) then bounces back and reaches its peak in the 5th period (Q1 2022). Afterward it plummets until the 7th period (Q3 2022) before it rises in the last period, albeit still in negative territory. This indicates that GDP will recover after the 3rd period but will slow down in the 6th period. It makes sense since economic growth is not a straight-line upward trend. Conversely, it is sensitive to the business cycle with boom-and-bust cycles (FSCC 2019).

Meanwhile, there is a negative reaction of inflation toward a shock in GDP for the first 4 periods (Q1 2021 to Q4 2021) then it gradually picks up again until the 7th period (Q3 2022) before slightly declining in the 8th quarter (see Fig. 5.10). Inflation may decrease in the near term due to higher interest rates during the onset of an economic downturn (Svensson 2018). The rise in interest rates is brought about by a phenomenon called

[4] Individual Impulse Response Function (IRF) graphs may be requested separately from the author.

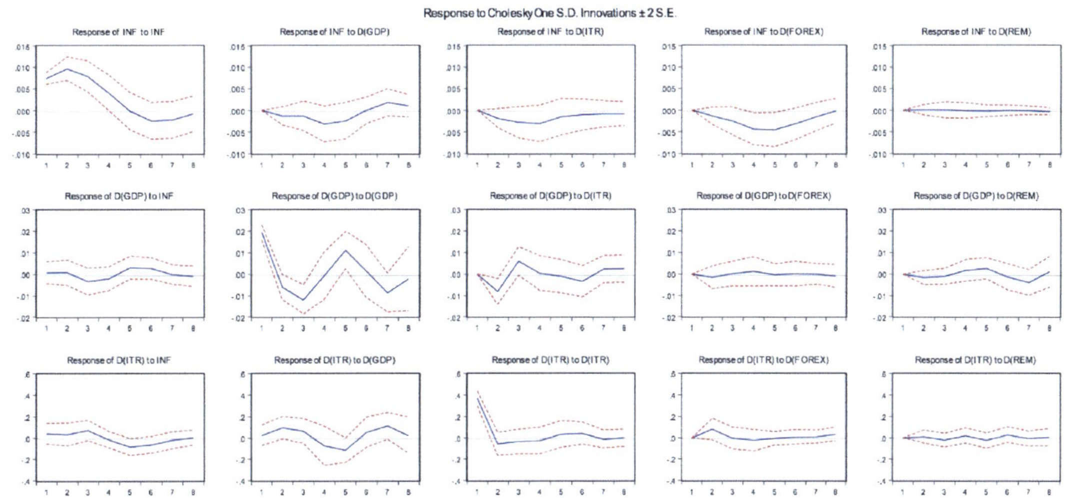

Fig. 5.8 Impulse response function (IRF) results (*Source* Author's Calculations. *Notes* (1) The magnitude of the shock: one standard deviation of x; (2) Red dots represent the standard error (SE) confidence bands. The confidence intervals are computed as +/− 2 SE confidence bands; (3) X axis represents the periods in quarters; Y axis shows the percentage variation)

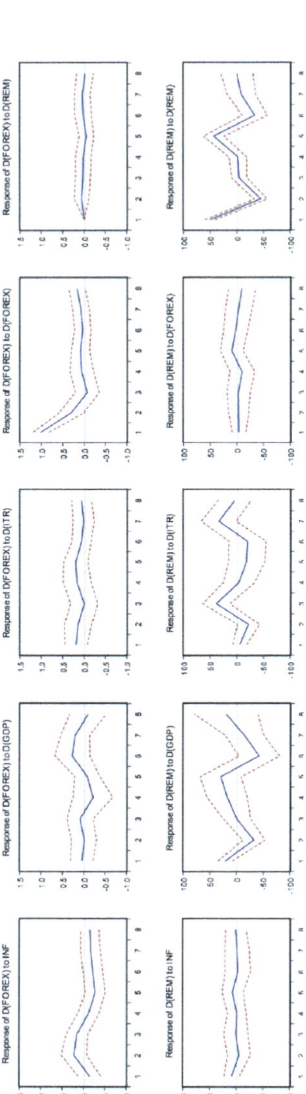

Fig. 5.8 (continued)

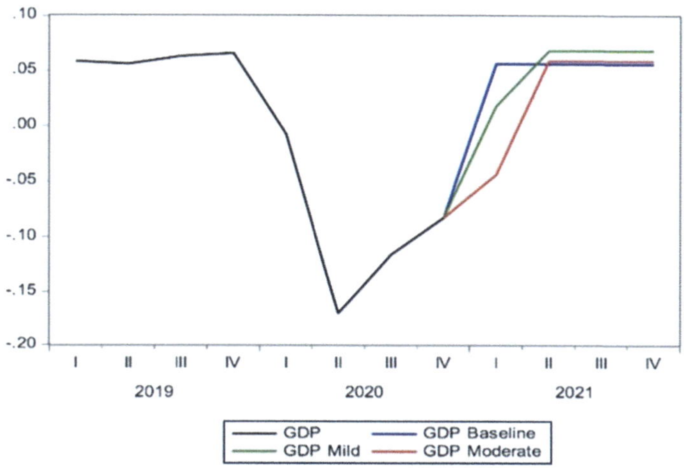

Fig. 5.9 GDP trend in 2019–2021(*Sources* Author's calculations. *Notes* (1) Data for 2021 is computed using VAR; (2) Simulation type: Deterministic, dynamic solution)

"credit crunch" where there is an increase in demand for borrowing but a decrease in willingness to lend (See Fig. 5.11). Businesses rely on credit to cover their operations in the face of falling sales while consumers run up credit cards or other sources of credit to make up for the loss of income. There's a decrease in supply at the same time, as banks curtail lending to increase reserves as a way to cover losses on loan defaults and as households draw down savings to cover living expenses when their jobs and other income dry up.

On the other hand, as shown in Fig. 5.11, the interest rate increases and remains elevated until the 3rd period (Q3 2021) then tumbles down and hits its lowest point in the 5th period (Q1 2022). Eventually, it goes back to positive territory until the final period. As previously mentioned, interest rates accelerate during the onset of economic distress just like any good in a market, when demand increases and supply decreases, prices rise sharply. So the normal expectation would be for interest rates to rise as the recession begins. However, rates decline later to stimulate demand

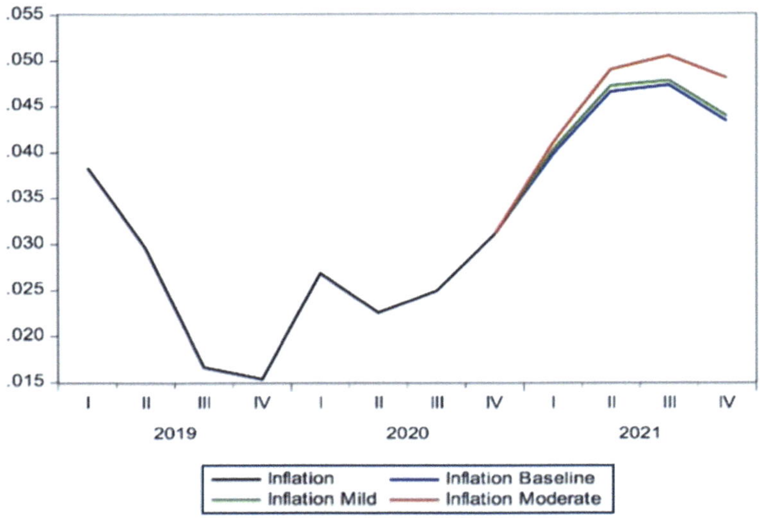

Fig. 5.10 Inflation Trend in 2019–2021 (*Sources* Author's calculations. *Notes* (1) Data for 2021 is computed using VAR; (2) Simulation type: Deterministic, dynamic solution)

by lowering the cost of borrowing (Kliesen 2010). It climbs again in the 7th period since GDP experiences another slump according to Fig. 5.9.

For the exchange rate (See Fig. 5.12), there is no noticeable impact in the first three periods (Q1 2021 to Q3 2021). However, it drops in the 4th period (Q4 2021) and begins its ascent until the 6th period (Q2 2022). In other words, the peso depreciates slightly at the beginning of the shock and then appreciates in the 4th period (Q4 2021). The devaluation of the peso can boost economic growth since a lower exchange rate makes exports cheaper and increases the demand for PH goods. In addition, the longer the shock persists, the movement of the exchange rate becomes pronounced making it more volatile. This is because a longer economic slowdown may contribute to economic instability, affecting the exchange rate and how businesses manage foreign exchange risk (Coppola 2020).

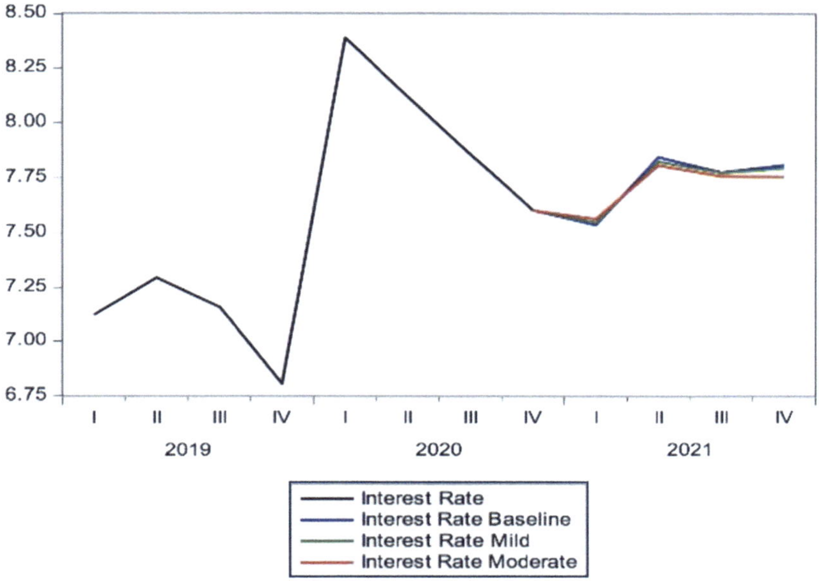

Fig. 5.11 Interest rate trend in 2019–2021 (*Sources* Author's calculations. *Notes* (1) Data for 2021 is computed using VAR; (2) Simulation type: Deterministic, dynamic solution)

Lastly, remittances plunged in the 2nd period (Q2 2021) then steadily increased before sharply falling in the 6th period (Q2 2022). It exits negative territory after the 7th period (Q3 2022) as observed in Fig. 5.13. Conversely, remittances have been countercyclical, where workers send more money home in times of crisis and hardship back home (WB 2020a). For instance, when GDP declines significantly in the 3rd and 7th periods, remittances diverge and increase instead.

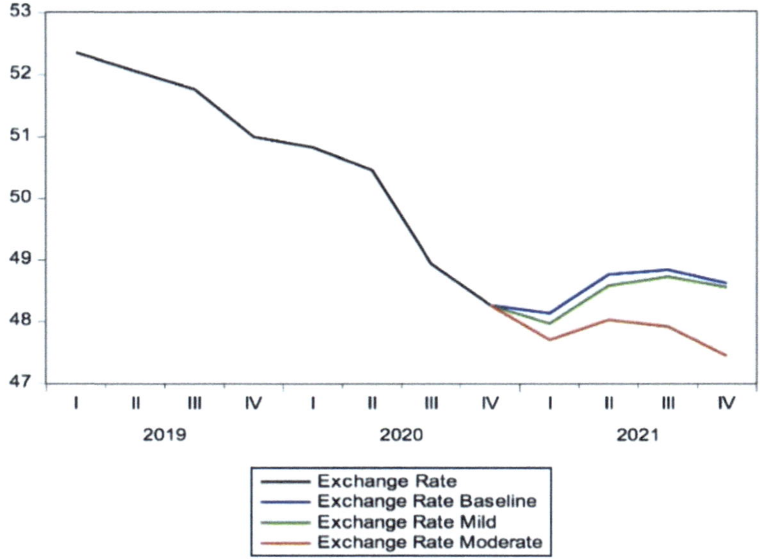

Fig. 5.12 Exchange rate trend in 2019–2021 (*Sources* Author's calculations. *Notes* (1) Data for 2021 is computed using VAR; (2) Simulation type: Deterministic, dynamic solution)

Objective 3: Macroeconomic Scenarios

After determining the relationship between the macroeconomic variables, the next objective is to forecast its values after subjecting it to mild and moderate stress scenarios (Objective 3). GDP is one of the most important macroeconomic indicators which measures national well-being (Vu et al. 2018). With this, real GDP is chosen to be the shock variable, and different scenarios are set up depending on the changes in this variable.

The country's GDP is projected to grow by 4.5% to 7% with an average of 5.7% according to different organizations as seen in Table 5.6. Only FocusEconomics and S&P Global have forecasts within the government's target range of 6% to 7%. The remaining agencies are cautiously optimistic about the Philippines' growth outlook. According to ADB, public spending on infrastructure and social assistance, progress in the country's COVID-19 vaccination drive, and a steady recovery in the global economy underpinned the growth of the Philippine economy in 2021

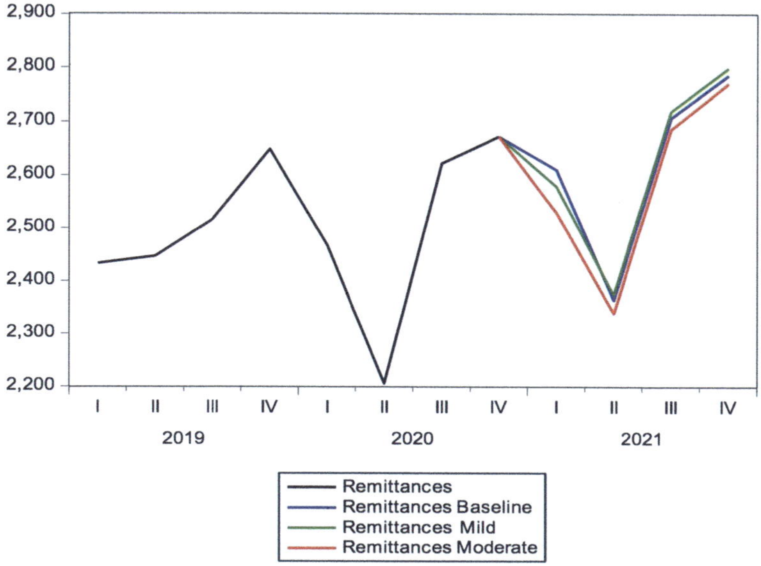

Fig. 5.13 Remittances trend in 2019–2021 (*Sources* Author's calculations, Bangko Sentral ng Pilipinas (BSP). *Notes* (1) Data for 2021 is computed using VAR; (2) Simulation type: Deterministic, dynamics: Dynamic solution)

(ADB 2021). Fitch Solutions' 5.3% GDP forecast is at the lower end of economists' estimates as the country continues to struggle to contain the COVID-19 pandemic and to normalize economic activity (Gonzales 2021b). They highlighted that the Philippines is highly vulnerable to lockdowns given its significant dependence on domestic activity for growth. Lastly, the World Bank's growth prospect of 4.7% is subject to significant downside risks (WB 2021). Several reasons include the ineffective containment of the virus or implementation of mass vaccination programs which contributed to the extension of mobility restrictions, resulting in further job and income losses, disrupting businesses, and delaying economic recovery.

The main objective of this paper is to use the macro stress testing technique to examine the effect of increased economic distress on the banks' credit quality. Therefore, the author created two scenarios of GDP shock for economic distress: mild and moderate. The mild scenario is

Table 5.6 GDP growth rate forecasts of organizations in 2021

Organization	*GDP forecast*
Development Budget Coordination Committee	6% to 7%
FocusEconomics	6.8%
S&P Global Ratings	6%
Bloomberg	5.5%
Fitch Solutions	5.3%
World Bank	4.7%
ADB	4.5%
Average	*5.6%*

Sources WB, ADB, Focus economics, S&P, Bloomberg, Fitch

established as the probability of 1 occurring every 10 years while the moderate scenario is the probability of 1 occurring every 25 years (Vu et al. 2018). Based on the quarterly data of the GDP growth rate for 16 years (2005–2020), the value of the shock was calculated through the Percentile Function. The generated shocks in Table 5.7 are used as the GDP for the first quarter of 2020.

The remaining quarters (Q2 to Q4) are computed from the time-series regression of GDP. The result of forecasted GDP per scenario is shown in Table 5.8 and Fig. 5.8. The baseline scenario depicts the future values of GDP without new significant interventions or events that will disrupt its trend based on its past performance. Under this scenario, GDP is predicted to grow by 5.7% in 2021, similar to the 5.6% average estimate by different organizations in Table 5.6. Meanwhile, there is not much difference compared to the mild scenario as it is forecasted to grow at 5.3%, still within the growth estimates. On the contrary, the 3.4% GDP outlook for the year under the moderate scenario indicates that the Philippines is recovering at a very slow pace, considering the low base

Table 5.7 Result of GDP shocks using percentile function

Scenarios	*Percentile*	*Generated value*
Mild	10th	1.8%
Moderate	4th	–4.3%

Sources Author's calculations, Philippine Statistics Authority (PSA)

Table 5.8 Computed GDP growth rate quarterly forecasts for 2021

	Baseline	*Mild*	*Moderate*
Mar-21	5.7%	1.8%	–4.3%
Jun-21	5.7%	6.5%	6.0%
Sep-21	5.7%	6.5%	6.0%
Dec-21	5.7%	6.5%	6.0%
Average	**5.7%**	**5.3%**	**3.4%**

Sources Author's calculations, Philippine Statistics Authority (PSA)

effect from the previous year. This setting may be possible if the government cannot efficiently contain the spread of the virus and deadly variants emerge to plague the country and dampen business and consumer confidence. Additionally, the shocks from both scenarios are still higher than the record-low contraction in 2020 of –9.5%.

Moving on, by replacing the forecasted GDP growth rate in the VAR model, the values for the other macroeconomic variables can be estimated individually. A simple forecast from the VAR is achieved by solving the model over the forecast period. It uses scenarios to perform a "what if" analysis.

Inflation is seen to continue its uptrend until the third quarter of 2021 before declining in the last quarter, higher than the government's inflation target of 2% to 4% for the year (Fig. 5.10). It will remain elevated due to rising global commodity prices and supply-side constraints brought about by the pandemic. The interest rate during the onset of the shock would drop slightly and then increase in the next period (Fig. 5.11). The remaining quarters would mirror this movement. Meanwhile, developments in exchange rates are more noticeable compared to the other variables as seen in Fig. 5.12. The peso mildly depreciates in the second and third quarters then it appreciates once the economy recovers, similar to the trend during the GFC. Lastly, in Fig. 5.13, remittances are forecasted to plunge in the second quarter before it significantly grows in the succeeding periods.

Objective 4: Credit Satellite Models

The macroeconomic model produced in the previous objectives does not include a credit risk measurement. Therefore in the last step of stress testing, a credit satellite model is used to link the credit risk measurement (NPL ratio) and the macroeconomic variables. The results of this objective will prove the second hypothesis, development of loan losses is linked to the macroeconomic environment, and the third hypothesis, an increase in macroeconomic growth leads to a decrease in NPL.

These models are estimated at the individual bank level as well as the whole UKB industry using the Generalized Method of Moments (GMM). The advantage of using this regression estimation procedure is that it controls for endogeneity heteroskedasticity, and inherent cross-section correlation of residuals due to interbank lending (Beck and Levine 2004; Dacanay 2017). GMM calculates robust estimators in an iterative process through a weighting procedure of regressors and an estimation of the covariance matrix which will allow the correction of cross-section dependence. For this study, the estimation weighting matrix used is the HAC (Newey-West) which is a heteroskedasticity and autocorrelation consistent estimator. Moreover, the Hansen J test is used to test the validity of the instruments.

Table 5.14 reports the GMM results under the mild scenario. The analysis will delve into the relationship, level of significance, and theory behind the effect of the macroeconomic variables on credit quality.[5] First, the impact of macroeconomic growth is only significant on BDO. The majority of the banks' NPL ratio shows a positive relationship with GDP, contrary to economic theory, albeit insignificant. This implies strong bank performance to withstand the changes in GDP. The impact of a 1% increase in GDP on the banks' credit quality is greater in UBP, PNB, and BDO while the least in LBP, PNB, and CBC.

Second, inflation significantly affects the ratio of non-performing loans of BPI, LBP, RCBC, and SBC. Apart from UBP, all banks showed a negative relationship which is inconsistent with economic theory. The impact of inflation on credit quality may be negative due to the direct as well as indirect effects on borrowing and lending (Dua et al. 2017).

[5] The author tried using lagged variables (up to three lags) to determine the longer impact of these variables on the NPL ratio. However, these models tested insignificant, thus the level form of the independent variables was utilized as the best-fit model instead.

The direct effect is the price effect which reduces the real interest rate through the Fishers' effect and thus promotes investment and economic growth in the economy. On the other hand, the indirect effect is the volume effect, due to which the real value of the borrowed amounts of debtors declines. Consequently, they are expected to gain during periods of inflation. Furthermore, when there is a significant increase in inflation, it affects RCBC, PNB, and DBP the most. On the contrary, MBT, CBC, and BDO are the least affected.

Third, the direct impact of monetary policy may be gauged by the coefficient of the nominal interest rate in the equations. This is an important result, with implications for a rise in the policy rate in a tightened monetary policy and its transmission to the bank default rate via pass-through effects to other rates in the economy, including lending rates. The interest rate is expected to have a positive association with NPL ratios due to the direct impact of the rise in the cost of borrowed funds. Thus, rising interest rate levels may adversely affect the Philippine economy and the financial condition and repayment ability of its corporate and retail borrowers, including holders of credit cards. This may lead to a deterioration in the banks' credit portfolio or quality. The majority of the banks exhibit a positive relationship and are significant at 1% (except PNB at 10%). Only LBP and UBP showed a negative relationship, but the results were insignificant. In addition, it Influences RCBC, PNB, and BDO the most while UBP, PNB, and MBT the least.

Fourth, for the exchange rate, the signs were mixed. BDO, CBC, and UBP displayed a negative relationship while the remaining banks were positive. Fluctuations in the peso-dollar exchange may affect the ability of the banks' customers to service debt obligations denominated in foreign currencies. Consequently, it could potentially increase NPLs depending on the pace of currency adjustment and the nature of the clients' enterprises. In addition, the implication of a depreciation of the nominal exchange rate (a rise in PHP/$) is expected to increase the competitiveness of exports and an increase in export earnings would favorably impact their ability to service their debt and promote export-oriented sectors and economic growth (Ibid.). However, the impact of a depreciation in the PHP on imports is expected to work in the opposite direction. It would imply dearer imports, rising oil or fuel prices, and an adverse debt-servicing capacity of borrowers who borrow in foreign currency. It is expected to worsen the repayment conditions of importers and borrowers and consequently raises NPL ratios. Therefore, the net impact of a change in the exchange rate on NPL ratios is ambiguous, meaning the relationship can be positive or negative. Moreover, it impacts PNB, MBT, and BDO the most while LBP, CBC, and SBC the least.

Lastly, remittances are confirmed to be negatively related to the banks' credit quality except for SBC. Over the years, redeployment and migration are seen to be preferred options for Filipino workers and professionals as long as the domestic economy cannot provide meaningful employment. An increase in remittances greatly explains the improvement of the credit quality of MBT, BPI, LBP, PNB, and CBC at 1% significance level and DBP at 5%. Meanwhile, it does not significantly affect BDO, RCBC, UBP, and SBC. Furthermore, the rise in remittances improves the credit quality of PNB, MBT, and CBC more compared to other banks and the SBC, BDO, and RCBC the least.

The impact of the macroeconomic variables varies per bank, making it difficult to create possible policies to improve the banks' credit quality. Therefore, the author estimated the effect of the shocks on the whole UKB industry. The results in Table 5.9 show that interest rate, exchange rate, and remittances significantly affect the industry's credit quality under the mild scenario. Meanwhile, GDP is still insignificant in explaining and predicting the movements of non-performing loans under both scenarios. Hence, the third hypothesis—an increase in macroeconomic growth leads to a decrease in NPL—is inconclusive. Moreover, it exhibits a relationship that is consistent with economic theory. This indicates that economic difficulties in the Philippines have a significant adverse effect on Philippine consumers and could result in reduced growth and deterioration in the credit quality of the whole universal and commercial banks. In particular, a 1% increase in GDP will lead to an improvement of 1.56 (mild scenario) and 2.43 (moderate scenario) in the ratio of significant non-performing loans. Similarly, inflation tested insignificant under both scenarios. Meanwhile, inflation, interest rates, and remittances exhibited the same signs that were presented in the previous tables. Lastly, the exchange rate significantly explains and has a positive relationship with the credit quality of the whole UKB industry. This means that when the peso depreciates, credit quality deteriorates. An appreciating exchange rate may decrease the value of credit and deposits denominated in foreign currencies and worsen the balance of foreign trade and GDP growth (Serwa 2010). Given the results, the second hypothesis—the development of loan losses is linked to the macroeconomic environment—is accepted.

Table 5.9 GMM results of the top 10 UKBs under mild scenario

Banks	*GDP*	*Inflation*	*Interest rate*	*Exchange rate*	*Remittances*	*Constant*
BDO	0.0680*	−0.0870	0.0100***	−0.0018***	−0.0035	0.0469
	(0.07)	(0.18)	(0.00)	(0.00)	(0.32)	
MBT	−0.0222	−0.0244	0.0050***	0.0024***	−0.0341***	−0.0616
	(0.71)	(0.82)	(0.04)	(0.00)	(0.00)	
BPI	0.0150	−0.1650**	0.0052***	0.0009**	−0.0221***	−0.0102
	(0.72)	(0.03)	(0.00)	(0.02)	(0.00)	
LBP	0.0082	−0.1848**	0.0087***	0.0000	−0.0112**	−0.0019
	(0.87)	(0.04)	(0.00)	(0.95)	(0.02)	
DBP	−0.0288	−0.2255	−0.0030	0.0018**	−0.0190**	0.0124
	(0.74)	(0.16)	(0.41)	(0.03)	(0.03)	
PNB	−0.0917	−0.3195	0.0154*	0.0059***	−0.0843***	−0.1476
	(0.65)	(0.37)	(0.06)	(0.00)	(0.00)	
RCBC	0.0259	−0.4396***	0.0180***	0.0013*	−0.0079	−0.1268
	(0.77)	(0.01)	(0.00)	(0.10)	(0.35)	
CBC	0.0167	−0.0809	0.0071***	−0.0001	−0.0332***	0.0501
	(0.70)	(0.30)	(0.00)	(0.87)	(0.00)	
UBP	0.1056	0.1903	−0.0008	−0.0007	−0.0083	0.0943
	(0.39)	(0.39)	(0.87)	(0.51)	(0.48)	
SBC	−0.0224	−0.1982**	0.0096***	0.0003	0.0029	−0.0614
	(0.69)	(0.05)	(0.00)	(0.60)	(0.60)	

Sources Bangko Sentral ng Pilipinas (BSP), Philippine Statistics Authority (PSA)
Notes (1) Superscripts *, **, and *** indicate statistical significance of the coefficients at 10, 5, and 1 percent levels of confidence, respectively; (2) *P*-values are indicated in parentheses (); (3) Banks: BDO—Banco de Oro Universal Bank, MBT—Metropolitan Bank & TCO, BPI—Bank of the Philippine Islands, LBP—Land Bank of the Philippines, PNB—Philippine National Bank, DBP—Development Bank of the Philippines, CBC—China Banking Corporation, RCBC—Rizal Commercial Banking Corporation, UBP—UnionBank of the Philippines, SBC—Security Bank Corporation; (4) Instrument specification: GDP(−1) INF(−1) ITR(−1) EXR(−1) REM(−1)

Given the regression results from the previous table, the value of NPL for 2021 is now forecasted under both adverse conditions as seen in Tables 5.10 and 5.11. The NPL ratio is forecasted to range between 1.4% and 2.4% under the mild scenario. Similarly, the ratio of non-performing loans is estimated to fall between 1.3% and 2.4%. The computed forecasts of 1.8% (mild) and 2.4% (moderate) are much lower than the actual reported NPL ratio for Q1 2021 which is at 3.5%. In other words, among the Top 10 UKBs, credit quality improves with a decrease in interest rates, remittances, and inflation as well as with an increase in the interest rate and exchange rate. This implies that the Top 10 banks may have better management of their credit quality as opposed to the other UKBs.

Results under the moderate scenario are like the estimates from the previous scenario as seen in Table 5.10. The differences are that first, the GDP growth rate is no longer significant on any banks' credit quality. Second, interest rate no longer affects PNB. Third, variations in exchange rates no longer influence RCBC. Lastly, the magnitude of the impact of macroeconomic factors differs per variable.

Table 5.10 GMM results of the Top 10 UKBs under moderate scenario

Banks	*GDP*	*Inflation*	*Interest rate*	*Exchange rate*	*Remittances*	*Constant*
BDO	0.0608	–0.0834	0.0098***	–0.0018***	–0.0037	0.0485
	(0.11)	(0.20)	(0.001)	(0.002)	(0.32)	
MBT	–0.0295	–0.0088	0.0047*	0.0024***	–0.0346***	–0.0587
	(0.64)	(0.93)	(0.08)	(0.002)	(0.002)	
BPI	0.0129	–0.1568**	0.0052***	0.0009**	–0.0219***	–0.0093
	(0.77)	(0.04)	(0.01)	(0.03)	(0.00)	
LBP	–0.0155	–0.1655*	0.0079***	0.00001	–0.0128**	0.0040
	(0.76)	(0.06)	(0.001)	(0.94)	(0.02)	
DBP	–0.0611	–0.1961	–0.0040	0.0019**	–0.0212**	0.0207
	(0.51)	(0.22)	(0.31)	(0.02)	(0.03)	
PNB	–0.1393	–0.2555	0.0137	0.0060***	–0.0877***	–0.1324
	(0.51)	(0.48)	(0.13)	(0.001)	(0.001)	
RCBC	0.0042	–0.4090***	0.0176***	0.0013	–0.0082	–0.1213
	(0.96)	(0.01)	(0.00)	(0.13)	(0.38)	
CBC	0.0179	–0.0754	0.0071***	–0.0001	–0.0333***	0.0513
	(0.69)	(0.33)	(0.00)	(0.83)	(0.001)	
UBP	0.0967	0.1945	–0.0009	–0.0008	–0.0083	0.0959
	(0.45)	(0.38)	(0.87)	(0.51)	(0.52)	
SBC	–0.0331	–0.1772*	0.0092***	0.0003	0.0024	–0.0572
	(0.58)	(0.09)	(0.001)	(0.64)	(0.70)	

Sources Bangko Sentral ng Pilipinas (BSP), Philippine Statistics Authority (PSA)

Notes (1) Superscripts *, **, and *** indicate statistical significance of the coefficients at 10, 5, and 1 percent levels of confidence, respectively; (2) *P*-values are indicated in parentheses (); (3) Banks: BDO—Banco de Oro Universal Bank, MBT—Metropolitan Bank & TCO, BPI—Bank of the Philippine Islands, LBP—Land Bank of the Philippines, PNB—Philippine National Bank, DBP—Development Bank of the Philippines, CBC—China Banking Corporation, RCBC—Rizal Commercial Banking Corporation, UBP—UnionBank of the Philippines, SBC—Security Bank Corporation; (4) Instrument specification: GDP(–1) INF(–1) ITR(–1) EXR(–1) REM(–1)

Table 5.11 GMM results of the UKB industry under mild and moderate scenarios

Scenarios	*GDP*	*Inflation*	*Interest rate*	*Exchange rate*	*Remittances*	*Constant*
Mild	−1.5596	−8.9855	0.5238**	0.1061**	−2.4464***	−0.5128
	(0.78)	(0.38)	(0.03)	(0.04)	(0.00)	
Moderate	−2.4335	−6.9286	0.5094**	0.1011*	−2.4349***	−0.2248
	(0.68)	(0.50)	(0.04)	(0.06)	(0.00)	

Sources Bangko Sentral ng Pilipinas (BSP), Philippine Statistics Authority (PSA)
Notes (1) Superscripts *, **, and *** indicate statistical significance of the coefficients at 10, 5, and 1 percent levels of confidence, respective; (2) *P*-values are indicated in parentheses (); (3) Instrument specification: GDP(−1) INF(−1) ITR(−1) EXR(−1) REM(−1)

To compare, Table 5.11 presents the actual full-year data of the NPL ratio for the entire UKB industry in 2019 and 2020 and the forecasted NPL for 2021 under mild and moderate scenarios. In 2020, NPL increased by 48%, almost half due to the pandemic. However, in 2021, NPL is predicted to decrease by 22% (Moderate) to 25% (Mild). This indicates that the credit quality of the Top 10 UKBs will improve rather than deteriorate as expected by other credit rating agencies. Take note that the model which produced the 1.8% forecast under both scenarios is based only on the critical macroeconomic variables. It did not account for any bank-specific factors that may capture the tepid demand for loans amidst the pandemic. Thus, the NPL ratio will decrease but is still higher than 1.6% in 2019 (Tables 5.12 and 5.13).

Table 5.12 Computed results using the forecasted values in 2021 under mild scenario versus actual 2020 data

Date	*NPL*	*GDP*	*INF*	*ITR*	*EXR*	*REM*
Q1 2020	1.8%	−0.7%	2.7%	8.4%	50.829	2.468
Q2 2020	2.0%	−17.0%	2.3%	8.1%	50.463	2.206
Q3 2020	2.5%	−11.6%	2.5%	7.9%	48.939	2.622
Q4 2020	3.2%	−8.3%	3.1%	7.6%	48.266	2.672
Q1 2021	1.8%	1.8%	4.0%	7.5%	47.969	2.579
Q2 2021	2.4%	6.9%	4.7%	7.8%	48.583	2.374
Q3 2021	1.5%	6.9%	4.8%	7.8%	48.730	2.719
Q4 2021	1.4%	6.9%	4.4%	7.8%	48.557	2.800

Sources Bangko Sentral ng Pilipinas (BSP), Philippine Statistics Authority (PSA)

Table 5.13 Computed results using the forecasted values in 2021 under moderate scenario versus actual 2020 data

Date	*NPL*	*GDP*	*INF*	*ITR*	*EXR*	*REM*
Q1 2020	1.8%	–0.7%	2.7%	8.4%	50.829	2.468
Q2 2020	2.0%	–17.0%	2.3%	8.1%	50.463	2.206
Q3 2020	2.5%	–11.6%	2.5%	7.9%	48.939	2.622
Q4 2020	3.2%	–8.3%	3.1%	7.6%	48.266	2.672
Q1 2021	2.1%	–4.3%	4.1%	7.6%	47.703	2.529
Q2 2021	2.4%	6.0%	4.9%	7.8%	48.030	2.340
Q3 2021	1.5%	6.0%	5.1%	7.8%	47.919	2.687
Q4 2021	1.3%	6.0%	4.8%	7.8%	47.443	2.772

Sources Bangko Sentral ng Pilipinas (BSP), Philippine Statistics Authority (PSA)

Table 5.14 Results using the forecasted values in 2021 under mild and moderate scenario versus actual 2019 and 2020 data

Date	*2019*	*2020*	*2021*
Mild	1.60%	2.4%	1.79%
Moderate			1.84%

Sources Bangko Sentral ng Pilipinas (BSP), Philippine Statistics Authority (PSA)

Summary of Findings

A summary of the results and findings for the three hypotheses are presented (Tables 5.14 and 5.15).

Summary, Conclusion, and Recommendations

Summary

The effect of a crisis on asset-credit quality is a critical dimension to pursue. This entails examining the effect of the crisis on non-performing loans and helps to note its sensitivity to different variables during the crisis period. Recognizing the banks' critical role in ensuring economic recovery, it is imperative to develop enhanced tools to assess risks and to better understand vulnerabilities in the financial system. One of the key techniques for quantifying risks is stress testing. This refers to a range of techniques used to assess the vulnerability of a financial system to "exceptional but plausible" macroeconomic shocks. Its main purpose is to

Table 5.15 Summary table of objectives, method and indicators, and results

Objectives, method and indicators	*Results*
Hypothesis 1:A more concentrated market will more likely result in higher credit quality of banks	
Objective 1: To review the historical influence of macroeconomic variables and bank competition on the credit quality of the Top 10 Universal and Commercial Banks (UKBs) individually Herfindahl–Hirschman Index (HHI) Computation Total Assets were used as the indicator which determined market share and market concentration It is plotted against non-performing loans (NPL) ratio to observe the relationship between market competition and credit quality	• There is an inverse relationship between the NPL ratio and market concentration ◦ This implies that increasing market concentration, marked by higher market share, would result in lower NPLs, hence better credit quality, and vice versa ◦ The first hypothesis—a more concentrated market will more likely result in higher credit quality of banks—is accepted • The Philippine UKB industry exhibits imperfect competition ◦ HHI > 1000 ◦ Out of 46 banks, the Top 10 UKBs accounted for 98% of the computed market share (in Q4 2020), signifying that these dominant banks hold a significant amount of market power despite the competitive industry • Historically, macroeconomic factors affect the banks' credit quality, particularly in periods of economic decline during the GFC and COVID-19 pandemic ◦ Banks' credit quality improved during the GFC as the country was not as affected by the financial crisis compared to other countries and the NPL ratios were relatively high before 2008. It displayed the bank's resiliency to withstand shocks ◦ Meanwhile, in 2020, the economy took the full brunt of the COVID-19 Pandemic crisis as GDP contracted by –9.5% since the country is heavily dependent on its domestic activity. Therefore, in this case, credit quality deteriorated

(continued)

Table 5.15 (continued)

Objectives, method and indicators	*Results*
Objective 2: To estimate the relationship between macroeconomic variables namely output growth, interest rates, inflation, exchange rate, and remittances Unit Root Test, Lag Length Criteria Test, inverse roots of the autoregressive (AR) characteristic polynomial, VAR Residual Serial Correlation Lagrange Multiplier (LM) test, Vector Autoregressive Regression (VAR), Impulse Response Function (IRF) Dependent Variables: GDP Growth Rate, Inflation Rate, Interest Rate, Exchange Rate, and Remittances Independent Variables: Dummy variables to account for the crisis periods during GFC and COVID-19 Pandemic, respectively	• The results of the Panel Unit Root Test showed that the variables except inflation exhibit non-stationary properties at level, thus the said variables were transformed in their first difference to make it stationary • The optimal lag length used is three according to the Lag Length Criteria Test • Additional tests such as inverse roots of the autoregressive (AR) characteristic polynomial and VAR Residual Serial Correlation Lagrange Multiplier (LM) were employed to make sure the model was stable and did not contain serial correlation at lag order three • Exchange rate has the strongest influence on the other variables whereas the variable Remittances are the most sensitive to the changes in macroeconomic conditions • According to the IRF results, a one standard deviation shock on GDP would exhibit a "W" pattern
Objective 3: To forecast the macroeconomic indicators under mild and moderate stress scenarios Percentile Function—Used to measure the shock for GDP growth rate Vector Autoregressive Regression (VAR)-Using the same indicators as Objective 2	• Using the percentile function, the generated value of shocks under mild and moderate scenarios was at 1.8% and –4.3%, respectively, for the first quarter of 2021 • By replacing the forecasted GDP growth rate in the VAR model, the values for the other macroeconomic variables were estimated individually

Objectives, method and indicators	*Results*
Hypothesis 2: Development of loan losses is linked to the macroeconomic environment	
Hypothesis 3: An increase in macroeconomic growth leads to a decrease in NPL	
Objective 4: To quantify the effect of economic distress on the credit quality of the Top 10 UKBs and the entire industry Generalized Method of Moments (GMM) – Using the same indicators as Objective 2	• The effect of macroeconomic variables affects the individual banks' credit quality differently as seen in their respective coefficients and signs • At the individual bank level, GDP does not significantly affect the banks' credit quality ◦ This implies that in the event of a crisis, GDP does not strongly influence the level of NPL but instead, by other factors such as interest rate, exchange rate, and remittances ◦ A reason for this is that GDP is a broad-based indicator of economic growth, hence economic growth does not affect the entirety of the banks' clients, unlike factors such as exchange rate, interest rate, and remittances which directly affect the loan portfolio and repayment ability of borrowers

(continued)

Table 5.15 (continued)

Objectives, method and indicators	*Results*
	• Inflation has a minor impact on the banks' credit quality as it only affected 4 banks (BPI, LBP, RCBC, SBC) and exhibited a negative relationship except for UBP • Rise in interest rates increases of NPL and affects the Top 10 banks the most as it greatly influences 8 banks (BDO, MBT, BPI, LBP, PNB, RCBC, CBC, SBC) • Exchange rate significantly affects 6 banks (BDO, MBT, BPI, DBP, PNB, RCBC). The relationship between exchange rate and credit quality is mixed as BDO, CBC, and UBP displayed a negative relationship while the remaining banks demonstrated a positive outcome • Remittances also affect 6 banks (MBT, BPI, LBP, DBP, PNB, and CBC) and it impacts NPL negatively • The difference between mild and moderate scenarios is that GDP is no longer significant on any of the banks' credit quality, interest rate no longer affects PNB while exchange rate no longer affects RCBC, and the magnitude of the impact of macroeconomic factors differ per variable • For the entire UKB industry, GDP proved to have a negative relationship with credit quality, although it does not necessarily predict its future values as it tested insignificant ◦ Thus, an increase in macroeconomic growth does not necessarily lead to a decrease in NPL. Hence, the third hypothesis—an increase in macroeconomic growth leads to a decrease in NPL—is inconclusive

Objectives, method and indicators	*Results*
	• Inflation negatively affects credit quality, and it is insignificant • Interest rate and exchange rate displayed a positive relationship with credit quality at 1% significance level • Remittances exhibited a negative relationship with credit quality at 1% significance level • Given the results, the second hypothesis—the development of loan losses is linked to the macroeconomic environment—is accepted

Source Author's results

evaluate the banks' performance in the light of a crisis which could help strengthen the banks' resiliency amidst uncertainties in the market. With this, the researcher came up with four objectives to answer the question: "Does increased economic distress, in the context of lower bank competition, lead to lower credit quality?". The first objective is to review the historical influence of macroeconomic variables and bank competition on the credit quality of the Top 10 Universal and Commercial Banks (UKBs) individually. Second is to estimate the relationship between macroeconomic variables namely output growth, interest rates, inflation, exchange rate, and remittances. Third is to forecast the macroeconomic indicators under mild and moderate stress scenarios. The last objective seeks to quantify the effect of economic distress on the credit quality of the Top 10 UKBs and the entire industry.

For the first objective, the Herfindahl–Hirschman Index (HHI) was employed to determine the degree of market competition in the UKB industry. The industry demonstrates an imperfectly competitive market as HHI for loans and deposits is 1100 to 1200 from 2020 to 2022, with the presence of dominant banks. The computed market share was also plotted against the banks' NPL ratio, the empirical measure used to proxy credit risk. It was observed that there is an inverse relationship between the NPL ratio and market concentration. It implies that increasing market concentration, marked by higher market share, would result in lower NPLs, hence an improvement in the bank's credit quality, and vice versa. This finding supports the competition-fragility theory and the first hypothesis which argues that a more concentrated market will more likely result in the higher credit quality of banks.

For the second objective, several pre-tests were conducted in order to make sure that the model is stable and did not contain serial correlation at lag order three (optimal lag length chosen). The macroeconomic variables were transformed into their first difference, except inflation, for it to be stationary. Results of the Vector Autoregressive (VAR) model showed that the exchange rate has the strongest influence on the other variables. On the contrary, the variable Remittances is the most sensitive to changes in macroeconomic conditions. Meanwhile, the Impulse Response Function presented that the path of recovery of GDP after experiencing a shock exhibits a "W" pattern.

For the third objective, the author applied the percentile function to determine the level of shock under the mild and moderate scenarios using GDP growth as the shock variable. The generated value of shocks under mild and moderate scenarios was at 1.8% and –4.3%, respectively, for the first quarter of 2021. Afterward a time-series regression was utilized to compute the remaining quarters of 2021 (Q2 to Q4). After completing the data required, the author employed VAR to forecast the macroeconomic variables individually.

For the last objective, a credit satellite model was applied using the Generalized Method of Moments as a means to link the macroeconomic model created from the previous objectives to the individual banks' and the entire UKB industry's credit quality. Results showed that the effect of macroeconomic variables affects the banks' credit quality differently as seen in their respective coefficients and signs under different adverse conditions. At the individual bank level, GDP does not significantly affect the banks' credit quality. Similarly, GDP tested insignificant in predicting its future values and exhibited a negative relationship with the entire UKB industry's ratio of NPL. This means that an increase in macroeconomic growth does not necessarily result in a decrease in NPL formation. Therefore, in the face of economic distress, GDP does not strongly influence the level of NPL but instead, by other factors such as interest rate, exchange rate, and remittances. This leads to refuting the third hypothesis which argues that an increase in macroeconomic growth leads to a decrease in NPL. However, this finding approves the second hypothesis which claims that the development of loan losses is linked to the macroeconomic environment. In particular. On the other hand, interest rate and exchange rate displayed a positive relationship with credit quality at 5% significance level. Lastly, remittances exhibited a negative relationship with credit quality at 1% significance level.

Conclusion

The paper created a macroeconomic model to estimate the values of the macroeconomic variables under stress scenarios and then applied a satellite model of credit risk to each bank under the Top 10 Universal and Commercial Banks (UKBs) and the entire industry to evaluate asset-credit quality under adverse conditions. With the application of stress testing, several conclusions were derived.

First, given the presence of the Top 10 UKBs and the way the banks behave from the indicated macroeconomic stress scenarios, this paper was able to show that a decrease in Remittances, GDP growth rate, and inflation, together with an increase in the interest rate and a level of exchange rate all contributed to forecasting an NPL ratio of 1.8% in both scenarios (below 5% forecasts of credit rating agencies & Basel III regulation) amidst the pandemic. Considering that the NPL is well within the Basel III regulation of 5%, the UKB industry will continue to be stable.

Second, the paper provided empirical evidence that the development of loan losses is linked to the macroeconomic environment as the selected macroeconomic variables tested significantly in predicting the future values of the banks' credit quality, specifically interest rate, exchange rate, remittances, and inflation. This calls for an appropriate mix of monetary, fiscal, and other structural policies which is crucial in achieving a stable and sound banking system. The results of the macroeconomic model provide a deeper understanding of how macroeconomic variables affect one another and react under stress scenarios. Meanwhile, the results of the credit satellite models impart insights into how these variables influence the ratio of non-performing loans per bank and the entire UKB industry. The said information can help in constructing structural policies that would mitigate the negative spillover effects brought about by the COVID-19 Pandemic.

Lastly, the macro stress tests were conducted at the individual bank level which provides awareness of various risk exposures experienced by each bank. Empirical evidence showed that macroeconomic factors affect banks differently as seen in the signs and coefficients of the regression analysis. Banking institutions are known to be integrated, thus exposure of one bank may pose risks to other banks and the entire financial system. By knowing the risks of other market participants, banks should collaborate in making sure the banking system is healthy and sound as it is beneficial in the long run. Every economic agent must work all together to achieve economic growth, most especially now with the presence of an unprecedented crisis.

To end, it is a difficult time for the country as the COVID-19 crisis continues to test the strength of its macroeconomic policies and reforms. Hence, the stakeholders must understand and assess the vulnerabilities of the banking system by running a macro stress test. The sooner the weaknesses are recognized, the quicker it is for policymakers and the banks' management to implement the right responses and recover.

Recommendations and Limitations of the Study

It is important to be aware of what a stress test can and cannot deliver. In that respect, managing expectations is part of the preparation for a stress test. This avoids the spreading of a false sense of security as well as complacency. The practical value of stress tests depends first and foremost on recognizing their limitations and defining appropriate objectives. There are several limitations to the use of the macro stress testing technique.

First, the connection to stress scenarios is not straightforward as risk is multidimensional (Siddique et al. 2013). The translation of a particular type of risk into a scenario seems feasible, but risks are correlated, so isolating a single type of risk may simplify the scenario unrealistically. However, designing a scenario based on correlations among types of risk poses implementation challenges and complicates the interpretation of stress test results. Second, stress tests rely on models that may generate erroneous predictions. They are generally based on experience as embodied in historical data, which may not be relevant to the next stress event. In other words, there can be no assurance either that future behavior under stress conditions will resemble past performance, or that the historical data incorporate a sufficiently diverse range of economic conditions to guarantee the accuracy of the prediction. Moreover, precision is unattainable concerning both assignments of probabilities to any scenario and estimation of credit quality conditional on assigned situations. Scenarios that are too mild or too intense may lead to failure to identify the impact of the interested variables on credit quality and generate excessive concerns. Lastly, the model does not capture the full effect of the pandemic given that the crisis is far from over.

Moving on, although the study used a complex, multi-step approach to study the relationships between the banking system's credit risk and macro-financial variables, it is recommended that future researchers explore other factors to improve the fit of the model as the real GDP growth rate tested insignificant. Several studies used other variables such as industrial production, money growth, consumption expenditure, unemployment rate, employee compensation, new car registrations, investment expenditures, and total gross fixed capital formation. Future researchers can also add bank-specific factors such as the deposit-to-loan ratio and loan-to-GDP ratio or other factors that may capture the tepid demand for loans during the pandemic to have a more accurate forecast. Likewise, future researchers

In addition, future researchers may develop a model that accounts for feedback loops between the banking system and the real economy. Furthermore, the study could be extended over a longer horizon as the paper was limited to a short-run analysis of the shocks (4 quarters). Historical experience, however, suggests that systemic episodes are the result of aggregate shocks that persist for several years (Sorge et al. 2006). It would be desirable, therefore, to lengthen the horizon of macro stress tests allowing for serially correlated shocks to build up economic imbalances over time. This entails capturing all second-round effects of a given stress scenario which requires the analysis of feedback effects both within the financial sector and between the financial sector and the real economy. Lastly, there exists a hidden correlation among financial institutions due to interbank exposures which can be a source of endogenous risk in addition to the exogenous risk generated by the initial macroeconomic shock. This would lead to a better understanding of the micro-dynamics of systemic risk in the financial sector. Currently, there are no models that capture the transmission of contagion, particularly how fast a bank failure influences other banks. However, it will be difficult to estimate this due to the unavailability of data on interbank exposure.

Appendix

Top 10 Banks Based on Total Assets from 2005 to 2020

1. Banco de Oro Universal Bank
2. Metropolitan Bank & TCO
3. Bank of the Philippine Islands
4. Land Bank of the Philippines
5. Philippine National Bank
6. Development Bank of the Philippines
7. China Banking Corporation
8. Rizal Commercial Banking Corporation
9. Union Bank of the Philippines
10. Security Bank Corporation

Note Ranking based on the historical performance of the banks' total assets

Epilogue

As of October 2023, the economies of the ASEAN, hailed as the fastest growing region in the world, are expected to grow by 4.2% in 2023 and 4.6% in 2024. These updated growth rates have already been downgraded in comparison to the April 2023 forecast for the ASEAN by the World Economic Outlook. Economists are expecting weaker growth due to monetary tightening, and lack luster external and domestic demand. The presence of conservative central banks in the region would result in well-managed inflation targets.

Even if the emerging economies of the ASEAN are vulnerable to external shocks, most of which affect the production side of the economy, UKBs remain stable and poised to withstand volatilities in loan payments and non-interest income with their NPL levels and sufficient capitalization.

As these economies face a new era of higher interest rates, managing risky investments would be a constant hurdle. Some countries are introducing high return investments, such as sovereign wealth funds which, due to their risky nature, would require higher risk-adjusted capitalization ratios. Nevertheless, macroprudential measures promptly implemented by bank managers are set to deal with any financial pressures, resulting in favorable liquidity and bank solvency levels.

The Philippines is expecting further increase in public infrastructure, i.e., subways, highways, road networks, railways, school buildings, and

J. C. Dacanay et al., *Bank Competition and the Effects on Financial Stability*, Palgrave Macmillan Studies in Banking and Financial Institutions, https://doi.org/10.1007/978-3-031-59599-8

health centers. All these shall be funded via syndicated loans, grants, and through the country's first sovereign development fund to provide additional financing support for its projects and demand the presence of well-capitalized UKBs to ensure a stability in the country's banking system.

Glossary

Adverse Selection refers to a situation where sellers have information that buyers do not, or vice versa, about some aspect of product quality. From the bank's point of view, a firm seeking a loan possesses information about the intended application of desired funding that is not necessarily readily discernible. Indeed, the bank faces a danger that firms and other borrowers most interested in obtaining credit are those desiring to pursue projects with highest risks. In the study, this behavior is called risk shifting, and results in higher non-performing loans for the bank.

Bank The distinctive function of banks is the transformation of short-term deposits into longer-term, less liquid, and riskier loans. By raising funds from depositors and providing credit, banks avoid the duplication of monitoring, which reduces the overall cost of transferring funds from capital suppliers to its users.

Bank Concentration (or Market Concentration in the Banking Industry) is defined as a measure of a firm's participation in total sales, total assets, and the equivalent market share, and, is usually determined by the number of companies in an industry vis-à-vis their relative size (Zingales and Raghuram 2003). It is usually determined by the number of firms in an industry and their relative size.

Bank Efficiency Efficiency refers to the utilization of resources in such a way as to maximize the production.

J. C. Dacanay et al., *Bank Competition and the Effects on Financial Stability*, Palgrave Macmillan Studies in Banking and Financial Institutions, https://doi.org/10.1007/978-3-031-59599-8

Bank Fragility is understood in the context of competition-fragility, that is, more bank competition erodes market power, decreases profit margins, and results in reduced franchise value—the on-going concern or market value of the banks beyond their book values. This encourages banking organizations to take on more risk to increase returns.

Banking Stability The term "banking stability" refers to the probability that banks do not default on their liabilities. In particular, for a bank that is funded by equity and deposits and invests solely in risky loans, the probability that the return on non-defaulting loan assets is greater than or equal to the bank's liabilities reflects the bank's stability. This definition does not consider bank default that is caused by a bank's liquidity problems, for example, a panic-based bank run. This idiosyncratic definition of banking stability does not reflect systemic risk (Schliephake 2016).

Buffer Effect A higher share of equity funding, *ceteris paribus*, increases the stability of banks. This is because higher equity funding provides a buffer (also called capital cushion) against losses and reduces the moral hazard of banks similar to the charter value effect of low competition. This is the so-called buffer effect of equity funding (Schliephake 2016, p. 1790). It is achieved through a higher equity-to-assets ratio (also called bank capitalization) or a higher risk-based capital adequacy ratio (ratio of total qualifying capital to risk-weighted assets).

Capital stock is the plant, equipment, and other assets that help with production. It is the total amount of capital goods (plant, offices, machinery, and equipment) currently available to a firm or an economy with which to produce goods and services. Capital formation or accumulation plays a crucial role in expanding the firm's/economy's productive capacity and hence its ability to sustain a high rate of business growth and economic growth.

Charter Value The charter value of the bank is the worth of the bank's capacity to continue operating. It refers to the value of a bank being able to continue to do business in the future reflected as part of its share price. Operationally, it is equal to the discounted value of future abnormal profits. In a perfectly competitive environment charter value would be equal to zero (Freixas and Rochet 2008). The value of the banking charter arises from monopoly rents obtained by banks within the imperfect competition market model defined by high barriers to entry in a highly regulated environment. Martinez-Miera and Repullo (2010) show that charter value arises from the opportunity to lend to a group of entrepreneurs by the bank that did not fail in the preceding time period.

Cost efficiency Capacity of banks to minimize average costs resulting from the expansion of scope and/or scale due to an expansion in loans and deposits. For the study, in the absence of bank-specific loan and deposit rates, the term cost-advantaged shall be used, which would imply cost efficiency through the Boone indicator. Cost efficiency measures how close a bank's cost is to the best-practice bank's cost which is producing the same output bundle and under the same conditions.

Countercyclical implies that the variable declines in the event of a slowdown in the economy.

Cournot-Nash Equilibrium (or Cournot Equilibrium) is an approach to examining banking markets between the extremes of perfect competition and monopoly is a Cournot–Nash framework—that is, a setting assuming quantity rivalry among banks offering homogeneous products. The theory assumes a finite number of loans offered in the loans market and whose equilibrium loan rates lie between the extremes of pure monopoly and perfect competition. The transfer of consumer surplus to banks and the deadweight loss are smaller than in the pure monopoly case (Van Hoose 2017, p. 38).

Credit Risk is the risk of financial loss of the banks if a counterparty (borrower) to a financial instrument fails to meet its contractual obligations. In other words, risk of loss due to a borrower or counterparty's nonpayment of a loan or other credit accommodations (either the principal or interest, or both). Potential impact to the bank includes: (1) Deterioration of the asset quality and (2) decrease in the banks' profitability due to an increase in loan losses. A fundamental asset risk faced by a bank is credit risk, or the probability that a portion of the institution's assets—loans in particular—will decrease in value. The ultimate form of credit risk is the possibility of full default by borrowers. Key measures of credit risk include the ratio of nonperforming loans (loans past due for at least 90 days) to total loans, the ratio of net loan charge-offs (loans declared valueless and no longer carried on the balance sheet) to total loans, and the ratios of loan loss provisions to total loans or to equity capital (Van Hoose 2017, p. 15).

Credit quality is used interchangeably with loan quality. As the term implies, it informs investors or stakeholders of the banks' portfolio credit worthiness or risk of default.

Crisis is typically defined as some event occurring if a set of macroeconomic variables (jointly) exceed critical thresholds. As a result, businesses have trouble meeting their financial obligations, and financial institutions lack sufficient cash or convertible assets to fund projects and meet immediate needs. Investors lose confidence in the value of their assets and consumers' incomes and assets are compromised, making it difficult for them to pay their debts.

Economic Distress is characterized by adverse economic conditions marked by a contraction in GDP.

External finance premium is the difference between the cost of funds raised externally and the opportunity cost of funds internal to the firm. External finance (raising funds from lenders) is virtually always more expensive than internal finance (using internally generated cash flows), because of the costs that outside lenders bear of evaluating borrowers' prospects and monitoring their actions.

Financial Fragility refers to the vulnerability of the financial environment and the macroeconomy to systemic risk. It is the proneness of the financial system, and the banking industry in particular, to financial market and credit risks, making banks illiquid and insolvent. This occurs when banks expose themselves to risky investments in contingent assets, and, when they loan to borrowers who are likely to engage in investments in risky business ventures.

Financial Stability For the study, financial stability would pertain to the capacity of the banking industry to withstand bank and regulatory distress. It refers to the stability of a financial system from the microeconomic standpoint, that is, from the point of view of a bank and the banking industry. Bank distress occurs when a bank becomes insolvent due to the large occurrence of loan default. Regulatory distress occurs when the largest banks in an industry become insolvent, brought about by several bank runs and/or losses, with the banks being unable to create liquidity due to very low levels of capitalization, i.e., equity-to-assets and risk-based capital adequacy ratio. Definitions of financial stability often encompass many elements, including the smooth and effective functioning of the financial system, the low probability of default, the absence of stress and disruptions in the financial system, and the absence of major financial imbalances in the economy.

Franchise Value The expected value of new business opportunities available to a bank. Traditional theory suggests that high franchise value limits bank risk-taking incentives. Empirically, however, a high franchise value allows the bank to borrow more, so it can take risk on a larger scale. This offsets lower incentives to take risk of given size. As a result, a bank with a higher franchise value may have higher risk-taking incentives (Martynova et al. 2014).

Friction is the total direct and indirect costs associated with the execution of a financial transaction.

Imperfect Competition occurs between the extremes of perfect competition and pure monopoly or pure monopsony and includes either oligopoly or monopolistic/monopsonistic competition. In typical Cournot–Nash oligopoly models, banks make their individual loan and deposit choices taking the choices of rivals offering identical loans and deposits as given. These oligopoly models yield equilibrium loan and deposit levels and rates between the extremes of perfect competition and monopoly/monopsony, with an increase in the number of banks pushing realized outcomes closer to those arising under perfect competition (VanHoose 2017, p. 40). It is sometimes characterized by the presence of dominant and fringe firms/banks.

Income Diversification The expansion into new income-earning financial services away from the traditional intermediation services.

Interest Rate Risk Another form of market risk is interest rate risk, which arises mainly through the potential for interest rates on liabilities to rise more rapidly than increases in interest rates on assets. The most common measure of a bank's exposure to interest rate risk is the ratio of interest-sensitive assets to interest-sensitive liabilities. If this ratio is significantly greater (less) than unity, then an institution is vulnerable to losses if the general level of interest rates declines (rises).

Kernel Density Estimation (KDE) is a non-parametric estimation of the probability density function of a random variable. Kernel density estimation is a fundamental data smoothing problem where inferences about the population are made, based on a finite data sample. Epanechnikov (1969) formulated a kernel that computes a non-parametric density for a multivariate random variable. Using a local fit, wherein errors from a central location parameter are achieved, a globalized error term is computed from the *n*-dimension random variable. For the study, an Epanechnikov Kernel fit was used as its residual estimates converge towards a standard normal density function. The basis for the stability criteria from the inflection points uses a Kernel fit from a Kernel local regression. A scatterplot would be done for the estimated values of bank capitalization and each of the financial stability indexes, all of which are multivariate random variables.

Leverage Leverage is the use of various financial instruments or borrowed capital, such as margin, to increase the potential return of an investment. For the study it is the ratio of assets to equity. In 1988, in an effort to take into account heterogeneities of risks across different sets of bank assets, bank regulators of various nations agreed to adopt the so-called Basel Accord. Under this agreement, now commonly called Basel I, participating nations imposed both a traditional leverage (asset-to-capital-ratio) requirement and "risk-based" requirements relating measures of bank capital to a "risk-weighted" measure of total assets (VanHoose 2017, p. 169).

Liberalization In this study, it refers to government policy encouraging or allowing the entry of more firms, especially foreign firms, to tighten competition and improve the overall financial industry. It also covers the government policy of allowing foreign firms to expand operations in the country.

Liquidity Risk is the current and prospective risk to earnings or capital arising from the inability to meet obligations when they come due. This may be caused by the inability to liquidate assets or to obtain funding to meet liquidity needs. This is the probability of having insufficient cash and borrowing capability to satisfy desired depositor withdrawals, to be able to extend loans to creditworthy borrowers, or to meet other cash requirements. In normal times, illiquidity events are rare and isolated. When such an event takes place, an affected bank typically must borrow funds at interest rates exceeding those paid by other institutions. Liquidity risk can also arise more generally as a consequence of concerns about the stability of the banking system, which induce large numbers of depositors to seek withdrawals (VanHoose 2017, p. 15).

Loans A financial product which provides capital to the borrower.

Market Power The ability of a market participant or group of participants (persons, firms, partnerships, or others) to influence price, quality, and the nature of the product in the marketplace.

Market risk refers to a bank's exposure of price risk, that is, the potential for a sudden drop in securities prices. Because banks hold a variety of securities alongside their loans, they encounter market risks on both types of assets: loans and securities. A bank's degree of exposure to such risks is usually measured as the ratio of the book value of assets to the estimated market value of those assets.

Margin Effect More competition leads to lower loan rates, and consequently lower revenues from performing loans, which provide a buffer against loan losses, thus, resulting to riskier banks (Martinez-Miera and Repullo 2010). The theoretical model calibration results of Martinez-Miera and Repullo (2010) show that the margin effect dominates in competitive markets.

Mild Scenario is established as the probability of 1, a certain event such as an economic distress, occurring in every 10 years.

Moderate Scenario is set up as the probability of 1, a certain event such as an economic distress, occurring in every 25 years.

Moral Hazard Problem is the idea that certain corporations, such as banks and automakers, are too big to fail. These companies usually take risks to become more profitable because they know the government will bail them out in the future.

Procyclical indicates that the variable rises in the event of a slowdown in the economy.

Satellite Model is a term used in stress testing which is used to translate a given macroeconomic scenario.

Product Differentiation is the capacity of a bank to position its products and services as either substitutes or complements to other financial products and services. Product differentiation is done in order to demonstrate the unique aspects of a firm's product and to create a sense of value. In economics, successful product differentiation is inconsistent with the conditions of perfect competition, which require products of competing firms to be perfect substitutes.

Profit Efficiency The profit efficiency referred to in this paper is the alternative profit efficiency which measures how close a bank is to earning maximum profits given its output level rather than its output prices.

Pump-priming is the action taken to stimulate an economy, usually during a recessionary period, through government spending and interest rate and tax reductions.

Quasibanks It refers to an entity or financial institution authorized by the Bangko Sentral ng Pilipinas to engage in quasi-banking functions or to borrow funds through issuance, endorsement, or assignment with recourse or acceptance of deposit.

Risk-Shifting Behavior or Effect The positive effect of loan rates on entrepreneurs' optimal choice of risk. The higher the loan rate, the higher the probability of failure chosen by the entrepreneurs, i.e., entrepreneurs may shift to risky projects (Martinez-Miera and Repullo 2010). The risk-shifting effect can also happen on the part of the bank's loan officers, who would opt to grant a loan to risk-taking borrowers. The theoretical model calibration results of Martinez-Miera and Repullo (2010) show that the risk-shifting effect tends to dominate in monopolistic markets.

Sunk Cost A sunk cost is a cost that has already been incurred and thus cannot be recovered. Sunk costs (past costs) are excluded from future business decisions, because the cost will be the same regardless of the outcome of a decision. Exogenous sunk costs are fixed size investments or investments that can only increase consumer utility for the product in a limited way: i.e., start-up costs, plant of minimum efficient scale, acquiring industry know-how. When an industry has exogenous sunk costs, i.e., set-up costs such as in opening a bank, filing fees, bank construction costs, legal fees, may lead to the appearance of indefinitely low levels of concentration in these industries (Sutton 1991, pp. 11–12). This result breaks down once we consider endogenous sunk costs. Endogenous sunk costs are variable size investments the returns to which increase with market size, e.g., advertising & R&D investments that proportionally increase demand. The bank might also incur "endogenous" fixed costs if it chooses to invest in advertising, developing a brand name, branch and ATM networks, installation costs of ATM networks, internet banking, most of which refer to costs to achieve certain types of bank quality. The key is that these investments should involve mostly an increase in fixed outlays, as opposed to unit variable costs (Dick 2007, p. 61).

Systemic Risk Systemic risk is the possibility that an event at the company level could trigger severe instability or collapse an entire industry or economy. Banks assume credit, market, and liquidity risks on an individual basis. Because payment flows among banks are interdependent, however, risks confronted by individual institutions have the potential to spill over onto others (VanHoose 2017, p. 16; De Bandt and Hartmann 2019, p. 849; Mishkin 2022, p. 336).

Universal and Commercial Banks (U/KBs) These are banks with expanded commercial banking license. These universal banks can perform the functions of investment house, such as securities under-taking, aside from the regular functions of commercial banks.

References

Aban, M. J. A. C. 2013 Transmission of Monetary Policy Through the Bank Lending Channel in the Philippines *International Journal of Trade, Economics and Finance* 4(1), 37–42 (http://www.ijtef.org.scihub.cc/index.php?m=content&c=index&a=show&catid=41&id=482 and https://doi.org/10.7763/IJTEF.2013.V4.257 Accessed July 16, 2016)

Abedifar, P., Molyneux, P. and Tarazi, A. 2018 Non-Interest Income and Bank Lending. *Journal of Banking & Finance* 87, 411–426

Adachi, Takanori 2019 Klein and Monti Meet Weyl and Fabinger: Imperfect Competition in the Banking Sector *Economic Research Center Discussion Paper* (E19–11), 1–5 (https://ci.nii.ac.jp/naid/120006725336/ Accessed August 24, 2021)

Admati, Anat and Hellwig, Martin 2013 *The Bankers' New Clothes: What's Wrong with Banking and What to Do About It* Princeton University Press, Princeton, NJ

Admati, Anat R., DeMarzo, Peter M., Hellwig, Martin F. and Pfleiderer, Paul C. 2013 *Fallacies, Irrelevant Facts, and Myths in the Discussion of Capital Regulation: Why Bank Equity Is Not Socially Expensive* Max Planck Institute for Research on Collective Goods 23 (https://pdfs.semanticscholar.org/9a0f/e635f7d16e6d70a6041a3ddc959b56967e72.pdf Accessed December 26, 2016)

Alberto, M. R., Tan, L. M. O., Regalado, M. K. L. and Reyes, M. J. W. 2018 The Effect of Foreign Bank Entry on the Performance of Philippine Domestic Banks In *Proceedings of the DLSU Research Congress*, June 20–22, 2018. https://www.dlsu.edu.ph/wp-content/uploads/pdf/conferences/research-congress-proceedings/2018/sep-03.pdf

J. C. Dacanay et al., *Bank Competition and the Effects on Financial Stability*, Palgrave Macmillan Studies in Banking and Financial Institutions, https://doi.org/10.1007/978-3-031-59599-8

Alhassan, Abdul Latif 2015 Income Diversification and Bank Efficiency in an Emerging Market *Managerial Finance* 41(12), 1318–1335. https://doi.org/10.1108/MF-12-2014-0304

Ali, Shoaib, Yousaf, Imran, Chughtai, Sumayya and Ali Shah, Syed Zulfiqar 2022 Role of Bank Competition in Determining Liquidity Creation: Evidence from GCC Countries *Journal of Applied Economics* 25(1), 242–259. https://doi.org/10.1080/15140326.2022.2043114

Allen, Franklin, and Gale, Douglas 2004 Competition and Financial Stability *Journal of Money, Credit, and Banking* 36(3), 453–480 (http://www.jstor.org/stable/3838946 Accessed December 22, 2016)

Amidu, M. and Wolfe, S. 2013 Does Bank Competition and Diversification Lead to Greater Stability? Evidence from Emerging Markets *Review of Development Finance* 3(3), 152–166

Arellano, M. and Bover, O. 1995 Another Look at the Instrumental Variable Estimation of Error-Components Models *Journal of Econometrics* 68(1), 29–51

Arrawatia, Rakesh, Misra, Arun and Dawar, Varun 2015 Bank Competition and Efficiency: Empirical Evidence from Indian Market *International Journal of Law and Management* 57(3), 217–231. https://doi.org/10.1108/IJLMA-03-2014-0029

Arrawatia, R., Dawar, V., Maitra, D. and Dash, S. R. 2019 Asset Quality Determinants of Indian Banks: Empirical Evidence and Policy Issues *Journal of Public Affairs* 19(4) https://doi.org/10.1002/pa.1937

Asian Development Bank 2012 *Assessing the Resilience of ASEAN Banking Systems: The Case of the Philippines*. February. https://www.adb.org/publications/assessing-resilience-asean-banking-systems-case-philippines

Asian Development Bank 2021 *Philippines: Economy*. https://www.adb.org/countries/philippines/economy

Bain, Joe S. 1951. Relation of Profit Rate to Industry Concentration: American Manufacturing 1936–1940 *The Quarterly Journal of Economics* 65(4), 602. https://doi.org/10.2307/1882581

Banco De Oro Unibank, Inc 2009 *BDO 2008 Annual Report*. https://www.bdo.com.ph/sites/default/files/pdf/BDO%20AR08%20VOL1%20full_B.pdf

Banco De Oro Unibank, Inc 2019 *BDO 2018 Annual Report*. https://www.bdo.com.ph/sites/default/files/pdf/BDO%20Unibank%202018%20Annual%20Report.pdf

Banerjee, S. and Murali, D. 2017 Stress Test of Banks in India Across Ownerships: A VAR Approach. *Studies in Economics and Finance* 34(4), 527–554. https://doi.org/10.1108/sef-11-2014-0213

Bangko Sentral ng Pilipinas (BSP) 2020 *BSP Unbound: Central Banking and the COVID-19 Pandemic in the Philippines* BSP, Manila, Philippines. https://www.bsp.gov.ph/Media_And_Research/Publications/BSP_Unbound.pdf

Bank for International Settlements (BIS) 2012 *82nd Annual Report*

Bank of the Philippine Islands (BPI) 2021 *BPI 2020 Integrated Report*. https://bpiexpressonline.com/media/uploads/609dfbfa31697_BPI_IR_20210513A1.pdf

Barros, P. 1999 Multimarket Competition in Banking with an Example from the Case of Portuguese Market *International Journal of Industrial Organization* 17, 335–352 (http://www.sciencedirect.com/science/article/pii/S0167718797000350 or https://doi.org/10.1016/S0167-7187(97)00035-0 Accessed December 22, 2016)

Basel Committee on Banking Supervision (BCBS) 2010a An Assessment of the Long-Term Economic Impact of Stronger Capital and Liquidity Requirements *Bank for International Settlements* August

Basel Committee on Banking Supervision (BCBS) 2010b The Basel Committee's Response to the Financial Crisis: Report to the G20 *Bank for International Settlements* October

Battese, G. E. and Coelli, T. J. 1992 Frontier Production Functions, Technical Efficiency and Panel Data: With Application to Paddy Farmers in India *Journal of Productivity Analysis* 3(1), 153–169.

Bayangos, Veronica B. 2010 Does the Bank Credit Channel of Monetary Policy Matter in the Philippines? In *Third Annual Asian Research Network Workshop* Japan. October (https://www.researchgate.net/profile/Veronica_Bayangos/publication/228593562_Does_the_bank_credit_channel_of_monetary_policy_matter_in_the_Philippines/links/540d5a270cf2df04e7548d23.pdf Accessed July 16, 2016)

Bayangos, Veronica B. 2022. Does Bank Competition Affect Bank Risk-Taking Differently? *Philippine Review of Economics* 59(2), 41–80 (https://pre.econ.upd.edu.ph/index.php/pre/article/viewFile/1028/953 Accessed March 23, 2023)

Beck, Thorsten, Demirguc-Kunt, Asli and Levine, Ross 2003 Bank Concentration and Crises. No. w9921. National Bureau of Economic Research (http://www.nber.org/papers/w9921 Accessed December 21, 2016)

Beck, T. and Levine, R. 2004 Stock Markets, Banks, and Growth: Panel Evidence *Journal of Banking & Finance* 28(3), 423–442 (https://doi.org/10.1016/S0378-4266(02)00408-9 Accessed March 23, 2023)

Beck, T., Demirguc-Kunt, A. and Levine, R. 2006 Bank Concentration, Competition, and Crises: First Results *Journal Banking and Finance* 30, 1581–1603 (http://www.sciencedirect.com/science/article/pii/S0378426605001044 or https://doi.org/10.1016/j.jbankfin.2005.05.010. Accessed July 16, 2016)

Beck, Thorsten, De Jonghe, Olivier and Schepens, Glenn 2013 Bank Competition and Stability: Cross-Country Heterogeneity *Journal of Financial*

Intermediation 22(2), 218–244 (https://doi.org/10.1016/j.jfi.2012.07.001 Accessed July 16, 2016)

Berger, A. N. 1995 The Profit–Structure Relationship in Banking: Tests of Market Power and Efficient Structure Hypotheses *Journal of Money, Credit and Banking* 27(2), 404–431

Berger, A. N. 2003 The Economic Effects of Technological Progress: Evidence from the Banking Industry *Journal of Money, Credit and Banking* 35(2), 141–176

Berger, A. N. and Bouwman, C. H. 2009 Bank Liquidity Creation. *The Review of Financial Studies* 22(9) http://web.mit.edu/cbouwman/www/downloads/BergerBouwmanBankLiquidityCreationRFSforthc.pdf

Berger, A. N., Espinosa-Vega, M. A., Frame, W. S. and Miller, N. H. 2005 Debt Maturity, Risk, and Asymmetric Information *The Journal of Finance* 60(6), 2895–2923

Berger, A. N. and Hannan, T. H. 1998 The Efficiency Cost of Market Power in the Banking Industry: A Test of the "Quiet Life" and Related Hypotheses *The Review of Economics and Statistics* 80(3), 454–465

Berger, Allen N., Klapper, Leora F. and Turk-Ariss, Rima 2008 Bank Competition and Financial Stability *World Bank Policy Research Working Paper No. 4696*. Available at SSRN: https://ssrn.com/abstract=1243102

Berger, Allen N., Klapper, Leora F. and Turk-Ariss, Rima 2009 Bank Competition and Financial Stability *Journal of Financial Services Research* 35(2), 99–118. (http://link.springer.com/article/10.1007/s10693-008-0050-7 and https://doi.org/10.1007/s10693-008-0050-7 Accessed July 16, 2016)

Berger, A. N., Klapper, L. F. and Turk-Ariss, R. 2017 Bank Competition and Financial Stability. In Jacob A. Bikker and Laura Spierdijk (eds) *Handbook of Competition in Banking and Finance*. Edward Elgar Publishing, Gloucestershire, UK pp. 185–204 (https://doi.org/10.4337/9781785363306.00018 Accessed August 24, 2021)

Berger, Allen N., and Mester, Loretta J. 1997 Inside the Black Box: What Explains Differences in the Efficiencies of Financial Institutions? *Journal of Banking and Finance* 21(7), 895–947. https://doi.org/10.1016/s0378-4266(97)00010-1

Berger, A. N. and Mester, L. J. 2003 Explaining the Dramatic Changes in Performance of US Banks: Technological Change, Deregulation, and Dynamic Changes in Competition *Journal of financial intermediation* 12(1), 57–95

Berger, Allen N., Molyneux, Philip and Wilson, John O. S. eds 2014 *The Oxford Handbook of Banking*. Second edition Oxford University Press, Oxford, UK http://www.oxfordhandbooks.com/view/10.1093/oxfordhb/9780199688500.001.0001/oxfordhb-9780199688500 or https://doi.org/10.1093/oxfordhb/9780199688500.001.0001 Accessed July 16, 2016)

Berger, Allen N., Molyneux, Philip, and Wilson, John O. S. eds 2019 *The Oxford Handbook of Banking*. Third edition Oxford University Press, Oxford, UK

Bernanke, B. S. 2007 *The Financial Accelerator and the Credit Channel* Federal Reserve Bank of Atlanta. https://fraser.stlouisfed.org/title/statements-speeches-ben-s-bernanke-453/financial-accelerator-credit-channel-8967

Bernanke, B., Gertler, M. and Gilchrist, S. 1996 The Financial Accelerator and the Flight to Quality *The Review of Economics and Statistics* 78(1), 1–15. https://doi.org/10.2307/2109844

Bernanke, B., Gertler, M. and Gilchrist, S. 1998 The Financial Accelerator in a Quantitative Business Cycle Framework *National Bureau of Economic Research* 6455. https://www.nber.org/system/files/working_papers/w6455/w6455.pdf

Bernanke, Ben S., Gertler, Mark, and Gilchrist, Simon 1999 The Financial Accelerator in a Quantitative Business Cycle Framework *Handbook of Macroeconomics* 1, 1341–1393 (https://doi.org/10.1016/S1574-0048(99)10034-X Accessed July 16, 2016)

Besanko, D. and A. Thakor 1995 Banking, Deposit Insurance and Bank Portfolio. In C. Mayer and X. Vives (eds) *Capital Markets and Financial Intermediation* Cambridge, UK, Cambridge University Press pp. 292–319 (http://www.cambridge.org/ph/academic/subjects/economics/finance/capital-markets-and-financial-intermediation?format=PB&isbn=9780521558532 Accessed August 15, 2016)

Boone, J., Griffith, R. and Harrison, R. 2005 Measuring Competition AIM Research Working Paper Series

Boone, J. and Van Leuvensteijn, M. 2010 Measuring Competition Using the Profit Elasticity: American Sugar Industry, 1890–1914 Center Discussion Paper No.2010–124

Boone, J. 2008 A New Way to Measure Competition *The Economic Journal* 118, 1245–1261

Boot, A., Greenbaum, S. and Thakor, A. 1993 Reputation and Discretion in Financial Contracting *American Economic Review* 83(5), 1165–1183. (http://www.jstor.org/stable/2117554 Accessed December 22, 2016)

Boot, A., and Greenbaum, S. 1995 Bank Regulation, Reputation and Rents: Theory and Policy Implications In C. Mayer and X. Vives (eds) *Capital Markets and Financial Intermediation* Cambridge University Press, Cambridge, UK (http://www.cambridge.org/ph/academic/subjects/economics/finance/capital-markets-and-financial-intermediation?format=PB&isbn=9780521558532 Accessed August 15, 2016)

Boot, A. W. A. and Thakor, A. V. 2019 Commercial Banking and Shadow Banking: The Accelerating Integration of Banks and Markets and Its Implications for Regulation. In Allen N. Berger, Philip Molyneux, John O. S. Wilson (eds) *The Oxford Handbook of Banking*. Third edition Oxford

University Press, Oxford pp. 62–94 (https://www.oxfordhandbooks.com/view/10.1093/oxfordhb/9780198824633.001.0001/oxfordhb-9780198824633 Accessed August 24, 2021)

Boot, Arnoud W. A. and Anjolein Schmeits 2000 Market Discipline and Incentive Problems in Conglomerate Firms with Applications to Banking *Journal of Financial Intermediation* 3, 240–273. https://doi.org/10.1006/jfin.2000.0287

Borio, Claudio 2016 Revisiting Three Intellectual Pillars of Monetary Policy *Cato Journal* 36(2) (https://object.cato.org/sites/cato.org/files/serials/files/cato-journal/2016/5/cj-v36n2-1.pdf Accessed July 16, 2016)

Bouvatier, Vincent, Lepetit, Laetitia, Rehault, Pierre-Nicholas and Strobel, Frank 2017 Bank Insolvency Risk and Z-Score Measures: Caveats and Best Practice, SSRN Working Paper January 2, 2017 (https://ssrn.com/abstract=2892672 and https://doi.org/10.2139/ssrn.2892672 Accessed February 2, 2017)

Boyd, J. H., Graham, S. L. and Hewitt, R. S. 1993 Bank Holding Company Mergers with Nonbank Financial Firms: Effects on the Risk of Failure *Journal of Banking & Finance* 17, 43–63

Boyd, John H. and De Nicolo, Gianni 2005 The Theory of Bank Risk Taking and Competition Revisited *The Journal of Finance* 60(3), 1329–1343. (http://www.jstor.org/stable/3694928 or https://doi.org/10.1111/j.1540-6261.2005.00763.x Accessed December 22, 2016)

Boyd, J. H. and Runkle, D. E. 1993 Size and Performance of Banking Firms. *Journal of Monetary Economics* 31(1), 47–67. https://doi.org/10.1016/0304-3932(93)90016-9

Bresnahan, T. F. 1982 The Oligopoly Solution Concept Is Identified *Economics Letters* 10(1–2), 87–92

Broecker, Thorsten 1990 Credit-Worthiness Tests and Interbank Competition *Econometrica: Journal of the Econometric Society*, 429–452. (http://www.jstor.org/stable/2938210 Accessed December 20, 2015)

Brooks, Chris 2014 *Introductory Econometrics for Finance.* Third edition Cambridge, UK, Cambridge University Press

Brooks, Chris 2019 *Introductory Econometrics for Finance.* Fourth edition Cambridge, UK, Cambridge University Press

Brunnermeier, M., Eisenbach, T. and Sannikov, Y. 2012 Macroeconomics with Financial Frictions: A Survey. *Macroeconomics with Financial Frictions: A Survey* 18102, 1–96. https://doi.org/10.3386/w18102

Business World 2021 *Philippine Banks' NPL Ratio May Rise Up to 5% by end-2021—Fitch.* https://www.bworldonline.com/philippine-banks-npl-ratio-may-rise-up-to-5-by-end-2021-fitch/

Business World 2021 *NPL Ratio Could Breach 5% by End-2021—BSP.* https://www.bworldonline.com/npl-ratio-could-breach-5-by-end-2021-bsp/

Caminal, Ramon and Matutes, Carmen 2002 Market Power and Banking Failures *International Journal of Industrial Organization* 20(9), 1341–1361 (https://doi.org/10.1016/S0167-7187(01)00092-3 or http://www.sciencedirect.com/science/article/pii/S0167718701000923 Accessed December 21, 2016)

Casu, B. and Girardone, C 2006 Bank Competition, Concentration, and Efficiency in the Single European Market *The Manchester School* 74(4), 441–468

Carletti, Elena 2008 Competition and Regulation in Banking *Handbook of Financial Intermediation and Banking* Elsevier, North Holland, Amsterdam pp. 449–482 (https://doi.org/10.1016/B978-044451558-2.50022-2 or http://www.sciencedirect.com/science/article/pii/B9780444515582500222 Accessed July 16, 2016)

Chen, J. 2021 *Bretton Woods Agreement and System: An Overview*. Investopedia. http://www.investopedia.com/terms/b/brettonwoodsagreement.asp

Chen, Chuling 2009 Bank Efficiency in Sub-Saharan African Middle Income Countries *IMF Working Papers* 9(14: 1). https://doi.org/10.5089/9781451871616.001

Chiorazzo, Vincenzo, Milani, Carlo, and Salvini, Francesca 2008 Income Diversification and Bank Performance: Evidence from Italian Banks *Journal of Financial Services Research* 33(3), 181–203. https://doi.org/10.1007/s10693-008-0029-4

Chortareas, G. E., Girardone, C. and Ventouri, A. 2011 Financial Frictions, Bank Efficiency and Risk: Evidence from the Eurozone. *Journal of Business Finance & Accounting* 38(1–2), 259–287. https://doi.org/10.1111/j.1468-5957.2010.02226.x

Choudhry, Moorad and Masek, Oldrich 2011 *An Introduction to Banking: Liquidity Risk and Asset-Liability Management*. Vol. 30 John Wiley & Sons, UK (http://as.wiley.com/WileyCDA/WileyTitle/productCd-0470687258.html Accessed October 2, 2016)

Claessens, Stijn and Laeven, Luc 2004 What Drives Bank Competition? Some International Evidence *Journal of Money, Credit, and Banking* 36(3), 563–583. https://doi.org/10.1353/mcb.2004.0044

Clark, Jeffrey Arthur and Siems, Tom 2002 X-Efficiency in Banking: Looking Beyond the Balance Sheet *Journal of Money, Credit, and Banking* 34(4), 987–1013. https://doi.org/10.1353/mcb.2002.0053

Clerides, S., Delis, M. D. and Kokas, S. 2015 A New Data Set on Competition in National Banking Markets *Financial Markets, Institutions & Instruments* 24, 267–311 (http://onlinelibrary.wiley.com/doi/10.1111/fmii.12030/full Accessed March 6, 2017)

Coppola, F. 2020 *Lower Long-Term Economic Growth May Affect the Dollar Exchange Rate Lower Long-Term Economic Growth May Affect the Dollar*

Exchange Rate. American Express. https://www.americanexpress.com/us/foreign-exchange/articles/long-term-economic-slowdown-affect-dollar-exchange-rate/

Dacanay, J. 2017 Does Bank Competition and Concentration Lead to Financial Stability? Ph.D. Dissertation, Department of Economics, Ateneo de Manila University

De Bandt, Olivier, and Hartmann, Philipp 2019 Systemic Risk in Banking After the Great Financial Crisis. In Allen N. Berger, Philip Molyneux, John O. S. Wilson (eds) *The Oxford Handbook of Banking*. Third edition Oxford University Press, Oxford pp. 847–884 (https://www.oxfordhandbooks.com/view/10.1093/oxfordhb/9780198824633.001.0001/oxfordhb-9780198824633 Accessed August 24, 2021)

De Groot, O. 2018 Financial Accelerator. In Palgrave Macmillan (eds) *The New Palgrave Dictionary of Economics*. Third edition Springer Nature, London, United Kingdom

De Nicolò, Gianni and Lucchetti, Marcella 2011 *Systemic Risks and the Macroeconomy*. No. w16998. National Bureau of Economic Research (http://www.nber.org/papers/w16998 or https://doi.org/10.3386/w16998 Accessed December 22, 2016)

DeYoung, R. and Roland, K. P. 2001 Product Mix and Earnings Volatility at Commercial Banks: Evidence from a Degree of Total Leverage Model *Journal of Financial Intermediation* 10(1), 54–84

Degryse, Hans and Ongena, Steven 2008 Competition and Regulation in the Banking Sector: A Review of the Empirical Evidence on the Sources of Bank Rents *Handbook of Financial Intermediation and Banking* Elsevier, North Holland, Amsterdam pp. 483–554 (http://www.sciencedirect.com/science/article/pii/B9780444515582500234 or https://doi.org/10.1016/B978-044451558-2.50023-4 Accessed July 16, 2016)

Degryse, Hans, Kim, Moshe, and Ongena, Steven 2009 *Microeconometrics of Banking: Methods, Applications, and Results*. Oxford University Press, Cambridge, USA

Degryse, H., Morales-Acevedo, P. and Ongena, S. 2019 Competition in the Banking Sector. In Allen N. Berger, Philip Molyneux, John O. S. Wilson (eds) *The Oxford Handbook of Banking*. Third edition Oxford University Press, Oxford, UK pp. 776–813 (https://www.oxfordhandbooks.com/view/10.1093/oxfordhb/9780198824633.001.0001/oxfordhb-9780198824633 Accessed August 24, 2021)

Demsetz, Rebecca S. and Strahan, Philip E. 1997 Diversification, Size, and Risk at Bank Holding Companies *Journal of Money, Credit, and Banking* pp. 300–313 (http://www.jstor.org/stable/2953695 Accessed December 23, 2016)

Development Bank of the Philippines (DBP) 2020 *Development Bank of the Philippines: P50 Billion Bond Programme*. Philippine Dealing

System. https://www.pds.com.ph/wp-content/uploads/2020/12/DBP-Series-2-Bonds-Due-2022-Final-OC.pdf

Dia, E. and VanHoose, D. 2017 Banking in Macroeconomic Theory and Policy. *Journal of Macroeconomics* 54, 149–160. https://doi.org/10.1016/j.jmacro.2017.07.009

Diamond, Douglas W. 1991 Monitoring and Reputation: The Choice Between Bank Loans and Directly Placed Debt *Journal of Political Economy* 99(4), 689–721. https://doi.org/10.1086/261775

Diamond, Douglas W. and Dybvig, Philip H. 1983 Bank Runs, Deposit Insurance, and Liquidity *The Journal of Political Economy* 401–419. (http://www.jstor.org/stable/1837095 Accessed December 23, 2016)

Dick, Astrid A. 2007 Market size, service quality, and competition in banking *Journal of Money, Credit and Banking* 39(1), 49–81. (http://www.jstor.org/stable/4123069 Accessed December 21, 2016)

Diokno, B. 2020a *Public Release of the Macroprudential Policy Strategy Framework: The Case of the Philippines*. Bangko Sentral ng Pilipinas. https://www.bsp.gov.ph/SitePages/MediaAndResearch/SpeechesDisp.aspx?ItemId=735

Diokno, B. 2020b *Q1 2020 BSP Inflation Report Press Briefing*. Bangko Sentral ng Pilipinas. https://www.bsp.gov.ph/SitePages/MediaAndResearch/SpeechesDisp.aspx?ItemId=687

Diokno, B. 2020 *The Philippines: Becoming An Economic Champion in the Post-COVID World*. Bangko Sentral ng Pilipinas. https://www.bsp.gov.ph/SitePages/MediaAndResearch/SpeechesDisp.aspx?ItemId=743

Doan, Anh-Tuan, Lin, Kun-Li, and Doong, Shuh-Chyi 2018 What Drives Bank Efficiency? The Interaction of Bank Income Diversification and Ownership *International Review of Economics and Finance* 55, 203–219. https://doi.org/10.1016/j.iref.2017.07.019

Dua, P. and Kapur, H. 2017 Macro Stress Testing of Indian Bank Groups. Ph.D. Dissertation, University of Delhi

Dumlao, Luis F. 2016 Too Big to Fail, Bail, Yet Frail Paper Presented in the ACERD Working Paper Series, February (http://ateneo.edu.ph Accessed February 14, 2016)

Dumlao, Luis F. 2017 The Cost of Doubling Capital in ASEAN-5 *International Journal of Research in Economics and Social Sciences* 7(2) February (http://euroasiapub.org Accessed April 4, 2017)

Dungey, M. and Gajurel, D. 2015 Contagion and Banking Crisis—International Evidence for 2007–2009 *Journal of Banking & Finance* 60, 271–283. https://doi.org/10.1016/j.jbankfin.2015.08.007

Duygun, M., Sena, V. and Shaban, M. 2013 Schumpeterian Competition and Efficiency Among Commercial Banks *Journal of Banking and Finance* 37(12), 5176–5185

Ebeke, C., Loko, B. and Viseth, A. 2014 Credit Quality in Developing Economies: Remittances to the Rescue? *IMF Working Paper* 14(144), 1–21. https://www.elibrary.imf.org/doc/IMF001/21555-9781498377911/21555-9781498377911/Other_formats/Source_PDF/21555-9781484338834.pdf

Edwards, F. R. and Mishkin, F. S. 1995 The Decline of Traditional Banking: Implications for Financial Stability and Regulatory Policy *Economic Policy Review* 1, 27–45

Elsas, Ralf, Hackethal, Andreas and Holzhäuser, Markus 2010 The Anatomy of Bank Diversification *Journal of Banking and Finance* 34(6), 1274–1287. https://doi.org/10.1016/j.jbankfin.2009.11.024

Epanechnikov, Vassiliy A. 1969 Non-Parametric Estimation of a Multivariate Probability Density *Theory of Probability & Its Applications* 14(1), 153–158 (http://epubs.siam.org/doi/abs/10.1137/1114019 or https://doi.org/10.1137/1114019 Accessed March 17, 2017)

Espinoza, R. and Prasad, A. 2010 Nonperforming Loans in the GCC Banking System and Their Macroeconomic Effects *IMF Working Paper* 10(224). https://www.imf.org/external/pubs/ft/wp/2010/wp10224.pdf

European Central Bank 2021 *Asset Quality*. European Central Bank—Banking Supervision. https://www.bankingsupervision.europa.eu/banking/priorities/assetquality/html/index.en.html#:%7E:text=Loans%20granted%20to%20businesses%20and%20households%20are%20assets%20for%20banks.&text=The%20higher%20this%20credit%20risk,prepare%20for%20the%20expected%20losses

Falkena, H. G., Hawkins, D., Llewellyn, P., Luus, D., Masilela, C., Parr, E., Pienaar, G. J. and Shaw, H. 2004 Competition in South African Banking: Task Group Report for National Treasury and the South African Reserve Bank

Federal Deposit Insurance Corporation (FDIC) 2012 *Asset Quality*. https://www.fdic.gov/regulations/safety/manual/section3-1.pdf in https://www.fdic.gov/regulations/safety/manual/

Felderer, B. and Homburg, S. 1992 *Macroeconomics and New Macroeconomics* Springer, Berlin

Financial Stability Coordination Council (FSCC) 2019 *Financial Stability Report 2018 H1–2019 H1*. http://www.pdic.gov.ph/files/ccd/2018%20H1-2019%20H1%20FSR%20(FINAL).pdf

Flamini, V., McDonald, C. and Schumacher, L. 2009 The Determinants of Commercial Bank Profitability in Sub-Saharan Africa. *IMF Working Paper* 9(15). https://www.imf.org/external/pubs/ft/wp/2009/wp0915.pdf

Focarelli, D. and Pozzolo, A. F. 2018 Banking Industry. In Palgrave Macmillan (eds) *The New Palgrave Dictionary of Economics* Third Edition Springer Nature, London, United Kingdom

Foglia, A. 2008. Stress Testing Credit Risk: A Survey of Authorities' Approaches. *SSRN Electronic Journal*. Published. https://doi.org/https://doi.org/10.2139/ssrn.1396243

Freixas, Xavier 2009 Monetary Policy in a Systemic Crisis *Oxford Review of Economic Policy* 25(4), 630–653 (http://oxrep.oxfordjournals.org/content/25/4/630.full.pdf+html or https://doi.org/10.1093/oxrep/grp035 Accessed May 15, 2015)

Freixas, Xavier and Rochet, Jean-Charles 2008 *Microeconomics of Banking*. MIT Press, USA (https://mitpress.mit.edu/books/microeconomics-banking Accessed January 25, 2015)

Freixas, Xavier and Ma, Kebin 2014 Banking Competition and Stability: The Role of Leverage (https://papers.ssrn.com/sol3/papers.cfm?abstract_id=2488426 Accessed October 6, 2016)

Fungacova, Zuzana, Pessarossi, Pierre and Weill, Laurent 2012 Is Bank Competition Detrimental to Efficiency? Evidence from China *China Economic Review* 27 https://doi.org/10.2139/ssrn.2206860

Gambacorta, Leonardo, Scatigna, Michela and Yang, Jing 2014 Diversification and Bank Profitability: A Nonlinear Approach *Applied Economics Letters* 21(6), 438–441. https://doi.org/10.1080/13504851.2013.866196

Gochoco-Bautista, Ma. Socorro 1999 The Past Performance of the Philippine Banking Sector and Challenges in The Postcrisis Period *Rising to the Challenge in Asia: A Study of Financial Markets* 10, 30–78

Gonzales, A. L. 2021a *Nonperforming Loan Ratio Seen Rising in 2021.* The Manila Times. https://www.manilatimes.net/2021/02/23/business/business-top/nonperforming-loan-ratio-seen-rising-in-2021/844365

Gonzales, A. L. 2021b *Fitch Lowers 2021 GDP Forecast to 5.3 Percent*. The Manila Times. https://www.manilatimes.net/2021/05/13/business/business-top/fitch-lowers-2021-gdp-forecast-to-5-3-percent/872617

Goyeau, D. and Tarazi, A. 1992 Evaluation du risque de defaillance bancaire en Europe *Revued'Economie Politique* 102, 249–280

Greenwald, B. and Stiglitz, J. 1993 New and Old Keynesians. *Journal of Economic Perspectives* 7(1), 23–44. https://doi.org/10.1257/jep.7.1.23

Gribbin, J. 1976 The Conglomerate Merger *Applied Economics* 8(1), 19–35. https://doi.org/10.1080/00036847600000003

Guinigundo, D. 2008 Transmission Mechanism of Monetary Policy in the Philippines *BIS Papers Chapters in: Bank for International Settlements (ed.), Transmission Mechanisms for Monetary Policy in Emerging Market Economies*, 35, Bank for International Settlements, Basel, Switzerland, pp. 413–425

Guinigundo, D. C. 2011 *The Impact of the Global Financial Crisis on the Philippine Financial System—An Assessment* 54, Bank for International Settlements, Basel, Switzerland pp. 317–342. https://www.bis.org/publ/bppdf/bispap54s.pdf

Guinigundo, D. C. 2015 Increased Financial Intermediation in the Philippines: Some Implications for Monetary Policy David Leung; Ceara Hui; Tom Fong and Alfred Wong, Hong Kong, 293

Hakenes, Hendrik, and Schnabel, Isabel 2011 Capital Regulation, Bank Competition, and Financial Stability *Economics Letters* 113(3), 256–258. (http://www.sciencedirect.com/science/article/pii/S0165176511002758 or https://doi.org/10.1016/j.econlet.2011.07.008 Accessed December 26, 2016)

Hakimi, A. and Zaghdoudi, K. 2017 Liquidity Risk and Bank Performance: An Empirical Test for Tunisian Banks *Business and Economic Research* 7(1), 46–57

Hamdaoui, Mekki, Zouari, Abir, and Maktouf, Samir 2016 The Effect of Financial Liberalization on Banking Sector Stability *International Review of Applied Economics* 30(5), 644–667

Hannan, T. H. and Hanweck, G. A. 1988 Bank Insolvency Risk and the Market for Large Certificates of Deposit *Journal of Money, Credit and Banking* 20, 203–211

Hauner, D. and Peiris, S. J. 2008 Banking Efficiency and Competition in Low-Income Countries: The Case of Uganda *Applied Economics* 40(21), 2703–2720

Hernández-Murillo, R., Llobet, G. and Fuentes, R. 2010 Strategic Online Banking Adoption *Journal of Banking and Finance* 34(7), 1650–1663

Hicks, J. R. 1935 Annual Survey of Economic Theory: The Theory of Monopoly *Econometrica: Journal of the Econometric Society* 3(1), 1–20

Hon, Lee Yoong, Eng Tuck, Cheah and Yu, Koay Lin. 2011 Efficiency in the Malaysian Banking Industry *ASEAN Economic Bulletin* 28(1), 16. https://doi.org/10.1355/ae28-1b

Horvath, R., Seidler, J. and Weill, L. 2016 How Bank Competition Influences Liquidity Creation *Economic Modelling* 52, 155–161

Isik, I. and Hassan, M. K. 2002 Technical, Scale and Allocative Efficiencies of Turkish Banking Industry *Journal of Banking and Finance* 26(4), 719–766

Iskandar-Datta, M. and McLaughlin, R. 2007 Global Diversification: Evidence from Corporate Operating Performance *Corporate Ownership and Control* 4(4), 228–242

Jensen, Michael C., and William H. Meckling 1976 Theory of the Firm: Managerial Behavior, Agency Costs and Ownership Structure *Journal of Financial Economics* 3(4), 305–360. https://doi.org/10.1016/0304-405x(76)90026-x

Jimenez, G., Lopez, J. and Saurina, J. 2013 How Does Competition Affect Bank Risk-Taking? *Journal of Financial Stability* 9, 185–195

Kagan, J. 2020 *What Is Friction Cost?* Investopedia. https://www.investopedia.com/terms/f/frictioncost.asp

Kalirai, H. and Scheicher, M. 2002 Macroeconomic Stress Testing: Preliminary Evidence for Austria *Financial Stability Report* 3, 58–86. https://www.oenb.at/dam/jcr:139c0d45-0098-4988-98cd-57458870452d/fsr_03_tcm16-8093.pdf

Keeley, Michael C. 1990 Deposit Insurance, Risk, and Market Power in Banking *The American Economic Review*, 1183–1200 (http://www.jstor.org/stable/2006769 Accessed December 23, 2016)

Kim, Moshe, Kristiansen, Eirik Gaard, and Vale, Bent 2005 Endogenous Product Differentiation in Credit Markets: What Do Borrowers Pay for? *Journal of Banking & Finance* 29(3), 681–699 (http://www.sciencedirect.com/science/article/pii/S1042957302000050 or https://doi.org/10.1016/S1042-9573(02)00005-0 Accessed October 2, 2016)

Klein, Michael A. 1971 A Theory of the Banking Firm *Journal of Money, Credit and Banking* 3(May), 205–218 (http://www.jstor.org/stable/1991279 Accessed August 24, 2021)

Klein, Peter G., and Marc R. Saidenberg 2010 Organizational Structure and the Diversification Discount: Evidence from Commercial Banking *The Journal of Industrial Economics* 58(1), 127–155. https://doi.org/10.1111/j.1467-6451.2010.00409.x

Kliesen, K. 2010 *Low Interest Rates Have Benefits … and Costs*. Federal Reserve Bank of St. Louis. October https://www.stlouisfed.org/publications/regional-economist/october-2010/low-interest-rates-have-benefits--and-costs

Koetter, M., Kolari, W. J. and Spierdijk, L. 2012 Enjoying the Quiet Life Under Deregulation? Evidence from Adjusted Lerner Indices for U.S. Banks *The Review of Economics and Statistics* 94(2), 462–480

König, T. 2020 The Financial Accelerator, Wages, and Optimal Monetary Policy *German Institute for Economic Research, 1860*. https://papers.ssrn.com/sol3/papers.cfm?abstract_id=3576407

Kopecky, K. J. and VanHoose, David 2004a Bank Capital Requirements and the Monetary Transmission Mechanism *Journal of Macroeconomics* 26(3), 443–464

Kopecky, K. J. and VanHoose, David 2004b A Model of the Monetary Sector With and Without Binding Capital Requirement *Journal of Banking & Finance* 28(3), 633–646

Kopecky, Kenneth, and VanHoose, David 2006 Capital Regulation, Heterogeneous Monitoring Costs, and Aggregate Loan Quality *Journal of Banking and Finance* 30, 1235–1255

Laeven, Luc, and Levine, Ross 2007 Is There a Diversification Discount in Financial Conglomerates? *Journal of Financial Economics* 85(2), 331–367. https://doi.org/10.1016/j.jfineco.2005.06.001

Landbank (n.d.) Landbank: Performance Highlights. https://www.landbank.com/about-us/about-landbank/performance-highlights

Lau, L. J. 1982 On Identifying the Degree of Competitiveness from Industry Price and Output Data *Economics Letters* 10(1–2), 93–99

Leibenstein, H. 1966. Allocative Efficiency vs. "X-Efficiency". *The American Economic Review* 56(3), 392–415

Lelissa, T. B. and Kuhil, A. M. 2018. The Structure Conduct Performance Model and Competing Hypothesis—A Review of Literature. *Structure* 9, 76–89

Leonida, Ella Mae O. 2021 Does Income Diversification Contribute to Achieving Bank Efficiency and Stability in Periods of Increased Competition? Master of Science in Industrial Economics, Master's Thesis, School of Economics, University of Asia and the Pacific

Lepetit, Laetitia, Nys, Emmanuelle, Rous, Philippe and Tarazi, Amine 2008 Bank Income Structure and Risk: An Empirical Analysis of European Banks *Journal of Banking and Finance* 32(8), 1452–1467. https://doi.org/10.1016/j.jbankfin.2007.12.002

Lepetit, L. and Strobel, F. 2015 Bank Insolvency Risk and Z-Score Measures: A Refinement. *Finance Research Letters* 13, 214–224

Lerner, A. P. 1934 The Concept of Monopoly and the Measurement of Monopoly Power *The Review of Economic Studies* 1, 157–175

Li, Li, and Zhang, Yu 2013 Are There Diversification Benefits of Increasing Noninterest Income in the Chinese Banking Industry? *Journal of Empirical Finance* 22, 151–165. https://doi.org/10.1016/j.jempfin.2013.10.004

Lown, C. S., Morgan, D. P. and Rohatgi, S. 2000 Listening to Loan Officers: The Impact of Commercial Credit Standards on Lending and Output *Economic Policy Review* 6(2)

Lucky, L. A. and Nwosi, A. A. 2015 Asset Quality and Profitability of Commercial Banks: Evidence from Nigeria. *Research Journal of Finance and Accounting* 6(18), 26–31. https://core.ac.uk/download/pdf/234631038.pdf

Macit, F. 2012 Recent Evidence on Concentration and Competition in Turkish Banking Sector *Theoretical and Applied Economics* 19(8), 573.

Macroeconomic Assessment Group (MAG) 2010a Interim Report: Assessing the Macroeconomic Impact of the Transition to Stronger Capital and liquidity Requirements *Bank for International Settlements* August

Macroeconomic Assessment Group (MAG) 2010b Final Report: Assessing the Macroeconomic Impact of the Transition to Stronger Capital and Liquidity Requirements *Bank for International Settlements* December

Macroeconomic Assessment Group (MAG) 2011 Assessment of the Macroeconomic Impact of Higher Loss Absorbency for Global Systemically Important Banks *Bank for International Settlements* October

Manlagñit, Maria Chelo V. 2011 The Economic Effects of Foreign Bank Presence: Evidence from the Philippines *Journal of International Money and Finance* 30(6), 1180–1194

Manlagnit, Maria Chelo V. 2015 Basel Regulations and Banks' Efficiency: The Case of the Philippines *Journal of Asian Economics* 39, 72–85

Manlagñit, M., Chelo, V. and Lamberte, M. B. 2004 Evaluating the Impacts of Competition Policy Reforms on the Efficiency of Philippine Commercial Banks (No. 2004–46). PIDS Discussion Paper Series

Marquez, R. 2002 Competition, Adverse Selection, and Information Dispersion in the Banking Industry *The Review of Financial Studies* 15(3), 901–926

Martens, Will. 2023. Exploring the Link Between Intellectual Capital, Technical Efficiency and Income Diversity and Banks Performance: Insights from Taiwan. *Qeios*. August 7. https://doi.org/10.32388/ITMIAU

Martinez-Miera, David 2009 Capital Requirements and Bank Failure CEMFI-UIMP Ph.D. Dissertation

Martinez-Miera, David and Repullo, Rafael 2008 DP6669 Does Competition Reduce the Risk of Bank Failure?

Martinez-Miera, David, and Repullo, Rafael 2010 Does Competition Reduce the Risk of Bank Failure? *Review of Financial Studies* 23(10), 3638–3664

Martinez Peria, Maria Soledad and Schmukler, Sergio L. 2001 Do Depositors Punish Banks for Bad Behavior? Market Discipline, Deposit Insurance, and Banking Crises *The Journal of Finance* 56(3), 1029–1051 (http://www.jstor.org/stable/222541 Accessed December 21, 2016)

Martynova, Natalya, Ratnovski, Lev and Vlahu, Razvan 2014 Franchise Value and Risk-Taking in Modern Banks De Nederlandsche Bank NV Working Paper No. 430 July (https://www.dnb.nl/binaries/Working%20Paper%20430_tcm46-309755.pdf Accessed December 31, 2016)

Matutes, C. and Padilla, A. J. 1994 Shared ATM Networks and Banking Competition *European Economic Review* 38, 1057–1069

Matutes, Carmen, and Vives, Xavier 2000 Imperfect Competition, Risk Taking, and Regulation in Banking *European Economic Review* 44(1), 1–34

Maudos, J., J. M. Pastor, Perez, F. and Quesada, J. 2002 Cost and Profit Efficiency in European Banks *Journal of International Financial Markets, Institutions and Money* 12(1), 33–58

Mercieca, Steve, Schaeck, Klaus, and Wolfe, Simon 2007 Small European Banks: Benefits from Diversification? *Journal of Banking and Finance* 31(7), 1975–1998. https://doi.org/10.1016/j.jbankfin.2007.01.004

Meriño, Michaela Nicole E. 2021 Macro Stress Testing of the Philippines' Top 10 UKBs: An Analysis of the Effect of Economic on the Bank's Credit Quality, Master of Science in Industrial Economics Master's Thesis, University of Asia and the Pacific

Meriño, M. N. and Dacanay, J. 2021 Bank Stability and Macro Stress Testing of the Top 24 Universal and Commercial Banks in the Philippines. In *Toward the Future of Asia: My Proposal. Best Papers of the 6th Asia Future Conference* (Forthcoming) The Japan Times, Tokyo

Meslier, Céline, Tacneng, Ruth and Tarazi, Amine 2014 Is Bank Income Diversification Beneficial? Evidence from an Emerging Economy *Journal of International Financial Markets, Institutions and Money* 31, 97–126. https://doi.org/10.1016/j.intfin.2014.03.007

Metropolitan Bank & Trust Company (MBTC) 2009 *Metropolitan Bank & Trust Company: P4,500,000,000 7.5% Unsecured Subordinated Notes Due 2019 Callable with Step-Up in 2014* Philippine Dealing System. https://www.pds.com.ph/wp-content/uploads/2013/12/Metrobank-Final-OC-Notes-due-2019.pdf

Meyer, A. P. 2018. Market Concentration and Its Impact on Community Banks. *The Regional Economist*, Federal Reserve Bank of St. Louis 26(1). (https://ideas.repec.org/a/fip/fedlre/00178.html Accessed March 23, 2023)

Miljković, Marko, Filipović, Sanja, and Tanasković, Svetozar 2013 Market Concentration in the Banking Sector: Evidence from Serbia *Industrija* 41(2), 7–25. (http://scindeks-clanci.ceon.rs/data/pdf/0350-0373/2013/0350-03731302007M.pdf Accessed March 10, 2017)

Milo, Melanie S. and Pasadilla, Gloria O. 2005 *Effect of Liberalization on Banking Competition*. No. DP 2005–03

Mishkin, F. 1996 The Channels of Monetary Transmission: Lessons for Monetary Policy NBER Working Paper Series. No. 5464 National Bureau of Economic Research

Mishkin, Frederic S. 1999 Financial Consolidation: Dangers and Opportunities *Journal of Banking & Finance* 23(2), 75–691

Mishkin, Frederic S. 2022 *The Economics of Money, Banking and Financial Markets* Thirteenth Edition, Global Edition Pearson Education Limited, London, UK (https://www.pearson.com/store/p/the-economics-of-money-banking-and-financial-markets/P100003054016/9780136893929 Accessed August 24, 2021)

Moenjak, Thammarak 2014 *Central Banking: Theory and Practice in Sustaining Monetary and Financial Stability*. John Wiley & Sons, UK

Molyneux, Philip, Fu, Xiaoqing Maggie and Lin, Yongjia Rebecca 2015 Bank Liquidity Creation and Regulatory Capital in Asia Pacific In *Bank Competition, Efficiency and Liquidity Creation in Asia Pacific* Palgrave Macmillan, UK pp. 96–124 (https://link.springer.com/chapter/10.1057/9781137533845_5 Accessed July 16, 2016)

Molyneux, Phil, Lloyd-Williams, D. Michael and Thornton, John 1994 Competitive Conditions in European Banking *Journal of Banking & Finance* 18(3), 445–459 (https://doi.org/10.1016/0378-4266(94)90003-5 Accessed December 21, 2016)

Molyneux, Phil and Forbes, William 1995 Market Structure and Performance in European Banking *Applied Economics* 27(2), 155–159 (https://doi.org/10.1080/00036849500000018 Accessed March 18, 2017)

Montgomery, C. 1994 Corporate Diversification *Journal of Economic Perspectives* 8(3), 163–178. https://doi.org/10.1257/jep.8.3.163

Monti, Mario 1972 Deposit, Credit and Interest Rate Determination Under Alternative Bank Objective Functions In Karl Shell and Giorgio P. Szegö (eds) *Mathematical Methods in Investment and Finance* North-Holland, Amsterdam pp. 431–454

Ncube, M. 2009 Efficiency of the Banking Sector in South Africa University of the Witwatersrand, 3 pp. 1–44. https://pdfs.semanticscholar.org/5b21/342a4c6af9ea6db1fe2b2610f3174c24f07b.pdf

Nguyen, T. P. T. and Nghiem, S. H. 2017 The Effects of Competition on Efficiency: The Vietnamese Banking Industry Experience. *The Singapore Economic Review* 65(6), 1507–1536

Njie, Matar 2006 The Impact of Financial Liberalization on Bank Spreads in Malaysia *Journal of Economic Cooperations* 27(3), 163–194. http://www.sesric.org/files/article/14.pdf

Oduor, Jacob, Ngoka, Kethi and Odongo, Maureen 2017 Capital Requirement, Bank Competition and Stability in Africa *Review of Development Finance* (article in press) (https://doi.org/10.1016/j.rdf.2017.01.002 and http://www.sciencedirect.com/science/article/pii/S1879933716301725 Accessed March 23, 2017)

Ogura, Y. 2006 Learning from a Rival Bank and Lending Boom. *Journal of Financial Intermediation* 15(4), 535–555. https://doi.org/10.1016/j.jfi.2005.10.002

Open Risk Management (n.d.) *Satellite Model*. https://www.openriskmanual.org/wiki/Satellite_Model#:~:text=5%20References-,Definition,Parameters%20at%20the%20firm%20level

Organization for Economic Co-operation and Development 2009 *Competition and the Financial Crisis* February https://www.oecd.org/competition/sectors/42538399.pdf

Pagaduan, Jesson A. and Majuca, Ruperto P. 2016 Macroprudential Regulation in a DSGE Model of the Philippines with Financial-Real Linkages *DLSU Business & Economics Review* 25(2)

Panzar, John C. and Rosse, James N. 1987 Testing for "Monopoly" Equilibrium *The Journal of Industrial Economics* 35(4), 443–456 (http://www.jstor.org/stable/2098582 Accessed December 21, 2016)

Parcon-Santos, Hazel C. and Bernabe Jr., Eufrocinio M. 2012 The Macroeconomic Effects of Basel III Implementation in the Philippines: A Preliminary Assessment

Park, Cyn-Young 2022 The Implications for Asia of US Monetary Policy *Asian Development Blog* (https://blogs.adb.org/blog/implications-asia-us-monetary-policy Accessed March 7, 2022)

Pasadilla, Gloria O. and Milo, Melanie 2005 *Effect of Liberalization on Banking Competition* Philippine Institute for Development Studies 2005–03. https://www.econstor.eu/bitstream/10419/127886/1/pids-dps2005-03.pdf

Perloff, Jeffrey M. 2011 *Microeconomics: Theory and Applications with Calculus* Prentice Hall, USA

Phan, Thi My Hanh 2015 Market Concentration, Bank Competition and Bank Efficiency in Emerging Asian Countries Ph.D. Dissertation, University of Western Sydney

Phan, Hanh Thi My, Daly, Kevin and Akhter, Selim 2016 Bank Efficiency in Emerging Asian Countries *Research in International Business and Finance* 38, 517–530 (http://www.sciencedirect.com/science/article/pii/S0275531916301520 or https://doi.org/10.1016/j.ribaf.2016.07.012 Accessed March 24, 2017)

Philippine National Bank (PNB) 2021 *Philippine National Bank: 2020 Annual Report*. https://www.pnb.com.ph/wp-content/uploads/docs/2020-Annual Report.pdf

Pruteanu-Podpiera, A., Weill, L. and Schobert, F. 2016 Banking Competition and Efficiency: A Micro-Data Analysis on the Czech Banking Industry In Josef C. Brada and Paul Wachtel (eds) *Global Banking Crises and Emerging Markets* Palgrave Macmillan, London, UK pp. 52–74

Qureshi, Z. 2019 *The Rise of Corporate Market Power*. Brookings Institution, USA. https://www.brookings.edu/blog/up-front/2019/05/21/the-rise-of-corporate-market-power/

Řepková, I. and Stavárek, D. 2013 Relationship Between Competition and Efficiency in the Czech Banking Industry *Acta Universitatis Agriculturae et Silviculturae Mendelianae Brunensis* 61(7), 2701–2707

Repullo, R. 2004 Capital Requirements, Market Power, and Risk-Taking in Banking *Journal of Financial Intermediation* 13, 156–182 (http://www.sciencedirect.com/science/article/pii/S1042957303001050 or https://doi.org/10.1016/j.jfi.2003.08.005 Accessed December 21, 2016)

Ribon, Sigal and Yosha, Oved 1999 Financial Liberalization and Competition in Banking: An Empirical Investigation. Bank of Israel Research Department Discussion Paper No. 99.05. https://www.boi.org.il/deptdata/mehkar/papers/dp9905e.pdf

Riordan, M. 1995 Competition and Bank Performance: A Theoretical Perspective In C. Mayer and X. Vives (eds) *Capital Markets and Financial Intermediation* Cambridge University Press, Cambridge, UK pp. 328–343 (http://www.cambridge.org/ph/academic/subjects/economics/finance/capital-markets-and-financial-intermediation?format=PB&isbn=9780521558532 Accessed August 15, 2016)

Rizal Commercial Banking Corporation (n.d.) *RCBC—Who We Are*. https://www.rcbc.com/our-company

Roberts, Michael R. and Whited, Toni M. 2013 Endogeniety in Empirical Finance Chapter 7 In George M. Constantinides, Milton Harris and Rene Stulza (eds) *Handbook of the Economics of Finance* Elsevier B.V., North Holland pp. 493–572. https://doi.org/10.1016/B978-0-44-453594-8.00007-0

Santander, B. (n.d.) *What Are the Differences Between Credit and a Loan?* Banco Santander. https://www.bancosantander.es/en/faqs/particulares/prestamos/diferencias-prestamo-credito#:%7E:text=Loans%20and%20credits%20are%20different%20finance%20mechanisms.&text=While%20a%20loan%20provides%20all,it%20or%20none%20at%20all

Sanya, Sarah, and Wolfe, Simon 2010 Can Banks in Emerging Economies Benefit from Revenue Diversification? *Journal of Financial Services Research* 40(1–2), 79–101. https://doi.org/10.1007/s10693-010-0098-z

Saunders, A. and Walter, Ingo 1994 *Universal Banking in the United States: What Could We Gain? What Could We Lose*? Oxford University Press, New York, USA

Schaeck, K. and Cihak, M. 2012. Banking Competition and Capital Ratios. *European Financial Management* 18(5), 836–866

Schliephake, Eva, and Kirstein, Roland 2013 Strategic Effects of Regulatory Capital Requirements in Imperfect Banking Competition *Journal of Money, Credit and Banking* 45(4), 675–700 (http://onlinelibrary.wiley.com/doi/10.1111/jmcb.12020/full or https://doi.org/10.1111/jmcb.12020 Accessed December 26, 2016)

Schliephake, Eva 2016 Capital Regulation and Competition as a Moderator for Banking Stability *Journal of Money, Credit and Banking* 48(8), 1787–1814 (http://onlinelibrary.wiley.com/doi/10.1111/jmcb.12371/full or https://doi.org/10.1111/jmcb.12371 Accessed December 26, 2016)

Sealey, C. W., Jr. and Lindley, James T. 1977 Inputs, Outputs, and Theory of Production Cost at Depository Financial Institutions *Journal of Finance* 32, 1251–1266

Security Bank (n.d.) *Security Bank Business Profile*. https://www.securitybank.com/about-us/business-profile/

Senior Supervisors Group (SSG) 2019 *Risk Management Lessons from the Global Banking Crisis of 2008*. Retrieved from https://www.sec.gov/news/press/2009/report102109.pdf

Serwa, D. 2010 Larger Crises Cost More: Impact of Banking Sector Instability on Output Growth *Journal of International Money and Finance* 29, 1463–1481. https://doi.org/10.1016/j.jimonfin.2010.05.011

Siddique, A. and Hasan, I. 2013 *Stress Testing: Approaches, Methods and Applications* Risk Books, USA

Silver, C. 2021 *Over 10 Years Later, Lessons from the 2008 Financial Crisis.* Investopedia. https://www.investopedia.com/news/10-years-later-lessons-financial-crisis/

Singh, M. 2021 *The 2007–2008 Financial Crisis in Review.* Investopedia. https://www.investopedia.com/articles/economics/09/financial-crisis-review.asp

Smirlock, Michael 1985 Evidence on the (Non) Relationship Between Concentration and Profitability in Banking *Journal of Money, Credit and Banking* 17(1), 69. https://doi.org/10.2307/1992507

Smirlock, M. and Brown, D. 1986 Collusion, Efficiency and Pricing Behavior: Evidence from the Banking Industry *Economic Inquiry* 24(1), 85–96

Sorge, M. and Virolainen, K. 2006 A Comparative Analysis of Macro Stress-Testing Methodologies with Application to Finland *Journal of Financial Stability* 2(2), 113–151. https://doi.org/10.1016/j.jfs.2005.07.002

Stiglitz, J. E. and Weiss A. 1981 Credit Rationing in Markets with Imperfect Information *American Economic Review* 71, 393–410. (http://www.jstor.org/stable/1802787 Accessed December 23, 2016)

Stiroh, Kevin J. and Adrienne Rumble 2006 The Dark Side Of Diversification: The Case of US Financial Holding Companies *Journal of Banking and Finance* 30(8), 2131–2161. https://doi.org/10.1016/j.jbankfin.2005.04.030.

Stiroh, Kevin J. 2004 Diversification in Banking: Is Noninterest Income the Answer? *Journal of Money, Credit, and Banking* 36(5), 853–882. https://doi.org/10.1353/mcb.2004.0076.

Svensson L. E. O. 2018 Inflation Targeting. In: Palgrave Macmillan (eds) *The New Palgrave Dictionary of Economics* Springer, London, United Kingdom

Sutton, John 1991 *Sunk Cost and Market Structure: Price Competition, Advertising, and the Evolution of Concentration* MIT Press, Cambridge, USA

Tarore, F. O. and Prasetyo, M. B. 2017 Diversification and Efficiency in the Indonesian Banking Industry *International Journal of Economics and Management* (IJEM) 11(S2), 473–486

Taskinsoy, J. 2020 Stress Testing: A Measure of Financial Stability Across ASEAN-5. *SSRN Electronic Journal* 1–83. https://doi.org/10.2139/ssrn.3543955

Toh, M. Y., Gan, C. and Li, Z. 2020 Bank Diversification, Competition and Liquidity Creation: Evidence from Malaysian Banks *The Singapore Economic Review* 65(4), 1127–1156

Tran, S., Nguyen, D. and Nguyen, L. 2022. Concentration, Capital, and Bank Stability in Emerging and Developing Countries *Borsa Istanbul Review* 22(6), 1251–1259.

Turk-Ariss, R. 2010 On the Implications of Market Power in Banking: Evidence from Developing Countries *Journal of Banking and Finance* 34(4), 765–775.

Tushaj, A. 2010 Market Concentration in the Banking Sector: Evidence from Albania In BERG Working Paper Series on Government and Growth. Bamberg Economic Research Group, Bamberg University

Union Bank of the Philippines (UBP) 2018 *Union Bank of the Philippines: Senior Fixed Rate Bonds* Philippine Dealing System. https://www.pds.com.ph/wp-content/uploads/2018/12/BB11-UnionBank-PHP-Bonds-OC-FINAL.pdf

UnionBank of the Philippines (UBP) 2013 *UnionBank Annual Report 2013.* https://www.unionbankph.com/about-us/disclosures

UnionBank of the Philippines (n.d.) *UnionBank of the Philippines: About Us.* https://www.unionbankph.com/about-us/who-we-are

Usman, M., Wang, Z., Mahmood, F. and Shahid, H. 2010 Scale Efficiency in Banking Sector of Pakistan *International Journal of Business and Management* 5(4), 104.

VanHoose, David 2010 *The Industrial Organization of Banking: Bank Behavior, Market Structure, and Regulation.* First Edition Springer Science & Business Media, Heidelberg, Berlin (http://www.springer.com/gp/book/9783642028205#otherversion=9783642425684 Accessed April 21, 2015)

VanHoose, D. 2013 Implications of Shifting Retail Market Shares for Loan Monitoring in a Dominant-Bank Model *Scottish Journal of Political Economy* 60(3), 291–316.

VanHoose, David 2017 *The Industrial Organization of Banking: Bank Behavior, Market Structure, and Regulation.* Second Edition Springer Science & Business Media, Heidelberg, Berlin (https://link.springer.com/book/10.1007/978-3-662-54326-9 Accessed May 28, 2017)

VanHoose, David, 2022 *The Industrial Organization of Banking: Bank Behavior, Market Structure, and Regulation.* Third Edition Springer Nature, Cham, Switzerland (https://link.springer.com/book/10.1007/978-3-031-16241-1 Accessed March 23, 2023)

Vennet, R. V. 2002 Cost and Profit Efficiency of Financial Conglomerates and Universal Banks in Europe *Journal of Money, Credit and Banking* 34(1), 254–282.

Vives, Xavier 2008 Competition and Regulation in Banking: Overview *Handbook of Financial Intermediation and Banking*. Amsterdam, Elsevier pp. 441–447. (http://www.sciencedirect.com/science/article/pii/B9780444515582500210 or https://doi.org/10.1016/B978-044451558-2.50021-0 Accessed July 16, 2016)

Vives, Xavier 2011 Competition and Stability in Banking *Central Banking, Analysis, and Economic Policies Book Series* 16, 455–502 (http://si2.bcentral.cl/public/pdf/banca-central/pdf/v16/Vol16_455-502.pdf Accessed December 23, 2016)

Vives, Xavier 2016 *Competition and Stability in Banking: The Role of Regulation and Competition Policy* Princeton University Press, New Jersey, USA (http://press.princeton.edu/titles/10741.html eBook | ISBN: 9781400880904 | Accessed August 16, 2016)

Vu, O. T. K., Vu, Y. H., Nguyen, T. T. T. and Bui, T. H. 2018 A Framework for Macro Stress-Testing the Credit Risk of Commercial Banks: The Case of Vietnam *Asian Social Science* 14(2), 1–11. https://doi.org/10.5539/ass.v14n2p1

Warue, B. N. 2013 The Effects of Bank Specific and Macroeconomic Factors on Nonperforming Loans in Commercial Banks in Kenya: A Comparative Panel Data Analysis *Advances in Management & Applied Economics* 2(3), 135–164 https://www.scienpress.com/Upload/AMAE/Vol%203_2_7.pdf

Waweru, N. M. and Kalani, V. M. 2009 Commercial Banking Crises in Kenya: Causes and Remedies *Global Journal of Finance and Banking* 4(4), 23–43. https://papers.ssrn.com/sol3/papers.cfm?abstract_id=1534205

Winton, Andrew 1999 Don't Put All Your Eggs in One Basket? Diversification and Specialization in Lending (September 27, 1999). Available at SSRN: https://ssrn.com/abstract=173615 or https://doi.org/10.2139/ssrn.173615

Wong, J., Choi, K.-F. and Fong, T. P.-W. 2008 A Framework for Stress Testing Banks' Credit Risk *The Banking Sector in Hong Kong* 240–260. https://doi.org/10.1057/9780230227378_11

Wooldridge, Jeffrey M. 2010 *Econometric Analysis of Cross Section and Panel Data* MIT Press, Cambridge, Massachusetts, USA

World Bank Group (n.d.) *World GDP Growth (Annual %).* World Bank. https://data.worldbank.org/indicator/NY.GDP.MKTP.KD.ZG?end=2020&start=2004

World Bank 1986 *The Philippines a Framework for Economic Recovery* The World Bank, Washington, D.C.

World Bank 2006 *Global Development Finance* The World Bank, Washington, D.C.

World Bank 2020a *World Bank Predicts Sharpest Decline of Remittances in Recent History.* https://www.worldbank.org/en/news/press-release/2020/04/22/world-bank-predicts-sharpest-decline-of-remittances-in-recent-history

World Bank 2020b *Philippines Economic Update, December 2020: Building a Resilient Recovery.* http://hdl.handle.net/10986/34899

World Bank 2021 *Navigating a Challenging Recovery in the Philippines (Philippines Economic Update June 2021).* https://www.worldbank.org/en/country/philippines/publication/navigating-a-challenging-recovery-in-the-philippines-philippines-economic-update-june-2021

Xu, Z. 2011 Technical, Pure Technical and Scale Efficiency of China's Banking Industry In *2011 International Conference on Information Management,*

Innovation Management, and Industrial Engineering 2, 198–201. IEEE, New Jersey, USA

Zhao, T., Casu, B. and Ferrari, A. 2010 The Impact of Regulatory Reforms on Cost Structure, Ownership and Competition in Indian Banking *Journal of Banking & Finance* 34(1), 246–254

Zingales, Luigi, and Raghuram G. Rajan 2003 Banks and Markets: The Changing Character of European Finance No. w9595. National Bureau of Economic Research

Index

A
adjusted Lerner index, 3, 51, 73, 74–77, 99–100, 102–105, 116–133, 135, 136–140, 151, 153, 155, 196, 202, 203, 206, 207, 212, 216, 220, 224
adverse selection, 52, 54, 254
ASEAN, 1, 2, 5, 8–16, 19–21, 24, 27, 28, 30, 31, 33–35, 47, 63, 168, 313
autocorrelation, 18, 195, 296

B
Bangko Sentral ng Pilipinas, 1, 188, 238, 239, 270, 274, 321
bank capitalization, 2, 3, 62, 63, 67, 77, 86, 88, 92, 93, 96, 101, 105, 108, 109, 140, 146, 153–160, 197, 222, 316, 320
bank concentration, 15, 17, 50, 56, 62, 63, 72, 135, 158
bank efficiency, 4, 18, 167, 170, 171, 173, 176, 180, 183, 184, 190, 191, 196, 197, 200, 203, 206, 213, 224, 229, 231, 247
bank fragility, 3, 56
banking stability, 4, 91, 95, 96, 236, 251, 316
bank risk, 3, 56, 77, 103–105, 319
bank size, 56, 120, 136, 141, 146, 176, 184, 197, 198, 206, 211, 213, 245
bank Z-score, 15, 16
Basel I, 58, 246, 320
Basel II, 58
Basel III, 5, 15, 24, 31, 58, 59, 62, 71, 72, 92, 109, 111, 159, 276, 310
Boone Indicator, 51, 68, 76, 100
buffer effect, 3, 86–89, 93, 94, 108, 111, 141, 151, 153, 160, 316

C
capital buffer, 3, 17, 58, 77, 85, 86, 151, 155, 218, 220, 221, 228

J. C. Dacanay et al., *Bank Competition and the Effects on Financial Stability*, Palgrave Macmillan Studies in Banking and Financial Institutions, https://doi.org/10.1007/978-3-031-59599-8

capitalization, 1–3, 15–17, 19–21, 24, 25, 27, 28, 30, 34, 39, 50, 66, 70, 78, 79, 85, 87–89, 91–93, 95, 97, 98, 102–104, 107–111, 151, 140–146, 153–156, 158–160, 197, 207–224, 228–229, 274, 313, 318
capital stock, 69, 151, 261
charter value, 54, 86, 89, 91, 94, 97, 241, 247, 316
competition-efficiency, 170, 209
competition-fragility, 3, 4, 49, 52, 54, 56, 77, 92, 103, 108, 146, 157, 217, 220, 221, 228, 242, 246–248, 263, 308, 316
competition-stability, 2, 3, 24, 52–54, 56, 77, 89, 92, 103, 105, 108, 146, 157, 218, 221, 228, 242, 246, 248, 263
conglomeration, 175, 185, 211, 216, 220, 226–228
conventional Lerner index, 98, 100, 127, 128, 130, 133, 135, 193, 198, 204, 208, 210, 214, 217, 218, 220, 223
cost efficiency, 1, 15–18, 20–30, 60, 74, 170–173, 176, 180–182, 192, 196, 200, 201, 203, 206, 209, 212–214, 228, 317
countercyclical, 58
credit, 4, 5, 13, 49–50, 55, 57, 61, 63, 78, 83, 93, 97, 140, 141, 151, 157, 179, 189, 212, 218, 220, 222, 224, 228, 237–266, 269–273, 276–285, 289, 293, 296–311, 315, 317, 318, 322
credit risk, 140, 141, 151, 160, 237, 238, 243, 244, 246, 249, 250, 257, 258, 270, 278, 284, 296, 308, 309, 311, 317, 318
crisis, 14, 33, 56, 62, 68, 167, 176, 209, 235, 240, 246, 250, 256, 258, 259, 272–276, 284, 291, 302–305, 310, 311

D

default, 3, 11, 21, 39, 52, 61–63, 69, 78, 79, 84, 85, 87, 88, 91, 94, 96, 97, 101, 109, 112, 114, 153, 157, 171, 176, 207, 213, 214, 218, 222, 228, 244, 249–252, 254, 263, 270, 276, 297, 316–318
dominant and fringe banks, 2, 58, 66, 77, 85, 92, 98, 100, 135, 169, 177–180, 197, 198, 201, 202, 208, 214, 216, 220, 222, 226–229
dominant banks, 3, 5, 49, 67, 76, 83, 85, 89, 91, 92, 95–97, 99, 101, 111, 116, 130, 131, 133–135, 151, 153, 158, 160, 178, 180, 201, 202, 209, 211, 213, 214, 216–218, 220, 221, 224, 228, 249, 277, 283, 303, 308

E

economic distress, 2, 4, 5, 237, 238, 243, 250, 254, 263, 264, 269, 271, 273, 283, 289, 293, 305, 308, 309, 321
efficient structure hypothesis, 17, 31
emerging capital markets, 2, 7, 8, 13–16
equilibrium, 50, 63, 65, 74, 75, 82, 85, 92, 134, 256, 259, 285, 317, 319
equity-to-assets, 19, 88, 103, 107, 108, 112, 114, 140, 146, 151, 153–155, 159, 316, 318
external finance premium, 57, 252, 256–258
external shocks, 2, 16, 17, 35, 313

F

financial fragility, 17, 56, 76
financial stability, 1–3, 5, 15, 17, 49–52, 54, 56, 62, 66–71, 73, 76–78, 89, 91–95, 97, 99, 104, 108–111, 120, 135, 136, 140, 141, 146–160, 185, 193, 198, 199, 216, 218, 220, 227, 228, 232, 318, 320
first differences, 16, 18
fixed assets to total assets, 107–109
flight for quality, 257
franchise value, 78, 263, 316, 318
friction, 248, 251, 252, 256–258, 262
fringe banks, 57, 66, 80–83, 93, 96, 133–135, 157, 159, 177–180, 200–203, 209, 212–214, 216, 220, 224

G

global financial crisis, 167, 176, 209, 235, 236, 238, 240, 246, 248, 249, 256, 258, 273, 277, 279
Global Financial Development Database, 16, 23, 68
global growth, 13
GMM panel estimation, 4, 195, 203
GMM regression, 3, 18, 77, 103, 160
gross domestic product, 16, 134, 264
growth projections, 10, 12

H

Herfindahl-Hirschman index, 3, 72, 117, 255, 264, 267, 272, 276, 277, 303, 308
heteroskedasticity, 18, 106, 195, 296

I

imperfect competition, 2, 3, 50, 55, 63, 66, 78–80, 85, 86, 89, 92, 97, 98, 105, 107, 109, 111, 136, 141, 157–160, 224, 249, 261, 277, 283, 303, 316
impulse response function, 255
income diversification, 3, 4, 168, 169, 174, 176–178, 180, 183, 184, 193, 197–200, 208, 209, 211–214, 216, 218, 220, 224, 226–229
industrial organization, 1, 50, 55, 66–68, 74, 77, 78, 92
inflation-targeting, 33, 50
inflection points, 107, 109, 153, 319
information generation, 4, 179, 180, 212
interest rate risk, 179, 319
intermediation, 13, 50, 51, 54, 57, 74, 83, 173, 200, 246, 255, 256, 259, 262, 319
inverted U, 2, 24, 85, 105, 107, 146, 157, 177, 179, 206, 218, 220
IS-LM model, 252

K

Keynesian model, 251

L

lag length criteria, 267, 272, 304
Lerner index, 2, 4, 196, 200, 202, 203, 206, 209, 212, 213, 216–218, 229, 231
leverage, 50, 54, 58, 59, 61, 63, 69, 70, 88, 89, 104, 111, 141, 146, 176, 249, 259, 260, 320
leverage ratio, 58, 63, 69, 104, 111, 141, 146
liberalization, 60
liquidity, 13–16, 24, 27, 34, 49, 50, 52, 54, 56, 59, 68, 167, 174, 186, 187, 190, 192, 200, 218, 231, 235, 236, 251, 257,

273–275, 285, 313, 316, 318, 320, 322
liquidity creation, 50, 54, 56, 174, 186, 190, 192, 200, 218, 231
liquidity risk, 49, 68, 174
loan quality, 30, 259, 317
loans, 2, 3, 13, 17, 49, 51, 55, 57, 58, 61, 63–67, 72–75, 77, 78–88, 91, 92, 95–98, 101, 103–105, 113, 115, 116–155, 157, 158, 179, 186–188, 200, 227, 228, 236, 238, 242–244, 248–254, 257, 259–264, 270, 274, 276–278, 280, 283, 284, 296, 298, 299, 301–303, 308, 310, 311, 314–317, 319–321
loans-to-assets ratio, 120, 133, 140, 146, 154

M
macroeconomic stabilization, 1–2, 33–35
macro stress testing, 2, 245, 293–296, 311–312
margin effect, 82–85, 91–98, 101, 111, 113, 115, 141, 146, 160, 241, 321
market power, 1–5, 17, 34, 55, 67–68, 75–82, 84–86, 92, 93–160, 170, 185–189, 192, 196–200, 203, 206, 209–213, 216–229, 241–242, 247, 276, 283, 316, 320
market risk, 319
market share, 3, 16, 51, 72, 116, 151–153, 156–160, 199, 218, 267, 284, 315
mark-up elasticity, 125
mild scenario, 299, 301–304, 321
moderate scenario, 272, 301–303, 306–307, 321
Monti-Klein model, 79–86, 92, 97, 133, 135

N
new empirical industrial organization (NEIO), 2, 49, 51, 67–68, 77
Next 5, 162, 278, 279
Next 10, 3, 73, 99–101, 105, 107–136, 137–154, 158–159, 161–166, 184–186, 209, 210
non-performing loans ratio (NPL), 165, 277–279
non-stationarity, 18
non-traditional methods, 51

O
operating expenses, 19–27, 28, 194
operational efficiency, 17–19, 30, 57, 209–213

P
Panzar-Rosse, 57, 171–173
portfolio risk, 3, 77, 101, 104–105
portfolio theory, 175, 180, 254
procyclical, 321
product differentiation, 55–60
profit efficiency, 3–5, 74, 169, 180–182, 210–221, 231, 321
profit elasticity indicator, 68, 76, 100
pump-priming, 274

Q
quiet life hypothesis (QLH), 27, 170, 241, 247

R
random effects model, 51, 160
return-on-assets, 3, 31, 32, 69, 78, 101, 146, 165, 166

return-on-equity (ROE), 3, 31, 32, 69, 74, 77, 78, 99, 110, 116, 129, 146, 153, 163–166, 199
risk-based capital adequacy framework, 59
risk-based capital adequacy ratio (RCAR), 60, 69, 71, 141–146

S
securitization, 239
solvency, 15–16, 25, 157–160, 313
stochastic frontier approach (SFA), 171–173, 176, 190–194
strategic focus, 211, 216
structure-conduct-performance (SCP), 67, 83
sunk cost, 51
systemic risk, 54, 96, 153, 159, 318

T
Tier1, 58–59, 69, 71–73, 104, 107, 109, 141–151, 149, 159
Top 5, 49, 116, 137, 162, 278, 279
Top 10, 2, 3–5, 63, 73, 97, 99–100, 105–153, 154–162, 166, 184, 198, 205, 209, 237–239, 263–265, 268–273, 276, 278, 281, 283, 299, 300, 303, 305, 306, 308
Top 20, 1–2, 51, 73, 98–100, 111–120, 136, 141–160, 161, 163, 167–169, 177, 180–187, 195–199, 208, 224, 225–227, 228, 278, 283–285
traditional methods, 51

V
vector autoregressive regression (VAR), 304
vulnerability, 4, 7, 16, 51, 235–237, 285, 318

W
World Bank, 16, 24, 26, 27–44, 45, 68, 293, 294

The manufacturer's authorised representative in the EU is Springer Nature Customer Service Centre GmbH, Europaplatz 3, 69115 Heidelberg, Germany. If you have any concerns regarding our products, please contact ProductSafety@springernature.com

Printed and bound by CPI Group (UK) Ltd, Croydon, CR0 4YY
30/09/2026
02225434-0009